CASES IN FINANCIAL REPORTING

SIXTH EDITION

ELLEN ENGEL
Graduate School of Business
UNIVERSITY OF CHICAGO

D. ERIC HIRST
McCombs School of Business
UNIVERSITY OF TEXAS AT AUSTIN

MARY LEA MCANALLY
Mays Business School
TEXAS A&M UNIVERSITY

Cambridge Business Publishers

CASES IN FINANCIAL REPORTING, Ellen Engel, D. Eric Hirst, Mary Lea McAnally.

COPYRIGHT © 2009 by Cambridge Business Publishers, LLC. Published by Cambridge Business Publishers, LLC. Exclusive rights by Cambridge Business Publishers, LLC for manufacture and export.

10 Digit ISBN 1-934319-19-8
13 Digit ISBN 978-1-934319-19-2

Bookstores & Faculty: to order this book, contact the company via email **customerservice@cambridgepub.com** or call 800-619-6473.

Students & Retail Customers: to order this book, please visit the book's website and order directly online.

Printed in Canada
10 9 8 7 6 5 4 3 2

CONTENTS

International cases are denoted ⊕.

BECOMING FAMILIAR WITH FINANCIAL REPORTING

Basics, Tools, and the Persistence of Earnings

Basics—Interpretation and Preparation of Financial Statements

Tools—Discounted Cash Flow

Tools—Basic Valuation and the Persistence of Earnings

EVALUATING FINANCIAL REPORTING DISCLOSURES

Balance Sheet Components and Issues in the Quality of Earnings

Assets

Liabilities

Owners' Equity

Financial Statement Analysis

CASES IN ALPHABETICAL ORDER

PREFACE

This book is a collection of financial accounting cases designed to help you become a user of financial reports. Learning accounting is very much like learning a new language. The best way to learn any language is to immerse oneself in the language and to converse with many people. Conversations speed up language acquisition and teach the nuances of the language. Conversations strengthen language skills and build breadth. This collection creates a set of conversational opportunities. You will learn accounting by reading financial statements and by responding to topical questions about those financials. By reading and using many different companies' financial statements, you will speed-up your acquisition of accounting concepts and skills. By observing the nuances of financial reporting, you will quickly learn to speak "accounting," the language of business.

These materials bridge a void in introductory financial statement materials at both the undergraduate and the graduate level. Typically, students are required to read a textbook chapter and do some exercises to ensure concept comprehension. Assigned end of chapter material, however, is often not sufficiently challenging to students with stronger analytical abilities. Questions often focus on financial statement preparation rather than, as appropriate for many students, financial statement use. At the other extreme, unstructured discussion cases can leave students with a weak grasp of the mechanics and subtleties of financial accounting. The cases here fill the void.

Each case deals with a specific financial accounting topic within the context of one (or more) corporation's financial statements. Each case contains financial statement information (a balance sheet, income statement, statement of cash flows, and footnotes) and a set of directed questions pertaining to one or two specific financial accounting issues. You will use the financial statement information to infer and interpret the economic events underlying the numbers. Some cases are accompanied by a related article taken from the business press. In those instances, information from the article is incorporated into the questions in the case. Some cases involve two or three companies within an industry and the case questions focus on intercompany comparisons of financial information. Some cases include industry-level information that you will use to assess the performance or position of the case company. Numerous cases are based on international companies.

WHAT MAKES THESE MATERIALS UNIQUE

These materials have a proven track record. The book was developed from the course materials used since 1991 at the University of Texas at Austin. The course (a semester-long, compulsory, first-year introductory class) has been extremely well-received by students each semester it is taught. The course consistently receives among the highest student evaluations in the UT and Texas A&M M.B.A. cores. The cases have been used with success internationally at ITESM in Mexico City and INSEAD in Fontainebleau, France.

Several unique features distinguish this casebook:

Financial Statement Diversity—This book comprises 28 cases. We believe that you will appreciate the exposure to many different companies and quickly learn that, while financial statements do not all look the same, you *can* understand and use them all.

Current Financial Statements—The cases are very current; primarily dated 2006 and 2007. This affords you the opportunity to read and use pertinent and timely financial information. Some older cases have been included because they explicate a concept particularly well or because they demonstrate an uncommon trend.

International Financial Statements—Cases cover companies from France, Austria, the Netherlands, the UK, India, as well as from the U.S. Many of the U.S. companies are major multinationals. The globalization of business necessitates your facility with financial statements other than those prepared in accordance with U.S. GAAP. The international cases will help you understand some of the recent harmonization efforts between the International Accounting Standards Board and the U.S. Financial Accounting Standards Board. Some international cases require you to compare U.S. GAAP financials to International Financial Reporting Standards (IFRS). Thus, you will become a sophisticated user of financial information.

Learning Objectives—Cases are prefaced with a set of learning objectives. These become your learning goals as you work through the cases. The focus of each case is made clear through these objectives.

Corporate Descriptions—Each case focuses on one or two sets of financial statements. A brief description of the companies in the case is designed to remind you that accounting information is used in specific business contexts. Reported financial accounting numbers are the result of a series of complex, professional estimates and judgments. Many of these are influenced by industry practice. Correctly reading and interpreting financial information is predicated on your awareness of a company's business and industry.

THE 'CPA' APPROACH—CONCEPTS, PROCESS, AND ANALYSIS

As in prior editions, the questions are organized in "C.P.A." order.

Concepts The typical case begins with a set of conceptual questions. As we introduce each topic area, we want to ensure that you are familiar with the vocabulary and the broader concepts before moving into the specific application to the case-corporation. These general questions focus each case on its topic area. For example, the Continental case on leases begins with the conceptual question, "what is a lease?" Several cases make explicit reference to the Concept Statements of the Financial Accounting Standards Board (available at www.fasb.org) or to International Financial Reporting (available at http://www.iasb.org/Home.htm).

Process Before you become a sophisticated consumer of accounting information you need an understanding of the accounting process and the basics of financial statement preparation. Thus, the second set of questions in each case focuses on the process. Process questions require you to retrieve specific information from the financial statements and to manipulate the information via calculations, journal entries, and T-accounts. It is at this point that many textbook exercises end. However, we believe that the accounting process is not the end but the means by which you will build a firm understanding of how financial accounting works the way it does.

Analysis With a strong understanding of the concepts and a solid knowledge of the accounting cycle, you are ready for higher level analytical questions. These questions have you synthesize, analyze, interpret information and formulate and defend your opinion on accounting policies, standards, and corporate behavior. Thus, analysis questions sharpen your higher-order thinking skills. In the 6th edition, there is increased use of the DuPont model of ROE analysis across cases. A number of cases encourage you to delve deeper by accessing original reports or finding current data on the internet.

By grouping the case questions into the C.P.A. categories, the text has broad audience. Taken alone, the Concept and Process questions are perfectly aimed at undergraduate introductory financial accounting classes. Because many M.B.A. students have taken some accounting and most have had some business experience, they are better prepared to handle the Analysis questions even at the introductory level. Several topics (e.g. pensions, leases, marketable securities, deferred taxes) included in this casebook are not typically covered in an introductory course. These can be used at the intermediate level for undergraduate and M.B.A. classes. For intermediate and financial statement analysis courses, the Concept questions can be used by your instructor to start class discussion. Taking up these questions first ensures that you are on firm ground before you tackle the more challenging Analysis questions. The full set of financial statements included with each case affords you and your class instructor the opportunity to explore issues the Analysis questions do not touch upon.

New in the 6th Edition

In keeping with the contemporary flavor of the earlier editions, we have added many new companies to the book (General Mills, Darden Restaurants, Molson Coors, Google, Borland, State Street, Abbott Labs, Palfinger, Corning, Johnson & Johnson, and others). Twenty of the cases are completely new or updated. We reviewed all of the continuing cases with an eye to improving their clarity. To that end, we reorganized the questions in several cases. We have included financial ratios and questions about management's incentives and motives in arriving at accounting choices in many cases. Several cases now include industry-level information. As well, we have included tables to many cases to guide the quantitative analysis especially when the questions require comparisons across years, to industry averages, or among firms. We continue to include a significant number of non-U.S. companies, denoted ⊕ in the table of contents.

How to Use These Materials

We've designed these cases to be used in conjunction with an introductory, intermediate, or financial statement analysis textbook. The order in which material is presented by your instructor does not affect the relevance of the cases. Each case stands alone and while some cases naturally precede others, there is no prescribed order.

As you use these materials, notice two main themes—earnings persistence and the quality of earnings. The first third of the cases in the book relate to the framework of financial reporting. In these cases you are acquiring skills in basic financial statement preparation, and in understanding how financial statements aid in the investment decision process. In achieving the latter, we emphasize how financial statements classify items and how such classifications are important in the prediction of the nature, uncertainty, and timing of future cash flows. Thus, we introduce the notion of earnings *persistence* and how it affects firm valuation. The remainder of the cases explores the accounting issues for the major financial statement line items. We place particular emphasis on the latitude and judgment management has in arriving at the reported numbers and the economic consequences of their choices. This introduces the notion of the *quality* of earnings. The cases are designed to help you acquire the skills necessary to identify quality of earnings issues and learn how to deal with them (for example, by restating the financials under different assumptions or accounting methods).

Instructor Resources

An electronic solutions manual with teaching notes is available to qualified **instructors**. To request a copy, please contact your sales representative or email Customer Service at customerservice@cambridgepub.com.

These cases can be custom published. For more information, please contact your sales representative or email Customer Service at customerservice@cambridgepub.com.

ACKNOWLEDGMENTS

We thank a number of people. First, the University of Texas at Austin, Texas A&M University, and INSEAD students who have used prior versions of the cases, have provided tremendous feedback. Each semester, they tell us how to improve the cases, and we listen. Second, our teaching assistants have helped craft some of the best questions in the book. Special thanks are due to A&M doctoral students Billy Strawser and Mike Neel who helped develop case questions and more importantly, related solutions. Bob May provided invaluable help in organizing and structuring the package as a whole. Feedback from reviewers, including Ashiq Ali, Robert Hartman, Philip Lewis, John Neill and Pamela Stuerke is also appreciated. Finally, the team at Cambridge Business Publishers, including George Werthman, Keith Chasse and Dennis Odom, kept the project going and saw it to completion. Thanks to all!

Although we have made every effort to avoid errors, any that remain are solely our responsibility. Should you have any suggestions for improving this product, we can be reached as follows:

Ellen Engel   Ellen.Engel@chicagogsb.edu

Eric Hirst   Eric.Hirst@mccombs.utexas.edu

Mary Lea McAnally   MMcAnally@mays.tamu.edu

ABOUT THE AUTHORS

Ellen Engel, PhD., is Adjunct Associate Professor of Accounting at the Graduate School of Business at the University of Chicago. She received her Ph.D. from Stanford University, M.B.A. from the University of Chicago and B.S. in Accounting from the University of Detroit Mercy. She is a Certified Public Accountant with experience in public practice. Her research interests include the role of accounting information in executive performance measurement and various corporate governance matters including executive and board of director incentives. Her research has been published in *The Journal of Accounting and Economics* and *The Journal of Accounting Research*. At the University of Chicago, she teaches financial reporting and financial statement analysis to M.B.A. students in the campus (full-time) and evening programs.

D. Eric Hirst, Ph.D., is the Associate Dean for Graduate Programs and John Arch White Professor of Accounting at the McCombs School of Business at the University of Texas at Austin. He received his Ph.D. from the University of Minnesota and M.Acc. and B.A. from the University of Waterloo. He worked as a Chartered Accountant with experience in public practice. His research on auditor, investor, and analyst judgment has been published in *The Journal of Accounting Research, The Accounting Review, Contemporary Accounting Research, The Journal of Financial Statement Analysis, Accounting Horizons, Auditing: A Journal of Practice & Theory, The International Tax Journal, CA Magazine, Organizational Behavior and Human Decision Processes* and others. At UT, Professor Hirst teaches financial accounting and financial statement analysis in the M.B.A and Executive M.B.A. programs. He has received numerous faculty-determined and student-initiated teaching awards at the University of Texas at Austin and INSEAD.

Mary Lea McAnally, Ph.D., CA, CIA is Associate professor and holder of the Carol and G. David Van Houten, Jr. '71 Professorship of Accounting at Mays Business School at Texas A&M University. She obtained her Ph.D. from Stanford University and B.Comm. from the University of Alberta. She is a Chartered Accountant (Canada) with experience in public practice and industry. She is also a Certified Internal Auditor. Her research concerns executive compensation, accounting choices and risk disclosures and has been published in *The Journal of Accounting and Economics, The Journal of Accounting Research, The Accounting Review, Contemporary Accounting Research, Accounting Horizons,* and *The Journal of Accounting, Auditing, and Finance*. At Texas A&M, Professor McAnally teaches financial accounting in the M.B.A. and executive programs. She has received numerous faculty-determined and student-initiated teaching awards at the University of Texas and Texas A&M University.

General Mills, Inc.—Understanding Financial Statements

> General Mills, Inc., incorporated in Delaware in 1928, is a leading producer of packaged consumer foods. The company has three segments: U.S. Retail, International, and Bakeries and Foodservice. U.S. Retail sells ready-to-eat cereals, meals, frozen dough products, baking products, snacks, yogurt and organic foods. The International segment includes retail business in Canada, Europe, Latin America and the Asia/Pacific region. Bakeries and Foodservice sells to retail and wholesale bakeries, and convenience stores. (Source: Company 2006 Form 10-K)

Learning Objectives
- Become familiar with a set of financial statements including auditor opinions and significant accounting policy footnotes.
- Perform a basic analysis and interpretation of the financial statements, including common-size income statements and balance sheets.
- Recognize the role of estimation in the preparation of financial statements.

Refer to the General Mills financial statements for fiscal year 2006 (that is, the year ended May 28, 2006).

Concepts

a. What is the nature of General Mills' business? That is, based on what you know about the company and on the accompanying financial statements, how does General Mills make money?

b. What financial statements are commonly prepared for external reporting purposes? What titles does General Mills give these statements? What does "consolidated" mean?

c. How often do publicly traded corporations typically prepare financial statements for external reporting purposes?

d. Who is responsible for the financial statements? Discuss the potential users of the General Mills financial statements and the type of information they are likely interested in.

e. Who are General Mills' external auditors? Describe the two "opinion" letters that General Mills received in 2006. In your own words, what do these opinions mean? Why are both opinions dated several months after General Mills' year-end?

Analysis

f. Use a spreadsheet to construct common-size income statements (which General Mills calls Statements of Earnings) and balance sheets for 2006 and 2005. Common-size income statements scale each income statement line item by *net* sales. Common-size balance sheets are created by dividing each figure on a given year's balance sheet by that year's total assets, thereby creating a balance sheet on a "percent of assets" basis. You will use these common-size statements in answering several of the questions below.

g. Refer to General Mills' balance sheet for fiscal 2006 (the year ended May 28, 2006).

   i. Show that the accounting equation holds for General Mills. Recall that the accounting equation is: Assets = Liabilities + Equity.

   ii. What are General Mills' major assets? Calculate the proportion of short-term and long-term assets for 2006. Does this seem appropriate for a company such as General Mills?

   iii. In general, what are intangible assets? What is goodwill? What specific intangible assets might General Mills have?

   iv. How is General Mills financed? What proportion of total financing comes from nonowners?

h. Refer to General Mills' Statement of Earnings for fiscal 2006 (the year ended May 28, 2006) and to the common-size income statement you developed in part f, above.

    i. Review the revenue recognition policies of General Mills discussed in Note 1 (Summary of Significant Accounting Policies). Discuss how the recognition policies for recording net sales and the treatment of returns and promotions are consistent with the revenue recognition criteria under Generally Accepted Accounting Principles.

    ii. What are General Mills' major expenses?

    iii. Were there any significant changes in the cost structure during the most recent year?

    iv. In fiscal 2005, General Mills separately reports the following three items: Restructuring and other exit costs, Divestitures, and Debt repurchase costs. Why didn't the company just include all of these amounts within the line item for Selling, general and administrative expenses?

    v. Was the company profitable during 2006? During 2005? Explain your definition of "profitable."

    vi. Compute the percentage change in Net Earnings from fiscal 2005 to 2006 and from fiscal 2004 to 2005. How would your answers change if the special items for Divestitures and Debt repurchase costs were excluded from fiscal 2005 Net Earnings? *Caution*: Divestitures and Debt repurchase costs are reported on the income statement before tax implications while Net Earnings is an after-tax number. Assume a marginal tax rate of 38.3% when considering the tax effects of the special items.

i. Refer to General Mills' fiscal 2006 Statement of Cash Flows.

    i. Compare General Mills' Net Earnings to Net Cash Provided by Operating Activities and explain the difference.

    ii. How much cash did General Mills use for expenditures for land, buildings and equipment during fiscal 2006?

    iii. What amount of dividends did General Mills pay during the year?

j. Several notes to the financial statements refer to the use of "estimates." Which accounts on General Mills' balance sheet require estimates? List as many accounts as you can. Are any accounts estimate-free?

ITEM 8 FINANCIAL STATEMENTS AND SUPPLEMENTARY DATA

MANAGEMENT'S REPORT ON INTERNAL CONTROL OVER FINANCIAL REPORTING

The management of General Mills, Inc. is responsible for establishing and maintaining adequate internal control over financial reporting, as such term is defined in Rule 13a-15(f) under the Securities Exchange Act of 1934. The Company's internal control system was designed to provide reasonable assurance to our management and the Board of Directors regarding the preparation and fair presentation of published financial statements. Under the supervision and with the participation of management, including our Chief Executive Officer and Chief Financial Officer, we conducted an assessment of the effectiveness of our internal control over financial reporting as of May 28, 2006. In making this assessment, management used the criteria set forth by the Committee of Sponsoring Organizations of the Treadway Commission (COSO) in Internal Control—Integrated Framework.

Based on our assessment using the criteria set forth by COSO in Internal Control—Integrated Framework, management concluded that our internal control over financial reporting was effective as of May 28, 2006.

KPMG LLP, an independent registered public accounting firm, has issued an audit report on management's assessment of the Company's internal control over financial reporting.

S. W. Sanger
Chairman of the Board
and
Chief Executive Officer

J. A. Lawrence
Vice Chairman and
Chief Financial Officer

July 27, 2006

REPORT OF INDEPENDENT REGISTERED PUBLIC ACCOUNTING FIRM REGARDING INTERNAL CONTROL OVER FINANCIAL REPORTING

The Board of Directors and Stockholders
General Mills, Inc.:

We have audited management's assessment, included in the accompanying Management's Report on Internal Control over Financial Reporting, that General Mills, Inc. and subsidiaries maintained effective internal control over financial reporting as of May 28, 2006, based on criteria established in Internal Control—Integrated Framework issued by the Committee of Sponsoring Organizations of the Treadway Commission (COSO). General Mills' management is responsible for maintaining effective internal control over financial reporting and for its assessment of the effectiveness of internal control over financial reporting. Our responsibility is to express an opinion on management's assessment and an opinion on the effectiveness of the Company's internal control over financial reporting based on our audit.

We conducted our audit in accordance with the standards of the Public Company Accounting Oversight Board (United States). Those standards require that we plan and perform the audit to obtain reasonable assurance about whether effective internal control over financial reporting was maintained in all material respects. Our audit included obtaining an understanding of internal control over financial reporting, evaluating management's assessment, testing and evaluating the design and operating effectiveness of internal control, and performing such other procedures as we considered necessary in the circumstances. We believe that our audit provides a reasonable basis for our opinion.

A company's internal control over financial reporting is a process designed to provide reasonable assurance regarding the reliability of financial reporting and the preparation of financial statements for external purposes in accordance with generally accepted accounting principles. A company's internal control over financial reporting includes those policies and procedures that (1) pertain to the maintenance of records that, in reasonable detail, accurately and fairly reflect the transactions and dispositions of the assets of the company; (2) provide reasonable assurance that transactions are recorded as necessary to permit preparation of financial statements in accordance with generally accepted accounting principles, and that receipts and expenditures of the company are being made only in accordance with authorizations of management and directors of the company; and (3) provide reasonable assurance regarding prevention or timely detection of unauthorized acquisition, use, or disposition of the company's assets that could have a material effect on the financial statements.

Because of its inherent limitations, internal control over financial reporting may not prevent or detect misstatements. Also, projections of any evaluation of effectiveness to future periods are subject to the risk that controls may become inadequate because of changes in conditions, or that the degree of compliance with the policies or procedures may deteriorate.

In our opinion, management's assessment that General Mills maintained effective internal control over financial reporting as of May 28, 2006, is fairly stated, in all material respects, based on criteria established in Internal Control—Integrated Framework issued by COSO. Also, in our opinion, General Mills maintained, in all material respects, effective internal control over financial reporting as of May 28, 2006, based on criteria established in Internal Control—Integrated Framework issued by COSO.

We also have audited, in accordance with the standards of the Public Company Accounting Oversight Board (United States), the consolidated balance sheets of General Mills, Inc. and subsidiaries as of May 28, 2006 and May 29, 2005, and the related consolidated statements of earnings, stockholders' equity and comprehensive income, and cash flows, for each of the fiscal years in the three-year period ended May 28, 2006, and our report dated July 27, 2006 expressed an unqualified opinion on those consolidated financial statements.

KPMG LLP

Minneapolis, Minnesota
July 27, 2006

REPORT OF MANAGEMENT RESPONSIBILITIES

The management of General Mills, Inc. is responsible for the fairness and accuracy of the consolidated financial statements. The statements have been prepared in accordance with accounting principles that are generally accepted in the United States, using management's best estimates and judgments where appropriate. The financial information throughout this Annual Report on Form 10-K is consistent with our consolidated financial statements.

Management has established a system of internal controls that provides reasonable assurance that assets are adequately safeguarded and transactions are recorded accurately in all material respects, in accordance with management's authorization. We maintain a strong audit program that independently evaluates the adequacy and effectiveness of internal controls. Our internal controls provide for appropriate separation of duties and responsibilities, and there are documented policies regarding use of our assets and proper financial reporting. These formally stated and regularly communicated policies demand highly ethical conduct from all employees.

The Audit Committee of the Board of Directors meets regularly with management, internal auditors and our independent auditors to review internal control, auditing and financial reporting matters. The independent auditors, internal auditors and employees have full and free access to the Audit Committee at any time.

The Audit Committee reviewed and approved the Company's annual financial statements and recommended to the full Board of Directors that they be included in the Annual Report. The Audit Committee also recommended to the Board of Directors that the independent auditors be reappointed for fiscal 2007, subject to ratification by the stockholders at the annual meeting.

S. W. Sanger
Chairman of the Board
and
Chief Executive Officer

J. A. Lawrence
Vice Chairman and
Chief Financial Officer

July 27, 2006

REPORT OF INDEPENDENT REGISTERED PUBLIC ACCOUNTING FIRM ON THE CONSOLIDATED FINANCIAL STATEMENTS AND RELATED FINANCIAL STATEMENT SCHEDULE

The Board of Directors and Stockholders
General Mills, Inc.:

We have audited the accompanying consolidated balance sheets of General Mills, Inc. and subsidiaries as of May 28, 2006 and May 29, 2005, and the related consolidated statements of earnings, stockholders' equity and comprehensive income, and cash flows for each of the fiscal years in the three-year period ended May 28, 2006. In connection with our audits of the consolidated financial statements we also have audited the accompanying financial statement schedule. These consolidated financial statements and financial statement schedule are the responsibility of the Company's management. Our responsibility is to express an opinion on these consolidated financial statements and financial statement schedule based on our audits.

We conducted our audits in accordance with the standards of the Public Company Accounting Oversight Board (United States). Those standards require that we plan and perform the audit to obtain reasonable assurance about whether the financial statements are free of material misstatement. An audit includes examining, on a test basis, evidence supporting the amounts and disclosures in the financial statements. An audit also includes assessing the accounting principles used and significant estimates made by management, as well as evaluating the overall financial statement presentation. We believe that our audits provide a reasonable basis for our opinion.

In our opinion, the consolidated financial statements referred to above present fairly, in all material respects, the financial position of General Mills, Inc. and subsidiaries as of May 28, 2006 and May 29, 2005, and the results of their operations and their cash flows for each of the fiscal years in the three-year period ended May 28, 2006 in conformity with U.S. generally accepted accounting principles. Also, in our opinion, the accompanying financial statement schedule, when considered in relation to the basic consolidated financial statements taken as a whole, presents fairly, in all material respects, the information set forth therein.

We also have audited, in accordance with the standards of the Public Company Accounting Oversight Board (United States), the effectiveness of General Mills' internal control over financial reporting as of May 28, 2006, based on criteria established in Internal Control—Integrated Framework issued by the Committee of Sponsoring Organizations of the Treadway Commission (COSO), and our report dated July 27, 2006 expressed an unqualified opinion on management's assessment of, and the effective operation of, internal control over financial reporting.

KPMG LLP

Minneapolis, Minnesota
July 27, 2006

GENERAL MILLS, INC. AND SUBSIDIARIES
CONSOLIDATED STATEMENTS OF EARNINGS

In Millions, Except per Share Data Fiscal Year Ended	May 28, 2006	May 29, 2005	May 30, 2004
Net Sales	$11,640	$11,244	$11,070
Costs and Expenses:			
Cost of sales	6,966	6,834	6,584
Selling, general and administrative	2,678	2,418	2,443
Interest, net	399	455	508
Restructuring and other exit costs	30	84	26
Divestitures (gain)	–	(499)	–
Debt repurchase costs	–	137	–
Total Costs and Expenses	10,073	9,429	9,561
Earnings before Income Taxes and After-tax Earnings from Joint Ventures	1,567	1,815	1,509
Income Taxes	541	664	528
After-tax Earnings from Joint Ventures	64	89	74
Net Earnings	$ 1,090	$ 1,240	$ 1,055
Earnings per Share – Basic	$ 3.05	$ 3.34	$ 2.82
Earnings per Share – Diluted	$ 2.90	$ 3.08	$ 2.60
Dividends per Share	$ 1.34	$ 1.24	$ 1.10

See accompanying notes to consolidated financial statements.

GENERAL MILLS, INC. AND SUBSIDIARIES
CONSOLIDATED BALANCE SHEETS

In Millions	May 28, 2006	May 29, 2005
ASSETS		
Current Assets:		
Cash and cash equivalents	$ 647	$ 573
Receivables	1,076	1,034
Inventories	1,055	1,037
Prepaid expenses and other current assets	216	203
Deferred income taxes	182	208
Total Current Assets	3,176	3,055
Land, Buildings and Equipment	2,997	3,111
Goodwill	6,652	6,684
Other Intangible Assets	3,607	3,532
Other Assets	1,775	1,684
Total Assets	$18,207	$18,066
LIABILITIES AND EQUITY		
Current Liabilities:		
Accounts payable	$ 1,151	$ 1,136
Current portion of long-term debt	2,131	1,638
Notes payable	1,503	299
Other current liabilities	1,353	1,111
Total Current Liabilities	6,138	4,184
Long-term Debt	2,415	4,255
Deferred Income Taxes	1,822	1,851
Other Liabilities	924	967
Total Liabilities	11,299	11,257
Minority Interests	1,136	1,133
Stockholders' Equity:		
Cumulative preference stock, none issued	–	–
Common stock, 502 shares issued	50	50
Additional paid-in capital	5,737	5,691
Retained earnings	5,107	4,501
Common stock in treasury, at cost, shares of 146 in 2006 and 133 in 2005	(5,163)	(4,460)
Unearned compensation	(84)	(114)
Accumulated other comprehensive income	125	8
Total Stockholders' Equity	5,772	5,676
Total Liabilities and Equity	$18,207	$18,066

See accompanying notes to consolidated financial statements.

GENERAL MILLS, INC. AND SUBSIDIARIES
CONSOLIDATED STATEMENTS OF CASH FLOWS

In Millions Fiscal Year Ended	May 28, 2006	May 29, 2005	May 30, 2004
Cash Flows – Operating Activities			
Net earnings	$ 1,090	$ 1,240	$ 1,055
Adjustments to reconcile net earnings to net cash provided by operating activities:			
Depreciation and amortization	424	443	399
Deferred income taxes	26	9	109
Changes in current assets and liabilities	184	258	(186)
Tax benefit on exercised options	41	62	63
Pension and other postretirement costs	(74)	(70)	(21)
Restructuring and other exit costs	30	84	26
Divestitures (gain)	–	(499)	–
Debt repurchase costs	–	137	–
Other, net	50	47	16
Net Cash Provided by Operating Activities	1,771	1,711	1,461
Cash Flows – Investing Activities			
Purchases of land, buildings and equipment	(360)	(434)	(653)
Investments in businesses	(26)	–	(10)
Investments in affiliates, net of investment returns and dividends	78	84	32
Purchases of marketable securities	–	(1)	(7)
Proceeds from sale of marketable securities	1	33	129
Proceeds from disposal of land, buildings and equipment	11	24	36
Proceeds from disposition of businesses	–	799	–
Other, net	4	(9)	2
Net Cash Provided (Used) by Investing Activities	(292)	496	(470)
Cash Flows – Financing Activities			
Change in notes payable	1,197	(1,057)	(1,023)
Issuance of long-term debt	–	2	576
Payment of long-term debt	(1,386)	(1,115)	(248)
Proceeds from issuance of preferred membership interests of subsidiary	–	835	–
Common stock issued	157	195	192
Purchases of common stock for treasury	(885)	(771)	(24)
Dividends paid	(485)	(461)	(413)
Other, net	(3)	(13)	(3)
Net Cash Used by Financing Activities	(1,405)	(2,385)	(943)
Increase (Decrease) in Cash and Cash Equivalents	74	(178)	48
Cash and Cash Equivalents – Beginning of Year	573	751	703
Cash and Cash Equivalents – End of Year	$ 647	$ 573	$ 751
Cash Flow from Changes in Current Assets and Liabilities:			
Receivables	$ (18)	$ (9)	$ (22)
Inventories	(6)	30	24
Prepaid expenses and other current assets	(7)	9	(15)
Accounts payable	14	(19)	(161)
Other current liabilities	201	247	(12)
Changes in Current Assets and Liabilities	$ 184	$ 258	$ (186)

See accompanying notes to consolidated financial statements.

GENERAL MILLS, INC. AND SUBSIDIARIES
NOTES TO CONSOLIDATED FINANCIAL STATEMENTS

1. Summary of Significant Accounting Policies

Basis of Presentation   Our consolidated financial statements include the accounts of General Mills, Inc. and all subsidiaries in which it has a controlling financial interest. Intercompany transactions and accounts are eliminated in consolidation. Certain prior years' amounts have been reclassified to conform to the current year presentation.

Our fiscal year ends on the last Sunday in May. Fiscal years 2006 and 2005 each consisted of 52 weeks, and fiscal 2004 consisted of 53 weeks. Our International segment, with the exception of Canada and our export operations, is reported for the 12 calendar months ended April 30.

Cash and Cash Equivalents   We consider all investments purchased with an original maturity of three months or less to be cash equivalents.

Inventories   Most U.S. inventories are valued at the lower of cost, using the last-in, first-out (LIFO) method, or market. Grain inventories are valued at market. The balance of the U.S. inventories and inventories of consolidated operations outside of the U.S. are valued at the lower of cost, using the first-in, first-out (FIFO) method, or market.

Shipping costs associated with the distribution of finished product to our customers are recorded as selling, general and administrative expense and are recognized when the related finished product is shipped to the customer.

Land, Buildings, Equipment and Depreciation   Land is recorded at historical cost. Buildings and equipment are recorded at historical cost and depreciated over estimated useful lives, primarily using the straight-line method. Ordinary maintenance and repairs are charged to operating costs. Buildings are usually depreciated over 40 to 50 years, and equipment is usually depreciated over three to 15 years. Accelerated depreciation methods generally are used for income tax purposes. When an item is sold or retired, the accounts are relieved of its cost and related accumulated depreciation; the resulting gains and losses, if any, are recognized in earnings.

Long-lived assets are reviewed for impairment whenever events or changes in circumstances indicate that their carrying amount may not be recoverable. An impairment loss would be recognized when estimated undiscounted future cash flows from the operation and disposition of the asset group are less than the carrying amount of the asset group. Asset groups are identifiable and largely independent of other asset groups. Measurement of an impairment loss would be based on the excess of the carrying amount of the asset group over its fair value. Fair value is measured using discounted cash flows or independent appraisals as appropriate.

Goodwill and Other Intangible Assets   Goodwill represents the difference between the purchase prices of acquired companies and the related fair values of net assets acquired. Goodwill is not subject to amortization and is tested for impairment annually for each of our reporting units and whenever events or changes in circumstances indicate that an impairment may have occurred. Impairment testing compares the carrying amount of goodwill for a reporting unit with its fair value. Fair value is estimated based on discounted cash flows. When the carrying amount of goodwill exceeds its fair value, an impairment has occurred. We have completed our annual impairment testing and determined none of our goodwill is impaired.

The costs of patents, copyrights and other intangible assets with finite lives are amortized over their estimated useful lives. Intangibles with indefinite lives, principally brands, are carried at cost. Finite and indefinite-lived intangible assets are also tested for impairment annually and whenever events or changes in circumstances indicate that their carrying value may not be recoverable. An impairment loss would be recognized when estimated undiscounted future cash flows are less than the carrying amount of the intangible. Measurement of an impairment loss would be based on the excess of the carrying amount of the intangible over its fair value. We have completed our annual impairment testing and determined none of our other intangible assets are impaired.

Investments in Joint Ventures   Our investments in companies over which we have the ability to exercise significant influence are stated at cost plus our share of undistributed earnings or losses. We also receive royalty income from certain joint ventures, incur various expenses (primarily research and development) and record the tax impact of certain joint venture operations that are structured as partnerships.

Variable Interest Entities   At May 28, 2006, we had invested in four variable interest entities (VIEs). We are the primary beneficiary (PB) of General Mills Capital, Inc. (GM Capital), a subsidiary that we consolidate as set forth in Note Eight. We also have an interest in a contract manufacturer at our former facility in Geneva, Illinois. Even though we are the PB, we have not consolidated this entity because it is not material to our results of operations, financial condition, or liquidity at May 28, 2006. This entity had property and equipment of $50 million and long-term debt of $50 million at May 28, 2006. We are not the PB of the remaining two VIEs. Our maximum exposure to loss from these VIEs is limited to the $150 million minority interest in GM Capital, the contract manufacturer's debt and our $6 million equity investments in the remaining two VIEs.

Revenue Recognition   We recognize sales revenue upon acceptance of the shipment by our customers. Sales are reported net of consumer coupon, trade promotion and other costs, including estimated returns. Coupons are expensed when distributed based on estimated redemptions. Trade promotions are expensed based on estimated participation and performance levels for offered programs. We generally do not allow a right of return. However, on a limited case-by-case basis with prior approval, we may allow customers to return product in saleable condition for redistribution to other customers or outlets. Returns are expensed as reductions of net sales.

Advertising Production Costs We expense the production costs of advertising the first time that the advertising takes place.

Research and Development All expenditures for research and development are charged against earnings in the year incurred.

Foreign Currency Translation Results of foreign operations are translated into U.S. dollars using the average exchange rates each month. Assets and liabilities of these operations are translated at the period-end exchange rates, and the differences from historical exchange rates are reflected within Accumulated Other Comprehensive Income in Stockholders' Equity as cumulative translation adjustments.

Derivative Instruments We use derivatives primarily to hedge our exposure to changes in foreign exchange rates, interest rates and commodity prices. All derivatives are recognized on the Consolidated Balance Sheets at fair value based on quoted market prices or management's estimate of their fair value and are recorded in either current or noncurrent assets or liabilities based on their maturity. Changes in the fair values of derivatives are recorded in earnings or other comprehensive income, based on whether the instrument is designated as a hedge transaction and, if so, the type of hedge transaction. Gains or losses on derivative instruments reported in other comprehensive income are reclassified to earnings in the period the hedged item affects earnings. If the underlying hedged transaction ceases to exist, any associated amounts reported in other comprehensive income are reclassified to earnings at that time. Any ineffectiveness is recognized in earnings in the current period.

Stock-based Compensation We use the intrinsic value method for measuring the cost of compensation paid in our common stock. This method defines our cost as the excess of the stock's market value at the time of the grant over the amount that the employee is required to pay. Our stock option plans require that the employee's payment (i.e., exercise price) be at least the market value as of the grant date.

Restricted share awards, including restricted stock and restricted stock units, are measured at the fair market value of our stock on the date of the award, and are initially recorded in Stockholders' Equity as unearned compensation, net of estimated forfeitures. Unearned compensation is amortized to compensation expense on a straight-line basis over the requisite service period.

The following table illustrates the pro forma effect on net earnings and earnings per share if we had applied the fair value recognition provisions of Statement of Financial Accounting Standard (SFAS) No. 123, (SFAS 123) "Accounting for Stock-Based Compensation," to all employee stock-based compensation, net of estimated forfeitures.

In Millions, Except per Share Data, Fiscal Year Ended	May 28, 2006	May 29, 2005	May 30, 2004
Net earnings, as reported	$1,090	$1,240	$1,055
Add: After-tax stock-based employee compensation expense included in reported net earnings	28	24	17
Deduct: After-tax stock-based employee compensation expense determined under fair value requirements of SFAS 123	(48)	(62)	(67)
Pro forma net earnings	$1,070	$1,202	$1,005
Earnings per share:			
Basic – as reported	$ 3.05	$ 3.34	$ 2.82
Basic – pro forma	$ 2.99	$ 3.24	$ 2.68
Diluted – as reported	$ 2.90	$ 3.08	$ 2.60
Diluted – pro forma	$ 2.84	$ 2.99	$ 2.49

The weighted-average grant date fair values of the employee stock options granted were estimated as $8.04 in fiscal 2006, $8.32 in fiscal 2005, and $8.54 in fiscal 2004 using the Black-Scholes option-pricing model with the following assumptions:

Fiscal Year	2006	2005	2004
Risk-free interest rate	4.3%	4.0%	3.9%
Expected life	7 years	7 years	7 years
Expected volatility	20.0%	21.0%	21.0%
Expected dividend growth rate	10.2%	9.8%	10.0%

In December 2004, the Financial Accounting Standards Board (FASB) issued SFAS No. 123(Revised) "Share-Based Payment" (SFAS 123R), which generally requires public companies to measure the cost of employee services received in exchange for an award of equity instruments based on the grant-date fair value and to recognize this cost over the period during which the employee is required to provide service in exchange for the award. The standard is effective for public companies for annual periods beginning after June 15, 2005, with several transition options regarding prospective versus retrospective application. We will adopt SFAS 123R in the first quarter of fiscal 2007, using the modified prospective method. Accordingly, prior year results will not be restated, but fiscal 2007 results will be presented as if we had applied the fair value method of accounting for stock-based compensation from the beginning of fiscal 1997. SFAS 123R also requires the benefits of tax deductions in excess of recognized compensation cost to be reported as a financing cash flow, rather than as an operating cash flow as currently required, thereby reducing net operating cash flows and increasing net financing cash flows in periods following adoption. While those amounts cannot be estimated for future periods, the amount of operating cash flows generated in prior periods for such excess tax deductions was $41 million for fiscal 2006, $62 million for fiscal 2005 and $63 million for fiscal 2004.

Certain equity-based compensation plans contain provisions that accelerate vesting of awards upon retirement, disability or death of eligible employees and directors. For the periods presented, we generally recognized stock compensation expense over the stated vesting period of the award, with any unamortized expense recognized immediately if an acceleration event occurred. SFAS No. 123R specifies that a stock-based award is vested when the employee's retention of the award is no longer contingent on providing subsequent service. Accordingly, beginning in fiscal 2007, we will prospectively revise our expense attribution method so that the related compensation cost is recognized immediately for awards granted to retirement-eligible individuals or over the period from the grant date to the date retirement eligibility is achieved, if less than the stated vesting period.

Use of Estimates Preparing our consolidated financial statements in conformity with accounting principles generally accepted in the United States requires us to make estimates and assumptions that affect reported amounts of assets and liabilities, disclosures of contingent assets and liabilities at the date of the financial statements, and the reported amounts of revenues and expenses during the reporting period. Actual results could differ from our estimates.

New Accounting Standards The FASB ratified in October 2004, Emerging Issues Task Force Issue No. 04-8, "The Effect of Contingently Convertible Debt on Diluted Earnings per Share" (EITF 04-8). EITF 04-8 was effective for us in the third quarter of fiscal 2005. The adoption of EITF 04-8 increased diluted shares outstanding to give effect to shares that were contingently issuable related to our zero coupon convertible debentures issued in October 2002. Also, net earnings used for earnings per share calculations were adjusted, using the if-converted method. See Note Eleven.

In the second quarter of fiscal 2006, we adopted SFAS No. 153, "Exchanges of Nonmonetary Assets – An Amendment of APB Opinion No. 29." SFAS 153 eliminates the exception from fair value measurement for nonmonetary exchanges of similar productive assets and replaces it with an exception for exchanges that do not have commercial substance. The adoption of SFAS 153 did not have any impact on our results of operations or financial condition.

In March 2005, the FASB issued FASB Interpretation No. 47, "Accounting for Conditional Asset Retirement Obligations" (FIN 47). FIN 47 requires that liabilities be recognized for the fair value of a legal obligation to perform asset retirement activities that are conditional on a future event if the amount can be reasonably estimated. We adopted FIN 47 in the fourth quarter of fiscal 2006 and it did not have a material impact on our results of operations or financial condition.

2. Acquisitions and Divestitures

On March 3, 2006, we acquired Elysées Consult S.A., the franchise operator of a *Häagen-Dazs* shop in France. On November 21, 2005, we acquired Croissant King, a producer of frozen pastry products in Australia. On October 31, 2005, we acquired a controlling financial interest in Pinedale Holdings Pte. Limited, an operator of *Häagen-Dazs* cafes in Singapore and Malaysia. The aggregate purchase price of our fiscal 2006 acquisitions was $26 million. The pro forma effect of these acquisitions was not material.

On February 28, 2005, Snack Ventures Europe (SVE), our snacks joint venture with PepsiCo, Inc., was terminated and our 40.5 percent interest was redeemed. On April 4, 2005, we sold our Lloyd's barbecue business to Hormel Foods Corporation. We received $799 million in cash proceeds from these dispositions and recorded $499 million in gains in fiscal 2005.

3. Restructuring and Other Exit Costs

In fiscal 2006, we recorded restructuring and other exit costs of $30 million pursuant to approved plans consisting of: $13 million related to the closure of our Swedesboro, New Jersey plant; $6 million related to the closure of a production line at our Montreal, Quebec plant; $4 million related to restructuring actions at our Allentown, Pennsylvania plant; $3 million of asset impairment charges for one of our plants; and $4 million related primarily to fiscal 2005 initiatives. The fiscal 2006 restructuring charges included $17 million to write down assets to fair value, $7 million of severance costs for 425 employees being terminated, and $6 million of other exit costs. The carrying value of the assets written down was $18 million. The fair values of the assets written down were determined using discounted cash flows.

The fiscal 2006 initiatives were undertaken to increase asset utilization and reduce manufacturing costs. The actions included decisions to: close our leased frozen dough foodservice plant in Swedesboro, New Jersey, affecting 101 employees; shut down a portion of our frozen dough foodservice plant in Montreal, Quebec, affecting 77 employees; realign and modify product and manufacturing

Darden Restaurants, Inc.—Preparing Financial Statements

Darden Restaurants, Inc. was incorporated in Florida in 1995 but its parent company, GMRI, began in 1968 as Red Lobster Inns of America. Now Darden Restaurants is the largest publicly held casual dining restaurant company in the world. In 2007, the company served over 350 million meals in 1,397 restaurants in the United States and Canada. The company operates the following restaurants: Red Lobster, Olive Garden, Bahama Breeze, Smokey Bones Barbeque & Grill and Seasons 52. (Source: Company Form 10-K)

Learning Objectives
- Determine how economic events affect a company's financial statements.
- Record economic events and prepare a simple set of financial statements.
- Understand how to adjust financial statements for accruals and reclassification.

In this case you will record basic transactions to recreate the May 27, 2007, balance sheet and income statement for Darden Restaurants, Inc. The company's actual financial statements are included at the end of the case. You can use them to guide your work. Note: All dollar figures are in millions.

To complete this case you need to develop a computerized spreadsheet. The structure of the spreadsheet follows after the case questions. Because of space constraints, the spreadsheet is reproduced on sequential pages here. However, you should create one worksheet with all the accounts across the top.

Use the numbers from Darden's actual financial statements to enter the opening (i.e., May 28, 2006) and ending (i.e., May 27, 2007) Balance Sheets and Statements of Earnings balances into the accounts on your spreadsheet. Create two separate accounts for "Land, building and equipment," one for the original cost of these assets (2006: $4,228.5 and 2007: $3,961.4) and a second account for the related accumulated depreciation (2006: $1,782.5 and 2007: $1,777). Show this second account as a negative amount (because it is a contra-asset account) so that the sum of the two accounts combined equals the "Land, building and equipment, net" amount on the balance sheet (2006: $2,446.0 and 2007: $2,184.4). Some smaller balance sheet accounts have been combined in the spreadsheet. The Statement of Earnings accounts should have opening balances of $0.

The row labeled "Unadjusted trial balance" should be defined so that each cell equals the sum of the opening balance and the transactions in that column. The row labeled "Pre-closing balances" should be defined so that each cell equals the sum of the "Unadjusted trial balance" and the adjustments and reclassifications in that column.

The last row (i.e., May 27, 2007, Actual Balance Sheets and Statements of Earnings) serves as a check that your year-end balances are correct. You can define another row that calculates the difference between the actual year-end balances and your calculated balances. A necessary (but not sufficient) condition for a correct spreadsheet is that the value in each cell of the "difference" row is equal to zero.

Some transactions will affect only the balance sheet (e.g. transaction #1), some will affect both the balance sheet and the income statement (e.g. transaction #2). Indicate increases in each account as positive numbers and decreases in each account as negative numbers.

Use the "Retained Earnings" account only for the dividend entry (#23) and the closing entry. Record the transactions and adjustments that affect Statement of Earnings accounts directly to the appropriate revenue and expense accounts. You will close these temporary accounts to "Retained Earnings" in part *g* of the case.

Concepts

a. Prior to examining Darden's balance sheet, think about what a restaurant chain does. What accounts do you expect to see on the balance sheet? Which are the major assets? Liabilities?

Process

b. Record each of the following transactions for the year ended May 27, 2007, in the spreadsheet. All figures are in millions of dollars.

   1. The company purchased $1,754.4 of food and beverage inventory on account.

Darden Restaurants, Inc.—Preparing Financial Statements
1

2. The company had $5,816.5 in sales to customers. Of this, $149.3 was on account.

3. The cost of the food and beverage sold (#2 above) was $1,663.4.

4. The company paid cash for restaurant employees' wages and other labor expenses totaling $1,875.6.

5. The company paid cash for restaurant expenses totaling $888.

6. The company sold gift cards for which it collected $117.6 in cash. The cards expire in one year. The company does not recognize this as revenue until customers actually use (redeem) the cards.

7. The company paid cash for selling, general and administrative expenses totaling $473.8.

8. The company collected $140 of accounts receivable.

9. The company paid cash of $345.2 to purchase new equipment and cash of $2.2 to acquire other long-term assets.

10. Darden Restaurants' management signed a new labor agreement with its employees. The two-year agreement takes effect on July 1, 2007, and calls for total wage and benefit increases of $120 per year.

11. Darden Restaurants disposed of equipment that had a net book value of $61 for cash proceeds of $57.9. The difference is considered an operating loss on the statement of earnings and is included in "Selling, general and administrative" expense. The equipment had an original cost of $110.

12. The company paid $1,752.5 to settle accounts payable.

13. During the year, the company paid bondholders $40.1 of interest.

14. Customers redeemed gift cards totaling $108.5.

15. On May 15, 2007, Darden paid $33.5 for casualty and property insurance policies. Coverage on these one-year policies begins June 1, 2007.

16. The company paid $59.5 to employees for wages and benefits relating to the prior-year. Of this, $56 related to accrued payroll and $3.5 to accrued payroll taxes.

17. The company received $167.4 when it borrowed short-term debt.

18. The company repurchased its own stock for $371.2 cash. Hint: Treasury stock is a contra-equity account, which is why it is bracketed on the balance sheet. Purchasing more treasury stock makes the negative balance grow more negative (that is, larger in absolute terms).

19. The company granted stock options to certain key executives. These options had a fair value of $31.6 and Darden recorded this as an expense ("Selling, general and administrative") and increased the common stock account by that amount. Cash was not affected.

20. During the year executives exercised previously-granted stock options. Darden collected cash of $95.9 from the executives and received a tax refund from the government. These transactions affected a number of accounts. These transactions have already been entered into the spreadsheet in aggregate.

21. The company repaid long-term debt amounting to $153. Hint: Part of this debt was classified as current portion of long-term debt on the May 28, 2006, balance sheet.

22. The company recorded income taxes expense of $153.7 which involved cash of $197.8 and other tax-related asset and liability accounts. This transaction has already been entered into the spreadsheet.

23. The company declared and paid $65.7 of dividends.

24. During the year, Darden Restaurants closed one Red Lobster location and one Olive Garden location. No cash was involved in these closures but the company recorded an impairment charge of $2.4. These restaurant properties had an original cost of $9.2 and accumulated depreciation of $6.8 at the time Darden closed them.

c. Prepare an unadjusted trial balance from the spreadsheet. *Hint*: the unadjusted balance for Retained Earnings is $1,619.

d. Based on the transactions you recorded in parts *b* and *c*, list at least three adjustments or reclassifications that need to be made prior to preparing the final financial statements.

e. Record in the spreadsheet, the following adjustments and reclassifications.

25. By the middle of May 2007, Darden Restaurants had decided to close certain under-performing restaurants. Even though these restaurants have not yet been closed, Darden must record the transactions in the current year. This necessitated three adjustments, as follows:

a) Darden must write down certain assets at the restaurants that will be closed such that the May 27, 2007, balance sheet reports the assets' (lower) fair value. To record this write-down, Darden must reduce asset accounts by the following amounts:

Land, buildings and equipment	396.0
Accumulated depreciation	145.8
Other assets (long-term)	3.9

In addition, Darden must accrue anticipated payroll-related severance costs of $12.5, which will be paid next year. The combined asset write-down and payroll accrual result in a total charge of $266.6, which Darden includes in an account labeled, "Loss from discontinued operations."

b) During the year, the discontinued restaurants generated profit of $90.9. However, Darden must reclassify this profit as discontinued for financial statement presentation purposes. On the income statement, Darden includes this profit in, "Loss from discontinued operations." Before any adjustments, the sales and expenses are recorded in the following accounts:

Sales	357.9
Food and beverage expense	82.8
Restaurant labor expense	96.2
Restaurant expenses	53.5
Selling, general and administrative expenses	34.5

c) For balance sheet presentation purposes, certain remaining assets and liabilities must be reclassified as discontinued assets and liabilities, respectively. Darden labels these discontinued accounts as, "Assets held for sale" and "Liabilities associated with assets held for sale". Before any adjustments, these assets and liabilities are included in the following accounts:

Inventories	44.6
Land, buildings and equipment	97.1
Other assets (long-term)	2.3
Accounts payable	37.1
Other liabilities (long-term)	5.2

26. The last payday for the company was May 22, 2007. Restaurant employees had earned, but the company had not yet paid, $28.8 of additional wages through May 27, 2007. Darden senior executives earned performance bonuses of $42.1, which the company will not pay until after 2010. Darden included the executives' compensation in Selling, general and administrative expense.

27. On May 15, 2006, Darden paid the casualty and property insurance premium of $29.9 and recorded the amount as a prepaid expense (a current asset). Coverage on these one-year policies began June 1, 2006. Adjust for this expired insurance premium at May 27, 2007 by recording the insurance expense in "Selling, general and administrative" expense.

28. Depreciation and amortization expense was $200.4 for the fiscal year. Of this, $196.1 pertained to buildings and equipment and $4.3 related to amortization of certain intangible assets, which Darden includes with "Other assets."

29. A review of the company's records revealed that $11.4 of previously deferred (unearned) rent had been earned during the year. Darden includes rent revenue as a reduction to "Selling, general and administrative expense."

30. On May 27, 2007, Darden Restaurant employees took a physical count of inventory. The cost of food and beverages at all continuing locations on that date was $209.6.

31. In May 2007, a consulting firm hired by Darden Restaurants issued a report stating that the "Olive Garden" brand name is worth $360.

f. Construct a statement of earnings for the year ended May 27, 2007. Use the headings from your spreadsheet columns as the account titles.

g. Close all the temporary accounts on the statement of earnings to retained earnings.

h. Prepare the May 27, 2007, balance sheet. Use the headings from your spreadsheet columns as the account titles.

i. For each of the transactions that involve cash, indicate whether the transaction would appear in the "operating," "investing," or "financing" section of the statement of cash flows.

Darden Restaurants, Inc. (Assets $ millions)	Cash and Equivalents	Receivables, net	Inventories, net	Prepaid expenses other curr assets	Deferred income taxes	Assets held for sale	Land, buildings equip, at cost	Accumulated depreciation	Other assets
Balance May 28, 2006	42.3	37.1	198.7	29.9	69.6	-	4,228.5	(1,782.5)	186.6
Transactions:									
1. Purchase inventory									
2. Sale for cash and on account									
3. Cost of food / beverages									
4. Pay restaurant wages									
5. Pay restaurant expenses									
6. Sell gift cards									
7. Pay SG&A expenses									
8. Collect accounts receivable									
9. Purchase equipment & other									
10. Sign labor agreement									
11. Dispose of equipment									
12. Settle accounts payable									
13. Pay interest expense									
14. Redeem gift cards									
15. Pay insurance premiums									
16. Settle accrued liabilities									
17. Borrow short-term debt									
18. Repurchase stock									
19. Grant stock options									
20. Executives exercise options	95.9								(27.3)
21. Repay long-term debt	(197.8)								
22. Record tax expense					12.1				
23. Pay dividends									
24. Close two restaurants									
Unadjusted trial balance									
Adjustments:									
25. a. Record discontinued ops									
25. b. Reclassify revenue/expenses									
25. c. Reclassify assets/liabilities									
26. Accrue wages and bonuses									
27. Adjust prepaid expenses asset									
28. Record depreciation expense									
29. Recognize rent revenue									
30. Adjust inventory									
31. Olive Garden brand name									
Pre-closing balances									
Closing entry									
Balance May 27, 2007	30.2	46.4	209.6	33.5	81.7	144.0	3,961.4	(1,777.0)	151.0

Darden Restaurants, Inc.—Preparing Financial Statements

4

Darden Restaurants, Inc. (Current liabilities $ millions)	Accounts payable	Short-term debt	Accrued payroll	Accrued income taxes	Other accrued taxes	Unearned revenues	Current portion of LT debt	Other current liabilities	Liabilities of assets for sale
Balance May 28, 2006	213.2	44.0	123.2	64.8	46.9	100.8	149.9	283.3	-
Transactions:									
1. Purchase inventory									
2. Sale for cash and on account									
3. Cost of food / beverages									
4. Pay restaurant wages									
5. Pay restaurant expenses									
6. Sell gift cards									
7. Pay SG&A expenses									
8. Collect accounts receivable									
9. Purchase equipment & other									
10. Sign labor agreement									
11. Dispose of equipment									
12. Settle accounts payable									
13. Pay interest expense									
14. Redeem gift cards									
15. Pay insurance premiums									
16. Settle accrued liabilities									
17. Borrow short-term debt									
18. Repurchase stock									
19. Grant stock options									
20. Executives exercise options									
21. Repay long-term debt				11.1					
22. Record tax expense								21.7	
23. Pay dividends									
24. Close two restaurants									
Unadjusted trial balance									
Adjustments:									
25. a. Record discontinued ops									
25. b. Reclassify revenue/expenses									
25. c. Reclassify assets/liabilities									
26. Accrue wages and bonuses									
27. Adjust prepaid expenses asset									
28. Record depreciation expense									
29. Recognize rent revenue									
30. Adjust inventory									
31. Olive Garden brand name									
Pre-closing balances									
Closing entry									
Balance May 27, 2007	178.0	211.4	108.5	75.9	43.4	109.9	-	305.0	42.3

Darden Restaurants, Inc.—Preparing Financial Statements

5

Darden Restaurants, Inc. (LT liabs. / Equity $ millions)	Long-term debt	Deferred income taxes	Deferred rent	Other liabilities	Common stock and surplus	Retained earnings	Treasury stock	Accum other comp income	Unearned comp and notes
Balance May 28, 2006	494.7	90.6	138.5	30.5	1,806.4	1,684.7	(2,211.2)	(5.5)	(44.6)
Transactions:									
1. Purchase inventory									
2. Sale for cash and on account									
3. Cost of food / beverages									
4. Pay restaurant wages									
5. Pay restaurant expenses									
6. Sell gift cards									
7. Pay SG&A expenses									
8. Collect accounts receivable									
9. Purchase equipment & other									
10. Sign labor agreement									
11. Dispose of equipment									
12. Settle accounts payable									
13. Pay interest expense									
14. Redeem gift cards									
15. Pay insurance premiums									
16. Settle accrued liabilities									
17. Borrow short-term debt									
18. Repurchase stock									
19. Grant stock options									
20. Executives exercise options					66.3		5.9	(27.3)	23.7
21. Repay long-term debt									
22. Record tax expense		(64.8)							
23. Pay dividends									
24. Close two restaurants									
Unadjusted trial balance									
Adjustments:									
25. a. Record discontinued ops									
25. b. Reclassify revenue/expenses									
25. c. Reclassify assets/liabilities									
26. Accrue wages and bonuses									
27. Adjust prepaid expenses asset									
28. Record depreciation expense									
29. Recognize rent revenue									
30. Adjust inventory									
31. Olive Garden brand name									
Pre-closing balances									
Closing entry									
Balance May 27, 2007	491.6	25.8	127.1	67.4	1,904.3	1,820.4	(2,576.5)	(32.8)	(20.9)

Darden Restaurants, Inc.—Preparing Financial Statements

6

Darden Restaurants, Inc. (Inc. Statement $ millions)	Sales	Food and beverage	Restaurant labor	Restaurant expenses	Selling general & admin	Depreciation and amort.	Interest, net	Asset impairment	Income taxes	Loss from discont ops
Balance May 28, 2006										
Transactions:										
1. Purchase inventory										
2. Sale for cash and on account										
3. Cost of food / beverages										
4. Pay restaurant wages										
5. Pay restaurant expenses										
6. Sell gift cards										
7. Pay SG&A expenses										
8. Collect accounts receivable										
9. Purchase equipment & other										
10. Sign labor agreement										
11. Dispose of equipment										
12. Settle accounts payable										
13. Pay interest expense										
14. Redeem gift cards										
15. Pay insurance premiums										
16. Settle accrued liabilities										
17. Borrow short-term debt										
18. Repurchase stock										
19. Grant stock options										
20. Executives exercise options										
21. Repay long-term debt										
22. Record tax expense									153.7	
23. Pay dividends										
24. Close two restaurants										
Unadjusted trial balance										
Adjustments:										
25. a. Record discontinued ops										
25. b. Reclassify revenue/expenses										
25. c. Reclassify assets/liabilities										
26. Accrue wages and bonuses										
27. Adjust prepaid expenses asset										
28. Record depreciation expense										
29. Recognize rent revenue										
30. Adjust inventory										
31. Olive Garden brand name										
Pre-closing balances	5,567.1	1,616.1	1,808.2	834.5	534.6	200.4	40.1	2.4	153.7	175.7
Closing entry	0.0	0.0	0.0	0.0	0.0	0.0	0.0	0.0	0.0	0.0
Balance May 27, 2007	0.0	0.0	0.0	0.0	0.0	0.0	0.0	0.0	0.0	0.0

Darden Restaurants, Inc.—Preparing Financial Statements

7

Consolidated Statements of Earnings

(In millions, except per share data)	May 27, 2007	May 28, 2006	May 29, 2005
		Fiscal Year Ended	
Sales	$ 5,567.1	$ 5,353.6	$ 4,977.6
Costs and expenses:			
Cost of sales:			
Food and beverage	1,616.1	1,570.0	1,490.3
Restaurant labor	1,808.2	1,722.1	1,594.2
Restaurant expenses	834.5	806.4	742.8
Total cost of sales, excluding restaurant depreciation and amortization of $186.4, $181.1 and $180.2, respectively	$ 4,258.8	$ 4,098.5	$ 3,827.3
Selling, general and administrative	534.6	504.8	467.3
Depreciation and amortization	200.4	197.0	194.7
Interest, net	40.1	43.9	44.7
Asset impairment, net	2.4	1.3	2.0
Total costs and expenses	$ 5,036.3	$ 4,845.5	$ 4,536.0
Earnings before income taxes	530.8	508.1	441.6
Income taxes	(153.7)	(156.3)	(141.7)
Earnings from continuing operations	$ 377.1	$ 351.8	$ 299.9
Losses from discontinued operations, net of tax benefit of $112.9, $12.1 and $8.3, respectively	(175.7)	(13.6)	(9.3)
Net earnings	$ 201.4	$ 338.2	$ 290.6
Basic net earnings per share:			
Earnings from continuing operations	$ 2.63	$ 2.35	$ 1.91
Losses from discontinued operations	(1.23)	(0.09)	(0.06)
Net earnings	$ 1.40	$ 2.26	$ 1.85
Diluted net earnings per share:			
Earnings from continuing operations	$ 2.53	$ 2.24	$ 1.84
Losses from discontinued operations	(1.18)	(0.08)	(0.06)
Net earnings	$ 1.35	$ 2.16	$ 1.78
Average number of common shares outstanding:			
Basic	143.4	149.7	156.7
Diluted	148.8	156.9	163.4

See accompanying notes to consolidated financial statements.

Consolidated Balance Sheets

(In millions)	May 27, 2007	May 28, 2006
Assets		
Current assets:		
Cash and cash equivalents	$ 30.2	$ 42.3
Receivables, net	46.4	37.1
Inventories, net	209.6	198.7
Prepaid expenses and other current assets	33.5	29.9
Deferred income taxes	81.7	69.6
Assets held for sale (Note 2)	144.0	–
Total current assets	$ 545.4	$ 377.6
Land, buildings and equipment, net	2,184.4	2,446.0
Other assets	151.0	186.6
Total assets	$ 2,880.8	$ 3,010.2
Liabilities and Stockholders' Equity		
Current liabilities:		
Accounts payable	$ 178.0	$ 213.2
Short-term debt	211.4	44.0
Accrued payroll	108.5	123.2
Accrued income taxes	75.9	64.8
Other accrued taxes	43.4	46.9
Unearned revenues	109.9	100.8
Current portion of long-term debt	–	149.9
Other current liabilities	305.0	283.3
Liabilities associated with assets held for sale (Note 2)	42.3	–
Total current liabilities	$ 1,074.4	$ 1,026.1
Long-term debt, less current portion	491.6	494.7
Deferred income taxes	25.8	90.6
Deferred rent	127.1	138.5
Other liabilities	67.4	30.5
Total liabilities	$ 1,786.3	$ 1,780.4
Stockholders' equity:		
Common stock and surplus, no par value. Authorized 500.0 shares; issued 277.7 and 274.7 shares, respectively; outstanding 141.4 and 147.0 shares, respectively	$ 1,904.3	$ 1,806.4
Preferred stock, no par value. Authorized 25.0 shares; none issued and outstanding	–	–
Retained earnings	1,820.4	1,684.7
Treasury stock, 136.3 and 127.7 shares, at cost, respectively	(2,576.5)	(2,211.2)
Accumulated other comprehensive income (loss)	(32.8)	(5.5)
Unearned compensation	(20.6)	(44.2)
Officer notes receivable	(0.3)	(0.4)
Total stockholders' equity	$ 1,094.5	$ 1,229.8
Total liabilities and stockholders' equity	$ 2,880.8	$ 3,010.2

See accompanying notes to consolidated financial statements.

$\mathcal{C}$onsolidated Statements of Cash Flows

	Fiscal Year Ended		
(In millions)	May 27, 2007	May 28, 2006	May 29, 2005
Cash flows – operating activities			
Net earnings	$ 201.4	$ 338.2	$ 290.6
Losses from discontinued operations, net of tax benefit	175.7	13.6	9.3
Adjustments to reconcile net earnings from continuing operations to cash flows:			
Depreciation and amortization	200.4	197.0	194.7
Asset impairment charges, net	2.4	1.3	2.0
Amortization of loan costs	1.7	3.0	3.6
Change in current assets and liabilities	(20.5)	127.3	19.6
Contribution to postretirement plan	(0.8)	(0.4)	(0.5)
Loss on disposal of land, buildings and equipment	3.1	2.4	1.1
Change in cash surrender value of trust-owned life insurance	(10.4)	(6.0)	(3.4)
Deferred income taxes	(27.1)	(30.7)	(33.6)
Change in deferred rent	2.5	4.8	5.2
Change in other liabilities	3.3	2.5	9.7
Income tax benefits credited to equity	–	34.3	43.0
Stock-based compensation expense	31.6	12.5	9.9
Other, net	6.5	(0.7)	(1.2)
Net cash provided by operating activities of continuing operations	$ 569.8	$ 699.1	$ 550.0
Cash flows – investing activities			
Purchases of land, buildings and equipment	(345.2)	(273.5)	(210.4)
Increase in other assets	(2.2)	(5.4)	(1.2)
Proceeds from disposal of land, buildings and equipment	57.9	20.6	18.0
Net cash used in investing activities of continuing operations	$(289.5)	$(258.3)	$(193.6)
Cash flows – financing activities			
Proceeds from issuance of common stock	56.6	61.8	74.7
Income tax benefits credited to equity	40.0	–	–
Dividends paid	(65.7)	(59.2)	(12.5)
Purchases of treasury stock	(371.2)	(434.2)	(311.7)
ESOP note receivable repayments	3.3	3.6	3.4
Increase (decrease) in short-term debt	167.4	44.0	(14.5)
Proceeds from issuance of long-term debt	–	294.7	–
Repayment of long-term debt	(153.3)	(303.6)	(3.4)
Net cash used in financing activities of continuing operations	$(322.9)	$(392.9)	$(264.0)
Cash flows – discontinued operations			
Net cash provided by operating activities of discontinued operations	36.6	17.9	33.2
Net cash used in investing activities of discontinued operations	(6.1)	(66.3)	(119.5)
Net cash provided by (used in) discontinued operations	$ 30.5	$ (48.4)	$ (86.3)
(Decrease) increase in cash and cash equivalents	(12.1)	(0.5)	6.1
Cash and cash equivalents – beginning of year	42.3	42.8	36.7
Cash and cash equivalents – end of year	$ 30.2	$ 42.3	$ 42.8
Cash flows from changes in current assets and liabilities			
Receivables	(5.9)	(0.7)	(5.4)
Inventories	(14.2)	37.0	(35.8)
Prepaid expenses and other current assets	(5.6)	(2.1)	(3.9)
Accounts payable	(23.6)	29.4	8.8
Accrued payroll	(8.2)	7.9	10.0
Accrued income taxes	11.1	12.4	3.7
Other accrued taxes	0.7	2.5	4.1
Unearned revenues	11.8	11.5	12.2
Other current liabilities	13.4	29.4	25.9
Change in current assets and liabilities	$ (20.5)	$ 127.3	$ 19.6

See accompanying notes to consolidated financial statements.

Darden Restaurants, Inc.—Transactions and Adjustments

Darden Restaurants, Inc. was incorporated in Florida in 1995 but its parent company, GMRI, began in 1968 as Red Lobster Inns of America. Now Darden Restaurants is the largest publicly held casual dining restaurant company in the world. In fiscal 2007, the company served over 350 million meals in 1,397 restaurants in the United States and Canada. The company operates the following restaurants: Red Lobster, Olive Garden, Bahama Breeze, Smokey Bones Barbeque & Grill and Seasons 52. (Source: Company Form 10-K)

Learning Objectives
- Use financial statement information to infer underlying transactions.
- Understand some common linkages between balance sheet and income statement accounts.
- Prepare accounting adjustments (adjusting journal entries) and closing entries.

Refer to the May 2007 financial statements of Darden Restaurants, Inc. Each part of this case is independent. Restrict the account titles used in your answers to those used in the financial statements.

Concepts

a. To prepare accrual-based financial statements, a company must adjust its accounts. This is accomplished with periodic adjustments (also known as adjusting journal entries or accounting adjustments). For each account below, explain the types of transactions or events that necessitate periodic adjustments to the account for the typical company.

    i.   "Inventories, net."

    ii.   "Receivables, net."

    iii.   "Accrued payroll."

    iv.   "Unearned revenues."

    v.   "Land, buildings and equipment, net."

b. In general, what other accounts typically require periodic adjustments?

c. Why do companies close their books at the end of each accounting period? What types of accounts are closed in this process?

Process

d. For each item in quotations, provide the year-end total disclosed in Darden's 2007 income statement. Write a journal entry to record the activity for the year. Assume that the company recorded a single (summary) journal entry.

    i.   "Sales." Assume that 5% of sales are on account, 3% of sales represent gift card redemptions, and the rest are cash sales.

    ii.   "Interest, net" expense. Assume that all these costs were paid in cash.

e. For each item in quotations, provide the amount and direction of the cash flow disclosed in Darden's 2007 statement of cash flows. Write a journal entry to record the cash inflow or outflow in 2007. Assume that the company recorded a single (summary) journal entry.

    i.   "Purchases of land, buildings and equipment."

    ii.   "Dividends paid." Assume that Darden recorded dividends as "payable" when they were declared.

iii.   "Purchase of treasury stock."

iv.   "Repayment of long-term debt."

f.   Assume that the following is an excerpt from Darden's unadjusted trial balance at May 27, 2007. The debits and credits indicated are the totals in each account before any accounting adjustments have been made for the year-end.

Account title	Debits	Credits
Receivables, net	48.5	
Inventories, net	221.9	
Prepaid expenses and other current assets	43.2	
Land, buildings and equipment, net	2,384.8	
Accrued payroll		91.7
Accrued income taxes		80.6
Unearned revenues		121.4

Use this information and Darden Restaurants' final balance sheet to prepare any required accounting adjustments for the year ending May 27, 2007.

g.   Consider the year-end totals disclosed in Darden Restaurants' 2007 income statement. Write a journal entry to close the temporary income statement accounts.

h.   Reconcile the activity in the retained earnings account for the year ending May 27, 2007.

Consolidated Statements of Earnings

(In millions, except per share data)	May 27, 2007	May 28, 2006	May 29, 2005
Sales	$ 5,567.1	$ 5,353.6	$ 4,977.6
Costs and expenses:			
Cost of sales:			
Food and beverage	1,616.1	1,570.0	1,490.3
Restaurant labor	1,808.2	1,722.1	1,594.2
Restaurant expenses	834.5	806.4	742.8
Total cost of sales, excluding restaurant depreciation and amortization of $186.4, $181.1 and $180.2, respectively	$ 4,258.8	$ 4,098.5	$ 3,827.3
Selling, general and administrative	534.6	504.8	467.3
Depreciation and amortization	200.4	197.0	194.7
Interest, net	40.1	43.9	44.7
Asset impairment, net	2.4	1.3	2.0
Total costs and expenses	$ 5,036.3	$ 4,845.5	$ 4,536.0
Earnings before income taxes	530.8	508.1	441.6
Income taxes	(153.7)	(156.3)	(141.7)
Earnings from continuing operations	$ 377.1	$ 351.8	$ 299.9
Losses from discontinued operations, net of tax benefit of $112.9, $12.1 and $8.3, respectively	(175.7)	(13.6)	(9.3)
Net earnings	$ 201.4	$ 338.2	$ 290.6
Basic net earnings per share:			
Earnings from continuing operations	$ 2.63	$ 2.35	$ 1.91
Losses from discontinued operations	(1.23)	(0.09)	(0.06)
Net earnings	$ 1.40	$ 2.26	$ 1.85
Diluted net earnings per share:			
Earnings from continuing operations	$ 2.53	$ 2.24	$ 1.84
Losses from discontinued operations	(1.18)	(0.08)	(0.06)
Net earnings	$ 1.35	$ 2.16	$ 1.78
Average number of common shares outstanding:			
Basic	143.4	149.7	156.7
Diluted	148.8	156.9	163.4

Fiscal Year Ended

See accompanying notes to consolidated financial statements.

Consolidated Balance Sheets

(In millions)	May 27, 2007	May 28, 2006
Assets		
Current assets:		
Cash and cash equivalents	$ 30.2	$ 42.3
Receivables, net	46.4	37.1
Inventories, net	209.6	198.7
Prepaid expenses and other current assets	33.5	29.9
Deferred income taxes	81.7	69.6
Assets held for sale (Note 2)	144.0	–
Total current assets	$ 545.4	$ 377.6
Land, buildings and equipment, net	2,184.4	2,446.0
Other assets	151.0	186.6
Total assets	$ 2,880.8	$ 3,010.2
Liabilities and Stockholders' Equity		
Current liabilities:		
Accounts payable	$ 178.0	$ 213.2
Short-term debt	211.4	44.0
Accrued payroll	108.5	123.2
Accrued income taxes	75.9	64.8
Other accrued taxes	43.4	46.9
Unearned revenues	109.9	100.8
Current portion of long-term debt	–	149.9
Other current liabilities	305.0	283.3
Liabilities associated with assets held for sale (Note 2)	42.3	–
Total current liabilities	$ 1,074.4	$ 1,026.1
Long-term debt, less current portion	491.6	494.7
Deferred income taxes	25.8	90.6
Deferred rent	127.1	138.5
Other liabilities	67.4	30.5
Total liabilities	$ 1,786.3	$ 1,780.4
Stockholders' equity:		
Common stock and surplus, no par value. Authorized 500.0 shares; issued 277.7 and 274.7 shares, respectively; outstanding 141.4 and 147.0 shares, respectively	$ 1,904.3	$ 1,806.4
Preferred stock, no par value. Authorized 25.0 shares; none issued and outstanding	–	–
Retained earnings	1,820.4	1,684.7
Treasury stock, 136.3 and 127.7 shares, at cost, respectively	(2,576.5)	(2,211.2)
Accumulated other comprehensive income (loss)	(32.8)	(5.5)
Unearned compensation	(20.6)	(44.2)
Officer notes receivable	(0.3)	(0.4)
Total stockholders' equity	$ 1,094.5	$ 1,229.8
Total liabilities and stockholders' equity	$ 2,880.8	$ 3,010.2

See accompanying notes to consolidated financial statements.

Consolidated Statements of Cash Flows

(In millions)	May 27, 2007	May 28, 2006	May 29, 2005
	Fiscal Year Ended		
Cash flows – operating activities			
Net earnings	$ 201.4	$ 338.2	$ 290.6
Losses from discontinued operations, net of tax benefit	175.7	13.6	9.3
Adjustments to reconcile net earnings from continuing operations to cash flows:			
Depreciation and amortization	200.4	197.0	194.7
Asset impairment charges, net	2.4	1.3	2.0
Amortization of loan costs	1.7	3.0	3.6
Change in current assets and liabilities	(20.5)	127.3	19.6
Contribution to postretirement plan	(0.8)	(0.4)	(0.5)
Loss on disposal of land, buildings and equipment	3.1	2.4	1.1
Change in cash surrender value of trust-owned life insurance	(10.4)	(6.0)	(3.4)
Deferred income taxes	(27.1)	(30.7)	(33.6)
Change in deferred rent	2.5	4.8	5.2
Change in other liabilities	3.3	2.5	9.7
Income tax benefits credited to equity	–	34.3	43.0
Stock-based compensation expense	31.6	12.5	9.9
Other, net	6.5	(0.7)	(1.2)
Net cash provided by operating activities of continuing operations	$ 569.8	$ 699.1	$ 550.0
Cash flows – investing activities			
Purchases of land, buildings and equipment	(345.2)	(273.5)	(210.4)
Increase in other assets	(2.2)	(5.4)	(1.2)
Proceeds from disposal of land, buildings and equipment	57.9	20.6	18.0
Net cash used in investing activities of continuing operations	$(289.5)	$(258.3)	$(193.6)
Cash flows – financing activities			
Proceeds from issuance of common stock	56.6	61.8	74.7
Income tax benefits credited to equity	40.0	–	–
Dividends paid	(65.7)	(59.2)	(12.5)
Purchases of treasury stock	(371.2)	(434.2)	(311.7)
ESOP note receivable repayments	3.3	3.6	3.4
Increase (decrease) in short-term debt	167.4	44.0	(14.5)
Proceeds from issuance of long-term debt	–	294.7	–
Repayment of long-term debt	(153.3)	(303.6)	(3.4)
Net cash used in financing activities of continuing operations	$(322.9)	$(392.9)	$(264.0)
Cash flows – discontinued operations			
Net cash provided by operating activities of discontinued operations	36.6	17.9	33.2
Net cash used in investing activities of discontinued operations	(6.1)	(66.3)	(119.5)
Net cash provided by (used in) discontinued operations	$ 30.5	$ (48.4)	$ (86.3)
(Decrease) increase in cash and cash equivalents	(12.1)	(0.5)	6.1
Cash and cash equivalents – beginning of year	42.3	42.8	36.7
Cash and cash equivalents – end of year	$ 30.2	$ 42.3	$ 42.8
Cash flows from changes in current assets and liabilities			
Receivables	(5.9)	(0.7)	(5.4)
Inventories	(14.2)	37.0	(35.8)
Prepaid expenses and other current assets	(5.6)	(2.1)	(3.9)
Accounts payable	(23.6)	29.4	8.8
Accrued payroll	(8.2)	7.9	10.0
Accrued income taxes	11.1	12.4	3.7
Other accrued taxes	0.7	2.5	4.1
Unearned revenues	11.8	11.5	12.2
Other current liabilities	13.4	29.4	25.9
Change in current assets and liabilities	$ (20.5)	$ 127.3	$ 19.6

See accompanying notes to consolidated financial statements.

Lucent Technologies, Inc.—Revenue Recognition

Lucent Technologies designs and delivers networks for the world's largest communications service providers. Backed by Bell Labs research and development, Lucent relies on its strengths in mobility, optical, data and voice networking technologies as well as software and services to develop next-generation networks. The company's systems, services and software are designed to help customers quickly deploy and better manage their networks and create new, revenue-generating services that help businesses and consumers. As of December 31, 2002, Lucent employed approximately 40,000 people worldwide (two years prior, the figure was close to 123,000). Lucent is listed on the New York Stock Exchange under the symbol LU. (Source: Company 2002 Form 10-K)

Learning Objectives
- Define revenues and gains. Explain the difference between the two.
- Critically assess the revenue recognition policies of a particular company.
- Consider the trade-offs between rules-based and principles-based accounting standards.
- Understand the role of audit committees in corporate governance and financial reporting.
- Explain how financial statement users can evaluate the quality of a company's reported revenue.

Refer to the 2002 financial statements of Lucent Technologies, Inc.

✧ Concepts ✧

a. In your own words, define "revenues." Explain how revenues are different from "gains."

b. Describe what it means for a business to "recognize" revenues. What specific accounts and financial statements are affected by the process of revenue recognition?

c. When does Lucent recognize revenues?

d. In general, what incentives do company managers have to make self-serving revenue recognition choices?

✧ Process ✧

e. Assume that all of Lucent's sales revenue is "on account." Prepare a journal entry that summarizes the sales activity for fiscal 2002.

f. Consider the following hypothetical revenue recognition scenarios and answer the associated questions. Note that there may be more than one acceptable answer. Support your answers with reasoned argumentation. Indicate where more information is required.

    i. In September 2002, Lucent contracted to provide services to a regional Bell operating company (RBOC) for a four-year period beginning November 1, 2002. The $50 million contract calls for annual payments of $12 million in monthly installments of $1 million. At the signing of the contract in September 2002, Lucent received $2 million. How much revenue will Lucent recognize in fiscal 2002? Provide a journal entry that records the receipt of the initial payment.

    ii. On June 30, 2002, Lucent sold telecom equipment to a small start-up company. The contract states that the sales price is $15 million. The equipment has been installed, tested, and accepted by the customer. Because the customer is short of cash, Lucent's sales team agreed to provide vendor financing for the sale. The customer is scheduled to make the $15 million payment in full on June 30, 2004, which represents the only cash Lucent will receive from the customer. Assume that Lucent's cost of borrowing is 10% and the customer's is 15%. Provide the journal entries recorded by Lucent on June 30 and September 30, 2002, as well as June 30, 2004. Assume that Lucent prepares formal financial statements quarterly.

iii. On December 31, 2002, Lucent learned that the customer in part *ii* failed to achieve success in the marketplace with its main product. The start-up company remains short of cash and is having trouble negotiating with its lenders. Provide the journal entry Lucent would make if they learned that the customer's borrowing cost had risen to 17%.

iv. At the end of September 2002, Lucent signed a $200 million contract to provide equipment, software, and services to an RBOC. By September 30, 2002, some of the equipment had been delivered and installed at the RBOC. Other equipment had been manufactured and shipped, but not yet received by the customer. Still other products are to be delivered over the following two fiscal years. All products contain a two-year warranty. Lucent has promised to maintain the products and provide software upgrades and a dedicated customer support team for a three-year period. How should Lucent recognize revenue on this contract?

v. For the contract in part *iv*, how would your answer change if you learned that there was a side agreement allowing the RBOC to return the products, no questions asked, through January 31, 2003? What if Lucent promised significant discounts on future purchases in return for signing the initial $200 million contract?

vi. How could Lucent manage its reported earnings through strategic revenue recognition choices for the contract in part *iv*?

✧ Analysis ✧

g. Evaluate the three-year trend in Lucent's sales and margins. Conduct an internet search to establish reasons for the change. Good starting points include the company's website www.lucent.com, the Securities and Exchange Commission's EDGAR service (where Lucent is required to file financial reports) at www.sec.gov, and online investing sites.

h. Refer to the accompanying article, Disparities in How U.K. Companies Report Sales Make Investors Wary, from the April 1, 2002 issue of *The Wall Street Journal*.

i. Why do markets "punish" firms that use unconventional or aggressive revenue recognition methods?

ii. What can companies do to avoid such outcomes?

iii. Nick Gomer, the Ernst and Young partner quoted in the article, suggests that the best practice is to follow detailed U.S. guidance. Why might he suggest that? How does his argument hold up against the call for accounting standards to be more principles-based and less rules-based?

i. Assume that you are a member of Lucent's audit committee. Your role, in part, is to evaluate the appropriateness of the company's financial reporting policies and choices. Each quarter, you meet with Lucent's external auditors and discuss financial reporting matters with them.

i. What questions would you ask Lucent's external auditors to assure yourself that the company's revenue recognition policy was reasonable?

ii. What signs might indicate that a company aggressively recognizes revenue? By those standards, does Lucent recognize revenue aggressively?

WSJ.com THE WALL STREET JOURNAL.
ONLINE

April 1, 2002

WORLD STOCK MARKETS

Disparities in How U.K. Companies Report Sales Make Investors Wary

BY GREN MANUEL

LONDON—When is a "sale" a sale?

Don't ask United Kingdom companies. The way in which these concerns report sales varies widely, according to a survey of 588 recent annual reports released last month by Company Reporting, a research house based in Edinburgh, Scotland. The disparities in the U.K. come as accounting has become a hot-button issue in the U.S., making global investors wary of companies that seem to bend the rules.

To get a sense of how critical this issue can be, look at British Airways. Although normally conservative about its financial reporting—it books sales only when a passenger has paid and is belted into the seat—it is a different story when it comes to reporting revenue from frequent-flier programs. British Airways books revenue as fliers rack up air miles, whereas U.S. accounting rules call for revenue to be recognized when air miles are exchanged for seats.

The result: In the year ended March 31, 2001, British Airways reported GBP 15 million ($21.4 million) of revenue that it couldn't have booked in the U.S. In a year when pretax profit was GBP 150 million, that is significant.

British Airways wasn't available to comment.

Company Reporting's study found that even U.K. companies in similar businesses report sales differently. For instance, of 100 companies in the consumer-goods sector, 26 reported revenue on delivery of service, 26 when an invoice is issued, 11 over the life of a contract, three on acceptance of a contract, and one on the completion of a contract. The rest of the companies surveyed didn't disclose a policy.

In particular, wide variations were found in the building industry, with some companies booking sales on the exchange of contracts, some when buildings are substantially complete and contracts are exchanged, and others only when a sale is complete and legal title is passed over. With sales in this sector often bracketed in the GBP 1 million range, even a small number of sales booked in a different year can make a big difference.

High-technology companies tended to disclose more information about how they book revenue than other sectors. Many of these tech companies were nudged along by the fact that they have U.S. investors or prepare accounts according to U.S. standards.

The sector includes Cable & Wireless PLC, a company that demonstrated how critical this issue can be after being panned by analysts for booking revenue upfront on long-term sales of network capacity even if the contracts span decades. Sales of such long-term network capacity have been cited as a factor in the downfall of Global Crossing Ltd., now in Chapter 11 bankruptcy proceedings. In Cable & Wireless's case, however, the company did disclose its policy in its annual report.

In terms of active disclosure, no company matches ARM Holdings PLC, a company whose core business is long-term licensing of chip technology. Its 20 paragraphs of explanation in its annual report seem designed to broadcast a message of conservatism and stability.

Nick Gomer, a partner for Ernst & Young in the U.K., says the real problem is companies that don't explain policy. "Having different policies is not in itself a problem, if it's very clearly explained how the numbers are arrived at," he said. "It does make it much more difficult to compare the performance of businesses."

He said that for simple businesses, there isn't much leeway in how revenue is recognized, but for other sectors, such as software, there are many options. The best practice is to follow the increasingly detailed guidance coming out of the U.S.

The clear risk to investors from this issue was demonstrated March 19, when Amey PLC, a services company heavily involved in long-term government contracts, was punished by the market when it switched its accounting, including its policy on revenue recognition. Analysts expecting a profit were instead shocked with an GBP 18.3 million loss due to more-conservative accounting. The stock fell 17% and caused widespread fallout in the sector. This was despite management protests that operating results were better than expected.

LUCENT TECHNOLOGIES INC. AND SUBSIDIARIES

CONSOLIDATED STATEMENTS OF OPERATIONS

(Amounts in Millions, Except Per Share Amounts)   *Years ended September 30,*

	2002	2001	2000
Revenues:			
Products	$ 9,632	$ 17,132	$23,978
Services	2,689	4,162	4,926
Total revenues	12,321	21,294	28,904
Costs:			
Products	8,452	15,596	13,265
Services	2,317	3,640	3,925
Total costs	10,769	19,236	17,190
Gross margin	1,552	2,058	11,714
Operating expenses:			
Selling, general and administrative	3,969	7,410	5,610
Research and development	2,310	3,520	3,179
Purchased in-process research and development	–	–	559
Business restructuring charges and asset impairments, net	2,252	10,157	–
Total operating expenses	8,531	21,087	9,348
Operating income (loss)	(6,979)	(19,029)	2,366
Other income (expense), net	292	(357)	333
Interest expense	382	518	342
Income (loss) from continuing operations before income taxes	(7,069)	(19,904)	2,357
Provision (benefit) for income taxes	4,757	(5,734)	924
Income (loss) from continuing operations	**(11,826)**	**(14,170)**	**1,433**
Income (loss) from discontinued operations, net	73	(3,172)	(214)
Income (loss) before extraordinary item and cumulative effect of accounting changes	(11,753)	(17,342)	1,219
Extraordinary gain, net	–	1,182	–
Cumulative effect of accounting changes, net	–	(38)	–
Net income (loss)	(11,753)	(16,198)	1,219
Conversion cost – 8% redeemable convertible preferred stock	(29)	–	–
Preferred stock dividends and accretion	(167)	(28)	–
Net income (loss) applicable to common shareowners	**$(11,949)**	**$(16,226)**	**$ 1,219**

EARNINGS (LOSS) PER COMMON SHARE – BASIC

	2002	2001	2000
Income (loss) from continuing operations	$ (3.51)	$ (4.18)	$ 0.44
Net income (loss) applicable to common shareowners	$ (3.49)	$ (4.77)	$ 0.38

EARNINGS (LOSS) PER COMMON SHARE – DILUTED

	2002	2001	2000
Income (loss) from continuing operations	$ (3.51)	$ (4.18)	$ 0.43
Net income (loss) applicable to common shareowners	$ (3.49)	$ (4.77)	$ 0.37

	2002	2001	2000
Weighted average number of common shares outstanding – basic	3,426.7	3,400.7	3,232.3
Weighted average number of common shares outstanding – diluted	3,426.7	3,400.7	3,325.9

See Notes to Consolidated Financial Statements.

LUCENT TECHNOLOGIES INC. AND SUBSIDIARIES

CONSOLIDATED BALANCE SHEETS

(Dollars in Millions, Except Per Share Amounts)   *September 30,*

	2002	2001
ASSETS		
Cash and cash equivalents	$ 2,894	$ 2,390
Short-term investments	1,526	–
Receivables, less allowance of $325 in 2002 and $634 in 2001	1,647	4,594
Inventories	1,363	3,646
Contracts in process, net	10	1,027
Deferred income taxes, net	–	2,658
Other current assets	1,715	1,788
Total current assets	9,155	16,103
Property, plant and equipment, net	1,977	4,416
Prepaid pension costs	4,355	4,958
Deferred income taxes, net	–	2,695
Goodwill and other acquired intangibles, net of accumulated amortization of $910 in 2002 and $832 in 2001	224	1,466
Other assets	2,080	2,724
Net long-term assets of discontinued operations	–	1,302
Total assets	**$17,791**	**$33,664**
LIABILITIES		
Accounts payable	$ 1,298	$ 1,844
Payroll and benefit-related liabilities	1,094	1,500
Debt maturing within one year	120	1,135
Other current liabilities	3,814	5,285
Net current liabilities of discontinued operations	–	405
Total current liabilities	6,326	10,169
Postretirement and postemployment benefit liabilities	5,230	5,481
Pension liability	2,752	80
Long-term debt	3,236	3,274
Company-obligated 7.75% mandatorily redeemable convertible preferred securities of subsidiary trust	1,750	–
Deferred income taxes, net	–	152
Other liabilities	1,551	1,651
Total liabilities	**20,845**	**20,807**
Commitments and contingencies		
8.00% redeemable convertible preferred stock	1,680	1,834
SHAREOWNERS' (DEFICIT) EQUITY		
Preferred Stock – par value $1.00 per share; authorized shares: 250,000,000; issued and outstanding none	–	–
Common stock – par value $.01 per share; Authorized shares: 10,000,000,000; 3,491,585,126 issued and 3,490,310,034 outstanding shares at September 30, 2002 and 3,414,815,908 issued and 3,414,167,155 outstanding shares at September 30, 2001	35	34
Additional paid-in capital	20,606	21,702
Accumulated deficit	(22,025)	(10,272)
Accumulated other comprehensive loss	(3,350)	(441)
Total shareowners' (deficit) equity	**(4,734)**	**11,023**
Total liabilities, redeemable convertible preferred stock and shareowners' (deficit) equity	**$17,791**	**$33,664**

See Notes to Consolidated Financial Statements.

LUCENT TECHNOLOGIES INC. AND SUBSIDIARIES

CONSOLIDATED STATEMENTS OF CASH FLOWS

(Dollars in Millions)		Years ended September 30,	
	2002	**2001**	**2000**
OPERATING ACTIVITIES			
Net income (loss)	$(11,753)	$(16,198)	$1,219
Less: Income (loss) from discontinued operations	73	(3,172)	(214)
Extraordinary gain	–	1,182	–
Cumulative effect of accounting changes	–	(38)	–
Income (loss) from continuing operations	(11,826)	(14,170)	1,433
Adjustments to reconcile income (loss) from continuing operations to net cash used in operating activities, net of effects of acquisitions and dispositions of businesses and manufacturing operations:			
Non-cash portion of business restructuring charges, net	827	9,322	–
Asset impairment charges	975	–	–
Depreciation and amortization	1,470	2,536	1,667
Provision for bad debts and customer financings	1,253	2,249	505
Tax benefit from employee stock options	–	18	1,064
Deferred income taxes	5,268	(5,935)	491
Purchased in-process research and development	–	–	559
Net pension and postretirement benefit credit	(972)	(1,083)	(802)
Gains on sales of businesses	(725)	(56)	(30)
Other adjustments for non-cash items	843	551	(222)
Changes in operating assets and liabilities:			
Decrease (increase) in receivables	2,493	3,627	(1,626)
Decrease (increase) in inventories and contracts in process	2,552	881	(2,242)
(Decrease) increase in accounts payable	(539)	(759)	263
Changes in other operating assets and liabilities	(2,375)	(602)	(1,763)
Net cash used in operating activities from continuing operations	**(756)**	**(3,421)**	**(703)**
INVESTING ACTIVITIES			
Capital expenditures	(449)	(1,390)	(1,915)
Dispositions of businesses and manufacturing operations, net of cash disposed	2,576	3,187	250
Sales or maturity of investments	31	57	820
Purchases of non-consolidated investments	(30)	(101)	(680)
Purchases of short-term investments	(1,518)	–	–
Proceeds from the sale or disposal of property, plant and equipment	194	177	26
Other investing activities	(47)	21	(60)
Net cash provided by (used in) investing activities from continuing operations	**757**	**1,951**	**(1,559)**
FINANCING ACTIVITIES			
Issuance of company-obligated 7.75% mandatorily redeemable convertible preferred securities of subsidiary trust	1,750	–	–
(Repayments of) proceeds from credit facilities	(1,000)	3,500	–
Net (repayments of) proceeds from other short-term borrowings	(104)	(2,147)	1,355
Issuance of long-term debt	–	302	72
Repayments of long-term debt	(47)	(754)	(387)
Issuance of 8% redeemable convertible preferred stock	–	1,831	–
Issuance of common stock	64	222	1,444
Dividends paid on preferred and common stock	(149)	(204)	(255)
Other financing activities	(46)	(125)	–
Net cash provided by financing activities from continuing operations	**468**	**2,625**	**2,229**
Effect of exchange rate changes on cash and cash equivalents	35	4	10
Net cash provided by (used in) continuing operations	504	1,159	(23)
Net cash used in discontinued operations	–	(236)	(196)
Net increase (decrease) in cash and cash equivalents	504	923	(219)
Cash and cash equivalents at beginning of year	2,390	1,467	1,686
Cash and cash equivalents at end of year	**$ 2,894**	**$ 2,390**	**$1,467**

See Notes to Consolidated Financial Statements.

(Dollars in Millions, Except Per Share Amounts)

1. SUMMARY OF SIGNIFICANT ACCOUNTING POLICIES

Basis of Consolidation

The consolidated financial statements include all majority-owned subsidiaries in which Lucent Technologies Inc. ("Lucent" or "the Company") exercises control. Investments in which Lucent exercises significant influence, but which it does not control (generally a 20% to 50% ownership interest), are accounted for under the equity method of accounting. All material intercompany transactions and balances have been eliminated. Except as otherwise noted, all amounts and disclosures reflect only Lucent's continuing operations.

Use of Estimates

The consolidated financial statements are prepared in conformity with generally accepted accounting principles. Management is required to make estimates and assumptions that affect the amounts reported in the consolidated financial statements and accompanying disclosures. Actual results could differ from those estimates. Among other things, estimates are used in accounting for long-term contracts, allowances for bad debts and customer financings, inventory obsolescence, restructuring reserves, product warranty, amortization and impairment of intangibles, goodwill, and capitalized software, depreciation and impairment of property, plant and equipment, employee benefits, income taxes, contingencies, and loss reserves for discontinued operations. Estimates and assumptions are periodically reviewed and the effects of any material revisions are reflected in the consolidated financial statements in the period that they are determined to be necessary.

Foreign Currency Translation

For operations outside the U.S. that prepare financial statements in currencies other than the U.S. dollar, results of operations and cash flows are translated at average exchange rates during the period, and assets and liabilities are translated at end-of-period exchange rates. Translation adjustments are included as a separate component of accumulated other comprehensive loss in shareowners' (deficit) equity.

Revenue Recognition

Revenue is recognized when persuasive evidence of an agreement exists, delivery has occurred, the fee is fixed and determinable, and collection of the resulting receivable, including receivables of customers to which Lucent has provided customer financing, is probable. For sales generated from long-term contracts, primarily those related to customized network solutions and network build-outs, Lucent generally uses the percentage of completion method of accounting. In doing so, Lucent makes important judgments in estimating revenue and costs and in measuring progress toward completion. These judgments underlie the determinations regarding overall contract value, contract profitability and timing of revenue recognition. Revenue and cost estimates are revised periodically based on changes in circumstances; any

losses on contracts are recognized immediately. Lucent also sells products through multiple distribution channels, including resellers and distributors. For products sold through these channels, revenue is generally recognized when the reseller or distributor sells the product to the end user.

Most sales are generated from complex contractual arrangements that require significant revenue recognition judgments, particularly in the areas of multiple element arrangements and collectibility. Revenues from contracts with multiple element arrangements, such as those including installation and integration services, are recognized as each element is earned based on the relative fair value of each element and when there are no undelivered elements that are essential to the functionality of the delivered elements. Lucent has determined that most equipment is generally installed by Lucent within 90 days, but can be installed by the customer or a third party, and as a result, revenue is recognized when title passes to the customer, which usually is upon delivery of the equipment, provided all other revenue recognition criteria are met. Services revenues are generally recognized at time of performance. The assessment of collectibility is particularly critical in determining whether revenue should be recognized in the current market environment. As part of the revenue recognition process, Lucent determines whether trade and notes receivables are reasonably assured of collection based on various factors, including the ability to sell those receivables and whether there has been deterioration in the credit quality of customers that could result in the inability to collect or sell the receivables. In situations where Lucent has the ability to sell the receivables, revenue is recognized to the extent of the value Lucent could reasonably expect to realize from the sale. Lucent defers revenue and related costs when it is uncertain as to whether it will be able to collect or sell the receivable. Lucent defers revenue but recognizes costs when it determines that the collection or sale of the receivables is unlikely.

Research and Development and Software Development Costs

Research and development costs are charged to expense as incurred. However, the costs incurred for the development of computer software that will be sold, leased or otherwise marketed are capitalized when technological feasibility has been established, generally when all of the planning, designing, coding and testing activities that are necessary in order to establish that the product can be produced to meet its design specifications including functions, features and technical performance requirements are completed. These capitalized costs are subject to an ongoing assessment of recoverability based on anticipated future revenues and changes in hardware and software technologies. Costs that are capitalized include direct labor and related overhead.

Amortization of capitalized software development costs begins when the product is available for general release. Amortization is provided on a product-by-product basis on the straight-line method over periods not exceeding 18 months. Unamortized capitalized software development costs determined to be in excess of the net realizable value of the product are expensed immediately.

Google Inc.—Earnings Announcements and Information Environment

Google Inc., incorporated in September, 1998, operates global Internet search engines and related services. It provides web, image, group, news, and shopping search services through its Google.com website. In 2006, Google acquired YouTube, a consumer media company for viewers to watch and share Internet videos worldwide. Google generates revenue primarily by delivering online advertising. Revenue is recognized equal to the fees charged advertisers each time a user clicks on an ad displayed next to the search results pages on the Google website and each time an ad is displayed on the YouTube site. (Source: Company 2007 Form 10-K)

Learning Objectives
- Understand the purpose and content of managers' use of pro forma earnings and earnings guidance.
- Understand the type of information included in managers' quarterly press releases of financial information.
- Understand the timing of the release of earnings information to investors.
- Explore how investors respond to earnings and other information about a firm's performance.

Refer to the 2007 Google Inc., financial statements and Note 1.

 **Concepts**

a. What type of opinion did the auditors issue on Google's financial statements for 2007? What is the date of the audit opinion? Explain why the opinion date is different than the date of the financial statements.

b. Managers often report "pro forma" or "non-GAAP" earnings as supplemental information when reporting their Generally Accepted Accounting Principles (GAAP) earnings.

   i.   What information can a pro forma earnings number provide that the GAAP earnings number does not? Give examples of possible differences that might exist between the two earnings numbers.

   ii. Discuss potential advantages and disadvantages to using pro forma earnings to assess a firm's performance.

   iii. Explain the SEC's position on pro forma earnings. Why might the SEC have instituted this sort of requirement?

c. What is meant by the term "earnings guidance"? Why might managers provide earnings guidance or an earnings forecast in advance of the release of the actual earnings number for a quarter? Why might managers choose not to provide earnings guidance in advance of earnings?

d. Security or financial analysts employed at brokerage houses are typically assigned to follow particular firms within an industry.

   i.   Explain briefly what security analysts do.

   ii. What information do analysts typically include in their reports? How might this information effect investors' decisions?

   iii. What is meant by the term "consensus analyst forecast?"

   iv. Go to the Investor Relations section of Google's web site. According to the Analyst Coverage link, approximately how many analysts follow Google? In your opinion, is Google a "widely followed" company?

e. Investors widely anticipate the release of quarterly earnings information by companies. Earnings announcements often trigger strong stock price reactions. Discuss why investors see earnings announcements as so important. Explain in your own words, the nature of the link between a firm's earnings and its stock price.

✧   **Analysis**   ✧

f. Consider Google's Statements of Income and the detailed revenue table in Note 1.

    i. What is the biggest source of total advertising revenue? How has Google's revenue composition changed since 2005?

    ii. Compute Google's revenue growth (in percentage terms) for fiscal 2007 and fiscal 2006.

    iii. Which type of advertising revenue is driving growth: Google web sites or Google Network web sites?

g. Consider Google's Income from operations for fiscal 2007 and 2006.

    i. Compute the annual percentage change in Income from operations for each fiscal year. *Note:* your calculation should exclude the "one-time" expense recorded in 2005 related to the contribution to the Google Foundation. Compare the growth in Income from Operations to Revenue growth from part *f* above. Assess whether expenses have grown at a faster or slower pace than revenues.

    ii. Which expenses explain the differences in growth rates between Revenues and Income from operations? *Hint:* look at the growth in each expense during 2007 and 2006.

h. Read the excerpts of the press release titled "Google Announces Fourth Quarter and Fiscal Year 2007 Results" and review Google's operating performance reported in the Statements of Income.

    i. How would you characterize Google's financial performance, especially revenues and profitability, for the fourth quarter of fiscal 2007? For fiscal 2007?

    ii. The press release includes information about non-GAAP financial measures for the fourth quarter of 2007. Consider the table that reconciles GAAP measures to the non-GAAP measures. What explains the difference between GAAP Income from operation and the non-GAAP equivalent? Do you agree with Google's adjustments in computing non-GAAP earnings? Why or why not?

i. Use the attached stock-market charts for Google for the period January 1, 2007, through May 1, 2008, to answer the following questions.

    i. Compare Google's fiscal 2007 earnings performance with the movement in Google's stock price over 2007.

    ii. Compare Google's 2007 stock price performance with the performance of the broader set of firms trading on the NASDAQ exchange (that is, the NASDAQ index).

    iii. Based on the stock market chart, did the market perceive the earnings news in Google's press release dated January 31, 2008, as "good news" or "bad news"? *Note*: the press release was made available after the close of trading for the day.

j. Read the *BusinessWeek Online* article titled "Google Disappoints the Street."

    i. According to the article, how did Google's fourth quarter earnings compare to the consensus analyst forecast at the time of the release?

    ii. What other factors does the article discuss that might explain the market's negative reaction to the earnings press release?

PRESS RELEASE EXCERPTS

Google Announces Fourth Quarter and Fiscal Year 2007 Results

MOUNTAIN VIEW, Calif. - January 31, 2008 - Google Inc. (NASDAQ: GOOG) today announced financial results for the quarter and fiscal year ended December 31, 2007.

"We're very pleased with our performance this quarter," said Eric Schmidt, CEO of Google. "It reflects strong momentum in our core business, growing receptivity to our new business initiatives, and improved discipline in managing our operating expenses."

Q4 Financial Summary

Google reported revenues of $4.83 billion for the quarter ended December 31, 2007, an increase of 51% compared to the fourth quarter of 2006 and an increase of 14% compared to the third quarter of 2007. Google reports its revenues, consistent with GAAP, on a gross basis without deducting traffic acquisition costs, or TAC. In the fourth quarter of 2007, TAC totaled $1.44 billion, or 30% of advertising revenues.

Q4 Financial Highlights

Revenues - Google reported revenues of $4.83 billion for the quarter ended December 31, 2007, representing a 51% increase over fourth quarter 2006 revenues of $3.21 billion and a 14% increase over third quarter 2007 revenues of $4.23 billion. Google reports its revenues, consistent with GAAP, on a gross basis without deducting TAC.

Paid Clicks - Aggregate paid clicks, which include clicks related to ads served on Google sites and the sites of our AdSense partners, increased approximately 30% over the fourth quarter of 2006 and approximately 9% over the third quarter of 2007.

Other Cost of Revenues - Other cost of revenues, which is comprised primarily of data center operational expenses, credit card processing charges as well as content acquisition costs, increased to $516 million, or 11% of revenues, in the fourth quarter of 2007, compared to $441 million, or 10% of revenues, in the third quarter of 2007.

Operating Expenses - Operating expenses, other than cost of revenues, were $1.43 billion in the fourth quarter of 2007, or 30% of revenues, compared to $1.25 billion in the third quarter of 2007, or 30% of revenues. The operating expenses in the fourth quarter of 2007 included $756 million in payroll-related and facilities expenses, compared to $659 million in the third quarter of 2007.

Stock-Based Compensation (SBC) - In the fourth quarter of 2007, the total charge related to SBC was $245 million as compared to $198 million in the third quarter of 2007.

Operating Income - GAAP operating income in the fourth quarter of 2007 was $1.44 billion, or 30% of revenues. This compares to GAAP operating income of $1.32 billion, or 31% of revenues, in the third quarter of 2007. Non-GAAP operating income in the fourth quarter of 2007 was $1.69 billion, or 35% of revenues. This compares to non-GAAP operating income of $1.52 billion, or 36% of revenues, in the third quarter of 2007.

Net Income - GAAP net income for the fourth quarter of 2007 was $1.21 billion as compared to $1.07 billion in the third quarter of 2007. Non-GAAP net income was $1.41 billion in the fourth quarter of 2007, compared to $1.24 billion in the third quarter of 2007. GAAP EPS for the fourth quarter of 2007 was $3.79 on 318 million diluted shares outstanding, compared to $3.38 for the third quarter of 2007, on 317 million diluted shares outstanding. Non-GAAP EPS for the fourth quarter of 2007 was $4.43, compared to $3.91 in the third quarter of 2007.

PRESS RELEASE EXCERPTS (continued)

ABOUT NON-GAAP FINANCIAL MEASURES

To supplement our consolidated financial statements, which statements are prepared and presented in accordance with GAAP, we use the following non-GAAP financial measures: non-GAAP operating income, non-GAAP operating margin, non-GAAP net income, non-GAAP EPS and free cash flow. The presentation of this financial information is not intended to be considered in isolation or as a substitute for, or superior to, the financial information prepared and presented in accordance with GAAP. For more information on these non-GAAP financial measures, please see the tables captioned "Reconciliations of non-GAAP results of operations measures to the nearest comparable GAAP measures" and "Reconciliation from net cash provided by operating activities to free cash flow" included at the end of this release.

We use these non-GAAP financial measures for financial and operational decision making and as a means to evaluate period-to-period comparisons. Our management believes that these non-GAAP financial measures provide meaningful supplemental information regarding our performance and liquidity by excluding certain expenses and expenditures that may not be indicative of our "recurring core business operating results," meaning our operating performance excluding not only non-cash charges, such as stock-based compensation, but also discrete cash charges that are infrequent in nature. We believe that both management and investors benefit from referring to these non-GAAP financial measures in assessing our performance and when planning, forecasting and analyzing future periods.

Non-GAAP operating income and operating margin. We define non-GAAP operating income as operating income plus stock-based compensation. Non-GAAP operating margin is defined as non-GAAP operating income divided by revenues. Google considers these non-GAAP financial measures to be useful metrics for management and investors because they exclude the effect of stock-based compensation so that Google's management and investors can compare Google's recurring core business operating results over multiple periods. Because of varying available valuation methodologies, subjective assumptions and the variety of award types that companies can use under FAS 123R, Google's management believes that providing a non-GAAP financial measure that excludes stock-based compensation allows investors to make meaningful comparisons between Google's recurring core business operating results and those of other companies, as well as providing Google's management with an important tool for financial and operational decision making and for evaluating Google's own recurring core business operating results over different periods of time. There are a number of limitations related to the use of non-GAAP operating income versus operating income calculated in accordance with GAAP. First, non-GAAP operating income excludes some costs, namely, stock-based compensation, that are recurring. Stock-based compensation has been and will continue to be for the foreseeable future a significant recurring expense in Google's business. Second, stock-based compensation is an important part of our employees' compensation and impacts their performance. Third, the components of the costs that we exclude in our calculation of non-GAAP operating income may differ from the components that our peer companies exclude when they report their results of operations. Management compensates for these limitations by providing specific information regarding the GAAP amounts excluded from non-GAAP operating income and evaluating non-GAAP operating income together with operating income calculated in accordance with GAAP.

Non-GAAP net income and EPS. We define non-GAAP net income as net income plus stock-based compensation, less the related tax effects. We define non-GAAP EPS as non-GAAP net income divided by the weighted average shares, on a fully-diluted basis, outstanding as of December 31, 2007. We consider these non-GAAP financial measures to be a useful metric for management and investors for the same reasons that Google uses non-GAAP operating income and non-GAAP operating margin.

The accompanying tables have more details on the GAAP financial measures that are most directly comparable to non-GAAP financial measures and the related reconciliations between these financial measures.

Investor Contact:
Maria Shim
650-253-7663
marias@google.com

Media Contact:
Jon Murchinson
650-253-4437
jonm@google.com

PRESS RELEASE EXCERPTS (continued)

Google Inc.
Consolidated Statements of Income
(in thousands, except per share amounts)

(unaudited)	Three Months Ended December 31,		Twelve Months Ended December 31,	
	2006	**2007**	**2006***	**2007**
Revenues	$ 3,205,498	$ 4,826,679	$ 10,604,917	$ 16,593,986
Costs and expenses:				
Cost of revenues (including stock-based compensation expense of $10,874, $6,255, $17,629, $22,335)	1,283,148	1,955,825	4,225,027	6,649,085
Research and development (including stock-based compensation expense of $82,122, $161,372, $287,485, $569,797)	386,806	630,783	1,228,589	2,119,985
Sales and marketing (including stock-based compensation expense of $14,502, $38,085, $59,389, $131,638)	255,206	422,291	849,518	1,461,266
General and administrative (including stock-based compensation expense of $26,929, $39,588, $93,597, $144,876)	219,744	377,046	751,787	1,279,250
Total costs and expenses	2,144,904	3,385,945	7,054,921	11,509,586
Income from operations	1,060,594	1,440,734	3,549,996	5,084,400
Interest income and other, net	124,139	167,294	461,044	589,580
Income before income taxes	1,184,733	1,608,028	4,011,040	5,673,980
Provision for income taxes	154,017	401,579	933,594	1,470,260
Net income	$ 1,030,716	$ 1,206,449	$ 3,077,446	$ 4,203,720
Net income per share - basic	$ 3.36	$ 3.86	$ 10.21	$ 13.53
Net income per share - diluted	$ 3.29	$ 3.79	$ 9.94	$ 13.29
Shares used in per share calculation - basic	306,906	312,251	301,403	310,806
Shares used in per share calculation - diluted	313,459	317,925	309,548	316,210

*Derived from audited financial statements.

PRESS RELEASE EXCERPTS (continued)

Reconciliations of non-GAAP results of operations measures to the nearest comparable GAAP measures

The following table presents certain non-GAAP results before certain material items (in thousands, except per share amounts, unaudited):

	Three months ended September 30, 2007					Three months ended December 31, 2007				
	GAAP Actual	Operating Margin (d)	Adjustments	Non-GAAP Results	Operating Margin (d)	GAAP Actual	Operating Margin (d)	Adjustments	Non-GAAP Results	Operating Margin (d)
Income from operations	$ 1,317,842	31.1%	$ 197,956 (a) 197,956 (a) (31,011) (c)	$ 1,515,798	35.8%	$ 1,440,734	29.8%	$ 245,300 (b) 245,300 (b) (42,253) (c)	$ 1,686,034	34.9%
Net income	$ 1,069,98		$ 166,945	$ 1,236,934		$ 1,206,449		$ 203,047	$ 1,409,496	
Net income per share - diluted	$ 3.38			$ 3.91		$ 3.79			$ 4.43	
Shares used in per share calculation - diluted	316,576			316,576						

(a) To eliminate $198.0 million of stock-based compensation charges recorded in the third quarter of 2007.
(b) To eliminate $245.3 million of stock-based compensation charges recorded in the fourth quarter of 2007.
(c) To eliminate income tax effects related to charges noted in (a) and (b).
(d) Operating margin is defined as income from operations divided by revenues.

Google (Ticker: *GOOG*) Stock Charts
For the period January 1, 2007 to March 31, 2008

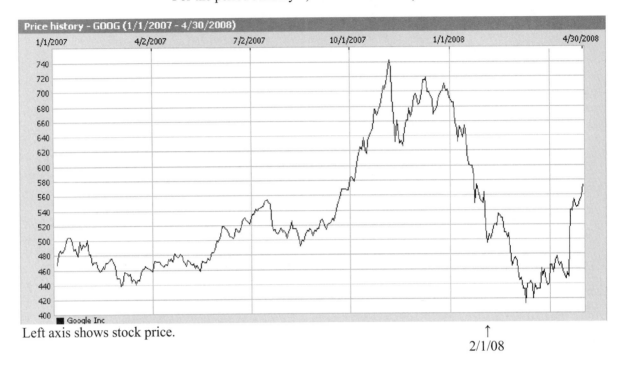

Left axis shows stock price.

2/1/08

Google (*GOOG*) vs. NASDAQ Index

Darker line reflects *GOOG*, lighter line reflects the NASDAQ Index.
Left axis shows cumulative stock return from January 1, 2007.

Google Inc.—Earnings Announcements and Information Environment

Technology

Google Disappoints the Street;
On news of Q4 results, the Web search giant's executives admit to issues with advertising on social networks, and defend R&D expenses

Catherine Holahan
1 February 2008
BusinessWeek.com
Copyright 2008 McGraw-Hill, Inc.

It's not the economy, stupid. That was the message from one Google (GOOG) executive after another on Jan. 31 as they tried to explain why the company's fourth-quarter results failed to match Wall Street expectations. "We have not yet seen any negative impact from the rumors of a possible recession," Google CEO Eric Schmidt said during a conference call after the figures were released. "We are quite optimistic about '08, and our model continues to work very well," he added.

And it's not like Google had a big miss either. The owner of the most highly trafficked Web search engine said fourth-quarter profit rose 17%, to $1.21 billion, as sales jumped 51%, to $4.83 billion. But net revenue, the amount Google retains after paying a share to partner Web sites, was $3.39 billion, about $60 million less than Wall Street's estimates. Per-share earnings, excluding stock paid to employees, were $4.43, a penny shy of analysts' forecasts.

Reassurances aside, the stock dropped 6.9%, to $525.50, in extended trading amid concerns that an economic slowdown will cause marketers to curtail online spending, depressing demand for ads on Google and its partner sites. Questions over the health of online advertising have already dragged on shares of Google, which dominates the market with an estimated 42% share of all Web marketing dollars, according to Jeffrey Rayport, founder and chairman of Marketspace Advisory, a strategy consulting firm.

Advertising Dollar Doldrums

The problem, Google executives said, was at least partly social networks. Google co-founder Sergey Brin said the company has yet to figure out the best way to make money from advertisements placed on the millions of personalized Web pages on such sites as News Corp.'s (NWS) MySpace. "We had a challenge in Q4 with social networking inventory as a whole," he said. "I don't think we have the killer best way to advertise on social networks. Some of the things that we were working on in Q4 didn't really pan out."

Brin's statements hint that News Corp. may have bad news when it reports earnings on Feb. 4. Though Google places ads on some 20 social networks, including its own Orkut, MySpace is by far the biggest. Google paid News Corp. $900 million in August, 2006, for the right to deliver ads to MySpace's 70 million-plus users.

BusinessWeek online Continued

Alarming for some investors was a slowdown in the rate at which ads are clicked on. That's important because Google's income from advertising hinges in part on how often Web surfers click on ads. Google said paid clicks increased 30% from a year earlier, compared with a 45% increase in the fourth quarter of 2006. Schmidt said the company has been reducing the clickable area around ads to decrease the number of accidental clicks, thus making the ads more valuable to marketers.

Expense Accounts

Expenses for research and development, as well as personnel, which both increased faster than revenue, are also to blame. R&D was up 63% from the prior quarter, and spending on sales and marketing increased 65%. General administrative costs, including stock-based compensation such as options, increased 72%.

Google executives stood behind their R&D strategy, claiming such investment is necessary to fuel the innovations that keep Google a leader, plus enable it to fuel the online ad industry's growth. The company is counting on the measurability of search advertising -- the business in which Google invests the most -- to help it weather any economic downturn that encourages marketing cutbacks.

Chief Financial Officer George Reyes noted that because search marketing is targeted so closely to consumers' interests, it aids direct sales, and that he's confident ad budgets will continue to emphasize search-related advertising. "Direct marketing tends to be less affected," said Reyes. "I think that has been true in past recessions and I think that will be true again."

As optimistic as Google is for now, even Reyes acknowledged the company would "certainly" be affected if online shopping takes a hit. He also stressed that Google has not yet seen any such weakening.

REPORT OF INDEPENDENT REGISTERED PUBLIC ACCOUNTING FIRM

The Board of Directors and Stockholders
Google Inc.

We have audited the accompanying consolidated balance sheets of Google Inc. as of December 31, 2006 and 2007, and the related consolidated statements of income, stockholders' equity, and cash flows for each of the three years in the period ended December 31, 2007. Our audits also included the financial statement schedule listed in the Index at Item 15(a)2. These financial statements and schedule are the responsibility of the Company's management. Our responsibility is to express an opinion on these financial statements and schedule based on our audits.

We conducted our audits in accordance with the standards of the Public Company Accounting Oversight Board (United States). Those standards require that we plan and perform the audit to obtain reasonable assurance about whether the financial statements are free of material misstatement. An audit includes examining, on a test basis, evidence supporting the amounts and disclosures in the financial statements. An audit also includes assessing the accounting principles used and significant estimates made by management, as well as evaluating the overall financial statement presentation. We believe that our audits provide a reasonable basis for our opinion.

In our opinion, the financial statements referred to above present fairly, in all material respects, the consolidated financial position of Google Inc. at December 31, 2006 and 2007, and the consolidated results of its operations and its cash flows for each of the three years in the period ended December 31, 2007, in conformity with U.S. generally accepted accounting principles. Also, in our opinion, the related financial statement schedule, when considered in relation to the basic financial statements taken as a whole, presents fairly in all material respects the information set forth therein.

As discussed in Note 1 to the consolidated financial statements, in 2006, Google Inc. changed its method of accounting for share-based payments in accordance with the guidance provided in Statement of Financial Accounting Standards No. 123(R), *Share-Based Payment.* As discussed in Note 13 to the consolidated financial statements, in 2007, the Company adopted Financial Accounting Standards Board Interpretation No. 48, *Accounting for Uncertainty in Income Taxes—an interpretation of FASB Statement No.109.*

We also have audited, in accordance with the standards of the Public Company Accounting Oversight Board (United States), the effectiveness of Google Inc.'s internal control over financial reporting as of December 31, 2007, based on criteria established in *Internal Control—Integrated Framework* issued by the Committee of Sponsoring Organizations of the Treadway Commission and our report dated February 14, 2008, expressed an unqualified opinion thereon.

/s/   ERNST & YOUNG LLP

San Jose, California
February 14, 2008

Google Inc.
CONSOLIDATED BALANCE SHEETS

	As of December 31,	
(In thousands, except par value per share)	2006	2007
Assets		
Current assets:		
Cash and cash equivalents	$ 3,544,671	$ 6,081,593
Marketable securities	7,699,243	8,137,020
Accounts receivable, net of allowance of $16,914 and $32,887	1,322,340	2,162,521
Deferred income taxes, net	29,713	68,538
Income taxes receivable	—	145,253
Prepaid revenue share, expenses and other assets	443,880	694,213
Total current assets	13,039,847	17,289,138
Prepaid revenue share, expenses and other assets, non-current	114,455	168,530
Deferred income taxes, net, non-current	—	33,219
Non-marketable equity securities	1,031,850	1,059,694
Property and equipment, net	2,395,239	4,039,261
Intangible assets, net	346,841	446,596
Goodwill.	1,545,119	2,299,368
Total assets	$ 18,473,351	$ 25,335,806
Liabilities and Stockholders' Equity		
Current liabilities:		
Accounts payable	$ 211,169	$ 282,106
Accrued compensation and benefits	351,671	588,390
Accrued expenses and other current liabilities	266,247	465,032
Accrued revenue share	370,364	522,001
Deferred revenue.	105,136	178,073
Total current liabilities	1,304,587	2,035,602
Deferred revenue, long-term	20,006	30,249
Deferred income taxes, net	40,421	—
Income taxes payable, long-term	—	478,372
Other long-term liabilities	68,497	101,904
Commitments and contingencies		
Stockholders' equity:		
Convertible preferred stock, $0.001 par value, 100,000 shares authorized; no	—	—
Class A and Class B common stock, $0.001 par value per share: 9,000,000 shares	309	313
Additional paid-in capital	11,882,906	13,241,221
Accumulated other comprehensive income	23,311	113,373
Retained earnings.	5,133,314	9,334,772
Total stockholders' equity	17,039,840	22,689,679
Total liabilities and stockholders' equity	$ 18,473,351	$ 25,335,806

See accompanying notes.

Google Inc.
CONSOLIDATED STATEMENTS OF INCOME
(In thousands, except per share amounts)

	Year Ended December 31,		
	2005	**2006**	**2007**
Revenues	$ 6,138,560	$ 10,604,917	$ 16,593,986
Costs and expenses:			
Cost of revenues (including stock-based compensation expense of $5,579, $17,629, $22,335)	2,577,088	4,225,027	6,649,085
Research and development (including stock-based compensation expense of $115,532, $287,485, $569,797).	599,510	1,228,589	2,119,985
Sales and marketing (including stock-based compensation expense of $28,411, $59,389, $131,638)	468,152	849,518	1,461,266
General and administrative (including stock-based compensation expense of $51,187, $93,597, $144,876)	386,532	751,787	1,279,250
Contribution to Google Foundation.	90,000	—	—
Total costs and expenses	4,121,282	7,054,921	11,509,586
Income from operations	2,017,278	3,549,996	5,084,400
Interest income and other, net	124,399	461,044	589,580
Income before income taxes	2,141,677	4,011,040	5,673,980
Provision for income taxes	676,280	933,594	1,470,260
Net income	$ 1,465,397	$ 3,077,446	$4,203,720
Net income per share of Class A and Class B common stock:			
Basic	$ 5.31	$ 10.21	$ 13.53
Diluted	$ 5.02	$ 9.94	$ 13.29

See accompanying notes.

Google Inc.

CONSOLIDATED STATEMENTS OF CASH FLOWS

(In thousands)

	Year Ended December 31,		
	2005	**2006**	**2007**
Operating activities			
Net income	$ 1,465,397	$ 3,077,446	$ 4,203,720
Adjustments:			
Depreciation and amortization of property and equipment	256,812	494,430	807,743
Amortization of intangibles and other	37,000	77,509	159,915
Stock-based compensation	200,709	458,100	868,646
Excess tax benefits from stock-based award activity	433,724	(581,732)	(379,206)
Deferred income taxes	21,163	(98,468)	(164,212)
Other, net	22,040	12,474	(39,741)
Changes in assets and liabilities, net of effects of acquisitions:			
Accounts receivable	(372,290)	(624,012)	(837,247)
Income taxes, net	66,237	496,882	744,802
Prepaid revenue share, expenses and other assets	(51,663)	(289,157)	(298,689)
Accounts payable	80,631	95,402	70,135
Accrued expenses and other liabilities	166,764	291,533	418,905
Accrued revenue share	93,347	139,300	150,310
Deferred revenue	39,551	30,801	70,329
Net cash provided by operating activities	2,459,422	3,580,508	5,775,410
Investing activities			
Purchases of property and equipment	(838,217)	(1,902,798)	(2,402,840)
Purchase of marketable securities	(12,675,880)	(26,681,891)	(15,997,060)
Maturities and sales of marketable securities	10,257,214	23,107,132	15,659,473
Investments in non-marketable equity securities	—	(1,019,147)	(34,511)
Acquisitions, net of cash acquired and purchases of intangible and other assets	(101,310)	(402,446)	(906,651)
Net cash used in investing activities	(3,358,193)	(6,899,150)	(3,681,589)
Financing activities			
Net proceeds from stock-based award activity	85,026	321,117	23,861
Excess tax benefits from stock-based award activity	—	581,732	379,206
Net proceeds from public offerings.	4,287,229	2,063,549	—
Payments of principal on capital leases and equipment loans	(1,425)	—	—
Net cash provided by financing activities	4,370,830	2,966,398	403,067
Effect of exchange rate changes on cash and cash equivalents	(21,758)	19,741	40,034
Net increase (decrease) in cash and cash equivalents	3,450,301	(332,503)	2,536,922
Cash and cash equivalents at beginning of year	426,873	3,877,174	3,544,671
Cash and cash equivalents at end of year	$ 3,877,174	$ 3,544,671	$ 6,081,593

See accompanying notes.

Google Inc.

NOTES TO CONSOLIDATED FINANCIAL STATEMENTS

Note 1.   Google Inc. and Summary of Significant Accounting Policies (excerpt)

Nature of Operations

We were incorporated in California in September 1998. We were re-incorporated in the State of Delaware in August 2003. We provide highly targeted advertising and global internet search solutions as well as intranet solutions via an enterprise search appliance.

Basis of Consolidation

The consolidated financial statements include the accounts of Google and our wholly-owned subsidiaries. All intercompany balances and transactions have been eliminated.

Use of Estimates

The preparation of consolidated financial statements in conformity with accounting principles generally accepted in the United States requires us to make estimates and assumptions that affect the amounts reported and disclosed in the financial statements and the accompanying notes. Actual results could differ materially from these estimates. On an ongoing basis, we evaluate our estimates, including those related to the accounts receivable and sales allowances, fair values of marketable and non-marketable securities, fair values of prepaid revenue share, intangible assets and goodwill, useful lives of intangible assets, property and equipment, fair values of options to purchase our common stock, and income taxes, among others. We base our estimates on historical experience and on various other assumptions that are believed to be reasonable, the results of which form the basis for making judgments about the carrying values of assets and liabilities.

Revenue Recognition

The following table presents our revenues:

| | Year Ended December 31, | | |
	2005	2006	2007
	(in thousands)		
Advertising revenues:			
Google web sites	$ 3,377,060	$ 6,332,797	$ 10,624,705
Google Network web sites	2,687,942	4,159,831	5,787,938
Total advertising revenues	6,065,002	10,492,628	16,412,643
Licensing and other revenues	73,558	112,289	181,343
Revenues	$ 6,138,560	$ 10,604,917	$ 16,593,986

In the first quarter of 2000, we introduced our first advertising program through which we offered advertisers the ability to place text-based ads on Google web sites targeted to users' search queries. Advertisers paid us based on the number of times their ads were displayed on users' search results pages, and we recognized revenue at the time these ads appeared. In the fourth quarter of 2000, we launched Google AdWords, an online self-service program that enables advertisers to place text-based ads on Google web sites. Ad Words is also available through our direct sales force. AdWords advertisers originally paid us based on the number of times their ads appeared on users' search results pages. In the first quarter of 2002, we began offering AdWords on a cost-per-click basis, so that an advertiser pays us only when a user clicks on one of its ads. From January 1, 2004, until the end of the first quarter of 2005, the AdWords cost-per-click pricing structure was the only structure available to our advertisers. However, during the second quarter of 2005, we launched an AdWords program that enables advertisers to pay us based on the number of times their ads appear on Google Network member sites specified by the advertiser.

Google AdSense is the program through which we distribute our advertisers' ads for display on the web sites of our Google Network members.

Google Inc.

NOTES TO CONSOLIDATED FINANCIAL STATEMENTS (continued)

Note 1.   Google Inc. and Summary of Significant Accounting Policies (excerpt – continued)

We recognize as revenues the fees charged advertisers each time a user clicks on one of the text-based ads that are displayed next to the search results pages on our site or on the search results pages or content pages of our Google Network members' web sites and, for those advertisers who use our cost-per impression pricing, the fees charged advertisers each time an ad is displayed on our members' sites. In addition, we recognize as revenues the fees charged advertisers when ads are published in the magazines or broadcasted by the radio stations (or each time a listener responds to that ad) of our Google Network members. We recognize these revenues as such because the services have been provided, and the other criteria set forth under Staff Accounting Bulletin Topic 13: *Revenue Recognition* have been met, namely, the fees we charge are fixed or determinable, we and our advertisers understand the specific nature and terms of the agreed-upon transactions and collectibility is reasonably assured. In accordance with Emerging Issues Task Force ("EITF") Issue No. 99-19, *Reporting Revenue Gross as a Principal Versus Net as an Agent* ("EITF 99-19"), we report our Google AdSense revenues on a gross basis principally because we are the primary obligor to our advertisers.

In the third quarter of 2005, we launched the Google Print Ads Program through which we distribute our advertisers' ads for publication in print media. We recognize as revenue the fees charged advertisers when their ads are published in print media. Also in the first quarter of 2006, we acquired dMarc Broadcasting, Inc. (dMarc), a digital solutions provider for the radio broadcast industry and launched our Google Audio Ads program, which distributes our advertisers' ads for broadcast in radio programs. We recognize as revenue the fees charged advertisers each time an ad is broadcasted or a listener responds to that ad. We consider the magazines and radio stations that participate in these programs to be members of our Google Network.

In the second quarter of 2006, we launched Google Checkout, an online shopping payment processing system for both consumers and merchants. We recognize as revenues any fees charged merchants on transactions processed through Google Checkout. Further, cash ultimately paid to merchants under Google Checkout promotions, including cash paid to merchants as a result of discounts provided to consumers on certain transactions processed through Google Checkout, are accounted for as an offset to revenues in accordance with EITF Issue No. 01-9, *Accounting for Consideration Given by a Vendor to a Customer (Including a Reseller of the Vendor's Products)*.

In the fourth quarter of 2006, we acquired YouTube, a consumer media company for people to watch and share videos worldwide through the web. We recognize as revenue the fees charged advertisers each time an ad is displayed on the YouTube site.

In the second quarter of 2007, we announced our trial to deliver Google TV ads to viewers and help advertisers, operators and programmers buy, schedule, deliver and measure ads on television. We recognize as revenue the fees charged advertisers each time an ad is displayed on TV in accordance with the terms of the related agreements. We consider the TV providers that participate in this program to be members of our Google Network.

In the third quarter of 2007, we acquired Postini, a provider of electronic communications security, compliance, and productivity software. We recognize as revenue the fees we charge customers for hosting enterprise applications and services ratably over the term of the service arrangement.

Revenues realized through the Google Print Ads Program, Google Audio Ads, Google TV Ads, Google Checkout, YouTube and Postini were not material in any of the years presented.

We generate fees from search services on a per-query basis. Our policy is to recognize revenues from per-query search fees in the period we provide the search results.

We also generate fees from the sale and license of our Search Appliance, which includes hardware, software and 12 to 24 months of post-contract support. We recognize revenue in accordance with Statement of Position 97-2, *Software Revenue Recognition*, as amended. As the elements are not sold separately, sufficient vendor- specific objective evidence does not exist for the allocation of revenue. As a result, the entire fee is recognized ratably over the term of the post-contract support arrangement.

Deferred revenue is recorded when payments are received in advance of our performance in the underlying agreement on the accompanying Consolidated Balance Sheets.

Weis Markets, Inc.—Statement of Cash Flows

Weis Markets, Inc., is a Pennsylvania business corporation formed in 1924. The Company is engaged principally in the retail sale of food. The business of the Company is highly competitive and the Company competes based on price and service with national retail food chains, local chains and independent food stores. Weis Markets operates 155 supermarkets primarily in Pennsylvania and Maryland under the names Weis Markets, Mr. Z's, Scot's, Cressler's Marketplace and King's, and 31 SuperPetz pet supply stores. (Source: Company 2007 Form 10-K)

Learning Objectives
- Contrast and compare the information in the statement of cash flows and income statement.
- Identify the three sections of the statement of cash flows.
- Understand the operations section of the statement of cash flows.
- Explain how operating cash flow line items relate to balance sheet and income statement accounts.
- Analyze the changes in balance sheet accounts by inferring transactions.
- Construct a complete statement of cash flows using the indirect method.
- Interpret the statement of cash flows, comparing key figures to net income.

Refer to the 2007 financial statements of Weis Markets, Inc.

 Concepts

a. What information does the statement of cash flows provide? How is this different from the information contained in the income statement?

b. What are the two different methods for preparing the statement of cash flows? Which method does Weis Markets use? How do you know? Why do you think most companies prepare their statement of cash flows using the indirect method?

c. What are the three sections of statement of cash flows?

d. How do each of the three sections of the statement of cash flows relate to the Balance Sheet?

e. The balance sheet includes an item called "Cash and cash equivalents." What are "cash equivalents"?

f. Net income is determined on an accrual basis. Yet, net income is the first item on the statement of cash flows. Explain this apparent inconsistency.

 Process

g. Construct the 2007 statement of cash flows for Weis Markets using the indirect method.

Recall that the change in cash (i.e., the statement of cash flows) is algebraically related to the balance sheet as follows:

Δ Cash = Δ Liabilities + Δ Owners' Equity – Δ All Other Assets

Thus, if you can "explain" the change in each of the noncash balance sheet accounts (and only those accounts), you will have generated a statement of cash flows.

Use a set of T-accounts for the balance sheet accounts (T-accounts are included at the end of the case) or a spreadsheet to help you organize your efforts. For each balance sheet account, consider what transactions and activities explain the change in the account. Classify each transaction and activity as operating, investing, or financing to prepare the statement of cash flows for Weis Markets.

The following five items provide additional information to help you prepare the statement of cash flows. All dollar amounts are in thousands.

1. Note 4 to Weis Markets' 2007 financial statements reveals the following:

(4) Property and Equipment

Property and equipment, as of December 29, 2007, and December 30, 2006, consisted of:

(dollars in thousands)	Useful Life (in years)	2007	2006
Land		$85,158	$84,094
Buildings and Improvements	10-60	404,784	391,357
Equipment	3-12	608,458	585,213
Leasehold Improvements	5-20	130,978	121,263
Total, at cost		1,229,378	1,181,927
Less accumulated depreciation and amortization		730,132	689,384
Property and equipment, net		$499,246	$492,543

In 2007, depreciation and amortization expense on property and equipment was $54,187. During 2007, the company purchased $64,233 of new property, plant, and equipment for cash. The company sold property and equipment for $11,374 in cash. No other property and equipment was acquired or sold in 2007.

Activities in the fixed asset accounts affect the statement of cash flows in four ways. Determine each of the four items, *i* through *iv*, below. To do this, create two T-accounts, one for property and equipment at cost and another for accumulated depreciation and amortization. Use the information from Weis' Note 4 to analyze the activity in both accounts during the year.

i. *Depreciation and amortization expense* is included in the operating section of the statement of cash flows. Explain why. Does depreciation expense actually generate cash for Weis Markets?

ii. *Capital expenditures* (i.e. cash used to purchase new property and equipment) are included in the investing section of the statement of cash flows as a use of cash.

iii. *Cash proceeds from the disposal of property and equipment* are included in the investing section as a source of cash.

iv. *Gains and losses on disposals of fixed assets* are included in the operating section of the statement of cash flows. *Hint*: To determine the gain or loss on disposal, determine the cost of the disposed property (the credit that balances the gross property and equipment T-account) and the related depreciation on the disposed property (the debit that balances the accumulated depreciation account). The difference between the cost of the disposed property and the related depreciation is the net book value of the disposed property. Compare the net book value to the cash proceeds to determine the amount of the gain or loss on disposal.

2. Weis did not purchase any new intangible assets in 2007. Amortization expense for the year was directly credited to the Intangible assets account. Create a T-account to analyze the activity in the Intangible and other assets, net account during 2007.

3. Create a T-account to analyze the activity in Marketable Securities during the year. The company sold marketable securities for $14,132 in 2007 and realized a gain of $6 on the sale. No additional marketable securities were purchased. Weis recorded the sale and realized a gain on the securities sold with this journal entry.

Dr.	Cash (B/S)	14,132
Cr.	Marketable Securities (B/S)	14,126
Cr.	Gain on Sale of Marketable Securities (I/S)	6

To record sales of marketable securities.

Each year-end, Weis Markets adjusts its Marketable Securities to market value by adding unrealized gains to, and subtracting unrealized from, a shareholders' equity account called Accumulated Other Comprehensive Income. These unrealized gains and losses affect neither net income nor cash. Therefore, they are not a reconciling item on the statement of cash flows. For 2007, the company recorded the following journal entry to reflect the net unrealized gains on marketable securities at the end of fiscal 2007. Use this journal entry to analyze the activity in the Marketable Securities and Accumulated Other Comprehensive Income accounts.

Dr.	Marketable Securities (B/S)	2,145	
Cr.	Accumulated Other Comprehensive Income (B/S)		1,255
Cr.	Deferred Income Taxes (B/S)		890

To record marketable securities at market value at year-end.

4. The Weis balance sheet reports Deferred Income Tax accounts in both the current and noncurrent liabilities sections but the statement of cash flows does not distinguish among the two. Combine them to create one T-account to analyze the Deferred Income Tax activities for the year.

According to Note 2—Income Taxes, Weis recorded a $1,252 reduction in the net deferred income tax liability in 2007. The company recorded the following journal entry to reflect the benefit:

Dr.	Deferred Income Taxes (B/S)	1,252	
Cr.	Provision for Income Taxes (I/S)		1,252

To record income tax expense for the year.

Use this journal entry and the one in part 3, above to explain the changes in the Deferred Income Tax, net liability account.

5. The footnotes discuss Weis' adoption of FIN 48[1] on December 31, 2006, whereby Weis recorded a prior period adjustment relating to income taxes. As a result, Weis recognized a $452 decrease to opening Retained Earnings with a corresponding increase in Income Taxes Payable for the cumulative effect of adoption. Prepare the journal entry to record this adjustment and use the entry to analyze the activity in the two accounts.

[1] FASB Interpretation No. 48, titled "Accounting for Uncertainty in Income Taxes: an Interpretation of FASB Statement No. 109" (FIN 48), establishes the necessary criterion for individual tax positions to be recognized in the company's financial statements.

✧　　　　　Analysis　　　　　✧

h. Use the 2007 statement of cash flows you constructed and the statements of income for 2005 through 2007, to evaluate Weis Markets' profitability and ability to generate cash. Comment on the nature of the differences between net income and cash from operations in each year.

i. Refer to the company's statements of cash flows for 2005 through 2007. Has Weis Markets maintained its productive capacity, expanded it or decreased it over the last three years? Explain.

j. Consider the following April 23, 2008, press release by Weis Markets relating to planned capital expenditures:

(Sunbury, PA) -- Weis Markets, Inc.'s (NYSE:WMK) Vice Chairman Jonathan Weis today said his company would invest $80 million in its growth over the next twelve months. Mr. Weis made the announcement at his company's annual shareholder meeting, which was held in Sunbury earlier today.

"For the coming year, we plan to invest nearly $80 million in our growth. We will target three quarters of this budget to our store base," said Mr. Weis. "We currently have 19 major projects in various stages of planning, including three new stores, two replacement units, nine additions and five remodels."

Mr. Weis noted this was a 23% increase over 2007, when his company made $64.2 million in capital expenditures.

Discuss Weis Markets' capacity for increasing its capital expenditures. What are the likely sources of cash to fund the increased level of investment in property and equipment?

The T-accounts for all the balance sheet accounts are as follows:

Cash

Opening Balance	27,545		
Operating activities			
Net Income			
Investing activities			
Financing activities			
Closing Balance	41,187		

T-accounts for all the balance sheet accounts (continued):

Marketable Securities	
38,163	
26,182	

Accounts Receivable, net	
41,885	
48,460	

Inventory	
189,468	
193,732	

Prepaid Expenses	
3,932	
3,317	

Income taxes recoverable	
0	
8,074	

Property and equipment, gross	
1,181,927	
1,229,378	

Accumulated Depreciation	
	689,384
	730,132

Goodwill	
15,722	
15,722	

Intangibles and Other Assets, net	
4,804	
4,149	

Accounts Payable	
	105,859
	111,555

Accrued Expenses	
	22,307
	23,036

Accrued Self-Insurance	
	22,778
	23,442

Payable to Employee Benefit Plans	
	1,435
	1,400

Income Taxes Payable	
	865
	0

Deferred Income Taxes (current + long-term)	
	18,743
	18,381

Postretirement benefit obligations	
	12,912
	14,027

Common Stock	
	8,595
	9,830

Retained Earnings	
	760,531
	779,760

Accumulated other comprehensive income	
	6,084
	7,339

Treasury Stock	
146,047	
148,701	

WEIS MARKETS, INC.
CONSOLIDATED BALANCE SHEETS
December 29, 2007 and December 30, 2006

(dollars in thousands)		2007		2006
Assets				
Current:				
Cash and cash equivalents	$	41,187	$	27,545
Marketable securities		26,182		38,163
Accounts receivable, net		48,460		41,885
Inventories		193,732		189,468
Prepaid expenses		3,317		3,932
Income taxes recoverable		8,074		---
Total current assets		320,952		300,993
Property and equipment, net		499,246		492,543
Goodwill		15,722		15,722
Intangible and other assets, net		4,149		4,804
Total assets	$	840,069	$	814,062
Liabilities				
Current:				
Accounts payable	$	111,555	$	105,859
Accrued expenses		23,036		22,307
Accrued self-insurance		23,442		22,778
Payable to employee benefit plans		1,400		1,435
Income taxes payable		---		865
Deferred income taxes		4,134		298
Total current liabilities		163,567		153,542
Postretirement benefit obligations		14,027		12,912
Deferred income taxes		14,247		18,445
Total liabilities		191,841		184,899
Shareholders' Equity				
Common stock, no par value, 100,800,000 shares authorized, 33,044,357 and 33,009,046 shares issued, respectively		9,830		8,595
Retained earnings		779,760		760,531
Accumulated other comprehensive income, net		7,339		6,084
		796,929		775,210
Treasury stock at cost, 6,077,311 and 6,016,291 shares, respectively		(148,701)		(146,047)
Total shareholders' equity		648,228		629,163
Total liabilities and shareholders' equity	$	840,069	$	814,062

WEIS MARKETS, INC.
CONSOLIDATED STATEMENTS OF INCOME
For Fiscal Years ended December 29 2007, December 30, 2006 and December 31, 2005

(dollars in thousands, except shares and per share amounts)

	2007 (52 Weeks)	2006 (52 Weeks)	2005 (53 Weeks)
Net sales	$2,318,551	$2,244,512	$2,222,598
Cost of sales, including warehousing and distribution expenses	1,716,424	1,647,233	1,634,874
Gross profit on sales	602,127	597,279	587,724
Operating, general and administrative expenses	527,378	515,675	491,499
Income from operations	74,749	81,604	96,225
Investment income	3,010	4,484	3,081
Income before provision for income taxes	77,759	86,088	99,306
Provision for income taxes	26,769	30,078	35,885
Net income	$ 50,990	$ 56,010	$ 63,421
Weighted-average shares outstanding, basic	26,987,786	27,016,877	27,026,748
Weighted-average shares outstanding, diluted	26,993,997	27,027,198	27,033,789
Cash dividends per share	$ 1.16	$ 1.16	$ 1.12
Basic and diluted earnings per share	$ 1.89	$ 2.07	$ 2.35

WEIS MARKETS, INC.
CONSOLIDATED STATEMENTS OF SHAREHOLDERS' EQUITY
For the Fiscal Years Ended December 29, 2007, December 30, 2006 and December 31, 2005

(dollars in thousands, except shares)

	Common Stock		Retained Earnings	Accum. Other Comprehensive Income	Treasury Stock		Total Shareholders' Equity
	Shares	Amount			Shares	Amount	
Balance at December 25, 2004	32,997,157	$8,199	$702,714	$4,747	5,964,330	$(143,960)	$ 571,700
Net income	---	---	63,421	---	---	---	63,421
Other comprehensive loss, net of reclassification adjustments and tax	---	---	---	(451)	---	---	(451)
Comprehensive income							62,970
Shares issued for options	5,200	172	---	---	---	---	172
Treasury stock purchased	---	---	---	---	18,131	(715)	(715)
Dividends paid	---	---	(30,270)	---	---	---	(30,270)
Balance at December 31, 2005	33,002,357	8,371	735,865	4,296	5,982,461	(144,675)	603,857
Net income	---	---	56,010	---	---	---	56,010
Other comprehensive income, net of reclassification adjustments and tax	---	---	---	1,788	---	---	1,788
Comprehensive income							57,798
Shares issued for options	6,689	224	---	---	3,498	(154)	70
Treasury stock purchased	---	---	---	---	30,332	(1,218)	(1,218)
Dividends paid	---	---	(31,344)	---	---	---	(31,344)
Balance at December 30, 2006	33,009,046	8,595	760,531	6,084	6,016,291	(146,047)	629,163
Net income	---	---	50,990	---	---	---	50,990
Other comprehensive income, net of reclassification adjustments and tax	---	---	---	1,255	---	---	1,255
Comprehensive income							52,245
Cumulative effect of change in accounting for income taxes	---	---	(452)	---	---	---	(452)
Shares issued for options	35,311	1,235	---	---	25,561	(1,155)	80
Treasury stock purchased	---	---	---	---	35,459	(1,499)	(1,499)
Dividends paid	---	---	(31,309)	---	---	---	(31,309)
Balance at December 29, 2007	33,044,357	$9,830	$779,760	$7,339	6,077,311	$(148,701)	$ 648,228

WEIS MARKETS, INC.
CONSOLIDATED STATEMENTS OF CASH FLOWS*
For the Fiscal Years ended December 29, 2007 December 30, 2006 and December 31, 2005

(dollars in thousands),	2007 (52 weeks)	2006 (52 weeks)	2005 (53 weeks)
Cash flows from operating activities:			
Net income	$	$ 56,010	$ 63,421
Adjustments to reconcile net income to net cash provided by operating activities:			
Depreciation and amortization expense		50,288	49,215
Amortization of intangible assets		732	891
(Gain) loss on disposition / impairment of fixed assets		974	519
Gain on sale of marketable securities		(431)	(422)
Changes in operating assets and liabilities:			
Accounts receivable		(3,509)	(2,318)
Inventories		(10,086)	(14,338)
Prepaid expenses		2,144	(1,106)
Income taxes recoverable		---	1,729
Accounts payable and other liabilities		4,964	5,152
Accrued expenses		2,228	(558)
Accrued self-insurance		1,225	1,381
Payable to employee benefit plans		(11,052)	1,661
Income taxes payable		(1,155)	2,020
Retirement benefits obligation		12,912	0
Deferred income taxes		(5,762)	(2,845)
Net cash provided by operating activities		99,482	104,402
Cash flows from investing activities:			
Purchase of property and equipment		(99,975)	(55,468)
Proceeds from the sale of property and equipment		2,696	291
Purchase of marketable securities		(33,020)	(8,248)
Proceeds from sales of marketable securities		21,554	902
Net cash used in investing activities		(108,745)	(62,523)
Cash flows from financing activities:			
Proceeds from issuance of common stock		224	172
Dividends paid		(31,344)	(30,270)
Purchase of treasury stock		(1,372)	(715)
Net cash used in financing activities		(32,492)	(30,813)
Net increase (decrease) in cash and cash equivalents		(41,755)	11,066
Cash and cash equivalents at beginning of year		69,300	58,234
Cash and cash equivalents at end of year	$	$ 27,545	$ 69,300

*Some accounts reclassified for presentation purposes.

Vodafone Group Plc—Time Value of Money

Vodafone Group Plc is the world's leading mobile telecommunications company, with a significant presence in Europe, the United States and the Asia Pacific region. The Group also has arrangements to market certain of its services, through its "Partner Networks" scheme. The Group provides a wide range of mobile telecommunications services, including voice and data telecommunications. The Company is listed on the London Stock Exchange and the Company's American Depositary Shares are listed on the New York Stock Exchange. The Company had a total market capitalization of approximately £92 billion at 24 May 2004, making it the second largest company in the Financial Times Stock Exchange (FTSE) 100 index and the eleventh largest company in the world. (Source: Company 2004 Annual Report)

Learning Objectives
- Calculate the present value and the future value of a single payment.
- Calculate the present value of a stream of payments.
- Understand the effect of compounding on present and future values.
- Determine the effective interest rate underlying a series of cash flows.

Refer to the 2004 financial statements and Note 18—Creditors of the Vodafone Group, Plc. Focus on the Group (i.e., consolidated) data. Vodafone's fiscal year ends on March 31st.

 Concepts

a. The following questions test your understanding of time value of money concepts.

    i.   Would you rather receive $100 today or $100 in exactly one year? Explain your choice.

    ii.   What is a lump-sum payment?

    iii.   What is an annuity? What is an ordinary annuity (annuity in arrears)? What is an annuity due?

    iv.   How does compound interest differ from simple interest?

 Process

b. Refer to Note 18—Creditors. Consider the 5.0% U.S. dollar bond due 2013. Assume that Vodafone issued this bond on March 31, 2004, and it matures in 9 years.

    i.   How much did Vodafone receive when it issued the bonds? (ignore issuance costs and fees)

    ii.   Where does this debt appear on Vodafone's balance sheet? Statement of cash flows? Where does the cost of this debt appear on Vodafone's income statement?

c. Because market conditions appeared favorable, Vodafone's Treasurer decided to raise funds through a debt issuance. Assume that on March 31, 2004, the company issued its 5.625% Sterling bonds due 2025. As the company had no immediate plans for the funds raised, the Treasurer placed the proceeds in an interest-bearing bank account.

    i.   Assume that the account pays 3% interest per year. The interest is paid annually on the anniversary date of the deposit and is left in the account. What will the balance of the bank account be on March 31, 2005? March 31, 2006? March 31, 2007? Use the first row in the table on the following page to tabulate your answers.

    ii.   Now assume that the account pays 5% per year. Complete the second row of the table.

    iii.   Now assume that the interest of 5% per year is paid semiannually (i.e., 2.5% every six months). Complete the third row of the table.

Interest rate	Balance March 31, 2005	Balance March 31, 2006	Balance March 31, 2007
3% annually			
5% annually			
2.5% semiannually			

d. Vodafone's Treasurer is considering issuing additional debt denominated in Japanese yen. The company wants to issue zero-coupon bonds. These are bonds that make no periodic interest payments. Rather, they pay a single lump sum at maturity. Vodafone is contemplating the issuance of 5-year zero-coupon bonds with a value at maturity (i.e., a face value) of ¥100 billion.

    i. If the effective (i.e., market) interest rate on this type of debt is 3% per annum, how much would Vodafone receive when it sells the bonds? How much would they receive if the market rate is 6%? Use the first column in the table below to tabulate your answers.

    ii. If instead, the bonds matured in 10 years, how much would Vodafone receive? Complete the second column in the table.

Interest rate	Proceeds on issuance of 5-year zero-coupon bond	Proceeds on issuance of 10-year zero-coupon bond
3% annually		
6% annually		

e. In Note 18, Vodafone indicates that it has some "Finance leases" included in its long-term debt. Finance leases are leases that are accounted for as though the company purchased an asset and borrowed funds for the purchase.

    i. Assume that one of Vodafone's finance leases requires the company to make payments of £10 on March 31st of each of the next 5 years. What is the present value of those lease payments if the appropriate discount (i.e., interest) rate is 7%?

    ii. Assume that another of Vodafone's finance leases requires the company to make payments of £12 on March 31st each year. The 15-year lease is structured so that there will be 10 payments made where the first payment will be made at the end of the fifth year (and annually thereafter). What is the present value of those lease payments if the appropriate discount (i.e., interest) rate is 7%? Drawing a time line that lays out the cash flows will make this analysis easier.

f. Consider the 5.0% Euro bond due 2018. Assume that this bond was issued on March 31, 2004, and matures in 14 years. Assume that the face value of the bond is (in Pounds Sterling) £550.

    i. If Vodafone pays interest on this bond annually, how much interest will the company pay each year?

    ii. What proceeds did Vodafone receive when it issued this bond?

    iii. What annual effective interest rate will Vodafone pay on this bond over the 14 years to maturity? To answer this question, calculate the rate at which the proceeds received exactly equals the annual interest payments plus the repayment of the face value at maturity.

    iv. How would your answer to part *iii* differ if the Vodafone paid 2.5% interest semiannually instead of 5% annually?

Consolidated Profit and Loss Accounts

For the years ended 31 March

	Note	2004 $m	2004 £m	2003 £m	2002 £m
Total Group turnover: Group and share of joint ventures and associated undertakings					
– Continuing operations		78,973	42,920	37,324	32,125
– Discontinued operations		1,505	818	1,828	1,416
		80,478	43,738	39,152	33,541
Less: Share of joint ventures		–	–	(8)	(3)
Share of associated undertakings		(18,729)	(10,179)	(8,769)	(10,693)
Group turnover	3	61,749	33,559	30,375	22,845
Group turnover	3				
– Continuing operations		60,244	32,741	28,547	21,767
– Discontinued operations		1,505	818	1,828	1,078
		61,749	33,559	30,375	22,845
Operating (loss)/profit	3, 4, 5				
– Continuing operations		(8,909)	(4,842)	(5,052)	(9,966)
– Discontinued operations		121	66	(243)	(411)
		(8,788)	(4,776)	(5,295)	(10,377)
Share of operating profit/(loss) in joint ventures and associated undertakings		1,005	546	(156)	(1,457)
Total Group operating loss					
Group and share of joint ventures and associated undertakings	3	(7,783)	(4,230)	(5,451)	(11,834)
Exceptional non-operating items	6	(190)	(103)	(5)	(860)
– Continuing operations		(81)	(44)	20	(860)
– Discontinued operations		(109)	(59)	(25)	–
Loss on ordinary activities before interest	3	(7,973)	(4,333)	(5,456)	(12,694)
Net interest payable and similar items	7	(1,314)	(714)	(752)	(845)
Group		(918)	(499)	(457)	(503)
Share of joint ventures and associated undertakings		(396)	(215)	(295)	(342)
Loss on ordinary activities before taxation		(9,287)	(5,047)	(6,208)	(13,539)
Tax on loss on ordinary activities	8	(5,803)	(3,154)	(2,956)	(2,140)
Group		(5,273)	(2,866)	(2,624)	(1,925)
Share of joint ventures and associated undertakings		(530)	(288)	(332)	(215)
Loss on ordinary activities after taxation		(15,090)	(8,201)	(9,164)	(15,679)
Equity minority interests		(1,386)	(753)	(593)	(415)
Non-equity minority interests		(112)	(61)	(62)	(61)
Loss for the financial year		(16,588)	(9,015)	(9,819)	(16,155)
Equity dividends	9	(2,535)	(1,378)	(1,154)	(1,025)
Retained loss for the Group and its share of joint ventures and associated undertakings	23	(19,123)	(10,393)	(10,973)	(17,180)
Basic and diluted loss per share	10	(24.36)¢	(13.24)p	(14.41)p	(23.77)p

The accompanying notes are an integral part of these Consolidated Financial Statements.

The unaudited US dollar amounts are prepared on the basis set out in note 1.

Balance Sheets

At 31 March

	Note	Group 2004 $m	Group 2004 £m	Group 2003 as restated £m	Company 2004 £m	Company 2003 £m
Fixed assets						
Intangible assets	11	172,264	93,622	108,085	–	–
Tangible assets	12	33,273	18,083	19,574	–	–
Investments		40,986	22,275	26,989	106,177	104,655
Investments in associated undertakings	13	39,056	21,226	25,825	–	–
Other investments	13	1,930	1,049	1,164	106,177	104,655
		246,523	133,980	154,648	106,177	104,655
Current assets						
Stocks	14	843	458	365	–	–
Debtors	15	12,698	6,901	7,460	65,627	44,699
Investments	16	8,061	4,381	291	–	287
Cash at bank and in hand		2,593	1,409	475	53	215
		24,195	13,149	8,591	65,680	45,201
Creditors: amounts falling due within one year	17	(27,648)	(15,026)	(14,293)	(95,679)	(76,087)
Net current liabilities		(3,453)	(1,877)	(5,702)	(29,999)	(30,886)
Total assets less current liabilities		243,070	132,103	148,946	76,178	73,769
Creditors: amounts falling due after more than one year	18	(23,874)	(12,975)	(13,757)	(9,271)	(8,171)
Provisions for liabilities and charges	21	(7,723)	(4,197)	(3,696)	–	–
		211,473	114,931	131,493	66,907	65,598
Capital and reserves						
Called up share capital	22	7,875	4,280	4,275	4,280	4,275
Share premium account	23	95,963	52,154	52,073	52,154	52,073
Merger reserve		182,026	98,927	98,927	–	–
Capital reserve		–	–	–	88	88
Own shares held	23	(2,090)	(1,136)	(41)	(1,088)	–
Other reserve	23	1,312	713	843	713	843
Profit and loss account	23	(79,146)	(43,014)	(27,447)	10,760	8,319
Total equity shareholders' funds		205,940	111,924	128,630	66,907	65,598
Equity minority interests		3,923	2,132	1,848	–	–
Non-equity minority interests	24	1,610	875	1,015	–	–
		211,473	114,931	131,493	66,907	65,598

The Consolidated Financial Statements were approved by the Board of directors on 25 May 2004 and were signed on its behalf by:

A SARIN   Chief Executive

K J HYDON   Financial Director

The accompanying notes are an integral part of these Consolidated Financial Statements.

The unaudited US dollar amounts are prepared on the basis set out in note 1.

Consolidated Cash Flows

For the years ended 31 March

	Note	2004 $m	2004 £m	2003 as restated £m	2002 as restated £m
Net cash inflow from operating activities	28	22,663	12,317	11,142	8,102
Dividends received from joint ventures and associated undertakings		3,314	1,801	742	139
Net cash outflow for returns on investments and servicing of finance	28	(81)	(44)	(551)	(936)
Taxation		(2,175)	(1,182)	(883)	(545)
Net cash outflow for capital expenditure and financial investment		(7,851)	(4,267)	(5,359)	(4,441)
Purchase of intangible fixed assets		(39)	(21)	(99)	(325)
Purchase of tangible fixed assets		(8,294)	(4,508)	(5,289)	(4,145)
Purchase of investments		(79)	(43)	(546)	(38)
Disposal of tangible fixed assets		291	158	109	75
Disposal of investments		226	123	575	319
Loans to joint ventures		–	–	(59)	(233)
Loans repaid by/(to) associated undertakings		44	24	–	(523)
Loans to businesses sold or acquired businesses held for sale		–	–	(50)	(116)
Loans repaid by acquired businesses held for sale		–	–	–	545
Net cash outflow from acquisitions and disposals		(2,414)	(1,312)	(4,880)	(7,691)
Purchase of interests in subsidiary undertakings		(3,797)	(2,064)	(3,519)	(3,078)
Net cash/(overdrafts) acquired with subsidiary undertakings		18	10	11	(2,514)
Purchase of interests in associated undertakings		–	–	(1,491)	(7,159)
Purchase of customer bases		–	–	(6)	(11)
Disposal of interests in subsidiary undertakings		1,831	995	125	–
Net cash disposed of with subsidiary undertakings		(475)	(258)	–	–
Disposal of interests in joint ventures and associated undertakings		9	5	–	–
Disposal of acquired businesses held for sale		–	–	–	5,071
Equity dividends paid		(2,315)	(1,258)	(1,052)	(978)
Cash inflow/(outflow) before management of liquid resources and financing		11,141	6,055	(841)	(6,350)
Management of liquid resources	29	(7,886)	(4,286)	1,384	7,042
Net cash outflow from financing	28	(1,288)	(700)	(150)	(681)
Issue of ordinary share capital		127	69	28	3,581
Increase/(decrease) in debt		515	280	(165)	(4,268)
Issue of shares to minorities		–	–	1	12
Purchase of treasury shares		(1,899)	(1,032)	–	–
Purchase of own shares in relation to employee share schemes		(31)	(17)	(14)	(6)
Increase in cash in the year		1,967	1,069	393	11
Reconciliation of net cash flow to movement in net debt					
Increase in cash in the year	29	1,967	1,069	393	11
Cash (inflow)/outflow from (increase)/decrease in debt	29	(515)	(280)	165	4,268
Cash outflow/(inflow) from increase/(decrease) in liquid resources	29	7,886	4,286	(1,384)	(7,042)
Decrease/(increase) in net debt resulting from cash flows	29	9,338	5,075	(826)	(2,763)
Net debt acquired on acquisition of subsidiary undertakings		(13)	(7)	–	(3,116)
Net debt disposed of on disposal of subsidiary undertakings		357	194	–	–
Translation difference		265	144	(826)	517
Premium on repayment of debt		(103)	(56)	(157)	–
Other movements		2	1	4	50
Decrease/(increase) in net debt in the year		9,846	5,351	(1,805)	(5,312)
Opening net debt		(25,464)	(13,839)	(12,034)	(6,722)
Closing net debt	29	(15,618)	(8,488)	(13,839)	(12,034)

The accompanying notes are an integral part of these Consolidated Financial Statements.

The unaudited US dollar amounts are prepared on the basis set out in note 1.

Vodafone Group Plc Annual Report 2004

72

Consolidated Statements of Total Recognised Gains and Losses

For the years ended 31 March

	2004 $m	2004 £m	2003 £m	2002 £m
Loss for the financial year				
Group	(16,553)	(8,996)	(9,049)	(14,131)
Share of joint ventures	–	–	(62)	(211)
Share of associated undertakings	(35)	(19)	(708)	(1,813)
	(16,588)	(9,015)	(9,819)	(16,155)
Currency translation				
Group	(4,530)	(2,462)	10,484	(1,980)
Share of joint ventures	–	–	2	4
Share of associated undertakings	(5,207)	(2,830)	(1,447)	(287)
	(9,737)	(5,292)	9,039	(2,263)
Total recognised losses relating to the year	(26,325)	(14,307)	(780)	(18,418)

The accompanying notes are an integral part of these Consolidated Financial Statements.

The unaudited US dollar amounts are prepared on the basis set out in note 1.

Movements in Total Equity Shareholders' Funds

For the years ended 31 March

	2004 $m	2004 £m	2003 as restated £m	2002 as restated £m
Loss for the financial year	(16,588)	(9,015)	(9,819)	(16,155)
Equity dividends	(2,535)	(1,378)	(1,154)	(1,025)
	(19,123)	(10,393)	(10,973)	(17,180)
Currency translation	(9,737)	(5,292)	9,039	(2,263)
New share capital subscribed, net of issue costs	158	86	31	5,984
Goodwill transferred to the profit and loss account in respect of business disposals	–	–	–	3
Shares to be issued	–	–	–	(978)
Purchase of treasury shares	(2,002)	(1,088)	–	–
Purchase of shares in relation to employee share schemes	(31)	(17)	(14)	(6)
Own shares released on vesting of share awards	18	10	6	1
Other	(22)	(12)	1	–
Net movement in total equity shareholders' funds	(30,739)	(16,706)	(1,910)	(14,439)
Opening total equity shareholders' funds (originally £128,671 million before prior year adjustment of £41 million)	236,679	128,630	130,540	144,979
Closing total equity shareholders' funds	205,940	111,924	128,630	130,540

The accompanying notes are an integral part of these Consolidated Financial Statements.

The unaudited US dollar amounts are prepared on the basis set out in note 1.

16. Investments

	Group		Company	
	2004 £m	2003 £m	2004 £m	2003 £m
Liquid investments	4,381	291	–	287

Liquid investments principally comprise collateralised deposits and investments in commercial paper.

Included within liquid investments of the Group and Company, at 31 March 2003, was a restricted deposit account of £287 million for the deferred purchase of 48,935,625 shares in Vodafone Portugal. This was released for payment on 4 April 2003.

17. Creditors: amounts falling due within one year

	Group		Company	
	2004 £m	2003 £m	2004 £m	2003 £m
Bank overdrafts	42	–	–	–
Bank loans and other loans	2,000	1,078	956	351
Commercial paper	–	245	–	245
Finance leases	12	107	–	–
Trade creditors	2,842	2,497	–	–
Amounts owed to subsidiary undertakings	–	–	93,553	74,242
Amounts owed to associated undertakings	8	13	–	–
Taxation	4,275	4,137	–	–
Other taxes and social security costs	367	855	–	–
Other creditors	741	1,342	71	460
Accruals and deferred income	4,011	3,407	371	177
Proposed dividend	728	612	728	612
	15,026	14,293	95,679	76,087

18. Creditors: amounts falling due after more than one year

	Group		Company	
	2004 £m	2003 £m	2004 £m	2003 £m
Bank loans	1,504	1,803	23	–
Other loans	10,596	11,191	8,795	7,807
Finance leases	124	181	–	–
Other creditors	7	19	–	–
Accruals and deferred income	744	563	453	364
	12,975	13,757	9,271	8,171

Bank loans are repayable as follows:

	Group		Company	
	2004 £m	2003 £m	2004 £m	2003 £m
Repayable in more than one year but not more than two years	105	128	6	–
Repayable in more than two years but not more than five years	1,398	1,602	16	–
Repayable in more than five years	1	73	1	–
	1,504	1,803	23	–

Other loans are repayable as follows:

	Group		Company	
	2004 £m	2003 £m	2004 £m	2003 £m
Repayable in more than one year but not more than two years	303	1,994	–	–
Repayable in more than two years but not more than five years	3,108	2,878	2,549	3,072
Repayable in more than five years	7,185	6,319	6,246	4,735
	10,596	11,191	8,795	7,807

Notes to the Consolidated Financial Statements continued

18. Creditors: amounts falling due after more than one year continued

Other loans falling due after more than one year primarily comprise bond issues by the Company, or its subsidiaries, analysed as follows:

	Group		Company	
	2004 £m	2003 £m	2004 £m	2003 £m
4.875% Euro bond due 2004	–	859	–	–
1.27% Japanese yen bond due 2005	134	139	–	–
1.93% Japanese yen bond due 2005	135	140	–	–
5.25% Euro bond due 2005	–	139	–	–
6.35% US dollar bond due 2005	34	125	–	–
7.625% US dollar bond due 2005	–	995	–	995
0.83% Japanese yen bond due 2006	16	16	16	16
1.78% Japanese yen bond due 2006	135	139	–	–
5.4% Euro bond due 2006	267	276	267	276
5.75% Euro bond due 2006	1,001	1,032	1,001	1,032
7.5% US dollar bond due 2006	121	258	–	–
4.161% US dollar bond due 2007	81	95	81	95
2.575% Japanese yen bond due 2008	136	140	–	–
3.95% US dollar bond due 2008	271	315	271	315
4.625% Euro bond due 2008	504	344	504	344
5.5% Euro bond due 2008	32	146	–	–
6.25% Sterling bond due 2008	249	248	249	248
6.25% Sterling bond due 2008	160	–	160	–
6.65% US dollar bond due 2008	135	316	–	–
4.25% Euro bond due 2009	1,266	1,306	1,266	1,306
4.75% Euro bond due 2009	548	567	–	–
2.0% Japanese yen bond due 2010	135	139	–	–
2.28% Japanese yen bond due 2010	133	136	–	–
2.5% Japanese yen bond due 2010	137	141	–	–
7.75% US dollar bond due 2010	1,473	1,711	1,487	1,711
5.0% US dollar bond due 2013	540	–	540	–
5.125% Euro bond due 2015	333	–	333	–
5.375% US dollar bond due 2015	495	251	495	251
5.0% Euro bond due 2018	499	–	499	–
4.625% US dollar bond due 2018	270	–	270	–
5.625% Sterling bond due 2025	246	–	246	–
7.875% US dollar bond due 2030	400	465	400	465
5.9% Sterling bond due 2032	443	443	443	443
6.25% US dollar bond due 2032	267	310	267	310
	10,596	11,191	8,795	7,807

Finance leases are repayable as follows:				
Repayable in more than one year but not more than two years	11	47	–	–
Repayable in more than two years but not more than five years	30	39	–	–
Repayable in more than five years	83	95	–	–
	124	181	–	–

Weis Markets, Inc.—Measurement Concepts & Valuation

Weis Markets, Inc., is a Pennsylvania business founded by Harry and Sigmund Weis in 1912 and incorporated in 1924. The company is engaged principally in the retail sale of food in Pennsylvania and surrounding states. The company's stock has been traded on the New York Stock Exchange since 1965 under the symbol "WMK." The company's retail food stores sell groceries, dairy products, frozen foods, meats, seafood, fresh produce, floral, prescriptions, deli/bakery products, prepared foods, fuel and general merchandise items, such as health and beauty care and household products. The company currently owns and operates 155 retail food stores and a chain of 31 SuperPetz, pet supply stores. (Source: Company 2007 Form 10-K)

Learning Objectives
- Explain how financial statements reflect important assumptions underlying GAAP.
- Understand the difference between net book value and fair market value.
- Perform and interpret basic balance sheet and income statement-based valuation analyses.
- Use information from the financial statements to estimate the intrinsic value of the firm using the residual income valuation model.

Refer to the 2007 financial statements of Weis Markets, Inc.

 Concepts

a. The Financial Accounting Standards Board's (FASB) Statement of Concepts No. 1, *Objectives of Financial Reporting by Business Enterprises*, discusses users and uses of financial reports.

   i.   Speculate on who uses the Weis Markets financial statements and what those users would like to know about the company.

   ii. For users interested in assessing the financial performance of an enterprise, which basis of accounting, accrual or cash-basis, generally provides a better measure of current period performance? Why? Does Weis Markets use accrual-basis or cash-basis accounting? How can you tell?

   iii. Financial statements are normally prepared under the assumption that the entity is a going concern. Explain what is meant by a "going concern" and how that assumption affects figures on the Weis Markets financial statements.

b. FASB Statement of Concepts No. 2, *Qualitative Characteristics of Accounting Information*, identifies attributes of financial reporting that enhance its usefulness. The primary qualities are that accounting information be relevant and reliable.

   Relevance is described as "the capacity of information to make a difference in a decision by helping users to form predictions about outcomes of past, present, and future events or to confirm or correct prior expectations." Reliability is described as "the quality of information that assures that information is reasonably free from error and bias and faithfully represents what it purports to represent."

   One way to enhance the relevance of financial reporting is to enhance its timeliness.

   i.   How often do public companies, like Weis Markets, typically report their financial performance, financial position, and cash flows?

   ii. How does increasing the frequency of reporting affect the reliability of financial reports?

   iii. Discuss some ways an enterprise can enhance the relevance and reliability of its financial reporting. What are the benefits to managers and shareholders of doing so?

c. FASB Statement of Concepts No. 6 (a replacement for SCON No. 3), *Elements of Financial Statements*, describes the building blocks with which financial statements are constructed.

Define each of the following elements and provide examples from Weis Markets' financial statements where possible.

  i.   Assets

  ii.   Liabilities

  iii. Owners' Equity

  iv.   Investments by Owners

  v.   Distributions to Owners

  vi.   Revenues

  vii. Expenses

  viii. Gains

  ix.   Losses

  x.   Comprehensive Income

d. FASB Statement of Concepts No. 5, *Recognition and Measurement in Financial Statements of Business Enterprises*, provides guidance on what information should be included in the financial statements and when. SCON No. 5 identifies four fundamental criteria for an item to be recognized in the financials: (1) the item should meet the *definition* of an element of financial statements (i.e., SCON No. 6), (2) the item is *relevant* to decision making, (3) the information is *reliable* (i.e., representationally faithful, verifiable, and neutral), and (4) it can be *measured* with sufficient reliability. Alternative measurement bases include historical cost, replacement cost, current market value, net realizable value, and the present value of future cash flows.

Explain how each of the following items are measured in Weis Markets' financial statements. You can learn more about each of these accounts in Weis Markets' Form 10-K available on the corporate website: www.weismarkets.com//financial_info.php

  i.   Cash

  ii.   Accounts receivable, net

  iii. Inventories

  iv.   Property and equipment, net

  v.   Accrued self-insurance

e. Why don't Weis Markets' financial statements measure all elements at their market, or fair, values?

✦   **Analysis**   ✦

f. For this question, refer only to the December 29, 2007, financial statements of Weis Markets.

  i.   What is the net book value of Weis Markets, Inc. (the company, not the individual assets or liabilities) at December 29, 2007? What does this amount represent?

  ii.   Which of Weis' individual asset and liability accounts most likely have fair values that differ significantly from the book values recorded on the balance sheet? What accounting principles give rise to these differences?

  iii. Assume that the market value of the company's inventories is $54,494 (in thousands) higher than its book value. Further, included under Property and equipment, net is land valued at an historic cost of $85,158 (in thousands). Recent real estate appraisals indicate that the land may be worth as much as $200,000 (in thousands). Also, Weis Markets has entered into long-term leases for some of its stores. A review of those leases suggests that they are very favorable to the company. In other words, the company is leasing assets at below market rates. The fair value of those favorable leases is estimated to be $4,500 (in thousands). Finally, assume that all other amounts recorded on the balance sheet approximate their fair market values.

Based on your restated balance sheet, what is the fair market value of Weis Markets, Inc.'s net assets at December 29, 2007?

iv. Compare your responses to parts *f i*. (net book value) and *f iii*. (fair market value of net assets). Why are these amounts different? What does the difference represent?

g. One way that financial analysts approximate the value of a company is by applying a "multiple" to the company's net income. This multiple is commonly known as the Price-Earnings (or PE) multiple. It is a simple, but easily applied, valuation method. For example, if a company had net income per share of $5 and analysts considered the appropriate PE multiple to be 12, the share would be valued at $60. The fair market value of the company would be $60 times the number of outstanding shares.

Conceptually, a PE multiple is akin to the factor for the present value of an annuity. When an annuity payment is expected to be perpetual (i.e., an infinite number of equal payments), the present value of an annuity factor converges to $(1 / r)$, where 'r' is the appropriate risk-adjusted discount rate for the firm. Thus, a PE multiple of 12 is equivalent to $1 / 0.083$. Applying the multiple of 12 to a given level of earnings is equivalent to valuing the company as though it would provide an annuity equal to its "earnings" every year, for an infinite number of years, using 8.3% as the discount rate.

i. If Weis Markets' shares are trading at a PE multiple (based on 2007 net income) of 21.11, what is the implied discount rate? (Assume, as above, an annuity paying for an infinite number of years.) Does this discount rate seem reasonable? Explain.

ii. Based on a PE multiple of 21.11, use Net Income to estimate the fair market value of Weis Markets' equity. In using Net Income for this calculation, what are you implicitly assuming?

iii. Compare your responses to parts *f iii*. (fair market value of net assets) and *g ii*. (fair market value of the equity). Why are these amounts so different? What do the differences represent?

iv. PE multiples can also accommodate earnings growth. If earnings are predicted to grow at a constant rate, g, then the PE multiple can be written as $(1 + g) / (r - g)$. (Note that in this formulation of the PE multiple, the earnings are last period's earnings, sometimes known as trailing earnings.) Assume that Weis Markets' shares have a PE multiple of 21.11 and that you believe that 8% is an appropriate discount rate for the company given its risk level. What is the implied growth rate embedded in the PE multiple of 21.11? Explain how you would assess whether the growth rate was reasonable.

h. A more sophisticated way to value a company is to forecast its future results for a number of periods and then make a simplifying assumption about results it will achieve over the rest of its life. For example, a security analyst could forecast specific figures for the next three years based on expectations about the economy and the company's competitive strategy. This period is known as the forecast horizon and can be as long or as short as the analyst feels comfortable forecasting. The period beyond the forecast horizon is called the terminal value. The simplifying assumptions used to calculate it usually rely on general trends expected to apply over the long-run; for example, that growth rates will move towards the general long run growth rates for the sector of the economy in which the firm operates and profits will be affected by the forces of competition and move towards their normal, or equilibrium, levels.

The residual income valuation model is a very powerful model that captures key economic variables in an intuitively appealing fashion. The model is algebraically equivalent to valuing a company by determining the present value of its future dividends to common shareholders. However, it allows analysts to focus on the *generation* of shareholder value rather than its *distribution*. The model demonstrates that the value of the equity of a firm is equal to its net book value plus the present value of its future residual income.

Residual income is an economic concept. It represents the profits a company earns above and beyond those "expected" by shareholders. Expected earnings are earnings that exactly compensate shareholders for taking on risky investments. In simple terms, when shareholders make an investment, they "demand" a return at least equal to the amount of their investment times the cost of equity capital (i.e., the amount they could earn on alternative investments of equivalent risk). If a firm's earnings are exactly equal to the value of beginning-of-the-period owners' equity times the cost of equity, then the firm has earned no residual income. When earnings are greater than (less than) beginning owners' equity times the cost of equity, the firm has positive (negative) residual income.

A firm's shareholders provide capital to the firm's managers. The managers' objective is to use that capital to earn long-run returns that exceed the cost of that capital. In others words, managers are tasked with generating residual income. When managers accomplish this, they are said to be creating shareholder value.

Algebraically, the residual income valuation model is:

$$V_0 = B_0 + \frac{B_0(ROE_1 - r_e)}{(1+r_e)^1} + \frac{B_1(ROE_2 - r_e)}{(1+r_e)^2} + \frac{B_2(ROE_3 - r_e)}{(1+r_e)^3} + \frac{B_3(ROE_4 - r_e)}{(r_e - g)(1+r_e)^3}$$

Where:

- V_0 is the intrinsic (estimated) value of the equity of the firm at time 0.

- B_t is the book value (i.e., owners' equity) of the firm at time t.

- ROE_t is return on common equity in period t.

- r_e is the firm's cost of equity capital.

- g is the appropriate long-run growth rate for residual income.

The first term on the right-hand side of the model is B_0, the owners' equity of the firm at the date of the valuation. Investors will pay only book value for a company that is not expected to earn a return over its cost of equity.

The remaining terms on the right-hand side are the analyst's estimate of the value that managers are expected to create over the rest of the life of the firm. These terms can be grouped into two categories: the present value of the residual income generated over the forecast horizon and the terminal value.

In the version of the model above, there are three periods in the forecast horizon. The numerator in each term is the residual income generated in periods 1, 2 and 3 respectively. The firm's book value grows from one period to the next by that period's earnings net of dividends paid and stock repurchased. Algebraically, this is: $B_{t+1} = B_t + (B_t \times ROE_{t+1}) \times (1 - dividend\ payout\ ratio - stock\ repurchase\ ratio)$. The denominator is the present value factor that brings the future residual income back to a present value at time 0.

The last term in the model is the terminal value and it has three parts. The numerator is the amount of residual income expected to be generated in period 4 and serves as the base from which all future residual income follows. The denominator takes that residual income and assumes that it grows in perpetuity at a constant rate, g, by dividing the numerator by $(r_e - g)$. Because that will generate the present value of an annuity at the beginning of period 4 (end of period 3), the amount needs to be discounted back to time 0 by further dividing the numerator by the present value factor for three periods (i.e., $(1 + r_e)^3$).

i.   Use information from the Weis Markets financial statements and the Five-Year Review of Operations to complete the table below that summarizes the inputs to the residual income valuation model. *Note*: different analysts will arrive at different model inputs. What is important is that you can justify your assumptions and the model inputs you choose.

Residual income valuation model input	Estimated model input
ROE_t – expected return on equity for year t. Assume that Weis Market's three-year average ROE approximates expected future ROEs. $ROE_t = Net\ Income_t / B_{t-1}$	
Dividend payout ratio. This ratio measures the dividends paid as a proportion of net income. Assume that Weis Market's three-year average dividend payout ratio approximates expected future payout ratios.	
Stock repurchase ratio. This ratio measures the stock repurchases, net of stock issuances, as a proportion of net income. Assume that Weis Market's three-year average stock repurchase ratio approximates future expectations.	
B_0 –book value of equity at December 29, 2007	
B_1 – expected book value of equity at December 29, 2008 $B_1 = B_0 + (B_0 \times ROE) \times (1 - dividend\ payout\ ratio - stock\ repurchase\ ratio)$	
B_2 – expected book value of equity at December 29, 2009	
B_3 – expected book value of equity at December 29, 2010	

ii. Assume that Weis Markets' cost of equity capital is 8% and that the company's expected terminal-period growth rate is 3.87%. Use the model inputs you estimated above, to compute the intrinsic value (i.e., V_0) of Weis Markets, Inc., at December 29, 2007.

iii. What is the intrinsic value per share of Weis Markets, Inc., at December 29, 2007?

iv. Explain why the net book value of equity (part *f i.*), the adjusted book value (part *f iii.*), the fair market value (part *g ii.*), and the intrinsic value (part *h iii.*) differ. Is there a "true" or "correct" value of the company?

i. Use an online investment site (such as http://finance.yahoo.com/) to find the stock price of Weis Markets, Inc. at December 29, 2007. Compare that stock price to your estimate of the company's intrinsic value per share, from part *h. iii.*, above. What might account for any difference? If you are very confident in your estimate of intrinsic value, what investment strategy might you undertake with respect to Weis Markets?

WEIS MARKETS, INC.
CONSOLIDATED BALANCE SHEETS
December 29, 2007 and December 30, 2006

(dollars in thousands)	2007	2006
Assets		
Current:		
Cash and cash equivalents	$ 41,187	$ 27,545
Marketable securities	26,182	38,163
Accounts receivable, net	48,460	41,885
Inventories	193,732	189,468
Prepaid expenses	3,317	3,932
Income taxes recoverable	8,074	---
Total current assets	320,952	300,993
Property and equipment, net	499,246	492,543
Goodwill	15,722	15,722
Intangible and other assets, net	4,149	4,804
Total assets	$ 840,069	$ 814,062
Liabilities		
Current:		
Accounts payable	$ 111,555	$ 105,859
Accrued expenses	23,036	22,307
Accrued self-insurance	23,442	22,778
Payable to employee benefit plans	1,400	1,435
Income taxes payable	---	865
Deferred income taxes	4,134	298
Total current liabilities	163,567	153,542
Postretirement benefit obligations	14,027	12,912
Deferred income taxes	14,247	18,445
Total liabilities	191,841	184,899
Shareholders' Equity		
Common stock, no par value, 100,800,000 shares authorized, 33,044,357 and 33,009,046 shares issued, respectively	9,830	8,595
Retained earnings	779,760	760,531
Accumulated other comprehensive income, net	7,339	6,084
	796,929	775,210
Treasury stock at cost, 6,077,311 and 6,016,291 shares, respectively	(148,701)	(146,047)
Total shareholders' equity	648,228	629,163
Total liabilities and shareholders' equity	$ 840,069	$ 814,062

See accompanying notes to consolidated financial statements.

WEIS MARKETS, INC.
CONSOLIDATED STATEMENTS OF INCOME
For Fiscal Years ended December 29 2007, December 30, 2006 and December 31, 2005

(dollars in thousands, except shares and per share amounts)	**2007** **(52 Weeks)**	**2006** **(52 Weeks)**	**2005** **(53 Weeks)**
Net sales	$2,318,551	$2,244,512	$2,222,598
Cost of sales, including warehousing and distribution expenses	1,716,424	1,647,233	1,634,874
Gross profit on sales	602,127	597,279	587,724
Operating, general and administrative expenses	527,378	515,675	491,499
Income from operations	74,749	81,604	96,225
Investment income	3,010	4,484	3,081
Income before provision for income taxes	77,759	86,088	99,306
Provision for income taxes	26,769	30,078	35,885
Net income	$ 50,990	$ 56,010	$ 63,421
Weighted-average shares outstanding, basic	26,987,786	27,016,877	27,026,748
Weighted-average shares outstanding, diluted	26,993,997	27,027,198	27,033,789
Cash dividends per share	$ 1.16	$ 1.16	$ 1.12
Basic and diluted earnings per share	$ 1.89	$ 2.07	$ 2.35

See accompanying notes to consolidated financial statements.

WEIS MARKETS, INC.
CONSOLIDATED STATEMENTS OF SHAREHOLDERS' EQUITY
For the Fiscal Years Ended December 29, 2007, December 30, 2006 and December 31, 2005

(dollars in thousands, except shares)	Common Stock Shares	Common Stock Amount	Retained Earnings	Accum. Other Comprehensive Income	Treasury Stock Shares	Treasury Stock Amount	Total Shareholders' Equity
Balance at December 25, 2004	32,997,157	$8,199	$ 702,714	$ 4,747	5,964,330	$ (143,960)	$ 571,700
Net income	---	---	63,421	---	---	---	63,421
Other comprehensive loss, net of reclassification adjustments and tax	---	---	---	(451)	---	---	(451)
Comprehensive income							62,970
Shares issued for options	5,200	172	---	---	---	---	172
Treasury stock purchased	---	---	---	---	18,131	(715)	(715)
Dividends paid	---	---	(30,270)	---	---	---	(30,270)
Balance at December 31, 2005	33,002,357	8,371	735,865	4,296	5,982,461	(144,675)	603,857
Net income	---	---	56,010	---	---	---	56,010
Other comprehensive income, net of reclassification adjustments and tax	---	---	---	1,788	---	---	1,788
Comprehensive income							57,798
Shares issued for options	6,689	224	---	---	3,498	(154)	70
Treasury stock purchased	---	---	---	---	30,332	(1,218)	(1,218)
Dividends paid	---	---	(31,344)	---	---	---	(31,344)
Balance at December 30, 2006	33,009,046	8,595	760,531	6,084	6,016,291	(146,047)	629,163
Net income	---	---	50,990	---	---	---	50,990
Other comprehensive income, net of reclassification adjustments and tax	---	---	---	1,255	---	---	1,255
Comprehensive income							52,245
Cumulative effect of change in accounting for income taxes	---	---	(452)	---	---	---	(452)
Shares issued for options	35,311	1,235	---	---	25,561	(1,155)	80
Treasury stock purchased	---	---	---	---	35,459	(1,499)	(1,499)
Dividends paid	---	---	(31,309)	---	---	---	(31,309)
Balance at December 29, 2007	33,044,357	$ 9,830	$ 779,760	$ 7,339	6,077,311	$ (148,701)	$ 648,228

See accompanying notes to consolidated financial statements.

WEIS MARKETS, INC.
CONSOLIDATED STATEMENTS OF CASH FLOWS
For the Fiscal Years Ended December 29, 2007, December 30, 2006 and December 31, 2005

(dollars in thousands)	2007 (52 Weeks)	2006 (52 Weeks)	2005 (53 Weeks)
Cash flows from operating activities:			
Net income	$ 50,990	$ 56,010	$ 63,421
Adjustments to reconcile net income to net cash provided by operating activities:			
Depreciation	47,511	45,000	43,875
Amortization	7,331	6,020	6,231
(Gain) loss on fixed asset disposition / impairment	(8,031)	974	519
Gain on sale of marketable securities	(6)	(431)	(422)
Changes in operating assets and liabilities:			
Inventories	(4,264)	(10,086)	(14,338)
Accounts receivable and prepaid expenses	(5,960)	(1,365)	(3,424)
Income taxes recoverable	(8,074)	---	1,729
Accounts payable and other liabilities	8,169	10,277	7,636
Income taxes payable	(1,317)	(1,155)	2,020
Deferred income taxes	(1,252)	(5,762)	(2,845)
Other	345	(201)	(98)
Net cash provided by operating activities	85,442	99,281	104,304
Cash flows from investing activities:			
Purchase of property and equipment	(64,233)	(99,975)	(55,468)
Proceeds from the sale of property and equipment	11,374	2,696	291
Purchase of marketable securities	---	(33,020)	(8,248)
Proceeds from maturities of marketable securities	13,780	15,745	---
Proceeds from sale of marketable securities	7	6,010	1,000
Net cash used in investing activities	(39,072)	(108,544)	(62,425)
Cash flows from financing activities:			
Proceeds from issuance of common stock	1,235	224	172
Dividends paid	(31,309)	(31,344)	(30,270)
Purchase of treasury stock	(2,654)	(1,372)	(715)
Net cash used in financing activities	(32,728)	(32,492)	(30,813)
Net increase (decrease) in cash and cash equivalents	13,642	(41,755)	11,066
Cash and cash equivalents at beginning of year	27,545	69,300	58,234
Cash and cash equivalents at end of year	$ 41,187	$ 27,545	$ 69,300

See accompanying notes to consolidated financial statements.

WEIS MARKETS, INC.

Item 6.   Selected Financial Data:

The following selected historical financial information has been derived from the company's audited consolidated financial statements. This information should be read in connection with the company's Consolidated Financial Statements and the Notes thereto, as well as "Management's Discussion and Analysis of Financial Condition and Results of Operations," included in Item 7.

Five Year Review of Operations

(dollars in thousands, except shares, per share amounts and store information)	52 Weeks Ended Dec. 29, 2007	52 Weeks Ended Dec. 30, 2006	53 Weeks Ended Dec. 31, 2005	52 Weeks Ended Dec. 25, 2004	52 Weeks Ended Dec. 27, 2003
Net sales	$ 2,318,551	$ 2,244,512	$ 2,222,598	$ 2,097,712	$ 2,042,499
Costs and expenses	2,243,802	2,162,908	2,126,373	2,011,331	1,955,119
Income from operations	74,749	81,604	96,225	86,381	87,380
Investment income	3,010	4,484	3,081	1,222	824
Income before provision for income taxes	77,759	86,088	99,306	87,603	88,204
Provision for income taxes	26,769	30,078	35,885	30,412	33,628
Net income	50,990	56,010	63,421	57,191	54,576
Retained earnings, beginning of year	760,531	735,865	702,714	702,961	678,294
	811,521	791,875	766,135	760,152	732,870
Less cumulative effect of change in accounting for income taxes	452	---	---	---	29,909
Cash dividends	31,309	31,344	30,270	57,438	
Retained earnings, end of year	$ 779,760	$ 760,531	$ 735,865	$ 702,714	$ 702,961
Weighted-average shares outstanding, diluted	26,993,997	27,027,198	27,033,789	27,098,276	27,186,277
Cash dividends per share	$ 1.16	$ 1.16	$ 1.12	$ 2.12	$ 1.10
Basic and diluted earnings per share	$ 1.89	$ 2.07	$ 2.35	$ 2.11	$ 2.01
Working capital	$ 157,385	$ 147,451	$ 170,100	$ 143,440	$ 167,154
Total assets	$ 840,069	$ 814,062	$ 784,128	$ 745,479	$ 740,920
Shareholders' equity	$ 648,228	$ 629,163	$ 603,857	$ 571,700	$ 575,448
Number of grocery stores	155	156	158	157	158
Number of pet supply stores	31	31	32	33	33

Molson Coors Brewing Company— Profitability and Earnings Persistence

On February 9, 2007, Adolph Coors Company merged with Molson Inc. to form Molson Coors Brewing Company. Molson was founded in 1786 in Canada and Coors was founded in 1873 in the U.S. Since the beginning, each company has been committed to producing the highest-quality beers. The Molson Coors brands are designed to appeal to a wide range of consumer tastes, styles and price preferences. The company's largest markets are Canada, the United States, and the United Kingdom. (Source: Company 2007 Form 10-K)

Learning Objectives
- Explain why income statements are "classified."
- Understand specific income statement items and interpret their impact on reported firm performance.
- Explain earnings persistence and use the income statement to calculate persistent income.
- Compute and interpret operating performance ratios.

Refer to the 2007 financial statements of Molson Coors Brewing Company.

 Concepts

a. What are the major classifications on an income statement?

b. Explain why, under GAAP, companies are required to provide "classified" income statements.

c. In general, why might financial statement users be interested in a measure of persistent income?

Process

d. The income statement reports "Sales" and "Net sales." What is the difference? Why does Molson Coors report these two items separately?

e. Consider the income statement item "Debt extinguishment costs" and the information in Note 13.

   i. Explain, in your own words, what these costs represent.

   ii. Prepare the journal entry to record the debt extinguishment costs.

f. Consider the income statement item "Special items, net" and information in Note 8.

   i. In general, what types of items does Molson Coors include in this line item?

   ii. Explain why the company reports these on a separate line item rather than including them with another expense item. Molson Coors classifies these special items as operating expenses. Do you concur with this classification? Explain.

   iii. What is the distinction between the "Special items" which Molson Coors classifies as operating expenses and "Other income (expense)" which is classified a nonoperating expenses?

g. Consider the income statement item "Loss from discontinued operations, net of tax" and information in Note 4.

   i. These operations were discontinued in 2006. Yet, Molson Coors shows a loss from discontinued operations of $91,826 in 2005 and a loss of $17,682 in 2007. Briefly explain why.

   ii. What total proceeds did Molson Coors receive for the sale of Kaiser? When did Molson Coors receive these proceeds? How do these proceeds affect the statement of cash flows?

h. In 2007, Molson Coors closed a brewery in Edmonton, Canada, and reported the loss as a special item (see Note 8). But when the company closed breweries in Brazil in 2006 it reported the loss as discontinued operations (see Note 4). Why the difference in accounting treatments?

i. Consider the "Cumulative effect of change in accounting principle" reported on the income statement. Explain in your own words what this item represents.

◆ Analysis ◆

A company's performance can be analyzed in many ways. Return on net operating assets (RNOA) is a common metric that compares the operating profit the company made during the period (the portion of net income attributable to continuing core operations) to the net operating resources invested in the company. We can break RNOA into two components: operating profit margin and net operating asset turnover. The RNOA decomposition can be written as:

$$RNOA = \frac{Net\ Operating\ Profit\ after\ Tax}{Average\ Net\ Operating\ Assets}$$

$$RNOA = \frac{Net\ Operating\ Profit\ after\ Tax}{Sales} \times \frac{Sales}{Average\ Net\ Operating\ Assets}$$

Where:

- *Net operating profit after tax* is profit from the firm's main, ongoing operating activities. Net operating profit after tax excludes any nonoperating income or expenses such as interest, gains or losses from marketable securities or disposals of investments. It also excludes discontinued operations (they are not ongoing).

- *Sales* are reported on the income statement. The appropriate sales number for this ratio would be net sales – that is after returns, discounts, and any excise taxes.

- *Net operating assets* are measured as all operating assets *less* all operating liabilities. Net operating assets exclude all nonoperating assets (including marketable securities, other investments, and assets of discontinued operations) and all nonoperating liabilities (including short and long-term debt, derivatives, and liabilities of discontinued operations).

j. Examine Molson Coors income statements for 2007 and 2006 and the relevant Notes to the financial statements.

   i. Identify items that you consider "nonoperating." Explain each item briefly.

   ii. Calculate the total after-tax amount of the nonoperating items you identified. For this calculation, assume that the company's marginal tax rate is 28% for nonoperating items. *Note*: some nonoperating items are reported net of tax on the income statement. Use the marginal tax only for the items that are reported "before tax" on the income statement.

   iii. Calculate net operating profit after tax for 2007 and 2006. *Hint*: net operating profit after tax is calculated as net income before the effect of the after-tax amount of nonoperating items.

k. Examine Molson Coors balance sheets 2007 and 2006. Footnotes to the financial statements (not included with the case) reveal that the Notes receivable (and the current portion thereof) relate to loans made to customers. These are considered nonoperating assets.

   i. Identify assets and liabilities that you consider "nonoperating." Explain each item briefly.

   ii. Calculate net operating assets for 2007 and 2006.

l. Calculate Molson Coors' return on net operating assets (RNOA) for 2007 and 2006. Compare the two returns. *Note*: to simplify the analysis, use year-end values for net operating assets rather than averages.

m. Compute the operating profit margin and net operating asset turnover components of Molson Coors' RNOA for 2007 and 2006. Use the components to explain the change in RNOA from 2006 to 2007.

n. Analysts and investors and other capital-market participants use the current income statement to predict income in future periods. However, a good prediction of future income requires an understanding of what factors determine current income. Analysts often begin their analysis by computing a measure of persistent or recurring income. Identify items on Molson Coors' income statement that you consider non-persistent. For each item indicate whether you do not expect the item itself to recur or whether the item might recur on future income statements but at potentially very different amounts.

o. Consider the information on income taxes, in Note 7.

   i.   What is Molson Coors' effective tax rate in 2007? Do you expect this rate to persist?

   ii. Determine a tax rate that you expect to persist for the company. Assume that Molson Coors' domestic operations will continue to be taxed at the combined statutory rate that prevailed in 2007. Molson Coors has foreign operations that are taxed at lower rates than in the U.S. Assume that the "Effect of foreign tax rates" can be expected to continue at the 2005 and 2006 levels. Assume that all other items in the tax rate reconciliation are not permanent.

p. Calculate an estimate of persistent income for Molson Coors. To assist you in this, make the following assumptions: Debt extinguishment and Loss on discontinued operations are nonrecurring items. "Special items" and "Other income" will recur and that the three-year average for these items approximates their respective future dollar amounts. Taxes on all items will be at the persistent rate you calculated in part *o*, above. All other items are considered persistent.

q. Recalculate Molson Coors' return on net operating assets (RNOA) for 2007, using the persistent income numbers from part *p*, above. Compare the RNOA to the one you calculated with the reported income statement numbers in part *l*, above. *Note*: your new RNOA calculations will use the same net operating assets as in part *l*, above. Which RNOA calculation better reflects Molson Coors' 2007 profitability? Which one is a better predictor of future profitability?

MOLSON COORS BREWING COMPANY AND SUBSIDIARIES
CONSOLIDATED STATEMENTS OF OPERATIONS AND COMPREHENSIVE INCOME
(IN THOUSANDS, EXCEPT PER SHARE DATA)

	For the Years Ended		
	December 30, 2007	December 31, 2006(1)	December 25, 2005(1)
Sales	$ 8,319,673	$ 7,901,614	$ 7,417,702
Excise taxes	(2,129,081)	(2,056,629)	(1,910,796)
Net sales	6,190,592	5,844,985	5,506,906
Cost of goods sold	(3,702,921)	(3,481,081)	(3,306,949)
Gross profit	2,487,671	2,363,904	2,199,957
Marketing, general and administrative expenses	(1,734,408)	(1,705,405)	(1,632,516)
Special items, net	(112,194)	(77,404)	(145,392)
Operating income	641,069	581,095	422,049
Other income (expense), net			
Interest expense	(126,462)	(143,070)	(131,106)
Interest income	26,587	16,289	17,503
Debt extinguishment costs	(24,478)	—	—
Other income (expense), net	17,662	17,736	(13,245)
Total other expense	(106,691)	(109,045)	(126,848)
Income from continuing operations before income taxes and minority interests	534,378	472,050	295,201
Income tax expense	(4,186)	(82,405)	(50,264)
Income from continuing operations before minority interests	530,192	389,645	244,937
Minority interests in net income of consolidated entities	(15,318)	(16,089)	(14,491)
Income from continuing operations	514,874	373,556	230,446
Loss from discontinued operations, net of tax	(17,682)	(12,525)	(91,826)
Income before cumulative effect of change in accounting principle	497,192	361,031	138,620
Cumulative effect of change in accounting principle, net of tax	—	—	(3,676)
Net income	$ 497,192	$ 361,031	$ 134,944
Other comprehensive income, net of tax:			
Foreign currency translation adjustments	795,060	157,207	122,971
Unrealized (loss) gain on derivative instruments	(3,428)	18,347	(19,276)
Realized loss (gain) reclassified to net income	2,933	(4,605)	(8,404)
Pension and other other postretirement benefit adjustments	(6,614)	131,126	(6,203)
Comprehensive income	$ 1,285,143	$ 663,106	$ 224,032

MOLSON COORS BREWING COMPANY AND SUBSIDIARIES
CONSOLIDATED BALANCE SHEETS
(IN THOUSANDS)

	As of	
	December 30, 2007	December 31, 2006
Assets		
Cash and cash equivalents	$ 377,023	$ 182,186
Accounts and notes receivable:		
Trade, less allowance for doubtful accounts of $8,827 and $10,363, respectively	758,526	679,507
Affiliates	—	4,002
Current notes receivable and other receivables, less allowance for doubtful accounts of $3,181 and $3,439, respectively	112,626	145,090
Inventories:		
Finished, less allowance for obsolete inventories of $995 and $1,057, respectively	163,955	138,449
In process	40,673	38,692
Raw materials	82,323	80,918
Packaging materials, less allowance for obsolete inventories of $579 and $1,807, respectively	82,570	61,479
Total inventories	369,521	319,538
Maintenance and operating supplies, less allowance for obsolete supplies of $10,556 and $9,554, respectively	34,782	32,639
Other current assets, less allowance for advertising supplies of $948 and $871, respectively	100,899	84,277
Deferred tax assets	17,901	6,477
Discontinued operations	5,536	4,640
Total current assets	1,776,814	1,458,356
Properties, less accumulated depreciation of $2,714,170 and $2,615,000, respectively	2,696,153	2,421,484
Goodwill	3,346,486	2,968,676
Other intangibles, less accumulated amortization of $312,067 and $221,867, respectively	5,039,363	4,395,294
Deferred tax assets	336,907	131,349
Notes receivable, less allowance for doubtful accounts of $7,930 and $10,318, respectively	71,239	75,243
Other assets	179,502	148,694
Discontinued operations	5,102	4,317
Total assets	$ 13,451,566	$ 11,603,413

MOLSON COORS BREWING COMPANY AND SUBSIDIARIES
CONSOLIDATED BALANCE SHEETS
(IN THOUSANDS)

	As of	
	December 30, 2007	December 31, 2006
Liabilities and stockholders' equity		
Accounts payable:		
Trade	$ 351,595	$ 388,281
Affiliates	29,104	31,369
Accrued expenses and other liabilities	1,189,134	1,225,406
Deferred tax liabilities	120,605	116,329
Short-term borrowings	55	432
Current portion of long-term debt	4,226	4,009
Discontinued operations	40,858	34,290
Total current liabilities	1,735,577	1,800,116
Long-term debt	2,260,596	2,129,845
Pension and post-retirement benefits	677,786	753,697
Derivative hedging instruments	477,450	269,253
Deferred tax liabilities	605,377	607,000
Unrecognized tax benefits	285,921	—
Other liabilities	90,926	93,721
Discontinued operations	124,791	85,643
Total liabilities	6,258,424	5,739,275
Commitments and contingencies (Note 20)		
Minority interests	43,751	46,782
Stockholders' equity		
Capital stock:		
Preferred stock, non-voting, no par value	—	—
Class A common stock, voting, $0.01 par value (authorized: 500,000,000 shares; issued and outstanding: 2,674,772 shares at 12/30/2007 and 12/31/2006, respectively)	27	27
Class B common stock, non-voting, $0.01 par value (authorized: 500,000,000 shares; issued and outstanding: 149,638,230 and 133,216,966 shares at 12/30/2007 and 12/31/2006, respectively)	1,496	1,332
Class A exchangeable shares (issued and outstanding: 3,315,899 and 3,314,250 shares at 12/30/2007 and 12/31/2006, respectively)	124,760	124,699
Class B exchangeable shares (issued and outstanding: 25,123,570 and 34,843,536 shares at 12/30/2007 and 12/31/2006, respectively)	945,275	1,310,989
Total capital stock	1,071,558	1,437,047
Paid-in capital	3,022,449	2,389,876
Retained earnings	1,950,455	1,673,455
Accumulated other comprehensive income	1,104,929	316,978
Total stockholders' equity	7,149,391	5,817,356
Total liabilities and stockholders' equity	$ 13,451,566	$ 11,603,413

MOLSON COORS BREWING COMPANY AND SUBSIDIARIES
CONSOLIDATED STATEMENTS OF CASH FLOWS
(IN THOUSANDS)

	For the Years Ended		
	December 30, 2007	December 31, 2006	December 25, 2005
Cash flows from operating activities:			
Net income	$ 497,192	$ 361,031	$ 134,944
Adjustments to reconcile net income to net cash provided by operating activities:			
Depreciation and amortization	345,843	438,354	392,814
Amortization of debt issuance costs and discounts	4,823	3,621	22,446
Share-based compensation	37,387	22,143	12,397
Loss (gain) on sale or impairment of properties and intangibles	66,317	(2,055)	11,116
Gain on sale of House of Blues Canada equity investment	(16,694)	—	—
Gain coincident with the sale of preferred equity holdings of Montréal Canadiens	—	(8,984)	—
Excess tax benefits from share-based compensation	(28,135)	(7,474)	—
Deferred income taxes	(97,948)	1,368	(23,049)
Loss (gain) on foreign currency fluctuations and derivative instruments	7,136	(4,578)	(9,266)
Cumulative effect of change in accounting principle, net of tax	—	—	3,676
Equity in net income of unconsolidated affiliates	(6,602)	(8,026)	(37)
Distributions from unconsolidated affiliates	9,350	10,164	8,612
Minority interest in net income of consolidated entities	15,318	16,089	14,491
Change in current assets and liabilities (net of assets acquired and liabilities assumed in business combinations) and other:			
Receivables	(47,715)	57,734	9,071
Inventories	(23,133)	7,825	47,233
Payables	(27,483)	4,151	16,724
Other assets and other liabilities	(137,236)	(71,527)	(281,460)
Operating cash flows of discontinued operations	17,617	13,408	62,563
Net cash provided by operating activities	616,037	833,244	422,275
Cash flows from investing activities:			
Additions to properties and intangible assets	(428,349)	(446,376)	(406,045)
Proceeds from sales of properties and intangible assets	8,046	29,118	42,450
Purchases of investment securities, net	(22,777)	—	—
Acquisition of subsidiaries, net of cash acquired	(26,700)	—	(16,561)
Proceeds in conjunction with the sale of preferred equity holdings of Montréal Canadiens	—	36,520	—
Proceeds from sale of House of Blues Canada investment	30,008	—	—
Cash recognized on Merger with Molson	—	—	73,540
Cash expended for Merger-related costs	—	—	(20,382)
Trade loan repayments from customers	32,352	34,152	42,460
Trade loans advanced to customers	(32,952)	(27,982)	(25,369)
Other	1,225	290	16
Discontinued operations—proceeds from sale of majority stake in Kaiser, net of costs to sell	—	79,465	—
Discontinued operations—additions to properties and intangible assets	—	—	(2,817)
Net cash used in investing activities	(439,147)	(294,813)	(312,708)

MOLSON COORS BREWING COMPANY AND SUBSIDIARIES
CONSOLIDATED STATEMENTS OF CASH FLOWS (Continued)
(IN THOUSANDS)

	For the Years Ended		
	December 30, 2007	December 31, 2006	December 25, 2005
Cash flows from financing activities:			
Exercise of stock options under equity compensation plans	209,531	83,348	55,229
Excess tax benefits from share-based compensation	28,135	7,474	—
Dividends paid	(114,783)	(110,563)	(109,960)
Dividends paid to minority interest holders	(16,986)	(17,790)	(10,569)
Proceeds from issuances of long-term debt	—	—	1,037,814
Proceeds from issuance of convertible debt	575,000	—	—
Debt issuance costs	(10,209)	(120)	(11,457)
Sale of warrants	56,991	—	—
Purchase of call options	(106,656)	—	—
Payments on long-term debt and capital lease obligations	(631,038)	(7,361)	(584,056)
Proceeds from short-term borrowings	179,187	83,664	1,050,686
Payments on short-term borrowings	(180,511)	(98,110)	(1,887,558)
Net proceeds from (payments on) commercial paper	—	(167,379)	165,795
Net proceeds from (payments on) revolving credit facilities	(6,109)	(166,177)	151,273
Change in overdraft balances and other	20,733	(1,441)	8,159
Settlements of debt-related derivatives	5,150	(5,900)	(11,285)
Financing cash flows of discontinued operations	—	(884)	(42,846)
Net cash provided by (used in) financing activities	8,435	(401,239)	(188,775)
Cash and cash equivalents:			
Net increase in cash and cash equivalents	185,325	137,192	(79,208)
Effect of foreign exchange rate changes on cash and cash equivalents	9,512	5,581	(4,392)
Balance at beginning of year	182,186	39,413	123,013
Balance at end of period	$ 377,023	$ 182,186	$ 39,413

MOLSON COORS BREWING COMPANY AND SUBSIDIARIES
NOTES TO CONSOLIDATED BALANCE SHEETS
(IN THOUSANDS)

Components of our Statement of Operations

Net sales—Our net sales represent almost exclusively the sale of beer and other malt beverages, the vast majority of which are brands that we own and brew ourselves. We import or brew and sell certain non-owned partner brands under licensing and related arrangements. We also sell certain "factored" brands, as a distributor, to on-premise customers in the United Kingdom (Europe segment).

Cost of goods sold—Our cost of goods sold include costs we incur to make and ship beer. These costs include brewing materials, such as barley, in the United States and United Kingdom where we manufacture the majority of our own malt. In Canada, we purchase malt from third parties. Hops and various grains are other key brewing materials purchased by all of our segments. Packaging materials, including costs for glass bottles, aluminum and steel cans, and cardboard and paperboard are also included in our cost of goods sold. Our cost of goods sold also include both direct and indirect labor, freight costs, utilities, maintenance costs, and other manufacturing overheads, as well as the cost of "factored" brands.

Marketing, general and administrative—These costs include media advertising (television, radio, print), tactical advertising (signs, banners, point-of-sale materials) and promotion costs planned and executed on both local and national levels within our operating segments. These costs also include our sales organizations, including labor and other overheads. This classification also includes general and administrative costs for functions such as finance, legal, human resources and information technology, which consist primarily of labor and outside services.

Special Items—These are unique, infrequent and unusual items which affect our statement of operations, and are discussed in each segment's Results of Operations discussion.

Interest expense, net—Interest costs associated with borrowings to finance our operations are classified here. Interest income in the Europe segment is associated with trade loans receivable from customers.

Debt extinguishment costs—The costs are associated with payments to settle the notes at fair value given interest rates at the time of extinguishment, incentive payments to note holders for early tendering of the notes, and a write-off of the proportionate amount of unamortized discount and issuance fees associated with the extinguished debt.

Cumulative Effect of Change in Accounting Principle—Molson Coors has adopted Financial Accounting Standards Board Interpretation No. 47, "*Accounting for Conditional Asset Retirement Obligations, an interpretation of FASB Statement No. 143*" (FIN 47) under which companies must recognize potential long-term liabilities related to the eventual retirement of assets. As a result of adopting FIN 47, we recorded a cumulative non-cash expense of $3.7 million, after tax, in the 2005 fourth quarter, reported as Cumulative Effect of Change in Accounting Principle in the Company's statement of operations. These liabilities represent accumulated remediation and restoration costs expected to be incurred up to 30 years in the future for anticipated asset retirements. Costs related to FIN 47 were not significant in 2007 or 2006. We do not expect FIN 47-related expense to have a significant impact on our on-going annual operating results.

4. Discontinued Operations

On January 13, 2006, we sold a 68% equity interest in our Brazilian unit, Cervejarias Kaiser Brasil S.A. ("Kaiser"), to FEMSA Cerveza S.A. de C.V. ("FEMSA") for $68.0 million cash, less $4.2 million of transaction costs, including the assumption by FEMSA of Kaiser-related debt and certain contingencies. Kaiser represented our previously-reported Brazil operating segment that we acquired on February 9, 2005 as part of the Merger. We retained a 15% interest in Kaiser throughout most of 2006, which we accounted for under the cost method, and had one seat out of seven on its board.

MOLSON COORS BREWING COMPANY AND SUBSIDIARIES
NOTES TO CONSOLIDATED BALANCE SHEETS (continued)
(IN THOUSANDS)

As part of the sale, we also received a put option to sell to FEMSA our remaining 15% interest in Kaiser for the greater of $15.0 million or fair market value through January 2009 and at fair market value thereafter. The value of the put option favorably impacted the calculation of the loss on the sale of Kaiser recorded in the first quarter of 2006. During the fourth quarter of 2006, we exercised the put option on our remaining 15% interest which had a carrying value of $2.0 million at the time of the sale, and received a cash payment of $15.7 million, including $0.6 million of accrued interest. As a result, we had no ownership interest remaining in Kaiser as of December 31, 2006. We sold Kaiser to allow us to focus on our Canada, United States and Europe markets. We have reflected the results of operations, financial position, and cash flows for the former Brazil segment in our financial statements as discontinued operations.

For the periods we had a controlling interest, Kaiser had $57.8 million and $244.7 million of net sales and $2.3 million and $100.5 million of pre-tax losses during the years ended December 31, 2006 and December 25, 2005, respectively. The 2006 period included the month of December 2005 and the first thirteen days of January 2006, since we reported Kaiser's results one month in arrears. The 2005 period included the period between February 9, 2005 (the date of the Merger) and November 30, 2005, again due to our reporting Kaiser one month in arrears in 2005.

The table below summarizes the loss from discontinued operations, net of tax, presented on our consolidated statements of operations:

	For the years ended		
	December 30, 2007	December 31, 2006	December 25, 2005
Loss from operations of Kaiser prior to sale on January 13, 2006 Kaiser	—	2,293	$91,826
(Gain) loss on sale of 68% Kaiser(1)	$ (2,693)	2,797	—
Loss on exercise of put option on remaining 15% interest in Kaiser	—	4,447	—
Adjustments to indemnity liabilities due to changes in estimates, foreign exchange gains and losses, and accretion expense	20,375	2,988	—
Loss from discontinued operations, tax affected	$17,682	$12,525	$91,826

(1) The $2.7 million gain recognized in 2007 resulted from a deferred tax liability adjustment related to the Kaiser transaction.

6. Other Income (Expense), net

	For the years ended		
	December 30, 2007	December 31, 2006	December 25, 2005
(Loss) gain on disposals of non-operating long-lived assets	$ (342)	$ 8,730	$ (2,665)
Gain coincident with the sale of preferred equity holdings of Montréal Canadiens	—	8,984	—
Gain on sale of House of Blues Canada investment	16,694	—	—
Equity in income (loss) of unconsolidated affiliates	4,318	3,911	(9,429)
(Loss) gain from foreign exchange and derivatives	(1,553)	(2,555)	3,454
Asset impairments	(1,706)	—	(1,259)
Loss on non-operating leases	(1,773)	(1,898)	(4,718)
Other, net	2,024	564	1,372
Other income (expense), net	$17,662	$17,736	$(13,245)

MOLSON COORS BREWING COMPANY AND SUBSIDIARIES
NOTES TO CONSOLIDATED BALANCE SHEETS (continued)
(IN THOUSANDS)

7. Income Taxes

Our income tax expense varies from the amount expected by applying the statutory federal corporate tax rate to income as follows:

	For the years ended		
	December 30, 2007	December 31, 2006	December 25, 2005
Statutory Federal income tax rate	35.0%	35.0%	35.0%
State income taxes, net of federal benefits	0.8%	(0.3)%	0.4%
Effect of foreign tax rates	(17.6)%	(7.8)%	(7.8)%
Effect of foreign tax law and rate changes	(15.1)%	(14.5)%	—
Effect of treating all past foreign subsidiary earnings as permanently reinvested	—	—	(11.8)%
Other, net	(2.3)%	5.1%	1.2%
Effective tax rate	0.8%	17.5%	17.0%

8. Special Items, net

We have incurred charges or gains that are not indicative of our core operations. As such, we have separately classified these costs as special operating items. The table below details special items recorded in the previous three years, by program.

	For the years ended		
	December 30, 2007	December 31, 2006	December 25, 2005
Canada			
Edmonton brewery asset impairment charge	$ 31,940	—	—
Foster's distribution right intangible asset impairment	24,131	—	—
Restructuring and related costs associated with the Edmonton brewery closure	14,573	—	—
Restructuring charge	4,515	—	$5,161
U.S.			
Costs associated with MillerCoors joint venture	6,724	—	—
Other restructuring charges	2,768	—	—
Memphis brewery accelerated depreciation	—	$60,463	36,471
Restructuring and other costs associated with the Golden and Memphis breweries	—	12,517	6,610
Memphis brewery pension withdrawal cost	—	3,080	25,000
Insurance recovery—environmental	—	(2,408)	—
Europe			
Gains on disposals of long-lived assets	—	—	(2,980)
Restructuring charge	10,187	13,042	14,332
Pension curtailment gain	—	(5,261)	—
Other, including certain exit costs	3,917	1,253	2,489
Corporate			
(Gain) loss on change in control agreements for Coors executives	(502)	(5,282)	38,802
Other severance costs for Molson executives	—	—	14,555
Costs associated with MillerCoors joint venture	13,941	—	—
Other costs	—	—	4,952
Total special items	$112,194	$77,404	$145,392

MOLSON COORS BREWING COMPANY AND SUBSIDIARIES
NOTES TO CONSOLIDATED BALANCE SHEETS (continued)
(IN THOUSANDS)

13. Debt and Credit Arrangements

On July 11, 2007, we repurchased $625.0 million aggregate principal amount of our 6.375% $850 million Senior Notes due 2012. The cash consideration paid of approximately $651 million included principal amounts of notes purchased and accrued but unpaid interest up to, but not including, the settlement date. The cash consideration paid also included an early tender payment of $20.00 for each $1,000 principal amount of Senior Notes tendered on or before June 22, 2007. This amount was in addition to the principal amounts of notes and interest, if any, paid to the bond holders whose bonds were repurchased. This early extinguishment of debt resulted in a charge of approximately $24.5 million in the third quarter of 2007. The loss comprised a $14.1 million payment to settle the notes at fair value given interest rates at the time of extinguishment, a $6.6 million incentive payment to note holders for early tendering of the notes, and a $3.8 million write-off of the proportionate amount of unamortized discount and issuance fees associated with the extinguished debt. The debt extinguishment was funded, in part, with proceeds from the issuance of $575 million aggregate principal amount of 2.5% Convertible Senior Notes, issued on June 15, 2007. The remaining source of funds for the early extinguishment was existing cash resources.

Alcatel—Accounts Receivable

Headquartered in Paris, France, Alcatel provides end-to-end communications solutions, enabling carriers, service providers and enterprises to deliver contents to any type of user, anywhere in the world. Leveraging its long-term leadership in telecommunications network equipment as well as expertise in innovative applications and network services, Alcatel enables its customers to focus on optimizing their service offerings and revenue streams. With sales of €16.5 billion in 2002, Alcatel operates in more than 130 countries. Shares trade in Paris and New York. (Source: Company Form 10-K)

Learning Objectives
- Understand accounts receivable terminology.
- Calculate annual and quarterly ratios for accounts receivable.
- Compare calculated ratios to those included in a press article and explore the differences.
- Learn about factoring and securitization of receivables.

Refer to the Alcatel financial statements released as part of a press release reporting fourth quarter and full year 2002 results. All figures are in millions of euros (€).

✧ Concepts ✧

a. What is an account receivable? What other names does this asset go by?

b. How do accounts receivable differ from notes receivable?

c. Alcatel's balance sheet reports a balance for trade receivables and related accounts, net. What are the trade receivables net of?

d. If Alcatel anticipates that some accounts are uncollectible, why did the company extend credit to those customers in the first place? Discuss the risks that must be managed with respect to accounts receivable and vendor financing.

✧ Process ✧

e. The balance in Alcatel's allowance for doubtful accounts (for trade receivables) was €1,092 at December 31, 2002 and €928 at December 31, 2001. Assume that Alcatel wrote off €115 of trade receivables as uncollectible during 2002. Create two T-accounts, one for gross trade receivables (that is, trade receivables before deducting the allowance) and another for the allowance for doubtful accounts. Analyze the change in both T-accounts between December 31, 2001 and 2002. Four journal entries are required to reconcile the two T-accounts: one to record sales, one to record the collection of trade receivables, one to record the write-off of trade receivables, and one to record bad debt expense.

✧ Analysis ✧

f. Refer to the accompanying *Wall Street Journal* article (Alcatel Allays Some Anxiety, Though Perils for Firm Persist). Chief Financial Officer Jean-Pascal Beaufret indicated that Alcatel collected its trade receivables in 104 days in 2002 (117 in 2001). The average collection period for accounts receivable (called trade receivables at Alcatel) can be estimated using the following formula (the denominator is referred to as the accounts receivable turnover ratio):

$$\text{Average Collection Period} = \frac{365\,\text{days}}{\left[\frac{\text{Credit Sales (annual)}}{\text{Accounts Receivable}}\right]}$$

Alcatel—Accounts Receivable
1

Confirm the figures reported by Alcatel's CFO using data for **trade receivables** from the accompanying financial statements. Assume that all sales are on account. That is, they are all "credit sales." Comment on the trend you observe. Provide possible reasons for the change.

g. What was the average collection period for the fourth quarter of 2002? For the same period in 2001? You will have to adjust the average collection period formula so that it appropriately considers quarterly data. Comment on the trend and the relation to the annual data.

h. In the *Wall Street Journal* article, the reporter refers to the practice of factoring receivables. Explain what factoring is and why some companies do it.

i. Data reported in Alcatel's 2002 financial statements (but not in the press release) indicate that the company effectively factored a portion of its trade receivables through a secured vendor financing agreement. In essence, under this agreement, Alcatel "sells" receivables to a trust that "buys" them by issuing bonds or other securities to investors. The trust's bonds are repaid using the cash flows from the receivables. According to note 29 of Alcatel's 2002 financial statements, $428 million and $700 million were outstanding under the securitization program at the end of 2002 and 2001, respectively (at December 31, 2002, $1 = €0.954, at December 31, 2001, $1 = €1.123).

    i. Explain in general terms how securitization of receivables affects the average collection period.

    ii. Assume that Alcatel had not securitized its receivables. Estimate the average collection period for 2002 and 2001 and compare it to the results you obtained in part *f.*

j. Under French GAAP, Alcatel treated the securitization of its receivables as a sale of receivables. Under U.S. GAAP, Alcatel's securitization would be considered secured borrowing (i.e. a loan secured by the receivables). How would Alcatel's balance sheet differ if the company had followed U.S. GAAP for its receivables securitization?

Consolidated income statements

in millions of euros except per share information

	Q4 2002 (unaudited)	Q4 2001* (unaudited)	2002	2001*	2000
Net sales	4,508	6,766	16,547	25,353	31,408
Cost of sales	(3,279)	(5,528)	(12,186)	(19,074)	(22,193)
Gross profit	**1,229**	**1,238**	**4,361**	**6,279**	**9,215**
Administrative and selling expenses	(647)	(893)	(2,862)	(3,773)	(4,136)
R&D costs	(562)	(713)	(2,226)	(2,867)	(2,828)
Income (loss) from operations	**20**	**(368)**	**(727)**	**(361)**	**2,251**
Interest expense on notes mandatorily redeemable for shares	(1)	-	(1)	-	-
Financial loss	(136)	(248)	(1,018)	(1,568)	(435)
Restructuring costs	(500)	(598)	(1,474)	(2,124)	(143)
Other revenue (expense)	(292)	(456)	(830)	(213)	623
Income (loss) before amortization of goodwill and taxes	**(909)**	**(1,670)**	**(4,050)**	**(4,266)**	**2,296**
Income tax	(62)	396	19	1,261	(497)
Share in net income of equity affiliates and discontinued operations	24	(16)	(107)	(16)	125
Consolidated net income (loss) before amortization of goodwill and purchased R&D	**(947)**	**(1,290)**	**(4,138)**	**(3,021)**	**1,924**
Amortization of goodwill	(147)	(185)	(589)	(1,933)	(576)
Purchased R&D	-	-	-	(4)	(21)
Minority interests	(25)	(23)	(18)	(5)	(3)
Net income (loss)	**(1,119)**	**(1,498)**	**(4,745)**	**(4,963)**	**1,324**
Ordinary Shares (A)*					
Basic earnings per share	*(0.93)*	*(1.28)*	*(3.99)*	*(4.33)*	*1.25*
Diluted earnings per share	*(0.93)*	*(1.28)*	*(3.99)*	*(4.33)*	*1.20*
*Alcatel tracking stock (O) (Optronics division)****					
Basic earnings per share	*(1.06)*	*(1.52)*	*(3.86)*	*(1.47)*	*0.14*
Diluted earnings per share	*(1.06)*	*(1.52)*	*(3.86)*	*(1.47)*	*0.14*

* In order to make comparisons easier, restated income statements are presented to take into account significant changes in consolidated companies du ring the second half of 2001 and the first half 2002.
** Net income per class A share for 2000 was restated to take into account the split by 5 of the nominal value of the class A shares approved by the shareholders' meeting of May 16, 2000.
*** For 2000, net income has been taken into account from October 20, 2000, issuance date of the class O shares.

Consolidated balance sheets at December 31

in millions of euros

ASSETS	2002	2001	2000
Goodwill, net	4,597	5,257	7,043
Other intangible as sets, net	312	472	504
Intangible assets, net	**4,909**	**5,729**	**7,547**
Property, plant and equipment	8,236	9,698	11,941
Depreciation	(5,737)	(5,496)	(7,283)
Property, plant and equipment, net	**2,499**	**4,202**	**4,658**
Share in net assets of equity affiliates and net assets and liabilities of discontinued operations	306	799	1,152
Other investments and miscellaneous, net	975	1,169	3,327
Investments and other financial assets	**1,281**	**1,968**	**4,479**
TOTAL FIXED ASSETS	**8,689**	**11,899**	**16,684**
Inventories and work in progress	**2,329**	**4,681**	**7,415**
Trade receivables and related accounts net	4,716	8,105	10,659
Other accounts receivable net	4,037	6,851	5,160
Accounts receivable	**8,753**	**14,956**	**15,819**
Marketable securities, net*	716	490	443
Cash (net)	5,393	4,523	2,617
Cash and cash equivalents*	**6,109**	**5,013**	**3,060**
TOTAL CURRENT ASSETS	**17,191**	**24,650**	**26,294**
TOTAL ASSETS	**25,880**	**36,549**	**42,978**

* Cash and cash equivalent as of December 31, 2002 includes in the marketab   le securities net line item, listed securities amounting to 44 million. Without listed securities, cash and cash equivalent amounts to 6,065 million as indicated in the consolidated statements of cash flows.

in millions of euros

LIABILITIES AND SHAREHOLDERS' EQUITY	2002		2001	2000*
	Before	After	After	After
	Appropriation		Appropriation	Appropriation
Capital stock (Euro 2 nominal value : 1,239,193,498 class A shares and 25,515,000 class O shares issued at December 31, 2002 ; 1,215,254,797 class A shares and 25,515,000 class O shares issued at December 31, 2001 and 1,212,210,685 class A shares and 16,500,000 class O shares at December 31, 2000)	2,529	2,529	2,481	2,457
Additional paid-in capital	9,573	9,573	9,565	9,558
Retained earnings	(333)	(5,078)	(389)	4,719
Cumulative translation adjustments	(283)	(283)	(185)	(350)
Net income	(4,745)	-	-	-
Less treasury stock at cost	(1,734)	(1,734)	(1,842)	(2,023)
SHAREHOLDERS' EQUITY	**5,007**	**5,007**	**9,630**	**14,361**
MINORITY INTERESTS	**343**	**343**	**219**	**435**
OTHER EQUITY				
Notes mandatorily redeemable for shares	**645**	**645**	**-**	**-**
Accrued pension and retirement obligations	1,016	1,016	1,120	1,292
Other reserves (a)	3,301	3,301	4,154	3,005
TOTAL RESERVES FOR LIABILITIES AND CHARGES	**4,317**	**4,317**	**5,274**	**4,297**
Bonds and notes issued	5,325	5,325	5,969	4,972
Other borrowings	458	458	1,706	2,418
TOTAL FINANCIAL DEBT	**5,783**	**5,783**	**7,675**	**7,390**
(of which medium and long-term portion)	*4,687*	*4,687*	*5,879*	*5,577*
Customers' deposits and advances	1,482	1,482	1,693	1,560
Trade payables and related accounts (a)	4,162	4,162	5,080	6,393
Debts linked to bank activity	246	246	660	932
Other payables	3,895	3,895	6,318	7,610
TOTAL OTHER LIABILITIES	**9,785**	**9,785**	**13,751**	**16,495**
TOTAL LIABILITIES AND SHAREHOLDERS' EQUITY	**25,880**	**25,880**	**36,549**	**42,978**

(a) Accrued contract costs previously under the line "accrued contracts costs and other reserves" have been reclassified under the line "trade payables" (650 million at December 31, 2000).

Consolidated statements of cash flows

in millions of euros

	Nine months 2002 (unaudited)	Q4 2002 (unaudited)	2002	2001	2000
Cash flows from operating activities					
Net income (loss)	(3,626)	(1,119)	(4,745)	(4,963)	1,324
Minority interests	(7)	25	18	5	3
Adjustments to reconcile income before minority interests to net cash provided by operating activities:					
- Depreciation and amortization, net	739	271	1,010	1,279	1,189
- Amortization and depreciation of goodwill and purchased R&D	442	147	589	1,937	597
- Net allowances in reserves for pension obligations	8	(11)	(3)	41	24
- Changes in valuation allowances and other reserves, net	1,374	(16)	1,358	2,001	(32)
- Net (gain) loss on disposal of non -current assets	(413)	126	(287)	(943)	(915)
- Share in net income of equity affiliates (net of dividends received)	214	(26)	188	88	(47)
Working capital provided (used) by operations	**(1,269)**	**(603)**	**(1,872)**	**(555)**	**2,143**
Net change in current assets and liabilities:					
- Decrease (increase) in inventories	1,244	756	2,000	1,186	(3,330)
- Decrease (increase) in accounts receivable	3,103	333	3,436	1,407	(1,192)
- Decrease (increase) in advances and progr ess payments	3	107	110	(99)	74
- Increase (decrease) in accounts payable and accrued expenses	(1,038)	(46)	(1,084)	(925)	898
- Increase (decrease) in customers deposits and advances	(279)	106	(173)	153	424
- Increase (decrease) in other rece ivables and debts	136	170	306	(622)	(262)
Net cash provided (used) by operating activities (a)	**1,900**	**823**	**2,723**	**545**	**(1,245)**
Cash flows from investing activities					
Proceeds from disposal of fixed assets	236	44	280	182	107
Capital expe nditures	(399)	(91)	(490)	(1,748)	(1,834)
Decrease (increase) in loans (b)	(720)	(119)	(839)	299	(962)
Cash expenditures for acquisition of consolidated companies, net of cash acquired, and for acquisition of unconsolidated companies	(206)	13	(193)	(743)	(834)
Cash proceeds from sale of previously consolidated companies, net of cash sold, and from sale of unconsolidated companies	797	16	813	3,627	1,579
Net cash provided (used) by investing activities	**(292)**	**(137)**	**(429)**	**1,617**	**(1,944)**
Net cash flows after investment	**1,608**	**686**	**2,294**	**2,162**	**(3,189)**
Cash flows from financing activities					
Increase (decrease) in short -term debt	(1,192)	(277)	(1,469)	(1,401)	(889)
Proceeds from issuance of long -term debt	-	645	645	1,744	2,565
Proceeds from issuance of shares	8	-	8	8	1,490
Dividends paid	(269)	(7)	(276)	(567)	(508)
Net cash provided (used) by financing activities	**(1,453)**	**361**	**(1,092)**	**(216)**	**2,658**
Net effect of exchange rate changes	(67)	(83)	(150)	7	(4)
Net increase (decrease) in cash and cash equivalents	**88**	**964**	**1,052**	**1,953**	**(535)**
Cash and cash equivalents at beginning of year	**5,013**	**5,101**	**5,013**	**3,060**	**3,595**
Cash and cash equivalents at end of year without listed securities	**5,101**	**6,065**	**6,065**	**5,013**	**3,060**
Operational cash flows (a) + (b) = Net cash provided (used) by operating activities + Decrease (increase) in loans (b)	**1,180**	**704**	**1,884**	**844**	**(2,207)**

THE WALL STREET JOURNAL.
O N L I N E

February 5, 2003

HEARD IN EUROPE

Alcatel Allays Some Anxiety, Though Perils for Firm Persist

By DAVID REILLY
Staff Reporter of THE WALL STREET JOURNAL

Alcatel SA is finally managing to squeeze some lemonade from this lemon of a market. Whether it's a beverage that's ready to be drunk, though, is an open question.

Europe's largest telecom-equipment maker did a surprisingly good job of reducing inventories and getting customers to pay their bills faster in the fourth quarter. As a result, Paris-based Alcatel said it generated €704 million ($759 million) in operating cash flow during the fourth quarter and moved to a small net cash position on its balance sheet by the end of 2002, although this was helped in part by a convertible-bond issue in December. The company also managed to eke out €20 million in operating profit in the fourth quarter even though sales were down 33% from a year earlier.

The good news didn't stop there. Alcatel reiterated its expectation of being able to break even on costs of €3 billion a quarter by the end of 2003, while Chairman and Chief Executive Serge Tchuruk said Alcatel expects to show a net profit by year-end.

Taken together, this is proof to some investors that the company is now turning the corner in its restructuring program. It should also finally put an end to worries the company could go belly up because it wouldn't be able to cut costs as quickly as sales are falling.

"Is this company going bankrupt? No," says Richard Windsor, an analyst at Nomura. He adds that Alcatel appears to be in a better position than rivals such as **Lucent Technologies** Inc., **Nortel Networks** Ltd. and **Telefon AB L.M. Ericsson**. "It's got more revenues, is much stronger financially, its sales are more geographically split, it has a more diverse product portfolio and its revenue stream should be stronger in the future."

That's not to say that the results were all sweetness and light. Mr. Tchuruk said sales could drop 25% to 30% in the first quarter compared with the same period of 2002, while the global market for telecommunications equipment could drop 15% in 2003.

So until there are signs that revenue can stabilize, the stock will remain volatile and is best avoided, Mustapha Omar, head of research at U.K. broker Collins Stewart, said in a note to clients.

Investors focused on this danger and shaved 7.7% off Alcatel's stock, which closed at €6.20 in Paris Tuesday.

Adding to the gloom, some analysts fretted about Alcatel's improvement in working capital, the money it needs to finance sales through inventory, outstanding customer bills and amounts due to suppliers. Alcatel said working capital as a portion of sales had fallen to just 9.4% of revenue at the end of the year, compared with 14.4% at the end of September and 24.6% at the end of 2001.

First, there were concerns about the contribution to cash flow from the sale of outstanding customer bills, a practice known as factoring receivables. Alcatel doesn't disclose how much money it raises through such sales. During a conference call with analysts, Mr. Tchuruk said there was "nothing new" on this front and that there was no change in the level of factoring from the third quarter. An Alcatel spokeswoman later said this meant that the level of factoring hadn't changed in absolute euro terms, although it would have increased as a percentage of the amount of overall receivables.

Second, it wasn't clear how much the reduction of inventory to €2.3 billion at the end of the year, compared with €3.2 billion at the end of September or €4.6 billion at the end of 2001, was helped by write-downs. The company said it wrote off €873 million in assets during 2002. While Chief Financial Officer Jean-Pascal Beaufret said the lion's share of this amount related to asset write-offs at the company's optronics division, he didn't give an exact figure. That led some analysts to worry that the write-downs could have flattered the figures that show how many times Alcatel turned over its inventory during the year, an efficiency measure.

The spokeswoman said the company didn't provide details about how much of the drop in inventories resulted from write-downs.

Finally, analysts questioned whether Alcatel could keep releasing cash by squeezing working capital, especially if sales start to rise. (A company generally needs more working capital to finance growth.)

Messrs. Tchuruk and Beaufret tried to allay these fears by saying the company still wasn't being run as efficiently as they would like or as well as some of its North American peers. Mr. Beaufret said during the conference call that at the end of 2002 the company was collecting on bills within 104 days. This was an improvement from 117 days at the end of 2001, but he said the company could still improve greatly on this level.

As for inventory turns, the spokeswoman said Alcatel has room to improve there: It had an inventory turn ratio of 5.2 times in 2002, compared with about 7.9 times for Nortel and about 8.2 times for Lucent.

Finally, the company has about €8 billion in liquid resources to draw on if it needs to finance a rise in sales.

All that is reassuring. But until sales stop falling, investors are to be forgiven for finding Alcatel's shares a bit too tart at this point.

Write to David Reilly at david.reilly@wsj.com;

Callaway Golf Company—Manufacturing Inventory

Callaway Golf Company is a California corporation formed in 1982. The Company designs, develops, manufactures and markets high-quality, innovative golf clubs and golf balls, and also sells golf footwear and accessories. Callaway operates two distinct segments: Golf Clubs and Golf Balls. The golf club segment consists primarily of woods, irons, wedges and putters under the Callaway Golf, Top-Flite and Ben Hogan brands and Odyssey putters. Callaway Golf's primary golf club products include the Big Bertha line of metal woods and drivers and the newer lines of FT woods and drivers using Callaway's patented Fusion Technology. Popular golf ball lines include the Tour i and HX series balls. Many of Callaway's golf ball products employ its proprietary HEX Aerodynamics, Dimple-in-Dimple and deep dimple technologies. (Source: Company Form 10-K)

Learning Objectives
- Disaggregate manufacturing inventory and understand its underlying components.
- Interpret the allowance for obsolete inventory.
- Trace product cost flows from raw materials through to finished goods inventory.
- Infer raw material purchases and calculate cash disbursements related to inventory.
- Calculate and analyze financial statement ratios related to inventory.

Refer to the 2007 financial statements of Callaway Golf Company.

Concepts

a. Note 5 reveals that the balance sheet inventory amount consists of three types of inventory. What types of costs do you expect to be in the raw materials inventory? In the work-in-process inventory? In the finished goods inventory?

b. The balance sheet inventory line item is called "Inventories, net." What are inventories *net* of?

Process

c. In its Form 10-K filed with the SEC, Callaway includes the following schedule that details the activity in an account titled "Reserve for obsolete inventory" (amounts in thousands):

Balance, December 31, 2006	$17,315
Provision	12,182
Write-offs, disposals and other	(9,368)
Balance, December 31, 2007	$20,129

   i. Where does this account appear on Callaway's financial statements?

   ii. What is the *gross* amount of inventory at the end of 2006? 2007?

   iii. What portion of the reserve for obsolete inventory do you think is attributable to each of the three types of inventory held by Callaway?

d. Recreate the journal entries Callaway prepared to record the activity in the reserve for obsolete inventory account during 2007.

e. Set up five separate T-accounts: one for each of the three inventory accounts, one for "Cost of sales" and one for "Accounts payable." Use the T-accounts to analyze inventory activity during 2007. Make the following simplifying assumptions.

   - The only activity in "Accounts payable" is for raw materials purchases and payments for those purchases. See Note 5 for account balances.

- During 2007, a total of $150,000 (in thousands) of manufacturing salaries and overhead was debited to "Work-in-process." All other activity in the work-in-process account is from raw materials transfers and transfers of completed products to "Finished goods."

- The reserve for obsolete inventory is included with the finished goods balance presented in Note 5.

Complete the five T-accounts to determine the following amounts. *Hint*: Be sure to consider the journal entries you made in part d, above.

i. The cost of finished goods sold in 2007.

ii. The cost of finished goods transferred from work-in-process in 2007 (i.e., the cost of goods manufactured).

iii. The cost of raw materials transferred to work-in-process in 2007.

iv. The cost of raw materials purchased during 2007.

v. The amount of cash disbursed for raw-material purchases during 2007.

Analysis

f. The inventory turnover ratio measures how efficiently Callaway manages its inventory. The ratio is defined as:

$$\text{Inventory turnover ratio} = \frac{\text{Cost of sales}}{\text{Average Inventories, net}}$$

Complete the table below to calculate Callaway Golf's inventory turnover ratio for 2007 and 2006. Note: the balance in "Inventories, net" was $241,577 thousand at December 31, 2005.

	2007	**2006**
Cost of sales		
Average Inventories, net		
Inventory turnover ratio		

g. The inventory holding period is another common inventory efficiency ratio. It measures the number of days that it takes to sell inventory, and is defined as:

$$\text{Inventory holding period} = \frac{365}{\text{Inventory turnover ratio}}$$

On average, how many days did it take for Callaway to manufacture and sell its inventory in 2007 and 2006? That is, what is the inventory holding period for 2007 and 2006? Compare Callaway's inventory efficiency for 2007 and 2006.

h. Assume that the reserve for obsolete inventory relates entirely to finished goods. Complete the table below to determine the percent of finished goods that Callaway estimated as obsolete in 2007 and 2006. What could explain the change from 2006 to 2007? As an investor or analyst, what additional information would you like from Callaway?

	2007	2006
Finished goods inventory, net		
+ Reserve for obsolete inventory		
Finished goods inventory, gross		
Portion obsolete	%	%

CALLAWAY GOLF COMPANY

CONSOLIDATED BALANCE SHEETS

(In thousands, except share and per share data)

	December 31,	
	2007	2006

ASSETS

Current assets:

	2007	2006
Cash and cash equivalents	$ 49,875	$ 46,362
Accounts receivable, net	112,064	118,133
Inventories, net	253,001	265,110
Deferred taxes	42,219	32,813
Income taxes receivable	9,232	9,094
Other current assets	30,190	21,688
Total current assets	496,581	493,200
Property, plant and equipment, net	128,036	131,224
Intangible assets, net	140,985	144,326
Goodwill	32,060	30,833
Deferred taxes	18,885	18,821
Other assets	40,416	27,543
	$856,963	$ 845,947

LIABILITIES AND SHAREHOLDERS' EQUITY

Current liabilities:

	2007	2006
Accounts payable and accrued expenses	$130,410	$ 111,360
Accrued employee compensation and benefits	44,245	18,731
Accrued warranty expense	12,386	13,364
Credit facilities	36,507	80,000
Total current liabilities	223,548	223,455
Long-term liabilities:		
Deferred taxes	21,252	16,256
Energy derivative valuation account	19,922	19,922
Income tax payable	13,833	—
Deferred compensation and other	8,200	7,210
Minority interest in consolidated subsidiary	1,978	1,987
Commitments and contingencies (Note 14)		
Shareholders' equity:		
Preferred Stock, $.01 par value, 3,000,000 shares authorized, none issued and outstanding at December 31, 2007 and 2006	—	—
Common Stock, $.01 par value, 240,000,000 shares authorized, 66,281,693 shares and 85,096,782 shares issued at December 31, 2007 and 2006, respectively	663	851
Additional paid-in capital	111,953	402,628
Unearned compensation	(2,158)	(3,566)
Retained earnings	470,469	435,074
Accumulated other comprehensive income	18,904	11,135
Less: Grantor Stock Trust held at market value, 1,813,010 shares and 5,184,601 shares at December 31, 2007 and 2006, respectively	(31,601)	(74,710)
Less: Common Stock held in treasury, at cost, 0 shares and 11,957,968 shares at December 31, 2007 and 2006, respectively	—	(194,295)
Total shareholders' equity	568,230	577,117
	$856,963	$ 845,947

The accompanying notes are an integral part of these financial statements.

CALLAWAY GOLF COMPANY

CONSOLIDATED STATEMENTS OF OPERATIONS
(In thousands, except per share data)

| | Year Ended December 31, | | | | | |
	2007		2006		2005	
Net sales	$1,124,591	100%	$1,017,907	100%	$998,093	100%
Cost of sales	631,368	56%	619,832	61%	583,679	58%
Gross profit	493,223	44%	398,075	39%	414,414	42%
Selling expenses	281,960	25%	254,526	25%	290,074	29%
General and administrative expenses	89,060	8%	79,709	8%	80,145	8%
Research and development expenses	32,020	3%	26,785	3%	26,989	3%
Total operating expenses	403,040	36%	361,020	35%	397,208	40%
Income from operations	90,183	8%	37,055	4%	17,206	2%
Interest and other income (expense), net	3,455		3,364		(390)	
Interest expense	(5,363)		(5,421)		(2,279)	
Income before income taxes	88,275	8%	34,998	3%	14,537	1%
Provision for income taxes	33,688		11,708		1,253	
Net income	$ 54,587	5%	$ 23,290	2%	$ 13,284	1%
Earnings per common share:						
Basic	$ 0.82		$ 0.34		$ 0.19	
Diluted	$ 0.81		$ 0.34		$ 0.19	
Common equivalent shares:						
Basic	66,371		67,732		68,646	
Diluted	67,484		68,503		69,239	

The accompanying notes are an integral part of these financial statements.

CALLAWAY GOLF COMPANY

CONSOLIDATED STATEMENTS OF CASH FLOWS
(In thousands)

	Year Ended December 31,		
	2007	2006	2005
Cash flows from operating activities:			
Net income	$ 54,587	$ 23,290	$ 13,284
Adjustments to reconcile net income to net cash provided by operating activities:			
Depreciation and amortization	35,326	32,274	38,260
Noncash compensation	10,851	11,921	6,527
(Gain) loss on disposal of long-lived assets	(4,731)	1,135	4,031
Deferred taxes	9,047	673	(3,906)
Tax benefit from exercise of stock options	—	—	2,408
Changes in assets and liabilities, net of effects from acquisitions:			
Accounts receivable, net	12,478	(12,128)	2,296
Inventories, net	17,292	(16,842)	(65,595)
Other assets	(7,410)	(4,475)	7,583
Accounts payable and accrued expenses	10,341	(4,525)	32,423
Accrued employee compensation and benefits	25,158	(6,376)	5,121
Accrued warranty expense	(978)	98	1,224
Income taxes receivable and payable	(10,573)	(6,936)	26,676
Other liabilities	594	(1,128)	(351)
Net cash provided by operating activities	151,982	16,981	69,981
Cash flows from investing activities:			
Capital expenditures	(32,930)	(32,453)	(33,942)
Proceeds from sale of capital assets	11,460	469	1,363
Investment in golf related ventures	(3,698)	(10,008)	—
Acquisitions, net of cash acquired	—	374	—
Net cash used in investing activities	(25,168)	(41,618)	(32,579)
Cash flows from financing activities:			
Issuance of common stock	48,035	9,606	14,812
Acquisition of treasury stock	(114,795)	(52,872)	(39)
Dividends paid, net	(18,755)	(19,212)	(19,557)
Proceeds from (payments on) credit facilities, net	(43,493)	80,000	(13,000)
Tax benefit from exercise of stock options	6,031	884	—
Other financing activities	(9)	1,971	(44)
Net cash provided by (used in) financing activities	(122,986)	20,377	(17,828)
Effect of exchange rate changes on cash and cash equivalents	(315)	1,141	(1,750)
Net increase (decrease) in cash and cash equivalents	3,513	(3,119)	17,824
Cash and cash equivalents at beginning of year	46,362	49,481	31,657
Cash and cash equivalents at end of year	$ 49,875	$ 46,362	$ 49,481
Supplemental disclosures:			
Cash paid for interest and fees	$ (5,633)	$ (4,502)	$ (2,096)
Cash paid for income taxes	$ (38,292)	$(18,859)	$(24,837)

The accompanying notes are an integral part of these financial statements.

CALLAWAY GOLF COMPANY

Note 2. Significant Accounting Policies (excerpt)

Inventories

Inventories are valued at the lower of cost or fair market value. Cost is determined using the first-in, first-out (FIFO) method. The inventory balance, which includes material, labor and manufacturing overhead costs, is recorded net of an estimated allowance for obsolete or unmarketable inventory. The estimated allowance for obsolete or unmarketable inventory is based upon current inventory levels, sales trends and historical experience as well as management's understanding of market conditions and forecasts of future product demand, all of which are subject to change. Actual inventory charges have been consistent with the Company's expectations.

Note 5. Selected Financial Statement Information

	December 31,	
	2007	2006
	(In thousands)	
Accounts receivable, net:		
Trade accounts receivable	$ 120,054	$ 126,672
Allowance for doubtful accounts	(7,990)	(8,539)
	$ 112,064	$ 118,133
Inventories, net:		
Raw materials	$ 82,185	$ 85,798
Work-in-process	1,932	4,195
Finished goods	168,884	175,117
	$ 253,001	$ 265,110
Property, plant and equipment, net:		
Land	$ 11,609	$ 12,815
Buildings and improvements	85,245	91,477
Machinery and equipment	143,994	135,573
Furniture, computers and equipment	112,079	113,982
Production molds	41,511	38,523
Construction-in-process	10,368	11,157
	404,806	403,527
Accumulated depreciation	(276,770)	(272,303)
	$ 128,036	$ 131,224
Accounts payable and accrued expenses:		
Accounts payable	$ 33,019	$ 40,947
Accrued expenses	97,391	70,413
	$ 130,410	$ 111,360
Accrued employee compensation and benefits:		
Accrued payroll and taxes	$ 31,882	$ 7,927
Accrued vacation and sick pay	10,752	9,600
Accrued commissions	1,611	1,204
	$ 44,245	$ 18,731

Caterpillar, Inc., and CNH Global N.V.—Inventory

Caterpillar operates in three principal lines of business: machinery (design, manufacture and marketing of construction, mining, agricultural and forestry machinery), engines (for Caterpillar machinery as well as free-standing electric power generation systems and on- and off-highway vehicles and locomotives), and financial products (providing loans and insurance products to customers and dealers). Caterpillar's products and support services are sold worldwide in a variety of highly competitive markets. (Source: Company Form 10-K)

CNH Global, headquartered in the Netherlands, is the power behind leading agricultural and construction equipment brands of the Case and New Holland brand families. Supported by more than 12,000 dealers in approximately 160 countries, CNH brings together the knowledge and heritage of its brands with the strength and resources of its worldwide commercial, industrial, product support and finance organizations. (Source: Company Form 10-K)

Learning Objectives
- Explain how cost flow assumptions affect inventory balances and cost of goods sold.
- Explain the financial statement effects of using different cost flow assumptions.
- Analyze the activity in inventory and related accounts.
- Restate a company's inventory balances and cost of sales to reflect alternative cost flow assumptions.
- Calculate inventory ratios under different cost flow assumptions.
- Understand the risks and benefits of holding inventory.

Refer to the fiscal 2007 financial statements of Caterpillar, Inc.

Concepts

a. Explain the risks and benefits associated with holding inventory.

b. Note 9 reveals that the balance sheet inventory amount consists of four types of inventory. What types of costs do you expect to be in the raw materials inventory? In the work-in-process inventory? In the finished goods inventory? In the supplies inventory?

c. In general, why do companies use cost flow assumptions to determine inventory cost? What cost flow assumption does Caterpillar use to determine inventory cost?

d. Assume that the prices Caterpillar pays for inventory typically increase over time. Explain, in general terms, how the Caterpillar balance sheet would have been different had the company used the first-in, first-out (FIFO) method of inventory costing instead of the last-in, first-out (LIFO) method. How would the income statement have differed? The statement of cash flows? What if prices typically *de*crease over time?

Process

e. Set up *one* T-account for Caterpillar's total Inventories (that is, combine the four inventory accounts for this analysis). Enter the 2006 and 2007 ending balances in the T-account. Use information from the financial statements to recreate the activity that took place in the account during fiscal 2007 and answer the following questions. Caterpillar credits the total Inventories account for the entire Cost of goods sold. Note that the income statement line item Cost of goods sold includes the labor and overhead needed to manufacture the inventory. Assume that the raw material costs represent half of the total cost of manufacturing the inventory.

  i. How much raw material inventory did Caterpillar purchase in fiscal 2007? Assume that raw material inventory was acquired in a single purchase. Provide the journal entry Caterpillar made to record that purchase.

ii. Now set up a T-account for Accounts payable. Enter the 2006 opening balance and 2007 ending balance in the T-account. Assume that Accounts payable includes only inventory-related transactions and that all raw material is purchased on account. How much did Caterpillar pay its suppliers for inventory in fiscal 2007? Assume that Caterpillar made a single payment to all its suppliers in fiscal 2007. Provide the journal entry Caterpillar made to record that payment.

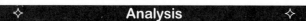

Analysis

f. You want to compare Caterpillar's operations for fiscal 2007 to those of an international competitor, CNH Global, headquartered in the Netherlands. (CNH Global financial statements follow the Caterpillar financial statements at the end of the case.) In particular you want to compare a number of inventory-related metrics. However, the two companies do not use the same inventory costing methods: Caterpillar uses LIFO for a large portion of its inventory whereas CNH Global uses FIFO to cost all of its inventory. International financial reporting standards (IFRS) do not permit companies to use the LIFO method.

To compare the two companies, you first must restate Caterpillar's relevant balance sheet and income statement numbers from LIFO to FIFO. To do this, we assume that Caterpillar had instead always used the FIFO method of inventory costing. Use the table below to aggregate the data you need to covert LIFO to FIFO for Caterpillar. For these calculations, assume that the marginal tax rate for Caterpillar is 35%.

Caterpillar, Inc.	2007	2006	2005
Sales			
LIFO Cost of goods sold (COGS)			
LIFO Net income			
LIFO Inventory from the balance sheet			
LIFO reserve from financial statement notes			
Total Assets from the balance sheet			

Calculations to convert LIFO to FIFO:	2007	2006	2005
FIFO Inventory = LIFO inventory + LIFO reserve			
FIFO Assets = LIFO Assets + LIFO reserve			
Increase in LIFO reserve during the year			
FIFO COGS = LIFO COGS - increase in LIFO reserve			
After-tax effect of LIFO method = (1-marginal tax rate) × increase in LIFO reserve			
FIFO Net income = LIFO net income + After-tax effect of LIFO method			

Complete the table below using information from the financial statements and from the table you completed above. Comment on the results comparing CNH Global with Caterpillar's 'As Reported' and 'As if FIFO' income statement and balance sheet information.

Year Ended December 31, 2007	Caterpillar		CNH Global
	As Reported	As if FIFO	As Reported
Common-size Cost of goods sold[1]			
Net income			
Growth in Net income			
Common-size Net income			
Total Assets			
Inventory			
Common-size Inventory[2]			

Notes:

[1] To common size items from the income statement, divide by total revenue attributable to equipment sales (that is, do not include revenues from each company's financing operations).

[2] To common size items from the balance sheet, divide by total assets.

g. The average inventory holding period is estimated using the following formula (the denominator is referred to as the inventory turnover ratio):

$$\text{Average Inventory Holding Period} = \frac{365 \, \text{days}}{\left[\dfrac{\text{Cost of Sales}}{\text{Average Inventory}} \right]}$$

Use data from the financial statements to estimate the average inventory holding period for Caterpillar and CNH Global for fiscal 2006 and 2007. Calculate the ratios for both companies with FIFO-based numbers. Additional information: CNH Global's inventory balance for fiscal 2005 was $2,466. Evaluate how well Caterpillar manages its inventory relative to its competitor.

Now recalculate the average holding period for Caterpillar using their as-reported (LIFO) numbers. Do you come to a different conclusion about their inventory turnover?

h. Assume that Caterpillar's inventory balances for accounting and for tax purposes are the same. Estimate the cumulative amount of income taxes through December 31, 2007, that Caterpillar has deferred by choosing the LIFO method of inventory costing instead of the FIFO method. For these calculations, assume that the marginal tax rate for Caterpillar is 35%.

i. Explain what is meant by the term "channel stuffing." Is channel stuffing likely to be a concern at a company like Caterpillar? Explain.

STATEMENT 1

Consolidated Results of Operations for the Years Ended December 31

(Dollars in millions except per share data)

Caterpillar Inc.

	2007	2006	2005
Sales and revenues:			
Sales of Machinery and Engines	$41,962	$38,869	$34,006
Revenues of Financial Products	2,996	2,648	2,333
Total sales and revenues	44,958	41,517	36,339
Operating costs:			
Cost of goods sold	32,626	29,549	26,558
Selling, general and administrative expenses	3,821	3,706	3,190
Research and development expenses	1,404	1,347	1,084
Interest expense of Financial Products	1,132	1,023	768
Other operating expenses	1,054	971	955
Total operating costs	40,037	36,596	32,555
Operating profit	4,921	4,921	3,784
Interest expense excluding Financial Products	288	274	260
Other income (expense)	320	214	377
Consolidated profit before taxes	4,953	4,861	3,901
Provision for income taxes	1,485	1,405	1,120
Profit of consolidated companies	3,468	3,456	2,781
Equity in profit (loss) of unconsolidated affiliated companies	73	81	73
Profit	$ 3,541	$ 3,537	$ 2,854
Profit per common share	$ 5.55	$ 5.37	$ 4.21
Profit per common share — diluted[1]	$ 5.37	$ 5.17	$ 4.04
Weighted-average common shares outstanding (millions)			
— Basic	638.2	658.7	678.4
— Diluted[1]	659.5	683.8	705.8
Cash dividends declared per common share	$ 1.38	$ 1.15	$ .96

[1] Diluted by assumed exercise of stock-based compensation awards, using the treasury stock method.

See accompanying notes to Consolidated Financial Statements.

STATEMENT 2
Consolidated Financial Position at December 31
(Dollars in millions)

	2007	2006	2005
Assets			
Current assets:			
Cash and short-term investments	$ 1,122	$ 530	$ 1,108
Receivables — trade and other	8,249	8,607	7,906
Receivables — finance	7,503	6,804	6,442
Deferred and refundable income taxes	816	733	255
Prepaid expenses and other current assets	583	638	2,250
Inventories	7,204	6,351	5,224
Total current assets	25,477	23,663	23,185
Property, plant and equipment — net	9,997	8,851	7,988
Long-term receivables — trade and other	685	860	1,037
Long-term receivables — finance	13,462	11,531	10,301
Investments in unconsolidated affiliated companies	598	562	565
Noncurrent deferred and refundable income taxes	1,553	1,949	857
Intangible assets	475	387	424
Goodwill	1,963	1,904	1,451
Other assets	1,922	1,742	1,745
Total assets	**$56,132**	**$51,449**	**$47,553**
Liabilities			
Current liabilities:			
Short-term borrowings:			
Machinery and Engines	$ 187	$ 165	$ 871
Financial Products	5,281	4,990	4,698
Accounts payable	4,723	4,085	3,412
Accrued expenses	3,178	2,923	2,617
Accrued wages, salaries and employee benefits	1,126	938	1,601
Customer advances	1,442	921	454
Dividends payable	225	194	168
Other current liabilities	951	1,145	1,012
Long-term debt due within one year:			
Machinery and Engines	180	418	340
Financial Products	4,952	4,043	4,159
Total current liabilities	22,245	19,822	19,332
Long-term debt due after one year:			
Machinery and Engines	3,639	3,694	2,717
Financial Products	14,190	13,986	12,960
Liability for postemployment benefits	5,059	5,879	3,161
Other liabilities	2,116	1,209	951
Total liabilities	**47,249**	**44,590**	**39,121**
Commitments and contingencies (Notes 22 and 23)			
Stockholders' equity			
Common stock of $1.00 par:			
Authorized shares: 900,000,000			
Issued shares: (2007, 2006 and 2005 — 814,894,624) at paid-in amount	2,744	2,465	1,859
Treasury stock (2007 — 190,908,490 shares; 2006 — 169,086,448 shares and 2005 — 144,027,405 shares) at cost	(9,451)	(7,352)	(4,637)
Profit employed in the business	17,398	14,593	11,808
Accumulated other comprehensive income	(1,808)	(2,847)	(598)
Total stockholders' equity	**8,883**	**6,859**	**8,432**
Total liabilities and stockholders' equity	**$56,132**	**$51,449**	**$47,553**

See accompanying notes to Consolidated Financial Statements.

C. Sales and revenue recognition

Sales of Machinery and Engines are generally recognized when title transfers and the risks and rewards of ownership have passed to customers or independently owned and operated dealers. Typically, where product is produced and sold in the same country, title and risk of ownership transfer when the product is shipped. Products that are exported from a country for sale typically pass title and risk of ownership at the border of the destination country.

No right of return exists on sales of equipment. Replacement part returns are estimable and accrued at the time a sale is recognized.

We provide discounts to dealers and original equipment manufacturers (OEM) through merchandising programs that are administered by our marketing profit centers. We have numerous programs that are designed to promote the sale of our products. The most common dealer programs provide a discount when the dealer sells a product to a targeted end user. OEM programs provide discounts designed to encourage the use of our engines. The cost of these discounts is estimated based on historical experience and known changes in merchandising programs and is reported as a reduction to sales when the product sale is recognized.

Our standard invoice terms are established by marketing region. When a sale is made to a dealer, the dealer is responsible for payment even if the product is not sold to an end customer and must make payment within the standard terms to avoid interest costs. Interest at or above prevailing market rates is charged on any past due balance. Our policy is to not forgive this interest. In 2007, 2006 and 2005 terms were extended to not more than one year for $219 million, $49 million and $287 million of receivables, respectively. For 2007, 2006 and 2005, these amounts represent less than 1% of consolidated sales.

Sales with payment terms of two months or more were as follows:

(Dollars in millions)

Payment Terms (months)	2007 Sales	2007 Percent of Sales	2006 Sales	2006 Percent of Sales	2005 Sales	2005 Percent of Sales
2	$ 1,747	4.2%	$ 1,481	3.8%	$ 261	0.8%
3	2,047	4.9%	636	1.6%	548	1.6%
4	524	1.2%	336	0.9%	262	0.8%
5	964	2.3%	1,228	3.2%	916	2.7%
6	4,499	10.7%	8,516	21.9%	8,147	23.9%
7-12	240	0.6%	272	0.7%	345	1.0%
	$10,021	23.9%	$12,469	32.1%	$10,479	30.8%

We establish a bad debt allowance for Machinery and Engines receivables when it becomes probable that the receivable will not be collected. Our allowance for bad debts is not significant. In 2006, we wrote off approximately $70 million of receivables in conjunction with settlement of various legal disputes with Navistar International Corporation. No significant write-offs of Machinery and Engines receivables were made during 2007 or 2005.

Revenues of Financial Products primarily represent the following Cat Financial revenues:

- Retail (end-customer) finance revenue on finance leases and installment sale contracts is recognized over the term of the contract at a constant rate of return on the scheduled outstanding principal balance. Revenue on retail notes is recognized based on the daily balance of retail receivables outstanding and the applicable effective interest rate.

- Operating lease revenue is recorded on a straight-line basis in the period earned over the life of the contract.

- Wholesale (dealer) finance revenue on installment contracts and finance leases is recognized over the term of the contract at a constant rate of return on the scheduled outstanding principal balance. Revenue on wholesale notes is recognized based on the daily balance of wholesale receivables outstanding and the applicable effective interest rate.

- Loan origination and commitment fees are deferred and then amortized to revenue using the interest method over the life of the finance receivables.

Recognition of income is suspended when collection of future income is not probable. Accrual is resumed, and previously suspended income is recognized, when the receivable becomes contractually current and/or collection doubts are removed. Cat Financial provides wholesale inventory financing to dealers. See Notes 7 and 8 for more information.

Sales and revenue recognition items are presented net of sales and other related taxes.

D. Inventories

Inventories are stated at the lower of cost or market. Cost is principally determined using the last-in, first-out (LIFO) method. The value of inventories on the LIFO basis represented about 75% of total inventories at December 31, 2007 and 2006, and about 80% of total inventories at December 31, 2005.

If the FIFO (first-in, first-out) method had been in use, inventories would have been $2,617 million, $2,403 million and $2,345 million higher than reported at December 31, 2007, 2006 and 2005, respectively.

E. Securitized receivables

We periodically sell finance receivables in securitization transactions. When finance receivables are securitized, we retain interests in the receivables in the form of interest-only strips, servicing rights, cash reserve accounts and subordinated certificates. The retained interests are recorded in "Other assets" at fair value. We estimate fair value based on the present value of future expected cash flows using key assumptions for credit losses, prepayment speeds and discount rates. See Note 8 for more information.

F. Depreciation and amortization

Depreciation of plant and equipment is computed principally using accelerated methods. Depreciation on equipment leased to others, primarily for Financial Products, is computed using the straight-line method over the term of the lease. The depreciable basis is the original cost of the equipment less the estimated residual value of the equipment at the end of the lease term. In 2007, 2006 and 2005, Cat Financial depreciation on equipment leased to others was $671 million, $631 million and $615 million, respectively, and was included in "Other operating expenses" in Statement 1. In 2007, 2006 and 2005 consolidated depreciation expense was $1,725 million, $1,554 million and $1,444 million, respectively. Amortization of purchased intangibles is computed principally using the straight-line method, generally not to exceed a period of 20 years.

Significant assumptions used to estimate the fair value of the retained interests and subordinated certificates at the time of the transaction were:

	2007	2006	2005
Discount rate	**8.4%**	11.2%	10.8%
Weighted-average prepayment rate	**14.0%**	14.0%	14.0%
Expected credit losses	**1.0%**	1.0%	1.0%

These assumptions are based on our historical experience, market trends and anticipated performance relative to the particular assets securitized.

The company receives annual servicing fees of approximately 1% of the unpaid note value.

As of December 31, 2007, 2006 and 2005, the subordinated retained interests in the public securitizations totaled $49 million, $68 million and $72 million, respectively. Key assumptions used to determine the fair value of the retained interests were:

	2007	2006	2005
Cash flow discount rates on retained interests and subordinated tranches	**10.1%**	7.3%	10.7%
Weighted-average maturity	**30 months**	31 months	30 months
Average prepayment rate	**14.0%**	14.0%	14.0%
Expected credit losses	**1.1%**	1.0%	1.0%

The investors and the securitization trusts have no recourse to Cat Financial's other assets for failure of debtors to pay when due.

We estimated the impact of individual 10% and 20% changes to the key economic assumptions used to determine the fair value of residual cash flow in retained interests on our income. An independent, adverse change to each key assumption had an immaterial impact on the fair value of residual cash flow.

We consider an account past due if any portion of an installment is due and unpaid for more than 30 days. Recognition of income is suspended when management determines that collection of future income is not probable (generally after 120 days past due). Accrual is resumed, and previously suspended income is recognized, when the receivable becomes contractually current and/or collection doubts are removed. Cash receipts on impaired loans or finance leases are recorded against the receivable and then to any unrecognized income. Investment in loans/finance leases on nonaccrual status were $232 million, $190 million and $175 million and past due over 90 days and still accruing were $47 million, $18 million and $31 million as of December 31, 2007, 2006 and 2005, respectively.

Cat Financial provides financing only when acceptable criteria are met. Credit decisions are based on, among other things, the customer's credit history, financial strength and intended use of equipment. Cat Financial typically maintains a security interest in retail financed equipment and requires physical damage insurance coverage on financed equipment.

Please refer to Table III for additional finance receivables information and Note 19 and Table IV for fair value information.

9. Inventories

		December 31,	
(Millions of dollars)	2007	2006	2005
Raw materials	**$2,474**	$2,182	$1,689
Work-in-process	**1,215**	977	814
Finished goods	**3,230**	2,915	2,493
Supplies	**285**	277	228
Total inventories	**$7,204**	$6,351	$5,224

We had long-term material purchase obligations of approximately $442 million at December 31, 2007.

10. Property, plant and equipment

	Useful Lives		December 31,	
(Millions of dollars)	(Years)	2007	2006	2005
Land	—	**$ 189**	$ 184	$ 154
Buildings and land improvements	20-45	**3,625**	3,407	3,195
Machinery, equipment and other	3-10	**9,756**	8,694	7,829
Equipment leased to others	1-10	**4,556**	3,957	3,988
Construction-in-process	—	**1,082**	1,036	696
Total property, plant and equipment, at cost		**19,208**	17,278	15,862
Less: Accumulated depreciation		**(9,211)**	(8,427)	(7,874)
Property, plant and equipment — net		**$9,997**	$ 8,851	$7,988

We had commitments for the purchase or construction of capital assets of approximately $570 million at December 31, 2007. Software assets with a carrying value of $50 million, primarily related to our dealer distribution support system, were abandoned in 2005. The write-off of these assets is included in "Other operating expense" in Statement 1.

Assets recorded under capital leases[1]:

		December 31,	
(Millions of dollars)	2007	2006	2005
Gross capital leases[2]	**$ 96**	$ 96	$ 91
Less: Accumulated depreciation	**(75)**	(65)	(55)
Net capital leases	**$ 21**	$ 31	$ 36

[1] Included in Property, plant and equipment table above.
[2] Consists primarily of machinery and equipment.

Equipment leased to others (primarily by Cat Financial):

		December 31,	
(Millions of dollars)	2007	2006	2005
Equipment leased to others — at original cost	**$4,556**	$ 3,957	$3,988
Less: Accumulated depreciation	**(1,487)**	(1,299)	(1,201)
Equipment leased to others — net	**$3,069**	$ 2,658	$2,787

At December 31, 2007, scheduled minimum rental payments to be received for equipment leased to others were:

(Millions of dollars)					
2008	2009	2010	2011	2012	After 2012
$736	$511	$309	$161	$57	$20

11. Investments in unconsolidated affiliated companies

Our investments in affiliated companies accounted for by the equity method consist primarily of a 50% interest in Shin Caterpillar Mitsubishi Ltd. (SCM) located in Japan. Combined financial information of the unconsolidated affiliated companies accounted for by the equity method (generally on a three-month lag, e.g., SCM results reflect the periods ending September 30) was as follows:

	Years ended December 31,		
(Millions of dollars)	2007	2006	2005
Results of Operations:			
Sales	**$4,007**	$ 4,420	$ 4,140
Cost of sales	**3,210**	3,526	3,257
Gross profit	**797**	894	883
Profit (loss)	**$ 157**	$ 187	$ 161
Caterpillar's profit (loss)	**$ 73**	$ 81	$ 73

CNH GLOBAL N.V.
CONSOLIDATED STATEMENTS OF INCOME
For the Years Ended December 31, 2007, 2006 and 2005

	Consolidated			Supplemental Information					
				Equipment Operations			Financial Services		
	2007	2006	2005	2007	2006	2005	2007	2006	2005
				(in millions, except per share data)					
Revenues:									
Net sales	$14,971	$12,115	$11,806	$14,971	$12,115	$11,806	$ —	$—	$—
Finance and interest income	993	883	769	190	177	129	1,131	952	801
	15,964	12,998	12,575	15,161	12,292	11,935	1,131	952	801
Costs and Expenses:									
Cost of goods sold	12,154	9,933	9,934	12,154	9,933	9,934	—	—	—
Selling, general and administrative	1,436	1,248	1,177	1,183	1,015	964	253	233	213
Research, development and engineering	409	367	303	409	367	303	—	—	—
Restructuring	85	96	73	85	94	71	—	2	2
Interest expense—Fiat affiliates	140	66	99	39	49	72	101	17	27
Interest expense—other	561	512	452	319	272	269	378	323	240
Interest compensation to Financial Services	—	—	—	247	235	159	—	—	—
Other, net	349	359	280	224	233	188	70	54	36
	15,134	12,581	12,318	14,660	12,198	11,960	802	629	518
Income (loss) before income taxes, minority interest and equity in income of unconsolidated subsidiaries and affiliates	830	417	257	501	94	(25)	329	323	283
Income tax provision	354	165	116	245	56	24	109	109	92
Minority interest	15	16	26	15	16	27	—	—	—
Equity in income of unconsolidated subsidiaries and affiliates:									
Financial Services	9	8	9	229	222	200	9	8	9
Equipment Operations	89	48	39	89	48	39	—	—	—
Net income	$ 559	$ 292	$ 163	$ 559	$ 292	$ 163	$ 229	$222	$200
Per Share Data:									
Basic earnings per share	$ 2.36	$ 1.37	$ 0.77						
Diluted earnings per share	$ 2.36	$ 1.23	$ 0.70						

2

CNH GLOBAL N.V.
CONSOLIDATED BALANCE SHEETS
As of December 31, 2007 and 2006

	Consolidated		Supplemental Information Equipment Operations		Financial Services	
	2007	2006	2007	2006	2007	2006
	(in millions, except share data)					
ASSETS						
Current Assets:						
Cash and cash equivalents	$ 1,025	$ 1,174	$ 405	$ 703	$ 620	$ 471
Deposits in Fiat affiliates cash management pools	1,231	497	1,157	496	74	1
Accounts and notes receivable, net	6,720	3,677	1,542	1,311	5,439	2,475
Intersegment notes receivable	—	—	1,831	1,348	—	—
Inventories, net	3,488	2,735	3,488	2,735	—	—
Deferred income taxes	584	587	377	424	207	163
Prepayments and other	220	114	200	110	20	4
Total current assets	13,268	8,784	9,000	7,127	6,360	3,114
Long-term receivables	3,873	2,872	2	3	3,871	2,869
Intersegment long-term notes receivable	—	—	—	97	—	—
Property, plant and equipment, net	1,510	1,306	1,505	1,297	5	9
Other Assets:						
Investments in unconsolidated subsidiaries and affiliates	528	457	420	354	108	103
Investment in Financial Services	—	—	2,099	1,788	—	—
Equipment on operating leases, net	511	254	—	—	511	254
Goodwill	2,382	2,365	2,231	2,220	151	145
Other intangible assets, net	760	780	742	776	18	4
Other assets	913	1,456	638	852	275	604
Total other assets	5,094	5,312	6,130	5,990	1,063	1,110
Total	$23,745	$18,274	$16,637	$14,514	$11,299	$7,102
LIABILITIES AND SHAREHOLDERS' EQUITY						
Current Liabilities:						
Current maturities of long-term debt—Fiat affiliates	$ 153	$ 33	$ —	$ —	$ 153	$ 33
Current maturities of long-term debt—other	1,334	1,027	2	53	1,332	974
Short-term debt—Fiat affiliates	2,562	438	263	260	2,299	178
Short-term debt—other	1,707	832	465	228	1,242	604
Intersegment short-term debt and current maturities of long-term debt	—	—	—	—	1,831	1,348
Accounts payable	2,907	1,881	2,989	1,939	161	42
Restructuring liability	10	85	10	82	—	3
Other accrued liabilities	2,575	2,144	2,160	1,879	433	274
Total current liabilities	11,248	6,440	5,889	4,441	7,451	3,456
Long-term debt—Fiat affiliates	1,515	19	800	—	715	19
Long-term debt—other	2,365	4,053	1,377	2,366	988	1,687
Intersegment long-term debt	—	—	—	—	—	97
Other Liabilities:						
Pension, postretirement and other postemployment benefits	1,810	2,288	1,804	2,279	6	9
Other liabilities	388	245	349	199	39	46
Total other liabilities	2,198	2,533	2,153	2,478	45	55
Commitments and contingencies						
Minority interest	117	109	116	109	1	—
Shareholders' equity:						
Preference shares, $1.00 par value; authorized and issued 74,800,000 shares in 2007 and 2006	—	—	—	—	35	35
Common shares, €2.25 par value; authorized 400,000,000 shares in 2007 and 2006, issued 237,324,183 in 2007 and 236,319,791 shares in 2006	595	592	595	592	205	205
Paid-in capital	6,168	6,117	6,168	6,117	1,224	1,205
Treasury stock, 154,813 shares in 2007 and 2006, at cost	(8)	(8)	(8)	(8)	—	—
Retained earnings (deficit)	(311)	(763)	(311)	(763)	359	211
Accumulated other comprehensive income (loss)	(142)	(818)	(142)	(818)	276	132
Total shareholders' equity	6,302	5,120	6,302	5,120	2,099	1,788
Total	$23,745	$18,274	$16,637	$14,514	$11,299	$7,102

State Street Corporation—Marketable Securities

State Street Corporation, tracing its beginnings to the founding of the Union Bank in 1792, is a major financial holding company with headquarters in Boston. State Street operates primarily through its principal banking subsidiary, State Street Bank and Trust with a focus on serving institutional investors. State Street operates two lines of business: Investment Servicing and Investment Management to support institutional investors worldwide , including brokerage and other trading services, securities finance, deposit and short-term investment facilities, performance, risk and investment research and investment management. (Source: Company 2007 Form 10-K)

Learning Objectives
- Distinguish among securities classified as trading, available-for-sale, and held-to-maturity.
- Interpret footnote disclosures of investment securities and analyze investment security accounts.
- Prepare journal entries for securities purchases, sales, and year-end market-value adjustments.
- Understand and critique the accounting treatment for marketable securities.

Refer to the 2007 financial statements and notes for State Street Corporation.

 Concepts

a. Consider trading securities. Note that financial institutions such as State Street typically call these securities "Trading account assets."

    i. In general, what are trading securities?

    ii. How would a company record $1 of dividends or interest received from trading securities?

    iii. If the market value of trading securities increased by $1 during the reporting period, what journal entry would the company record?

b. Consider securities available-for-sale. Note that State Street calls these, "Investment securities available for sale."

    i. In general, what are securities available-for-sale?

    ii. How would a company record $1 of dividends or interest received from securities available-for-sale?

    iii. If the market value of securities available-for-sale increased by $1 during the reporting period, what journal entry would the company record?

c. Consider securities held-to-maturity. Note that State Street calls these, "Investment securities held to maturity."

    i. In general, what are these securities? Why are equity securities never classified as held-to-maturity?

    ii. If the market value of securities held-to-maturity increased by $1 during the reporting period, what journal entry would the company record?

Process

d. Consider the "Trading account assets" on State Street's Balance Sheet.

    i. What is the balance in this account on December 31, 2007? What is the market value of these securities on that date?

    ii.   Assume that the 2007 unadjusted trial balance for trading account assets was $436 million. What adjusting journal entry would State Street make to adjust this account to market value? Ignore any income tax effects for this part.

e. Consider the balance sheet account "Investment securities held to maturity" and the related disclosures in Note 3.

    i.   What is the 2007 year-end balance in this account?

    ii.   What is the market value of State Street's Investment securities held to maturity?

    iii.   What is the amortized cost of these securities? What does "amortized cost" represent? How does amortized cost compare to the original cost of the securities?

    iv.   What does the difference between the market value and the amortized cost represent? What does the difference suggest about how the average market rate of interest on held-to-maturity securities has changed since the purchase of the securities held by State Street?

f. Consider the balance sheet account "Investment securities available for sale" and the related disclosures in Note 3.

    i.   What is the 2007 year-end balance in this account? What does this balance represent?

    ii.   What is the amount of net *unrealized* gains (losses) on the available-for-sale securities held by State Street at December 31, 2007? Be sure to note whether the amount is a net gain or loss.

    iii.   What was the amount of net *realized* gains (losses) from sales of available-for-sale securities for 2007? How would this amount impact State Street's statements of income and cash flows for 2007?

g. State Street's statement of cash flow for 2007 (not included) shows the following line items in the "Investing Activities" section relating to available-for-sale securities (in millions):

Proceeds from sales of available-for-sale securities	$ 4,731
Purchases of available-for-sale securities	$27,578

    i.   Show the journal entry State Street made to record the purchase of available-for-sale securities for 2007.

    ii.   Show the journal entry State Street made to record the sale of available-for-sale securities for 2007. Assume that the book (or carrying) value of the securities was $4,652 (in millions) at the time of the sale. *Hint:* be sure to consider the amount of net unrealized gains or losses recorded in prior periods for these securities.

    iii.   Use the information in part *g. ii* to determine the original cost of the available-for-sale securities sold during 2007.

    iv.   Use Note 3 and your solution to part *g. ii*, to determine the amount of net unrealized gains (losses) during 2007 for the available-for-sale securities on hand at December 31, 2007. How would this amount impact State Street's statement of cash flows for 2007? Show the journal entry that State Street would have made to mark the available-for-sale securities portfolio to market value at year end. Ignore any tax considerations for this analysis. *Hint:* use a T-account to analyze the changes in the net unrealized gains (losses) activity in Note 3.

✦   Analysis   ✦

h. Consider the statements of shareholders' equity and the column labeled "Accumulated Other Comprehensive (Loss) Income." This account captures the year-over-year changes in all assets and liabilities that are not reflected in income for the year (other than transactions with the shareholders during the year). For example, State Street's unrealized increases and decreases in the market value of available-for-sale securities are included in total assets at the end of the year. Yet, these increases or decreases are not included in net income for the year. They are however, included in "Comprehensive income" for the year. The accumulated other comprehensive income account is the accumulation of many years' comprehensive income. Because the account is in a loss (that is, debit) position at the end of 2006 and 2007, State Street calls the account "Accumulated Other Comprehensive Loss" on the balance sheet.

    i.   What is the 2007 year-end balance in State Street's accumulated other comprehensive loss account? The 2006 balance?

    ii.   What is the amount of the net change in the "Accumulated Other Comprehensive (Loss) Income" account relating to net unrealized gains (losses) on available-for-sale securities during 2007?

    iii.   Compare the net unrealized gain (loss) amount in part *h. ii.*, to the information about changes in net unrealized gains (losses) shown in Note 3 (and analyzed in part *g*, above). What likely accounts for the difference in the two amounts?

i.   What would State Street have reported as income before income tax expense in 2007 had the company classified its securities available-for-sale as trading account assets instead? Assume that all of the securities available-for-sale had also been reclassified as trading securities as of January 1, 2007. By what amount would total shareholders' equity at December 31, 2007, differ with this change in classification?

j.   Early versions of SFAS No. 115 would have required all marketable securities to be carried at market value on the balance sheet.

    i.   Prepare a brief argument against this method of accounting.

    ii.   Now, prepare a brief argument in support of this method of accounting.

    iii.   Which position would you have supported if you had been CFO of State Street in 2007? How would your answer differ if you were an investor?

State Street Corporation

CONSOLIDATED FINANCIAL STATEMENTS

Consolidated Statement of Income

Years ended December 31, (Dollars in millions, except per share amounts)	2007	2006	2005
Fee revenue:			
Servicing fees	$ 3,388	$ 2,723	$ 2,474
Management fees	1,141	943	751
Trading services	1,152	862	694
Securities finance	681	386	330
Processing fees and other	237	272	302
Total fee revenue	6,599	5,186	4,551
Net interest revenue:			
Interest revenue	5,212	4,324	2,930
Interest expense	3,482	3,214	2,023
Net interest revenue	1,730	1,110	907
Provision for loan losses	—	—	—
Net interest revenue after provision for loan losses	1,730	1,110	907
Gains (Losses) on sales of available-for-sale investment securities, net	7	15	(1)
Gain on sale of Private Asset Management business	—	—	16
Total revenue	8,336	6,311	5,473
Operating expenses:			
Salaries and employee benefits	3,256	2,652	2,231
Information systems and communications	546	501	486
Transaction processing services	619	496	449
Occupancy	408	373	391
Provision for legal exposure	600	—	—
Merger and integration costs	198	—	—
Other	806	518	484
Total operating expenses	6,433	4,540	4,041
Income from continuing operations before income tax expense	1,903	1,771	1,432
Income tax expense from continuing operations	642	675	487
Income from continuing operations	1,261	1,096	945
Income (Loss) from discontinued operations before income tax expense	—	16	(165)
Income tax expense (benefit) from discontinued operations	—	6	(58)
Income (Loss) from discontinued operations	—	10	(107)
Net income	$ 1,261	$ 1,106	$ 838
Earnings per share from continuing operations:			
Basic	$ 3.50	$ 3.31	$ 2.86
Diluted	3.45	3.26	2.82
Income (Loss) per share from discontinued operations:			
Basic	—	$ .03	$ (.33)
Diluted	—	.03	(.32)
Earnings per share:			
Basic	$ 3.50	$ 3.34	$ 2.53
Diluted	3.45	3.29	2.50
Average shares outstanding (in thousands):			
Basic	360,675	331,350	330,361
Diluted	365,488	335,732	334,636

The accompanying notes are an integral part of these consolidated financial statements.

State Street Corporation

Consolidated Statement of Condition

As of December 31, (Dollars in millions, except per share amounts)	2007	2006
Assets		
Cash and due from banks	$ 4,733	$ 2,368
Interest-bearing deposits with banks	5,579	5,236
Securities purchased under resale agreements	19,133	14,678
Federal funds sold	4,540	—
Trading account assets	589	785
Investment securities available for sale	70,326	60,445
Investment securities held to maturity (fair value of $4,225 and $4,484)	4,233	4,547
Loans and leases (less allowance of $18)	15,784	8,928
Premises and equipment (net of accumulated depreciation of $2,650 and $2,415)	1,894	1,560
Accrued income receivable	2,096	1,617
Goodwill	4,567	1,384
Other intangible assets	1,990	434
Other assets	7,079	5,371
Total assets	$142,543	$107,353
Liabilities		
Deposits:		
Noninterest-bearing	$ 15,039	$ 10,194
Interest-bearing—U.S.	14,790	1,272
Interest-bearing—Non-U.S.	65,960	54,180
Total deposits	95,789	65,646
Securities sold under repurchase agreements	14,646	19,147
Federal funds purchased	425	2,147
Other short-term borrowings	5,557	2,835
Accrued taxes and other expenses	4,392	3,143
Other liabilities	6,799	4,567
Long-term debt	3,636	2,616
Total liabilities	131,244	100,101
Commitments and contingencies (note 10)		
Shareholders' equity		
Preferred stock, no par: authorized 3,500,000 shares; issued none		
Common stock, $1 par: authorized 750,000,000 shares; issued 398,366,000 and 337,126,000 shares	398	337
Surplus	4,630	399
Retained earnings	7,745	7,030
Accumulated other comprehensive loss	(575)	(224)
Treasury stock, at cost (12,082,000 and 4,688,000 shares)	(899)	(290)
Total shareholders' equity	11,299	7,252
Total liabilities and shareholders' equity	$142,543	$107,353

The accompanying notes are an integral part of these consolidated financial statements.

State Street Corporation

Consolidated Statement of Changes in Shareholders' Equity

(Dollars in millions, except per share amounts, shares in thousands)	COMMON STOCK Shares	Amount	Surplus	Retained Earnings	Accumulated Other Comprehensive (Loss) Income	TREASURY STOCK Shares	Amount	Total
Balance at December 31, 2004	337,126	$337	$ 289	$5,590	$ 92	3,481	$ (149)	$ 6,159
Comprehensive income:								
Net income				838				838
Change in net unrealized gains/losses on available-for-sale securities, net of related taxes of $(150) and reclassification adjustment					(229)			(229)
Foreign currency translation, net of related taxes of $(54)					(140)			(140)
Change in unrealized gains/losses on hedges of net investments in non-U.S. subsidiaries, net of related taxes of $20					37			37
Change in unrealized gains/losses on cash flow hedges, net of related taxes of $6					9			9
Total comprehensive income				838	(323)			515
Cash dividends declared—$.72 per share				(239)				(239)
Common stock acquired						13,130	(664)	(664)
Common stock issued under SPACES			(73)			(8,712)	418	345
Common stock awards and options exercised, including tax benefit of $20			50			(4,319)	197	247
Other						(79)	4	4
Balance at December 31, 2005	337,126	337	266	6,189	(231)	3,501	(194)	6,367
Comprehensive income:								
Net income				1,106				1,106
Change in net unrealized gains/losses on available-for-sale securities, net of related taxes of $40 and reclassification adjustment					58			58
Foreign currency translation, net of related taxes of $56					124			124
Change in unrealized gains/losses on hedges of net investments in non-U.S. subsidiaries, net of related taxes of $(10)					(18)			(18)
Change in minimum pension liability, net of related taxes of $2					4			4
Change in unrealized gains/losses on cash flow hedges, net of related taxes of $2					3			3
Total comprehensive income				1,106	171			1,277
Adjustment to apply provisions of SFAS No. 158, net of related taxes of $(109)					(164)			(164)
Cash dividends declared—$.80 per share				(265)				(265)
Common stock acquired						5,782	(368)	(368)
Common stock received under COVERS contracts			30			1,199	(26)	4
Common stock awards and options exercised, including tax benefit of $43			103			(5,782)	300	403
Other						(12)	(2)	(2)
Balance at December 31, 2006	337,126	337	399	7,030	(224)	4,688	(290)	7,252
Adjustment for effect of applying provisions of FASB Staff Position No. FAS 13-2				(226)				(226)
Adjusted balance at January 1, 2007	337,126	337	399	6,804	(224)	4,688	(290)	7,026
Comprehensive income:								
Net income				1,261				1,261
Change in net unrealized gains/losses on available-for-sale securities, net of related taxes of $(276) and reclassification adjustment					(451)			(451)
Change in net unrealized gains/losses on fair value hedges of available-for-sale securities, net of related taxes of $(37)					(55)			(55)
Foreign currency translation, net of related taxes of $62					134			134
Change in unrealized gains/losses on cash flow hedges, net of related taxes of $(7)					(11)			(11)
Change in unrealized gains/losses on hedges of net investments in non-U.S. subsidiaries, net of related taxes of $(4)					(8)			(8)
Change in minimum pension liability, net of related taxes of $28					40			40
Total comprehensive income				1,261	(351)			910
Cash dividends declared—$.88 per share				(320)				(320)
Common stock acquired						13,369	(1,002)	(1,002)
Common stock awards and options exercised, including tax benefit of $52	401	—	65			(5,975)	393	458
Common stock issued in connection with acquisition	60,839	61	4,166					4,227
Balance at December 31, 2007	398,366	$398	$4,630	$7,745	$(575)	12,082	$ (899)	$11,299

The accompanying notes are an integral part of these consolidated financial statements.

STATE STREET CORPORATION

Note 1. Summary of Significant Accounting Policies (excerpt)

The accounting and financial reporting policies of State Street Corporation conform to accounting principles generally accepted in the United States of America, referred to as "GAAP." Unless otherwise indicated or unless the context requires otherwise, all references in these Notes to Consolidated Financial Statements to "State Street," "we," "us," "our" or similar references mean State Street Corporation and its subsidiaries on a consolidated basis. The parent company is a financial holding company headquartered in Boston, Massachusetts. We report two lines of business:

- Investment Servicing provides services for U.S. mutual funds and collective investment funds, corporate and public retirement plans, insurance companies, foundations, endowments and other investment pools worldwide. Products include custody, product- and participant-level accounting; daily pricing and administration; master trust and master custody; recordkeeping; foreign exchange, brokerage and other trading services; securities finance; deposit and short-term investment facilities; loans and lease financing; investment manager and hedge fund manager operations outsourcing; and performance, risk and compliance analytics to support institutional investors.

- Investment Management offers a broad array of services for managing financial assets, including investment management and investment research services, primarily for institutional investors worldwide. These services include passive and active U.S. and non-U.S. equity and fixed-income strategies, and other related services, such as securities finance.

Investment Securities Available for Sale and Held to Maturity:

Securities held in our investment securities portfolio are classified at the time of purchase, based on management's intentions, as available for sale or held to maturity. Securities available for sale are those that management intends to hold for an indefinite period of time, including securities used as part of our asset and liability management strategy that may be sold in response to changes in interest rates, pre-payment risk, liquidity needs or other similar factors. Debt and marketable equity securities classified as available for sale are reported at fair value, and after-tax net unrealized gains and losses are reported in accumulated other comprehensive income, a component of shareholders' equity. Gains or losses on sales of available-for-sale securities are computed using the specific identification method. Securities held to maturity are debt securities that management has the positive intent and ability to hold to maturity. Securities classified as held to maturity are reported at cost, adjusted for amortization of premiums and accretion of discounts.

Management reviews the fair value of the portfolio at least quarterly, and evaluates individual securities for declines in fair value that may be other than temporary, considering factors such as current and expected future interest rates, external credit ratings, dividend payments, the performance of underlying collateral, if any, the financial health of the issuer and other pertinent information, including current developments with respect to the issuer, as well as the duration of the decline and management's intent and ability to hold the security. If declines are deemed other than temporary, an impairment loss is recognized and the amortized cost basis of the investment security is written down to its current fair value, which becomes the new cost basis. Other-than-temporary unrealized losses on available-for-sale and held-to-maturity securities, if any, are recorded as a reduction of processing fees and other revenue.

In March 2007, we completed our acquisition of Currenex, Inc., an independently owned electronic foreign exchange trading platform. We paid approximately $564 million, net of liabilities assumed, and recorded the following significant assets: goodwill—$437 million; customer relationship and other intangible assets—$174 million; and other tangible assets—$25 million. The customer relationship and other intangible assets are being amortized on a straight-line basis over periods ranging from eight to twelve years. Financial results of Currenex are included in the accompanying consolidated financial statements beginning on March 2, 2007.

During the first quarter of 2006, we agreed to a plan of sale to finalize the divestiture of our ownership interest in Bel Air Investment Advisors LLC, and recorded income of approximately $16 million, or $10 million after-tax, related to the finalization of legal, selling and other costs recorded in connection with the divestiture. We completed the divestiture in July 2006.

Note 3. Investment Securities

(In millions)	2007 Amortized Cost	2007 Gross Unrealized Gains	2007 Gross Unrealized Losses	2007 Fair Value	2006 Amortized Cost	2006 Gross Unrealized Gains	2006 Gross Unrealized Losses	2006 Fair Value
Available for sale:								
U.S. Treasury and federal agencies:								
Direct obligations	$ 8,163	$ 32	$ 14	$ 8,181	$ 7,701		$ 89	$ 7,612
Mortgage-backed securities	14,631	54	100	14,585	11,685	$ 15	246	11,454
Asset-backed securities	26,100	2	1,033	25,069	25,646	28	40	25,634
Collateralized mortgage obligations	12,018	41	167	11,892	8,538	17	79	8,476
State and political subdivisions	5,756	79	22	5,813	3,740	20	11	3,749
Other debt investments	4,041	27	27	4,041	3,043	7	23	3,027
Money-market mutual funds	243	—	—	243	201	—	—	201
Other equity securities	479	24	1	502	269	24	1	292
Total	$71,431	$259	$1,364	$70,326	$60,823	$111	$489	$60,445
Held to maturity:								
U.S. Treasury and federal agencies:								
Direct obligations	$ 757	$ 9	$ 1	$ 765	$ 846		$ 15	$ 831
Mortgage-backed securities	940	7	6	941	1,084	$ 5	17	1,072
Collateralized mortgage obligations	2,190	5	24	2,171	2,357	5	41	2,321
Other investments	346	2	—	348	260	1	1	260
Total	$ 4,233	$ 23	$ 31	$ 4,225	$ 4,547	$ 11	$ 74	$ 4,484

Aggregate investment securities carried at $39.84 billion and $23.28 billion at December 31, 2007 and 2006, respectively, were designated as pledged for public and trust deposits, short-term borrowings and for other purposes as provided by law.

Gross unrealized losses on investment securities on a pre-tax basis consisted of the following as of December 31, 2007:

(In millions)	Less than 12 continuous months		12 continuous months or longer		Total	
	Fair Value	Gross Unrealized Losses	Fair Value	Gross Unrealized Losses	Fair Value	Gross Unrealized Losses
U.S. Treasury and federal agencies:						
Direct obligations	$ 2,414	$ 11	$ 1,350	$ 4	$ 3,764	$ 15
Mortgage-backed securities	2,501	19	6,682	87	9,183	106
Asset-backed securities	2,277	46	20,965	987	23,242	1,033
Collateralized mortgage obligations	2,603	53	7,388	138	9,991	191
State and political subdivisions	1,010	20	134	2	1,144	22
Other debt investments	758	9	928	18	1,686	27
Other equity securities	18	1	—	—	18	1
Total	$11,581	$159	$37,447	$1,236	$49,028	$1,395

As described in note 1, management periodically reviews the investment securities portfolio to determine if other-than-temporary impairment has occurred. This review encompasses all investment securities and includes such quantitative factors as current and expected future interest rates, the length of time the cost basis has exceeded the fair value and the severity of the impairment measured as the ratio of fair value to amortized cost, and includes all investment securities for which we have issuer-specific concerns regardless of quantitative factors. After a full review of all investment securities, taking into consideration current economic conditions, adverse situations that might affect our ability to fully collect interest and principal, the timing of future payments, the credit quality and performance of the underlying collateral of asset-backed securities, and other relevant factors, management considers the aggregate decline in fair value and the resulting gross unrealized losses of $1.40 billion on 2,702 securities at December 31, 2007 to be temporary. The losses are not considered to be the result of any material changes in the credit characteristics of the investment securities. Management has the ability and the intent to hold the securities until recovery in market value.

Gross gains and losses realized from sales of available-for-sale securities were as follows for the years indicated:

(In millions)	2007	2006	2005
Gross gains	$24	$33	$ 9
Gross losses	17	18	10
Net gains (losses)	$ 7	$15	$(1)

Palfinger AG—Property, Plant, & Equipment

Headquartered in Bergheim, Austria, Palfinger AG manufactures hydraulic lifting, loading, and handling solutions worldwide. Founded in 1932, Palfinger offers various products, including knuckle boom cranes, timber and recycling cranes, and telescopic cranes. The company also provides container handling systems, tailgates, aerial work platforms, transportable forklifts, and railway system solutions. The company primarily serves construction, transport, agriculture and forestry, recycling, and haulage industries. (Source: Company 2007 Annual Report)

Learning Objectives
- Use information from the financial statements to analyze fixed asset and depreciation transactions.
- Understand why and how certain costs are capitalized.
- Compute depreciation expenses using common accounting methods.
- Calculate gains and losses on fixed asset disposals.
- Calculate and interpret the fixed asset turnover ratio.

Refer to the 2007 financial statements of Palfinger AG.

 Concepts

a. Based on the description of Palfinger above, what sort of property and equipment do you think the company has?

b. The 2007 balance sheet shows Property, plant, and equipment of €149,990. What does this number represent?

c. What types of equipment does Palfinger report in notes to the financial statements?

d. In the notes, Palfinger reports "Prepayments and assets under construction." What does this sub-account represent? Why does this account have no accumulated depreciation? Explain the reclassification of €14,958 in this account during 2007.

e. How does Palfinger depreciate its property and equipment? Does this policy seem reasonable? Explain the trade-offs management makes in choosing a depreciation policy.

f. Palfinger routinely opts to perform major renovations and value-enhancing modifications to equipment and buildings rather than buy new assets. How does Palfinger treat these expenditures? What is the alternative accounting treatment?

 Process

g. Use the information in the financial statement notes to analyze the activity in the "Property, plant and equipment" and "Accumulated depreciation and impairment" accounts for 2007. Determine the following amounts:

  i. The purchase of new property, plant and equipment in fiscal 2007.

  ii. Government grants for purchases of new property, plant and equipment in 2007. Explain what these grants are and why they are deducted from the property, plant, and equipment account.

  iii. Depreciation expense for fiscal 2007.

  iv. The net book value of property, plant, and equipment that Palfinger disposed of in fiscal 2007.

h. The statement of cash flows (not presented) reports that Palfinger received proceeds on the sale of property, plant, and equipment amounting to €1,655 in fiscal 2007. Calculate the gain or loss that Palfinger incurred on this transaction. Hint: use the net book value you calculated in part g *iv*, above. Explain what this gain or loss represents in economic terms.

i. Consider the €10,673 added to "Other plant, fixtures, fittings, and equipment" purchased during fiscal 2007. Assume that these net assets have an expected useful life of five years and a salvage value of €1,273. Prepare a table showing the depreciation expense and net book value of this equipment over its expected life assuming that Palfinger recorded a full year of depreciation in 2007 and the company uses:

    i.   Straight-line depreciation.

    ii.   Double-declining-balance depreciation.

j. Assume that the equipment from part *i.* was sold on the first day of fiscal 2008 for proceeds of €7,500. Assume that Palfinger's accounting policy is to take no depreciation in the year of sale.

    i.   Calculate any gain or loss on this transaction assuming that the company used straight-line depreciation. What is the total income statement impact of the equipment for the two years that Palfinger owned it? Consider the gain or loss on disposal as well as the total depreciation recorded on the equipment (i.e. the amount from part *i. i.*).

    ii.   Calculate any gain or loss on this transaction assuming the company used double-declining-balance depreciation. What is the total income statement impact of this equipment for the two years that Palfinger owned them? Consider the gain or loss on disposal as well as the total depreciation recorded on the equipment (i.e. the amount from part *i. ii.*).

    iii.   Compare the total two-year income statement impact of the equipment under the two depreciation policies. Comment on the difference.

✧ Analysis ✧

k. Suppose you want to compare Palfinger AG to another heavy equipment manufacturer, Caterpillar, Inc. To compare the companies, complete the table below and calculate common-sized numbers. To common-size balance sheet numbers, divide by total assets and to common-size income statement numbers, divide by net sales. Comment on the trends over time and levels across companies.

	Palfinger (€ thousands)		Caterpillar ($ millions)	
	2007	*2006*	*2007*	*2006*
Net PPE			$ 9,997	$8,851
Total Assets			$56,132	$51,449
Common-size				
Depreciation*			$1,797	$1,602
Sales / Revenue			$41,962	$38,869
Common-size				

* Include only the depreciation expense from Palfinger's footnotes and not "Depreciation, amortisation, and impairment expenses" from the income statement.

l. A ratio that analysts use to gauge the efficiency with which management is using its invested capital is the fixed asset turnover ratio. The ratio is defined as:

$$\text{Fixed Asset Turnover} = \frac{\text{Net Sales}}{\text{Average Net PPE}}$$

Use the table below to determine the fixed asset turnover ratios for fiscal 2006 and 2007 for Palfinger and Caterpillar. Explain what this ratio measures. Comment on the trends over time and levels across companies.

	Palfinger (€ thousands)		Caterpillar ($ millions)	
	2007	*2006*	*2007*	*2006*
Sales / Revenue			$41,962	$38,869
Average net PPE			$9,424	$8,420
Turnover				

m. Annually, companies must assess the book (carrying) value of Property, plant, and equipment. If assets are impaired in value, the company must record an impairment charge (expense) on the income statement and reduce the net book value of the impaired assets to their lower fair value. In 2006, Palfinger recorded an impairment to "Land and buildings." Use the information in Note 2 to the annual report, to prepare the journal entry to record the 2006 asset impairment.

n. Under International Financial Reporting Standards (IAS 16), firms are permitted to revalue assets upward to fair market value. The notes to Palfinger's 2007 annual report include the following.

> In connection with the implementation of the business location concept in Austria and the planned demolition of some parts of the building, an impairment loss in the amount of TEUR 1,960 was recognised for the company building in Bergheim, Salzburg in the 2006 financial year. Due to changes in the business location concept and the plans to continue to use the company building, a write-up of TEUR 1,755 was recognised in the 2007 financial year.

    i. Explain in your own words, Palfinger's asset revaluation during 2007. Is this revaluation significant?

    ii. Use the information in Note 2 to prepare the journal entry to record the 2007 asset revaluation. Speculate on how the journal entry would have been different if Palfinger had not previously recorded an impairment on this building.

    iii. Suppose you want to compare Palfinger AG to another heavy equipment manufacturer such as Caterpillar, Inc. U.S. GAAP does not permit upward asset revaluations. How might you adjust the financial numbers of either company to more closely compare the ratios you calculated above?

Consolidated Balance Sheet

TEUR	Note	31 Dec 2007	31 Dec 2006
ASSETS			
Non-current assets			
Intangible assets	1	54,609	31,420
Property, plant, and equipment	2	149,990	98,130
Investments in associated companies	3	11,951	8,054
Deferred tax assets	4	19,663	14,043
Other non-current assets	5	2,732	2,942
		238,945	**154,589**
Current assets			
Inventories	6	151,894	114,249
Receivables and other current assets	7	133,112	104,004
Current tax receivables		1,121	5,988
Cash and cash equivalents	8	2,559	30,536
		288,686	**254,777**
Non-current assets held for sale	9	683	0
		289,369	**254,777**
Total assets		**528,314**	**409,366**
EQUITY AND LIABILITIES			
Equity			
Share capital	10	37,135	18,568
Additional paid-in capital	11	35,190	53,757
Retained earnings	12	221,607	171,034
Revaluation reserve	13	(112)	0
Valuation reserves pursuant to IAS 39	14	519	776
Foreign currency translation reserve	15	(4,923)	(6,053)
		289,416	**238,082**
Minority interests	16	5,640	3,882
		295,056	**241,964**
Non-current liabilities			
Non-current financial liabilities	17	38,315	31,566
Non-current provisions	18	21,103	15,426
Deferred tax liabilities	4	5,668	259
Other non-current liabilities	19	1,176	4,174
		66,262	**51,425**
Current liabilities			
Current financial liabilities	20	43,598	15,241
Current provisions	21	14,063	16,402
Current tax liabilities		10,059	8,133
Other current liabilities	22	99,276	76,201
		166,996	**115,977**
Total equity and liabilities		**528,314**	**409,366**

TEUR	Note	Jan–Dec 2007	Jan–Dec 2006
Revenue	23	695,623	585,205
Changes in inventories and own work capitalised	24	11,302	15,158
Other operating income	25	11,738	12,643
Materials and external services	26	(371,047)	(316,363)
Staff costs	27	(141,183)	(122,887)
Depreciation, amortisation, and impairment expenses	28	(15,638)	(15,100)
Other operating expenses	29	(91,157)	(81,630)
Earnings before interest and taxes (EBIT)		99,638	77,026
Income from associated companies	30	5,755	2,106
Interest and other financial expenses	31	(3,001)	(3,549)
Net financial result		2,754	**(1,443)**
Profit before income tax		102,392	75,583
Income tax expense	32	(24,324)	(15,904)
Profit after income tax		78,068	59,679
attributable to			
Minority interests		4,090	3,076
Shareholders of PALFINGER AG (consolidated net profit for the period)		73,978	56,603

EUR			
Earnings per share (undiluted and diluted) [2]	12	2.09	1.60
Dividend per share [2]	12	0.70 [1]	0.55

[1] Proposal of the Management Board to the Supervisory Board for presentation to the Annual General Meeting for resolution.

[2] Previous year's figures were converted pursuant to the stock split.

Notes to the Consolidated Financial Statements 2007

Accounting and Valuation Principles

Property, Plant, and Equipment

Property, plant, and equipment are reported at cost, adjusted for straight-line depreciation. Besides direct costs, production costs also contain appropriate proportions of materials and manufacturing overhead costs. General administrative expenses as well as interest on borrowings are not capitalised.

Assets are depreciated as soon as they are put into operation. Depreciation is performed on a straight-line basis over the prospective useful lives of the relevant assets. The anticipated economic or technical useful life is used to determine the expected useful life of property, plant, and equipment.

	Years
Own buildings and investments in third-party buildings	8–50
Plant and Machinery	3–15
Fixtures, fittings, and equipment	3–10

To the extent the nature of the asset concerned is not modified and no additional future benefit arises, maintenance and repair work are booked as current expenses in the year in which they occur. Replacement investments and value-enhancing investments are capitalised and depreciated over either the new or the original useful life. In the case of asset disposals, the difference between the carrying amounts and the net realisable value is booked through the income statement in either other operating income or other operating expenses.

When a decision to sell property, plant, and equipment is made and the conditions set out in IFRS 5 are met, the performance of an impairment test is mandatory. If necessary, the asset is written down to the realisable amount less costs to sell still to be incurred and is then no longer depreciated until the date of sale.

Government Grants

According to IAS 20 government grants for property, plant, and equipment are presented as reductions of the acquisition and/or manufacturing costs.

Leases

In keeping with IAS 17, the allocation of a leased asset to the lessor or lessee is based on the transfer of all material risks and rewards incidental to ownership of the asset.

Assets obtained through finance leases are capitalised at the fair value or lower present value of the minimum lease payments at the acquisition date from the viewpoint of the lessee, and depreciated over their useful lives. The capitalised value of assets corresponds to the present value of the lease payments outstanding at the balance sheet date.

Assets obtained through operating leases are allocated to the lessor. The lessee recognises the lease payments as an expense in equal instalments over the term of the lease.

Notes to the Consolidated Financial Statements 2007

(2) Property, Plant, and Equipment

Changes in property, plant, and equipment were as follows:

TEUR	Land and buildings	Undeveloped	Plant and machinery	Other plant, fixtures,fittings, and equipment	Prepayments and assets under construction	Total
Acquisition cost						
At 1 Jan 2006	**76,880**	**1,375**	**56,919**	**24,660**	**3,826**	**163,660**
Additions	3,661	0	4,714	2,803	10,173	**21,351**
Disposals	(2)	0	(2,157)	(4,582)	(238)	**(6,979)**
Reclassifications	455	39	3,269	(533)	(3,287)	**(57)**
Foreign currency translation	(379)	(4)	(129)	(94)	(6)	**(612)**
At 31 Dec 2006	**80,615**	**1,410**	**62,616**	**22,254**	**10,468**	**177,363**
At 1 Jan 2007	**80,615**	**1,410**	**62,616**	**22,254**	**10,468**	**177,363**
Change in scope of consolidation	920	0	4,667	2,380	16	**7,983**
Additions	12,139	2,020	15,612	10,673	21,000	**61,444**
Additional capitalisation	0	0	108	26	0	**134**
Government grants	(417)	0	(316)	0	0	**(733)**
Disposals	(1,409)	0	(6,733)	(4,936)	(721)	**(13,799)**
Reclassifications	4,007	0	9,951	826	(14,958)	**(174)**
Reclassification to held for sale	(3,499)	0	0	0	0	**(3,499)**
Foreign currency translation	446	17	77	(14)	14	**540**
At 31 Dec 2007	92,802	3,447	85,982	31,209	15,819	229,259
Accumulated depreciation and impairment						
At 1 Jan 2006	**23,502**	**0**	**33,686**	**16,420**	**0**	**73,608**
Depreciation	2,146	0	5,219	2,615	0	**9,980**
Impairment	1,960	0	0	0	0	**1,960**
Disposals	0	0	(2,153)	(3,910)	0	**(6,063)**
Reclassifications	0	0	112	(112)	0	**0**
Foreign currency translation	(108)	0	(70)	(74)	0	**(252)**
At 31 Dec 2006	**27,500**	**0**	**36,794**	**14,939**	**0**	**79,233**
At 1 Jan 2007	**27,500**	**0**	**36,794**	**14,939**	**0**	**79,233**
Change in scope of consolidation	98	0	2,559	1,548	0	**4,205**
Depreciation	2,826	0	6,869	2,862	0	**12,557**
Write-up	(1,755)	0	0	0	0	**(1,755)**
Additional capitalisation	0	0	116	28	0	**144**
Disposals	(1,011)	0	(6,548)	(4,739)	0	**(12,298)**
Reclassifications	(328)	0	30	263	0	**(35)**
Reclassification to held for sale	(2,886)	0	0	0	0	**(2,886)**
Foreign currency translation	162	0	(28)	(30)	0	**104**
At 31 Dec 2007	24,606	0	39,792	14,871	0	79,269
Carrying amounts						
At 31 Dec 2006	**53,115**	**1,410**	**25,822**	**7,315**	**10,468**	**98,130**
At 31 Dec 2007	68,196	3,447	46,190	16,338	15,819	149,990

Borland Software Corporation— Goodwill and Other Intangible Assets

Borland Software Corporation was organized in 1983 and is a leading vendor of Open Application Lifecycle Management solutions, or ALM, which represents the segment of the ALM market in which vendors' solutions are flexible enough to support a customer's specific processes, tools and platforms. Open ALM is a new, customer-centric approach to helping IT organizations transform software delivery into a managed, efficient and predictable business process. Borland operates two segments: Enterprise and CodeGear. Enterprise provides a combination of software products as well as consulting and education services to help customers manage their software development. The CodeGear segment focuses on developing tools for individual developers and currently offers a number of Integrated Developer Environment, or IDE, and database products for Java, .NET and Windows. (Source: Company 2007 Form 10-K)

Learning Objectives
- Understand when and how intangible assets are recorded in the balance sheet.
- Understand how goodwill impairments are recorded in the financial statements.
- Consider how investors may use the financial statements to gather information about intangible assets that are not recorded in the balance sheet.
- Understand how the purchase of a company leads to goodwill and intangible assets and the expensing of in-process research and development costs.

Refer to the 2007 financial statements and notes of Borland Software Corporation.

Concepts

a. What is an intangible asset? Give several examples of intangible assets. Which intangible assets appear on a company's balance sheet under Generally Accepted Accounting Principles (GAAP)? Describe how GAAP determines whether an intangible asset is included in the balance sheet. Be sure to discuss the concepts of relevance and reliability in your answer.

b. What does the value of goodwill on a balance sheet capture (that is, how does a company determine when and at what amount to record the value of goodwill)?

Process

c. Refer to Borland's balance sheet and note 4 relating to goodwill.

   i. What percentage of total assets consists of goodwill at December 31, 2007? At December 31, 2006?

   ii. What is the primary cause of the decrease in the value of goodwill on Borland's balance sheet from 2006 to 2007?

   iii. Which business unit experienced an impairment of goodwill in 2007? What percentage of the beginning balance of goodwill of this unit was deemed to be impaired?

   iv. Borland's notes describe that the company tests for goodwill impairment by comparing the carrying value of a business unit and its goodwill to its fair value. Describe how Borland might determine the fair value of a business unit and its goodwill in order to make this comparison.

   v. Show the journal entry that Borland made to record the impairment of goodwill during 2007. Ignore any income tax effects.

   vi. Describe how the impairment of goodwill impacts the statement of cash flows for 2007.

vii. Goodwill impairments are sometimes referred to as noncash charges. Often, in press releases and other corporate communications, managers encourage readers to ignore these noncash charges. Comment on whether and when that makes sense.

d. Refer to Borland's balance sheet and note 4 relating to intangible assets, net.

   i. What percentage of total assets consists of intangible assets, net, at December 31, 2007? At December 31, 2006? What type of events likely triggered the existence of the intangible assets?

   ii. What is the gross amount of recorded intangible assets at December 31, 2007?

   iii. What is the primary cause of the decrease in the value of intangible assets, net on Borland's balance sheet from 2006 to 2007?

   iv. Show the journal entry that Borland made to record the amortization of intangible assets for 2007. Ignore any income tax effects.

e. In Note 2, Borland explains that expenditures relating to research and development of new software products are expensed as they are incurred until "technological feasibility" is established. Under SFAS 86, costs incurred after this point may be capitalized as software development assets and subsequently amortized over the period in which the software generates revenue. What amount of capitalized software development costs is included in Borland's balance sheet at December 31, 2007? Does this amount seem reasonable to you?

✧ Analysis ✧

f. Describe how Borland accounts for expenditures for advertising activities including "funded advertising" for resellers of Borland's products.

   i. Complete the following table relating to advertising expenses reported by Borland:

	2007	2006	2005
Total advertising expense, including funded advertising			
Total advertising expense / Total revenues			
Total advertising expense / Selling, general, and administrative expense			

   ii. Comment on the trends in the advertising expense and related ratios in the table above. What events might explain the trends you observe?

   iii. In following generally accepted accounting principles, Borland's balance sheet does not include an intangible asset for the value of the brand name of its software products. Describe how investors might use the information in the table above to gain insights about changes in the value of Borland's branded products.

g. Note 6 describes Borland's 2006 acquisition of Segue Software, Inc., for cash totaling $115.9 million and reports the allocation of the purchase price to specific asset and liability accounts.

   i. How did Borland determine the allocation of the purchase price to specific tangible and intangible assets?

   ii. What percentage of the total (gross) assets acquired related to goodwill and other intangible assets?

iii. $4.8 million of the purchase price of Segue was attributed to "in-process research and development." Describe what these costs represent and how Borland accounted for these costs in the purchase transaction.

iv. Show the journal entry that Borland made to record the purchase of Segue Software, Inc., in 2006. Be sure to note whether each account is a balance sheet or income statement account.

v. How does Borland report the purchase transaction in the statement of cash flows in 2006? Why does the amount reported in the statement of cash flows differ from the total cash purchase price disclosed in Note 6?

h. i. Use information from Borland's financial statements to describe Borland's financial performance over the past three years and its current financial condition. Be specific about the accounting numbers you use to make your assessment.

ii. Use the stock price chart below to describe the market's perception of Borland's value over the last year. Estimate Borland's market capitalization at December 31, 2007, using information in the balance sheet about shares outstanding and the chart below. *Hint:* market capitalization equals total common shares outstanding times stock price. How does this market value estimate compare to the book value of equity (that is, shareholders' equity) at December 31, 2007?

iii. What might the trends you observed in parts *h. i* and *h. ii* suggest about current and future value of goodwill and other intangible assets?

iv. Locate Borland's May 7, 2008, news release about the first quarter 2008 financial results in the Investor Relations section of Borland's website (www.borland.com, follow the "Company" link). Comment on Borland's assessment of the value of goodwill during Q1 2008 in the news release.

Borland Stock Price – April 1, 2007 through March 31, 2008

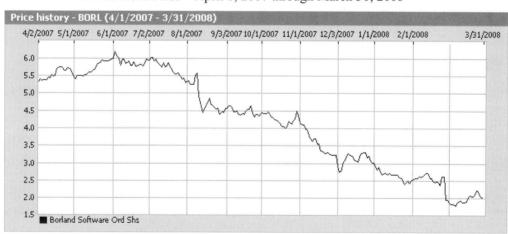

Source: http://moneycentral.msn.com/

BORLAND SOFTWARE CORPORATION
CONSOLIDATED BALANCE SHEETS

(In thousands, except par value and share amounts)

ASSETS

	December 31, 2007	December 31, 2006
Current assets:		
Cash and cash equivalents	$90,805	$55,317
Short-term investments	68,061	—
Accounts receivable, net of allowances of $6,096 and $5,413, respectively	54,640	62,154
Prepaid expenses	9,207	13,341
Other current assets	5,106	1,329
Total current assets	227,819	132,141
Property and equipment, net	9,996	11,176
Goodwill	226,688	253,356
Intangible assets, net	31,658	40,521
Long-term investments	37,970	—
Other non-current assets	9,886	6,705
Total assets	$544,017	$443,899

LIABILITIES AND STOCKHOLDERS' EQUITY

	December 31, 2007	December 31, 2006
Current liabilities:		
Accounts payable	$ 7,622	$ 15,591
Accrued expenses	31,605	36,438
Short-term restructuring	9,867	9,582
Income taxes payable	2,315	14,925
Deferred revenue	51,390	58,930
Other current liabilities	7,575	7,264
Total current liabilities	110,374	142,730
Convertible senior notes	200,000	—
Long-term restructuring	5,823	6,231
Long-term deferred revenue	1,774	1,610
Other long-term liabilities	23,976	7,848
Total liabilities	341,947	158,419
Commitments and Contingencies		
Stockholders' equity:		
Preferred stock; $.01 par value; 1,000,000 shares authorized; 0 shares issued and outstanding	—	—
Common stock; $.01 par value; 200,000,000 shares authorized; 72,975,972 and 78,704,764 shares issued, respectively	730	787
Additional paid-in capital	666,910	659,932
Accumulated deficit	(335,478)	(273,892)
Cumulative other comprehensive income	10,317	9,121
	342,479	395,948
Less common stock in treasury at cost, 21,158,980 and 15,275,899 shares, respectively	(140,409)	(110,468)
Total stockholders' equity	202,070	285,480
Total liabilities and stockholders' equity	$544,017	$443,899

The accompanying notes are an integral part of these consolidated financial statements.

BORLAND SOFTWARE CORPORATION
CONSOLIDATED STATEMENTS OF OPERATIONS

	Year Ended December 31,		
	2007	2006	2005
	(In thousands, except per share data)		
License and other revenues	$137,358	$165,886	$163,182
Service revenues	131,423	138,774	113,561
Total revenues	268,781	304,660	276,743
Cost of license and other revenues	6,014	7,439	8,884
Cost of service revenues	40,918	55,381	40,491
Amortization of acquired intangibles and other charges	8,445	6,972	10,043
Cost of revenues	55,377	69,792	59,418
Gross profit	213,404	234,868	217,325
Selling, general and administrative	176,206	195,710	174,002
Research and development	57,795	70,178	57,687
Restructuring, amortization of other intangibles, acquisition-related expenses and other charges	13,934	22,073	20,611
Impairment of goodwill	26,509	—	—
Total operating expenses	274,444	287,961	252,300
Operating loss	(61,040)	(53,093)	(34,975)
Gain on sale of investment, net	—	—	4,372
Gain on sale of fixed assets	—	1,658	—
Interest income	8,742	3,168	5,509
Interest expense	(5,449)	(374)	(302)
Other expense	(790)	(790)	(52)
Loss before income taxes	(58,537)	(49,431)	(25,448)
Income tax provision	3,136	2,522	4,384
Net loss	(61,673)	(51,953)	(29,832)
Net loss per share:			
Net loss per share — basic and diluted	(0.85)	(0.67)	(0.38)
Shares used in computing basic and diluted net loss per share	$72,875	$77,096	$77,557

The accompanying notes are an integral part of these consolidated financial statements.

BORLAND SOFTWARE CORPORATION
CONSOLIDATED STATEMENTS OF STOCKHOLDERS' EQUITY

	Common Stock		Additional Paid in Capital	Accumulated (Deficit)	Treasury Stock		Cumulative Other Comprehensive Income	Deferred Compensatio	Total
	Number of Shares	Amount			Number of Shares	Amount			
Balance at December 31, 2004	80,937	$809	$638,077	($198,826)	9,999	($75,349)	$12,671	($1,002)	$376,380
Employee stock option, employee stock purchase plan and other, net	1,013	10	5,726	—	—	—	—	—	5,736
Issuance of restricted stock in connection with TeraQuest acquisition	87	1	849	—	—	—	—	(850)	—
Issuance of restricted stock, net	1,041	11	6,295	—	34	—	—	(6,385)	(79)
Repurchase of Common Stock	(5,270)	(53)	—	—	5,276	(35,119)	—	—	(35,172)
Amortization of TogetherSoft option value	—	—	—	—	—	—	—	41	41
Release of TogetherSoft escrow shares	(1)	—	—	—	1	—	—	—	—
Amortization of TeraQuest deferred compensation	—	—	—	—	—	—	—	212	212
Amortization of deferred compensation	—	—	—	—	—	—	—	793	793
Fair market value adjustment available-for-sale securities	—	—	—	—	—	—	(72)	—	(72)
Foreign currency translation adjustments	—	—	—	—	—	—	(6,067)	—	(6,067)
Net Loss	—	—	—	(29,832)	—	—	—	—	(29,832)
Balance at December 31, 2005	77,807	778	650,947	(228,658)	15,310	(110,468)	6,532	(7,191)	311,940
Cumulative effect of adjustments from the adoption of SAB No. 108, net of taxes	—	—	1,460	6,719	—	—	—	—	8,179
Adjusted balances as of December 31, 2005	77,807	778	652,407	(221,939)	15,310	(110,468)	6,532	(7,191)	320,119
Employee stock option, employee stock purchase plan and other, net	1,076	11	4,863	—	—	—	—	—	4,874
Issuance of restricted stock	363	—	—	—	—	—	—	—	—
Repurchase of Common Stock	—	—	—	—	(34)	—	—	—	—
Cancellation of restricted stock	(390)	—	—	—	—	—	—	—	—
Repurchases and retirements of restricted stock	(151)	(2)	(835)	—	—	—	—	—	(837)
Amortization of restricted stock	—	—	3,515	—	—	—	—	—	3,515
Stock-based compensation	—	—	7,173	—	—	—	—	—	7,173
Reclassification of unearned stock-based compensation upon adoption of SFAS 123R	—	—	(7,191)	—	—	—	—	7,191	—
Fair market value adjustment available-for-sale securities	—	—	—	—	—	—	72	—	72
Foreign currency translation adjustments	—	—	—	—	—	—	2,517	—	2,517
Net Loss	—	—	—	(51,953)	—	—	—	—	(51,953)
Balance at December 31, 2006	78,705	787	659,932	(273,892)	15,276	(110,468)	9,121	—	285,480
Employee stock option, employee stock purchase plan and other, net	453	4	1,805	—	—	—	—	—	1,809
Issuance of restricted stock	—	—	—	—	—	—	—	—	—
Repurchase of Common Stock	(5,883)	(60)	—	—	5,883	(29,941)	—	—	(30,001)
Cancellation of restricted stock	(129)	—	—	—	—	—	—	—	—
Repurchases and retirements of restricted stock	(170)	(1)	(820)	—	—	—	—	—	(821)
Amortization of restricted stock	—	—	—	—	—	—	—	—	—
Stock-based compensation	—	—	4,405	—	—	—	—	—	4,405
Amortization of TeraQuest deferred compensation	—	—	66	—	—	—	—	—	66
Amortization of deferred compensation	—	—	1,563	—	—	—	—	—	1,563
Fair market value adjustment available-for-sale securities	—	—	—	—	—	—	14	—	14
Foreign currency translation adjustments	—	—	(41)	—	—	—	1,182	—	1,141
Net Loss	—	—	—	(61,673)	—	—	—	—	(61,673)
Balance at December 31, 2007	72,976	730	666,910	(335,565)	21,159	(140,409)	10,317	—	201,983
Cumulative effect of adjustments from the adoption of FIN 48	—	—	—	87	—	—	—	—	87
Adjusted balances as of December 31, 2007	72,976	$730	$666,910	($335,478)	21,159	($140,409)	$10,317	—	$202,070

The accompanying notes are an integral part of these consolidated financial statements.

BORLAND SOFTWARE CORPORATION
CONSOLIDATED STATEMENTS OF CASH FLOWS

	2007	2006	2005
CASH FLOWS FROM OPERATING ACTIVITIES:			
Net loss	($61,673)	($51,953)	($29,832)
Adjustments to reconcile net loss to net cash provided by (used in) operating			
Depreciation and amortization	14,709	12,773	18,403
Stock-based compensation	6,033	10,688	1,046
Provision for accounts receivable allowances	1,570	(2,952)	3,005
Acquired in-process research & development charge	—	4,800	300
Developed technology impairment charge	—	497	—
Impairment of goodwill	26,509	—	—
Gain on sale of investment	—	—	(4,680)
Loss (gain) on disposal of fixed assets	751	(1,658)	30
Loss on sale of subsidiary	226	—	—
Changes in assets and liabilities, net of acquisitions:			
Accounts receivable	7,497	960	4,435
Prepaid expenses and other assets	(2,856)	5,456	420
Accounts payable and accrued expenses	(12,213)	3,400	(1,509)
Income taxes payable	297	(1,747)	363
Short-term restructuring	192	2,513	2,041
Deferred revenues	(7,853)	(7,559)	7,738
Long-term restructuring	(408)	(3,208)	—
Other liabilities	8,914	(120)	6,854
Cash provided by (used in) operating activities	(18,305)	(28,110)	8,614
CASH FLOWS FROM INVESTING ACTIVITIES:			
Purchases of property and equipment	(5,495)	(6,187)	(7,190)
Proceeds from sale of fixed assets	—	11,015	—
Acquisition of Legadero, net of cash acquired	—	—	(12,744)
Acquisition of TeraQuest, net of cash acquired	—	—	(4,436)
Acquisition of Segue Software, net of cash acquired	—	(102,457)	—
Acquisition of developed technology	—	(497)	—
Proceeds from the sale of an investment	—	—	4,680
Proceeds from the sale of subsidiary	178	—	—
Purchases of investments	(155,859)	—	(328,000)
Sales and maturities of investments	49,878	125,944	346,706)
Cash provided by (used in) investing activities	(111,298)	27,818	(984)
CASH FLOWS FROM FINANCING ACTIVITIES:			
Issuance of convertible senior notes	194,230	—	—
Proceeds from issuance of stock options, employee stock purchase plan and	1,612	4,863	5,657
Repurchase of common stock	(29,941)	—	(35,172)
Cash provided by (used in) financing activities	165,901	4,863	(29,515)
Effect of exchange rate changes on cash	(810)	1,671	(5,472)
Net increase (decrease) in cash and cash equivalents	35,488	6,242	(27,357)
Beginning cash and cash equivalents	55,317	49,075	76,432
Ending cash and cash equivalents	$90,805	$55,317	$49,075
Cash paid during the year for:			
Interest	$3,291	$300	$302
Income taxes, net of refunds	$2,209	$3,715	$752
Supplemental disclosure of non-cash transactions:			
Assets acquired under capital lease	—	—	—
Deferred tax asset effect of acquired tax attributes, net of valuation allowance	$12,470	$17,835	$1,977

The accompanying notes are an integral part of these consolidated financial statements.

BORLAND SOFTWARE CORPORATION
NOTES TO THE CONSOLIDATED FINANCIAL STATEMENTS — (continued)

NOTE 2.   SUMMARY OF SIGNIFICANT ACCOUNTING POLICIES (excerpt)

Research and Development

Costs incurred in the research and development of new software products are expensed as incurred until technological feasibility is established. Software localization projects are outsourced to third-party developers. We capitalize software development in accordance with the provisions of SFAS 86, "*Accounting for the Costs of Computer Software to be Sold, Leased, or Otherwise Marketed.*" Software development costs begin to be capitalized at the time a product's technological feasibility is established and end when the product reaches the working model stage. To date, products and enhancements have generally reached technological feasibility and have been released for sale at substantially the same time and all research and development costs have been expensed.

Goodwill and Acquired Intangibles

Goodwill represents the excess of the aggregate purchase price over the fair value of the tangible and identifiable intangible assets acquired in various acquisitions, net of assumed liabilities. Amortization of both purchased technology and maintenance contracts along with impairment of purchase technology charged to cost of revenues during the years ended December 31, 2007, 2006 and 2005 totaled $8.4 million, $7.0 million and $10.0 million, respectively. Amortization of other acquired intangibles charged to operating expenses during the years ended December 31, 2007, 2006 and 2005 was $0.4 million, $0.6 million and $2.9 million, respectively. We had $31.7 million and $40.5 million in unamortized acquired intangibles at December 31, 2007 and 2006, respectively. We also had $226.7 million and $253.4 million of unimpaired goodwill at December 31, 2007 and 2006, respectively.

Advertising Costs

We expense the production costs of advertising, including direct response, the first time the advertising takes place. Advertising expense was $1.8 million, $1.9 million and $3.2 million during the years ended December 31, 2007, 2006 and 2005, respectively. We also fund certain advertising activities of our reseller channel. These costs are treated as advertising expenses under EITF Issue No. 01-09, "*Accounting for Consideration Given by a Vendor to a Customer or a Reseller of the Vendor's Products,*" or EITF 01-09, as we have deemed that the identifiable benefit is sufficiently separable from the customer's purchase of our product and the fair value of that benefit is reasonably estimable. The amounts related to funded advertising were $0.5 million, $0.9 million and $1.2 million during the years ended December 31, 2007, 2006 and 2005, respectively.

BORLAND SOFTWARE CORPORATION
NOTES TO THE CONSOLIDATED FINANCIAL STATEMENTS — (continued)

NOTE 4.   GOODWILL AND INTANGIBLE ASSETS

The change in the carrying amount of goodwill is as follows (in thousands):

	Goodwill		
	Enterprise	CodeGear	Consolidated
Balance as of January 1, 2007	$ 186,016	$ 67,340	$ 253,356
Impairment of goodwill	—	(26,509)	(26,509)
Purchase accounting adjustments — Segue	(539)	—	(539
Effect of exchange rates	380	—	380
Balance as of December 31, 2007	$ 185,857	$ 40,831	$ 226,688

Goodwill and identifiable intangibles are accounted for in accordance with SFAS No. 141 *"Business Combinations",* or SFAS 141 and SFAS No. 142 *"Goodwill and Other Intangible Asset.",* or SFAS 142. Effective January 1, 2007, we changed from reporting one segment to reporting two segments (Enterprise and CodeGear). As of January 1, 2007, we began utilizing a combination of a discounted cash flow and market approach and goodwill was allocated to each of the reporting segments. Please refer to Note 15 "Reportable Segments" below for more information on the accounting related to the reportable segments. Under SFAS 142, goodwill and other long-lived assets must be tested for impairment annually or in interim periods, if conditions indicate possible impairment. Impairment testing of goodwill is performed in two steps. First, the carrying value of the reporting unit is compared to the fair value of the reporting unit including the goodwill. If the carrying amount of the reporting unit is greater than the fair value of the reporting unit, we perform the second step. The second step of the impairment test, used to measure the amount of impairment loss, compares the implied fair value of the reporting unit goodwill with the carrying amount of that goodwill. If the carrying amount of the reporting unit goodwill exceeds the implied fair value of the goodwill, the impairment loss shall be recognized as an operating expense in an amount equal to that excess. We performed our annual testing of goodwill for impairment during the third quarter of 2007 and no impairment was indicated as of September 30, 2007. At December 31, 2007, we took into consideration various data points when determining the implied fair value including discounted cash flows and market comparable transactions. Our estimated fair value requires management to make estimates and assumptions that impact the reporting value of goodwill and may result in future write downs beyond the current reduction. As a result of this testing, impairment of $26.5 million was recorded against our CodeGear reporting segment.

The initial purchase price allocation for the Segue acquisition resulted in $65.5 million of goodwill. The adjustments to goodwill during the year ended December 31, 2007 are related to purchase consideration adjustments determined during post-closing reviews of the Segue acquisition for accounts receivable, deferred revenues and customer deposits. Additionally, fluctuations in foreign currency exchange rates impact our foreign goodwill balances.

BORLAND SOFTWARE CORPORATION
NOTES TO THE CONSOLIDATED FINANCIAL STATEMENTS — (continued)

NOTE 4. GOODWILL AND INTANGIBLE ASSETS (continued)

The following tables summarize our intangible assets, net (in thousands):

	December 31, 2007		
	Gross Amount	Accumulated Amortization	Net Amount
Acquired technology	$ 46,330	($ 30,187)	$ 16,143
Maintenance agreements	11,300	(2,735)	8,565
Trade names and trademarks	1,100	(499	601
Customer relationship	9,075	(2,726)	6,349
Other	400	(400)	—
	$ 68,205	($ 36,547)	$ 31,658

	December 31, 2006		
	Gross Carrying Amount	Accumulated Amortization	Net Carrying Amount
Acquired technology	$ 46,330	($ 24,701)	$ 21,629
Maintenance agreements	11,300	(1,121)	10,179
Trade names and trademarks	1,100	(215	885
Customer relationship	9,075	(1,376)	7,699
Other	400	(271)	129
	$ 68,205	($ 27,684)	$ 40,521

The intangible assets are all amortizable and have original estimated useful lives as follows: acquired developed technology — 3 to 6 years; maintenance agreements — 7 years; trade names and trademarks — 4 years; customer relationships — 7 years; other — 1 to 3 years. Based on the current amount of intangibles subject to amortization, the estimated future amortization expense related to our intangible assets at December 31, 2007 is as follows (in thousands):

	Future Amortization
2008	$ 8,468
2009	7,315
2010	6,465
2011	5,272
2012	3,317
Thereafter	821
Total	$ 31,658

BORLAND SOFTWARE CORPORATION
NOTES TO THE CONSOLIDATED FINANCIAL STATEMENTS — (continued)

NOTE 6. ACQUISITIONS

Segue Software, Inc.

In April 2006, we completed the acquisition of Segue Software, Inc., or Segue, pursuant to an Agreement and Plan of Merger, dated as of February 7, 2006, or the Merger Agreement. Segue is now a wholly-owned subsidiary of Borland. Segue was a Massachusetts-based provider of quality and testing solutions which defined, measured, managed and improved software quality throughout the entire application lifecycle. Under the terms of the Merger Agreement, we paid $8.67 per share in cash for all outstanding shares of Segue. The purchase price was approximately $115.9 million and consisted of fixed consideration of $105.4 million in cash used to purchase all of Segue's outstanding common shares, $8.1 million in cash paid to eligible Segue employees who held vested common stock options on the closing date of the acquisition and $2.5 million of direct acquisition-related costs. The purchase price of the transaction was allocated to the acquired assets and liabilities based on their estimated fair values as of the date of the acquisition, including identifiable intangible assets, with the remaining amount being classified as goodwill. Additionally, we expect to pay contingent consideration through 2009 of up to a maximum of $1.3 million, of which a total of $0.6 million has been paid to eligible former Segue employees who held unvested common stock options on the closing date of the acquisition and were retained as Borland employees. The contingent consideration is based upon continued employment with Borland and paid in accordance with the vesting schedules of the original Segue common stock options. This contingent consideration is recognized as compensation expense in the periods when it is earned and paid. Cash acquired in the acquisition was $13.5 million. The results of operations for Segue have been included in our consolidated financial statements from the date of acquisition. The acquisition was accounted for as a purchase and the total purchase price was recorded as follows (in thousands):

Cash paid for outstanding common shares	$105,358
Cash paid for outstanding vested common stock options	8,130
Direct transaction costs	2,451
Total purchase price	$115,939

Based upon the purchase price of the acquisition, the purchase price allocation is as follows (in thousands):

Current assets and other tangible assets:	
Cash	$ 13,482
Accounts receivable	$ 4,199
Other current assets	1,210
Property and equipment	902
Deferred tax assets, net of valuation allowance	17,835
Goodwill	65,528
Amortizable intangible assets:	
Developed technology	23,400
In-process research and development	4,800
Customer relationships	7,500
Trademarks	1,000
Non-compete agreements	300
Maintenance agreements	11,300
Total assets acquired	151,456
Liabilities assumed:	
Deferred revenues	(9,042)
Current liabilities	7,276)
Deferred tax liabilities	(17,835)
Other long-term liabilities	(1,364)
Net assets acquired	$ 115,939

BORLAND SOFTWARE CORPORATION
NOTES TO THE CONSOLIDATED FINANCIAL STATEMENTS — (continued)

NOTE 6.   ACQUISITIONS (continued)

The developed technology is being amortized over three to six years, the customer relationships and maintenance agreements over seven years, the trademarks over four years and the non-compete agreements over a one year life from the date of acquisition. The amortizable intangible assets were calculated using the income approach by estimating the expected cash flows from the projects once commercially viable and discounting the net cash flows back to their present value. The discount rates used in the valuation were 11% to 21%.

Of the purchase price, $4.8 million represented acquired in-process research and development, or IPR&D, that had not yet reached technological feasibility and had no alternative future use. Accordingly, this amount was immediately charged to operating expense upon completion of the acquisition. Independent third-party sources assisted us in calculating the value of the intangible assets, including the IPR&D. The value of the IPR&D was calculated using the income approach by estimating the expected cash flows from the projects once commercially viable and discounting the net cash flows back to their present value. The discount rates used in the valuation of IPR&D were 18% to 20% and factored in the costs expected to complete each project.

In accordance with SFAS 109, "*Accounting for Income Taxes*," deferred tax liabilities of $11.9 million have been recorded for the tax effect of the amortizable intangible assets. We have recorded an offsetting deferred tax asset of $11.9 million to reflect future deductible differences that could be allocable to offset future taxable income. We are releasing a portion of the valuation allowance to the extent the realization of deferred tax assets becomes assured as a result of the additional taxable income generated by the non-deductible amortizable intangible assets and other taxable temporary differences. Any future release of valuation allowance against deferred tax assets of Segue will be recorded against goodwill. None of the goodwill recorded as a result of the acquisition of Segue is deductible for tax purposes.

Additionally, subsequent to the completion of the acquisition, options to purchase approximately 843,000 shares of common stock pursuant to our 2003 Supplemental Stock Option Plan were issued to Segue employees who became our employees. These options will vest over a four year period.

Abbott Laboratories—Equity Method Investments

Founded by Chicago physician Wallace Calvin Abbott in 1888, Abbott Laboratories is a diversified pharmaceutical and healthcare company specializing in prescription drugs and diagnostic equipment. In 2007, Abbott spent $2,506 million on research to discover and develop new pharmaceutical products and processes. In 1978, Abbott and Takeda Pharmaceutical Company Limited of Japan, created a 50-50 joint venture: TAP Pharmaceutical Products Inc. TAP develops and markets pharmaceutical products primarily for the United States. (Source: Company 2007 Form 10-K)

Learning Objectives
- Understand why firms undertake joint ventures and other strategic investments.
- Account for equity method investments.
- Use financial statements and footnotes to analyze joint-venture activity.
- Calculate and interpret financial ratios.
- Evaluate the impact of proportionate consolidation accounting treatment on financial statements.

Refer to the 2007 financial statements and notes of Abbott Laboratories.

 Concepts

a. In general, why do firms enter into joint-venture agreements?

b. What accounting method does Abbott use to account for its joint venture in TAP Pharmaceutical Products (TAP)? Briefly explain this accounting method.

Process

c. Consider Abbott Laboratories' statement of earnings.

    i. How did the TAP joint-venture affect Abbott Laboratories' earnings before taxes in 2007? In 2006?

    ii. Prepare the journal entry to record Abbott Laboratories' share of TAP's 2007 earnings.

d. Consider the information in Note 12 – Equity Method Investments.

    i. What amount did Abbott include on its 2007 and 2006 balance sheets for the TAP joint venture? Where does this appear on Abbott Laboratories' balance sheet?

    ii. Prepare the journal entry to record the dividends that Abbott received from TAP in 2007.

e. Use your responses to parts c and d, above along with information in Note 12, to prepare a T-account that summarizes the 2007 activity in Abbott Laboratories' investment in TAP account (that is, the investment asset account). This T-account reflects the joint-venture transactions from Abbott Laboratories' perspective.

f. Use information in Note 12 to prepare a T-account that summarizes the 2007 activity in TAP's combined equity accounts. This T-account reflects the joint-venture transactions from the joint venture's perspective. Recall that TAP's equity is equal to its total assets less total liabilities.

g. Compare the two T-accounts you prepared in parts e and f. What regularity do you notice? Is this a coincidence?

h. How would you expect the TAP joint venture to affect Abbott Laboratories' statement of cash flows for 2007? Where does Abbott Laboratories report the effects on its statement of cash flows?

i. International Financial Reporting Standards (IAS31R) permits an alternate method of accounting for joint ventures: proportionate consolidation. Under this method, the investor includes in its financial statements its share of the joint-venture assets, liabilities, revenue, and expenses rather than the net amounts on the balance sheet and income statement. Consider the effects on Abbott's 2007 financial statements if the company used proportionate consolidation instead of the equity method to account for the TAP joint venture.

    i. Use the table below to show how total assets, total liabilities, revenue, and expenses would be affected by proportionate consolidation. (*Hint*: Assume that Total Expenses = Net Sales – Net Earnings.)

	Gross amount that would be added	*Net amount currently included*	*Net amount that would be added*
Total Assets			
Total Liabilities			
Net Sales			
Cost of products sold			
Total Expenses			
Net Earnings			

    ii. Determine the amounts and ratios below using Abbott Laboratories' reported numbers. Then, recompute the amounts and ratios on a pro forma basis taking into account the restated balance sheet and income statement items you calculated in part i above, to reflect the proportionate consolidation method. For purposes of these calculations, use year-end balance sheet numbers and assume that the company's marginal tax rate, as approximated by the combined federal and state statutory rates is 35%.

	As reported	*Pro forma*
Total Assets		
Total Liabilities		
Total Equity		
Net Sales		

Cost of products sold		
Total Expenses		
Liabilities to equity ratio		
Gross margin percentage		
Return on assets[#]		
Return on equity		

\# Assume that TAP has no interest expense in 2007.

iii. Would Abbott Laboratories' financial statements and ratios be affected in a material way if the company implemented proportionate consolidation?

iv. In your opinion, which accounting treatment better reflects the economic reality of Abbott's joint-venture investment, the equity method or the proportionate consolidation? Explain.

Consolidated Statement of Earnings

(dollars and shares in thousands except per share data)

Year Ended December 31	2007	2006	2005
Net Sales	$25,914,238	$22,476,322	$22,337,808
Cost of products sold	11,422,046	9,815,147	10,641,111
Research and development	2,505,649	2,255,271	1,821,175
Acquired in-process and collaborations research and development	—	2,014,000	17,131
Selling, general and administrative	7,407,998	6,349,685	5,496,123
Total Operating Cost and Expenses	21,335,693	20,434,103	17,975,540
Operating Earnings	4,578,545	2,042,219	4,362,268
Interest expense	593,142	416,172	241,355
Interest (income)	(136,752)	(123,825)	(87,693)
(Income) from TAP Pharmaceutical Products Inc. joint venture	(498,016)	(475,811)	(441,388)
Net foreign exchange (gain) loss	14,997	28,441	21,804
Other (income) expense, net	135,526	(79,128)	8,270
Earnings Before Taxes	4,469,648	2,276,370	4,619,920
Taxes on Earnings	863,334	559,615	1,247,855
Net Earnings	$ 3,606,314	$ 1,716,755	$ 3,372,065
Basic Earnings Per Common Share	$ 2.34	$ 1.12	$ 2.17
Diluted Earnings Per Common Share	$ 2.31	$ 1.12	$ 2.16
Average Number of Common Shares Outstanding Used for Basic Earnings Per Common Share	1,543,082	1,529,848	1,552,457
Dilutive Common Stock Options and Awards	16,975	6,876	11,646
Average Number of Common Shares Outstanding Plus Dilutive Common Stock Options and Awards	1,560,057	1,536,724	1,564,103
Outstanding Common Stock Options Having No Dilutive Effect	6,406	23,567	22,469

The accompanying notes to consolidated financial statements are an integral part of this statement.

Consolidated Statement of Cash Flows

(dollars in thousands)

Year Ended December 31	2007	2006	2005
Cash Flow From (Used in) Operating Activities:			
Net earnings	$ 3,606,314	$ 1,716,755	$ 3,372,065
Adjustments to reconcile net earnings			
to net cash from operating activities —			
Depreciation	1,072,855	983,485	868,808
Amortization of intangible assets	782,031	575,265	490,131
Share-based compensation	429,677	329,957	30,140
Acquired in-process research and development	—	1,927,300	17,131
Investing and financing (gains) losses, net	356,331	277,388	125,328
Trade receivables	(431,846)	(101,781)	(98,216)
Inventories	131,324	104,653	(88,257)
Prepaid expenses and other assets	(418,344)	(283,455)	(406,858)
Trade accounts payable and other liabilities	(82,960)	(183,203)	199,703
Income taxes	(261,539)	(84,275)	537,429
Net Cash From Operating Activities	5,183,843	5,262,089	5,047,404
Cash Flow From (Used in) Investing Activities:			
Acquisitions of businesses and technologies, net of cash acquired	—	(7,923,163)	(295,123)
Acquisitions of property and equipment	(1,656,207)	(1,337,818)	(1,207,493)
Sales of (investment in) Boston Scientific common stock;			
and (investments in) note receivable and derivative financial instruments	568,437	(2,095,780)	—
Purchases of investment securities	(32,852)	(33,632)	(15,670)
Proceeds from sales of investment securities	17,830	18,476	783,599
Other	(33,485)	(25,712)	14,600
Net Cash (Used in) Investing Activities	(1,136,277)	(11,397,629)	(720,087)
Cash Flow From (Used in) Financing Activities:			
(Repayments of) net proceeds from issuance of short-term debt and other	(3,603,481)	5,183,225	(1,528,180)
Proceeds from issuance of long-term debt	3,500,000	4,000,000	1,851,013
(Repayment) of long-term debt	(441,012)	(3,532,408)	(150,000)
Purchases of common shares	(1,058,793)	(754,502)	(1,302,314)
Proceeds from stock options exercised, including income tax benefit	1,249,804	502,782	223,637
Dividends paid	(1,959,150)	(1,777,170)	(1,686,472)
Net Cash (Used in) From Financing Activities	(2,312,632)	3,621,927	(2,592,316)
Effect of exchange rate changes on cash and cash equivalents	200,258	73,966	(193,954)
Net cash provided by operating activities of discontinued operations of Hospira, Inc.	—	67,152	127,012
Net Increase (Decrease) in Cash and Cash Equivalents	1,935,192	(2,372,495)	1,668,059
Cash and Cash Equivalents, Beginning of Year	521,192	2,893,687	1,225,628
Cash and Cash Equivalents, End of Year	$ 2,456,384	$ 521,192	$ 2,893,687

The accompanying notes to consolidated financial statements are an integral part of this statement.

Consolidated Balance Sheet

(dollars in thousands)

December 31	2007	2006	2005
Assets			
Current Assets:			
Cash and cash equivalents	$ 2,456,384	$ 521,192	$ 2,893,687
Investments, including $307,500 of investments measured at fair value at December 31, 2007	364,443	852,243	62,406
Trade receivables, less allowances of — 2007: $258,288; 2006: $215,443; 2005: $203,683	4,946,876	4,231,142	3,576,794
Inventories:			
Finished products	1,677,083	1,338,349	1,203,557
Work in process	681,634	686,425	630,267
Materials	592,725	781,647	708,155
Total inventories	2,951,442	2,806,421	2,541,979
Deferred income taxes	2,109,872	1,716,916	1,248,569
Other prepaid expenses and receivables	1,213,716	1,153,969	1,062,593
Total Current Assets	14,042,733	11,281,883	11,386,028
Investments	1,125,262	1,229,873	134,013
Property and Equipment, at Cost:			
Land	494,021	488,342	370,949
Buildings	3,589,050	3,228,485	2,655,356
Equipment	10,393,402	9,947,503	8,813,517
Construction in progress	1,121,328	737,609	920,599
	15,597,801	14,401,939	12,760,421
Less: accumulated depreciation and amortization	8,079,652	7,455,504	6,757,280
Net Property and Equipment	7,518,149	6,946,435	6,003,141
Intangible Assets, net of amortization	5,720,478	6,403,619	4,741,647
Goodwill	10,128,841	9,449,281	5,219,247
Deferred Income Taxes and Other Assets	1,178,461	867,081	1,657,127
	$39,713,924	$36,178,172	$29,141,203

The accompanying notes to consolidated financial statements are an integral part of this statement.

Consolidated Balance Sheet

(dollars in thousands)

December 31	2007	2006	2005
Liabilities and Shareholders' Investment			
Current Liabilities:			
Short-term borrowings	$ 1,827,361	$ 5,305,985	$ 212,447
Trade accounts payable	1,219,529	1,175,590	1,032,516
Salaries, wages and commissions	859,784	807,283	625,254
Other accrued liabilities	3,713,104	3,850,723	2,783,473
Dividends payable	504,540	453,994	423,335
Income taxes payable	80,406	262,344	488,926
Current portion of long-term debt	898,554	95,276	1,849,563
Total Current Liabilities	9,103,278	11,951,195	7,415,514
Long-term Debt	9,487,789	7,009,664	4,571,504
Post-employment Obligations and Other Long-term Liabilities	3,344,317	3,163,127	2,155,837
Deferred Income Taxes	—	—	583,077
Commitments and Contingencies			
Shareholders' Investment:			
Preferred shares, one dollar par value			
Authorized — 1,000,000 shares, none issued	—	—	—
Common shares, without par value			
Authorized — 2,400,000,000 shares			
Issued at stated capital amount —			
Shares: 2007: 1,580,854,677;			
2006: 1,550,590,438; 2005: 1,553,769,958	6,104,102	4,290,929	3,477,460
Common shares held in treasury, at cost —			
Shares: 2007: 30,944,537;			
2006: 13,347,272; 2005: 14,534,979	(1,213,134)	(195,237)	(212,255)
Earnings employed in the business	10,805,809	9,568,728	10,404,568
Accumulated other comprehensive income (loss)	2,081,763	389,766	745,498
Total Shareholders' Investment	17,778,540	14,054,186	14,415,271
	$39,713,924	$36,178,172	$29,141,203

Notes to Consolidated Financial Statements

In addition, Abbott will also pay to Boston Scientific $250 million each upon government approvals to market the *Xience V* drug-eluting stent in the U.S. and in Japan. Government approvals are anticipated in 2008 for the U.S. and in 2009 for Japan. Each $250 million payment will result in the recording of additional goodwill. The allocation of the purchase price resulted in a charge of $665 million for acquired in-process research and development, intangible assets of $1.2 billion, goodwill (primarily deductible) of $1.7 billion and tangible net assets of $580 million. Acquired intangible assets are being amortized over 4 to 15 years. Deductible acquired in-process research and development was charged to income in 2006. The net tangible assets acquired consist primarily of property and equipment of approximately $530 million, trade accounts receivable of approximately $250 million and inventories of approximately $120 million, net of assumed liabilities, primarily trade accounts payable, litigation reserves and other liabilities.

A substantial amount of the acquired in-process research and development charge relating to the Guidant acquisition related to drug eluting and bioabsorbable stents. The research efforts ranged from 35 percent to 85 percent complete at the date of acquisition. The valuation method used to fair value the projects was the Multi-period Excess Earnings Method (Income Approach) and the risk-adjusted discount rates used ranged from 16 percent to 25 percent. In developing assumptions for the valuation model, comparable Abbott products or products marketed by competitors were used to estimate pricing, margins and expense levels. As of December 31, 2007, the research efforts were primarily on schedule. The estimated projected costs to complete totaled approximately $390 million as of December 31, 2007, with anticipated product launch dates from 2008 through 2013. There have been no significant changes in the development plans for the acquired incomplete projects. Significant net cash inflows will commence within one to two years after product launch.

In order to facilitate Boston Scientific's acquisition of Guidant, Abbott also acquired 64.6 million shares of Boston Scientific common stock directly from Boston Scientific and loaned $900 million to a wholly-owned subsidiary of Boston Scientific. The common stock was valued at $1.3 billion and the note receivable was valued at $829 million at the acquisition date. In connection with the acquisition of the shares, Boston Scientific is entitled to certain after-tax gains upon Abbott's sale of the shares. In addition, Boston Scientific agreed to reimburse Abbott for certain borrowing costs on debt incurred to acquire the Boston Scientific shares. Abbott recorded a net derivative financial instruments liability of $59 million for the gain-sharing derivative financial instrument liability and the interest derivative financial instrument asset. The effect of recording the shares, the loan to Boston Scientific and the derivative financial instruments at fair value on the date of acquisition resulted in the recording of additional goodwill of approximately $204 million. Changes in the fair value of the derivative financial instruments, net are recorded in Other (income) expense, net.

In 2005, Abbott acquired the remaining interest in a small medical products company and a less than 50 percent equity interest in a small medical products company for $25 million. In 2005, Abbott also acquired additional rights related to *HUMIRA* for approximately $270 million, which are being amortized over 13 years.

Had the above acquisitions taken place on January 1 of the previous year, consolidated net sales and income would not have been significantly different from reported amounts.

Note 11 — Goodwill and Intangible Assets
(dollars in millions)

Abbott recorded goodwill of $53, $3,721 and $69 in 2007, 2006 and 2005, respectively, related to acquisitions. Goodwill adjustments recorded in 2007 allocated to the Pharmaceutical Products segment amounted to $194 and goodwill allocated to the Vascular Products segment amounted to $(141). Acquired goodwill allocated to the Pharmaceutical Products segment amounted to $1,590 in 2006 and goodwill allocated to the Vascular Products segment amounted to $1,688 in 2006. Foreign currency translation and other adjustments increased (decreased) goodwill in 2007, 2006 and 2005 by $627, $509 and $(535), respectively. The amount of goodwill related to reportable segments at December 31, 2007 was $6,221 for the Pharmaceutical Products segment, $210 for the Nutritional Products segment, $261 for the Diagnostic Products segment, and $2,086 for the Vascular Products segment. There were no reductions of goodwill relating to impairments or disposal of all or a portion of a business.

The gross amount of amortizable intangible assets, primarily product rights and technology, was $9,043, $8,988 and $6,776 as of December 31, 2007, 2006 and 2005, respectively, and accumulated amortization was $3,323, $2,602 and $2,053 as of December 31, 2007, 2006 and 2005, respectively. The estimated annual amortization expense for intangible assets is $710 in 2008, 2009 and 2010; $690 in 2011 and $680 in 2012. Intangible assets are amortized over 4 to 25 years (average 11 years).

Note 12 — Equity Method Investments
(dollars in millions)

Abbott's 50 percent-owned joint venture, TAP Pharmaceutical Products Inc. (TAP), is accounted for under the equity method of accounting. The investment in TAP was $159, $162 and $167 at December 31, 2007, 2006 and 2005, respectively, and dividends received from TAP were $502, $487 and $343 in 2007, 2006 and 2005, respectively. Abbott performs certain administrative and manufacturing services for TAP at negotiated rates that approximate fair value. Summarized financial information for TAP is as follows:

Year Ended December 31	2007	2006	2005
Net sales	$3,002	$3,363	$3,260
Cost of sales	720	836	883
Income before taxes	1,564	1,524	1,379
Net income	996	952	883

December 31	2007	2006	2005
Current assets	$1,101	$1,181	$1,339
Total assets	1,354	1,333	1,470
Current liabilities	914	955	1,082
Total liabilities	1,037	1,009	1,136

Undistributed earnings of investments accounted for under the equity method amounted to approximately $136 as of December 31, 2007.

WorldCom, Inc.—Capitalized Costs and Earnings Quality

Organized in 1983, WorldCom, Inc. provides a broad range of communications services to both U.S. and non-U.S. based businesses and consumers. The company's strategy is to provide service through their own facilities throughout the world instead of being restricted to a particular geographic location. The company's core business is communications services, which include voice, data, Internet and international services. During the second quarter of 2002, WorldCom announced that costs totaling $3.9 billion had been improperly capitalized in five preceding quarters which overstated pretax earnings by the same amount. Subsequently, the magnitude of the fraudulent accounting entries has increased and WorldCom filed for Chapter 11 bankruptcy protection. (Source: Company 2001 Form 10-K)

Learning Objectives
- Distinguish between costs and expenses.
- Distinguish between costs that should be capitalized and costs that should be expensed.
- Restate earnings to reflect generally accepted accounting principles.
- Understand management's incentives to engage in "aggressive accounting."

Refer to the 2001 financial statements and notes for WorldCom, Inc. and to the *Wall Street Journal* article dated June 27, 2002.

✧ Concepts ✧

a. FASB Statement of Concepts No. 6 (a replacement for SCON No. 3), *Elements of Financial Statements*, describes the building blocks with which financial statements are constructed.

    i.   Explain, in your own words, how SCON 6 defines "asset" and "expense."

    ii.   In general, when should costs be expensed and when should they be capitalized as assets?

b. What becomes of "costs" after their initial capitalization? Describe, in general terms, how the balance sheet and the income statement are affected by a decision to capitalize a given cost.

✧ Process ✧

c. Refer to WorldCom's statement of operations. What did the company report as line costs for the year ended December 31, 2001? Prepare the journal entry to record these transactions for the year. Explain in your own words, what these "line costs" are.

d. Refer to the *Wall Street Journal* article. Describe the types of costs that were improperly capitalized at WorldCom. Explain, in your own words, what transactions give rise to these costs. Do these costs meet your definition of assets in part *a* above?

e. Prepare a single journal entry to record the improperly capitalized line costs of $3.055 billion for the year. Where did these costs appear on the balance sheet? Where on the statement of cash flows?

✧ Analysis ✧

f. In a sworn statement to the Securities and Exchange Commission, WorldCom revealed details of the improperly capitalized amounts (in millions) in 2001: $771 in the first quarter, $610 in the second quarter, $743 in the third quarter, and $931 in the fourth quarter. Assume that WorldCom planned to depreciate these capitalized costs over the midpoint of the range for transmission equipment as disclosed in note 1. Further assume that depreciation begins in the quarter that assets are acquired (or costs capitalized). Calculate the related depreciation expense for 2001. Prepare the journal entry to record this depreciation.

g. Use your answers to parts e and f above, to determine what WorldCom's net income would have been in 2001 had line-costs not been improperly capitalized. Use 35% as an approximation of WorldCom's 2001 marginal income tax rate, in your calculations. State any other assumptions you make. Is the difference in net income material?

h. "… *former employees and people familiar with WorldCom's operations, reveal a grow-at-any-cost culture that made it possible for employees and managers to game the system internally and to deceive investors about the health of the business.*" (Washington Post, August 29, 2002). Why would WorldCom's management engage in such deception (i.e., capitalizing costs that are normally immediately expensed)? That is, what incentives did WorldCom management have to defer costs?

i. In your opinion, what rules and internal controls might have been put in place at WorldCom to detect this sort of improper accounting?

j. What economic consequences arise when a publicly traded company's financial reports are revealed as fraudulent?

June 27, 2002 1:33 p.m. EDT

PAGE ONE

Accounting Spot-Check Unearthed A Scandal in WorldCom's Books

By JARED SANDBERG, DEBORAH SOLOMON and REBECCA BLUMENSTEIN
Staff Reporters of THE WALL STREET JOURNAL

NEW YORK -- It all started a few weeks ago with a check of the books by Cynthia Cooper, an internal auditor for **WorldCom** Inc. The telecom giant's newly installed chief executive had asked for a financial review, and her job was to spot-check records of capital expenditures.

According to people familiar with the matter, Ms. Cooper soon found something that caught her eye. In quarter after quarter, starting in 2001, WorldCom's chief financial officer, Scott Sullivan, had been using an unorthodox technique to account for one of the long-distance company's biggest expenses: charges paid to local telephone networks to complete calls.

Instead of marking them as operating expenses, he moved a significant portion into the category of capital expenditures. The maneuver was worth hundreds of millions of dollars to WorldCom's bottom line, effectively turning a loss for all of 2001 and the first quarter of 2002 into a profit.

Ms. Cooper contacted Max Bobbitt, the head of WorldCom's auditing committee, setting in motion a chain of events that resulted in Mr. Sullivan's firing late Tuesday. The company said that it had turned up $3.8 billion of expenses that were improperly booked and will now be restated.

Even in a season when one giant company after another has been laid low by accounting scandals, WorldCom's disclosure stands out. The coming financial restatement will almost certainly be one of the largest in corporate history -- more than six times that of Enron Corp. More important, it offers the clearest warning sign yet of the ease with which telecom companies, operating on the frontiers of accounting amidst a huge speculative excess, could manipulate their books to inflate their earnings.

President Bush himself called for a full investigation into the spiraling scandal, calling the accounting irregularities "outrageous."

The loss of trust by investors, customers and financial institutions has been profound. Shareholders have lost more than $2 trillion, and more than 500,000 telecom workers have lost their jobs.

"There was so much pressure on companies to continue to grow and support those share prices," says Charles H. Noski, who is a vice chairman of **AT&T** Corp. and its former chief financial officer. AT&T hasn't come under fire for its accounting, although its stock has tumbled amid the general industry malaise. "People are going to try to figure out how do you know enough to trust what corporations are telling investors. There is an overhang on the market now."

Stock markets around the world reacted swiftly Wednesday to a growing sense of unease that, like WorldCom itself, much of the explosive, double-digit growth of the stock market boom may have been a mirage. The Dow Jones Industrial Average fell 6.7 points. **Qwest Communications International** Inc., a big Denver telecom company under investigation by the Securities and Exchange Commission for alleged accounting irregularities, saw its stock fall nearly 60% Wednesday, to $1.79 a share. The company has denied wrongdoing.

For WorldCom, the development could well spell the end of the nation's No. 2 long-distance company, which sells to consumers under the MCI brand name. WorldCom's banks said they wouldn't immediately act on debt covenants that could allow them to call their loans. But people familiar with the matter said a bankruptcy-court filing remains an option. Nasdaq halted trading in WorldCom's stock all day Wednesday. It currently stands at 83 cents, far from its high of $64.50 in 1999.

The SEC Wednesday <u>filed civil fraud charges</u> against WorldCom, saying the company "falsely portrayed itself as a profitable business." The U.S. Justice Department has launched a probe that could result in criminal charges, according to people familiar with the situation. These people said WorldCom and Mr. Sullivan could potentially face charges including securities fraud, bank fraud and mail fraud.

Andrew J. Graham, Mr. Sullivan's attorney, said he wouldn't comment. But people familiar with Mr. Sullivan say he firmly believes he didn't do anything wrong.

Brad Burns, a spokesman for WorldCom, declined to comment on the SEC charges but said the company is "very focused on serving our customers, working with our bank lenders and ensuring our employees that we'll get through these difficult times."

Scott Sullivan

WorldCom had already been reeling under a heavy debt load and declining revenues. In April, the board ousted the long-time chief executive, Bernard J. Ebbers, in part because of a controversy surrounding a $408 million loan WorldCom extended to him to cover margin calls on loans secured by company stock. Since then, its new chief executive, John Sidgmore, has been trying to hold off a financial crisis and restore investor confidence.

Internal Investigation

At this point, it's unclear whether anyone else at WorldCom knew what Mr. Sullivan was doing. The company has launched an internal investigation and is trying to determine who knew what and when. WorldCom has hired William McLucas, an SEC former enforcement chief who assisted in an internal probe of Enron's accounting, to help in the WorldCom investigation. One of the people under scrutiny is Mr. Ebbers, a close confidant of Mr. Sullivan. The two men shared an adjoining office at their Clinton, Miss., headquarters.

Mr. Ebbers couldn't be reached for comment, and his attorney didn't have any immediate comment.

What is clear is that over the past five quarters as the market softened, Mr. Sullivan undertook an aggressive approach to the company's way of accounting for one of its biggest expenses.

This happened just as WorldCom's acquisition machine was grinding to a halt. Mr. Ebbers had cobbled together his empire from modest roots as a long-distance reseller and motel owner in Mississippi. Mr. Sullivan became a trusted ally after Mr. Ebbers acquired his company, Advanced Telecommunications Corp., in 1992. The two executives worked in tandem as WorldCom, then known as LDDS, acquired dozens of companies, seemingly springing out of nowhere to snag MCI Communications Corp. in 1998. WorldCom's double-digit growth rates helped it win a takeover battle for MCI, trumping a bid by GTE Corp.

But by early 2001, the growth had started to slow. The booming telecommunications market was beginning to falter from a glut of capacity after a frenzied investment in fiber-optic networks. Suddenly, it found it had too much capacity. It had signed multibillion-dollar contracts with third-party telecommunications firms such as Baby Bells to insure it would be able to complete calls for its customers. An appraisal commissioned by WorldCom showed that roughly 15% of these costs weren't producing revenue, according to a WorldCom insider.

Mr. Sullivan made an important decision, says a person familiar with his thinking. Instead of reducing profits by those costs whenever WorldCom issued results in 2001, Mr. Sullivan would spread those costs to a future time when the anticipated revenue might arrive.

He was in a murky area. One of accounting's most basic rules is that capital costs have to be connected to long-term investments, not ongoing activities.

CREATIVE ACCOUNTING

By booking certain costs as a capital expense, WorldCom was able to boost its bottom line. A look at how the company conducted such accounting in 2001.

WorldCom's accounting

1. Accounts $3.1 billion in 'line costs,' including telecom access and transport charges, as capital expenditure.

2. Plans to amortize $3.1 billion over a period of time, possibly as much as 10 years.

3. Reports net income of $1.38 billion for 2001.

Expense

Capital Expense	Operating Expense
Amortization	Cost of Business
Higher Net Income	Lower Net Income

Generally accepted accounting principles

1. The $3.1 billion 'line-cost' expense is booked as an operating expense.

2. The entire $3.1 billion would have been counted as a cost of business for that quarter.

3. Net income for 2001 would have been a loss, amount to be determined.

According to WorldCom, the company transferred more than $3.8 billion in "line cost" expenses to its capital accounts. WorldCom hasn't provided more detail about what those costs included, or what portions of their line costs were improperly capitalized. But line costs, according to the company's most recent annual report filed with the SEC, consist principally of access charges and transport charges. WorldCom's "line costs" totaled $8.12 billion in 2001, according to the company's income statement.

While companies can capitalize some costs like installation and labor, the magnitude of WorldCom's capitalization appears to be far beyond its industry peers.

A person familiar with the matter says Mr. Sullivan didn't appear to have realized any personal financial gain from his strategy. At WorldCom's peak in 1999, his shares were worth more than $150 million, and he currently owns about 3.2 million shares. But he hasn't sold any WorldCom stock in nearly two years, according to Thomson Financial/Lancer Analytics, a data service.

Mr. Sullivan never attempted to cover up the aggressive accounting method, the person familiar with the matter says. Details are spelled out clearly enough in internal company documents, this person says, that "other people had to see it unless they were blind." Still, Arthur Andersen, WorldCom's auditor at the time, said it wasn't consulted or notified about the capitalized expenses.

The CFO capitalized costs in amounts ranging from $540 million to $797 million each quarter. When April results came out this year, though, he began to doubt whether some of his revenue projections related to the line costs would be realized. In May, according to people familiar with his thinking, Mr. Sullivan was contemplating taking a charge. On May 23, the board was notified that a charge would include the line costs, but didn't signal how much it would be, a person familiar with the matter said.

Then in early June, Ms. Cooper called Mr. Bobbitt, chairman of the board's audit committee, notifying him that she had found suspect entries in the books.

Mr. Bobbitt had been under fire for months for his controversial role in extending Mr. Ebbers the $408 million personal loan from WorldCom. He quickly notified the newly hired accountants, KPMG LLP, of the discrepancy. The firm set to work.

Two weeks ago, KPMG came to WorldCom's offices in Washington and told the committee there was a problem. The investigation continued through the week and last Thursday the audit committee met at KPMG's Washington offices to ask Mr. Sullivan and company controller David Myers to justify their accounting treatment. Mr. Sullivan, according to people familiar with the situation, gave an impassioned defense of his decision, saying that since WorldCom wasn't receiving revenue, he could defer the costs of leasing the lines until they produced revenue. But KPMG officials weren't satisfied, citing accounting rules that clearly dictate that the costs of operating leases can't be delayed. The KPMG partner in charge of the WorldCom account, told Mr. Sullivan that he couldn't "get past the theory" but gave him the weekend to produce a so-called white paper that would set out his justification, a person close to the matter said.

Accounting experts say the rules are clear on what costs can be capitalized and what has to be expensed. "If the amounts being paid out are going to have created a long-lasting asset, then the costs depreciate and can be amortized over several years," says Carr Conway, a former SEC official and senior forensic accountant with Dickerson Financial Group in Denver. Unless the asset is going to generate value in future years, the cost for it can't be capitalized, he adds.

Weekend Huddle

Mr. Sullivan spent the weekend huddled with his team in Clinton, Miss., reviewing documents and constructing the white paper. But it wasn't going well. "He was becoming increasingly pessimistic" that he would have enough time to satisfy KPMG, said one person familiar with the matter.

At a board meeting Monday night at WorldCom's offices, Mr. Sullivan again made his case. A national practice specialist at KPMG said, however, that the issue was "an open-and-shut case," said one person who attended. "The KPMG people left no door open." After asking Mr. Sullivan to leave the room, board members concluded at the meeting that they would have to restate earnings. The meeting ended without a vote, which was postponed until Tuesday when Mr. Sullivan was fired and Mr. Myers was asked to resign.

Through it all, Mr. Sullivan was "very calm and articulate," says one person who attended the meetings. "He handled himself very well, though you could tell he was pained." As far as the board members, added another person, "most people were absolutely flabbergasted."

In a speech Wednesday, Mr. Sidgmore tried to make the most out of a bad situation. "We want to make clear that WorldCom reported itself in this matter and moved swiftly to do so," he said. "We turned ourselves in, in other words."

Write to Jared Sandberg at jared.sandberg@wsj.com, Deborah Solomon at deborah.solomon@wsj.com and Rebecca Blumenstein at rebecca.blumenstein@wsj.com

URL for this article:
http://online.wsj.com/article/0,,SB102512901721030520,00.html

WORLDCOM, INC. AND SUBSIDIARIES

CONSOLIDATED BALANCE SHEETS

(In Millions, Except Share Data)

	December 31, 2000	December 31, 2001
ASSETS		
Current assets:		
Cash and cash equivalents	$ 761	$ 1,416
Accounts receivable, net of allowance for bad debts of $1,532 in 2000 and $1,086 in 2001	6,815	5,308
Deferred tax asset	172	251
Other current assets	2,007	2,230
Total current assets	9,755	9,205
Property and equipment:		
Transmission equipment	20,288	23,814
Communications equipment	8,100	7,878
Furniture, fixtures and other	9,342	11,263
Construction in progress	6,897	5,706
	44,627	48,661
Accumulated depreciation	(7,204)	(9,852)
	37,423	38,809
Goodwill and other intangible assets	46,594	50,537
Other assets	5,131	5,363
	$ 98,903	$ 103,914
LIABILITIES AND SHAREHOLDERS' INVESTMENT		
Current liabilities:		
Short-term debt and current maturities of long-term debt	$ 7,200	$ 172
Accrued interest	446	618
Accounts payable and accrued line costs	6,022	4,844
Other current liabilities	4,005	3,576
Total current liabilities	17,673	9,210
Long-term liabilities, less current portion:		
Long-term debt	17,696	30,038
Deferred tax liability	3,611	4,066
Other liabilities	1,124	576
Total long-term liabilities	22,431	34,680
Commitments and contingencies		
Minority interests	2,592	101
Company obligated mandatorily redeemable and other preferred securities	798	1,993
Shareholders' investment:		
Series B preferred stock, par value $.01 per share; authorized, issued and outstanding: 10,693,437 shares in 2000 and none in 2001 (liquidation preference of $1.00 per share plus unpaid dividends)	—	—
Preferred stock, par value $.01 per share; authorized: 31,155,008 shares in 2000 and 30,967,637 shares in 2001; none issued	—	—
Common stock:		
WorldCom, Inc. common stock, par value $.01 per share; authorized: 5,000,000,000 shares in 2000 and none in 2001; issued and outstanding: 2,887,960,378 shares in 2000 and none in 2001	29	—
WorldCom group common stock, par value $.01 per share; authorized: none in 2000 and 4,850,000,000 shares in 2001; issued and outstanding: none in 2000 and 2,967,436,680 shares in 2001	—	30
MCI group common stock, par value $.01 per share; authorized: none in 2000 and 150,000,000 shares in 2001; issued and outstanding: none in 2000 and 118,595,711 in 2001	—	1
Additional paid-in capital	52,877	54,297
Retained earnings	3,160	4,400
Unrealized holding gain (loss) on marketable equity securities	345	(51)
Cumulative foreign currency translation adjustment	(817)	(562)
Treasury stock, at cost, 6,765,316 shares of WorldCom, Inc. in 2000, 6,765,316 shares of WorldCom group stock and 270,613 shares of MCI group stock in 2001	(185)	(185)
Total shareholders' investment	55,409	57,930
	$ 98,903	$ 103,914

The accompanying notes are an integral part of these statements.

F-3

WORLDCOM, INC. AND SUBSIDIARIES

CONSOLIDATED STATEMENTS OF OPERATIONS

(In Millions, Except Per Share Data)

	For the Years Ended December 31,		
	1999	**2000**	**2001**
Revenues	$35,908	$39,090	$35,179
Operating expenses:			
Line costs	14,739	15,462	14,739
Selling, general and administrative	8,935	10,597	11,046
Depreciation and amortization	4,354	4,878	5,880
Other charges	(8)	—	—
Total	28,020	30,937	31,665
Operating income	7,888	8,153	3,514
Other income (expense):			
Interest expense	(966)	(970)	(1,533)
Miscellaneous	242	385	412
Income before income taxes, minority interests and cumulative effect of accounting change	7,164	7,568	2,393
Provision for income taxes	2,965	3,025	927
Income before minority interests and cumulative effect of accounting change	4,199	4,543	1,466
Minority interests	(186)	(305)	35
Income before cumulative effect of accounting change	4,013	4,238	1,501
Cumulative effect of accounting change (net of income tax of $50 in 2000)	—	(85)	—
Net income	4,013	4,153	1,501
Distributions on mandatorily redeemable preferred securities and other preferred dividend requirements	72	65	117
Net income applicable to common shareholders	$ 3,941	$ 4,088	$ 1,384
Net income attributed to WorldCom group before cumulative effect of accounting change	$ 2,294	$ 2,608	$ 1,407
Cumulative effect of accounting change	$ —	$ (75)	$ —
Net income attributed to WorldCom group	$ 2,294	$ 2,533	$ 1,407
Net income (loss) attributed to MCI group before cumulative effect of accounting change	$ 1,647	$ 1,565	$ (23)
Cumulative effect of accounting change	$ —	$ (10)	$ —
Net income (loss) attributed to MCI group	$ 1,647	$ 1,555	$ (23)

	Pro Forma		
Earnings (loss) per common share:			
WorldCom group:			
Net income attributed to WorldCom group before cumulative effect of accounting change:			
Basic	$ 0.81	$ 0.91	$ 0.48
Diluted	$ 0.78	$ 0.90	$ 0.48
Cumulative effect of accounting change	$ —	$ (0.03)	$ —
Net income attributed to WorldCom group:			
Basic	$ 0.81	$ 0.88	$ 0.48
Diluted	$ 0.78	$ 0.87	$ 0.48
MCI group:			
Net income (loss) attributed to MCI group before cumulative effect of accounting change:			
Basic	$ 14.32	$ 13.61	$ (0.20)
Diluted	$ 14.32	$ 13.61	$ (0.20)
Cumulative effect of accounting change	$ —	$ (0.09)	$ —
Net income (loss) attributed to MCI group:			
Basic	$ 14.32	$ 13.52	$ (0.20)
Diluted	$ 14.32	$ 13.52	$ (0.20)

The accompanying notes are an integral part of these statements.

WORLDCOM, INC. AND SUBSIDIARIES
CONSOLIDATED STATEMENTS OF CASH FLOWS
(In Millions)

	For the Years Ended December 31,		
	1999	2000	2001
Cash flows from operating activities:			
Net income	$ 4,013	$ 4,153	$ 1,501
Adjustments to reconcile net income to net cash provided by operating activities:			
Cumulative effect of accounting change	—	85	—
Minority interests	186	305	(35)
Other charges	(8)	—	—
Depreciation and amortization	4,354	4,878	5,880
Provision for deferred income taxes	2,903	1,649	1,104
Change in assets and liabilities, net of effect of business combinations:			
Accounts receivable, net	(875)	(1,126)	281
Other current assets	143	(797)	164
Accounts payable and other current liabilities	692	(1,050)	(1,154)
All other operating activities	(403)	(431)	253
Net cash provided by operating activities	11,005	7,666	7,994
Cash flows from investing activities:			
Capital expenditures	(8,716)	(11,484)	(7,886)
Acquisitions and related costs	(1,078)	(14)	(206)
Increase in intangible assets	(743)	(938)	(694)
Decrease in other liabilities	(650)	(839)	(480)
All other investing activities	1,632	(1,110)	(424)
Net cash used in investing activities	(9,555)	(14,385)	(9,690)
Cash flows from financing activities:			
Principal borrowings (repayments) on debt, net	(2,894)	6,377	3,031
Common stock issuance	886	585	124
Distributions on mandatorily redeemable and other preferred securities and dividends paid on other equity securities	(72)	(65)	(154)
Redemptions of preferred stock	—	(190)	(200)
All other financing activities	—	(84)	(272)
Net cash provided by (used in) financing activities	(2,080)	6,623	2,529
Effect of exchange rate changes on cash	(221)	(19)	38
Net increase (decrease) in cash and cash equivalents	(851)	(115)	871
Cash and cash equivalents at beginning of period	1,727	876	761
Deconsolidation of Embratel	—	—	(216)
Cash and cash equivalents at end of period	$ 876	$ 761	$ 1,416

The accompanying notes are an integral part of these statements.

WORLDCOM, INC. AND SUBSIDIARIES
NOTES TO CONSOLIDATED FINANCIAL STATEMENTS (Continued)
DECEMBER 31, 2001

(1) The Company and Significant Accounting Policies—(Continued)

Our equity in Embratel's loss for 2001 is included in miscellaneous income/(expense) in the accompanying consolidated financial statements.

Fair Value of Financial Instruments:

The fair value of long-term debt and company obligated mandatorily redeemable and other preferred securities is determined based on quoted market rates or the cash flows from such financial instruments discounted at our estimated current interest rate to enter into similar financial instruments. The carrying amounts and fair values of these financial instruments were $25.7 billion and $25.3 billion, respectively, at December 31, 2000 and $32.2 billion and $32.9 billion, respectively, at December 31, 2001. The carrying values for all our other financial instruments approximate their respective fair values.

Cash and Cash Equivalents:

We consider cash in banks and short-term investments with original maturities of three months or less as cash and cash equivalents.

Property and Equipment:

Property and equipment are stated at cost. Depreciation is provided for financial reporting purposes using the straight-line method over the following estimated useful lives:

Transmission equipment (including conduit)	4 to 40 years
Communications equipment	5 to 10 years
Furniture, fixtures, buildings and other	4 to 39 years

We evaluate the recoverability of property and equipment when events and circumstances indicate that such assets might be impaired. We determine impairment by comparing the undiscounted future cash flows estimated to be generated by these assets to their respective carrying amounts. In the event an impairment exists, a loss is recognized based on the amount by which the carrying value exceeds the fair value of the asset. If quoted market prices for an asset are not available, fair market value is determined primarily using the anticipated cash flows discounted at a rate commensurate with the risk involved. Losses on property and equipment to be disposed of are determined in a similar manner, except that fair market values are reduced for the cost to dispose.

Maintenance and repairs are expensed as incurred. Replacements and betterments are capitalized. The cost and related reserves of assets sold or retired are removed from the accounts, and any resulting gain or loss is reflected in results of operations.

We construct certain of our own transmission systems and related facilities. Internal costs directly related to the construction of such facilities, including interest and salaries of certain employees, are capitalized. Such internal costs were $625 million ($339 million in interest), $842 million ($495 million in interest) and $858 million ($498 million in interest) in 1999, 2000 and 2001, respectively.

Dr. Reddy's Laboratories Limited— Research & Development Costs

Dr. Reddy's Laboratories Limited is a leading India-based pharmaceutical company headquartered in Hyderabad, India. The Company's principal areas of operation are formulations, active pharmaceutical ingredients and intermediates, generics, critical care, biotechnology, and drug discovery. The Company's principal research and development and manufacturing facilities are located in Andhra Pradesh, India, with marketing facilities in India, Russia, the United States, the United Kingdom and Brazil. The Company's shares trade on several stock exchanges in India and, since April 11, 2001, on the New York Stock Exchange. (Source: Company 2004 Form 20-F)

Learning Objectives
* Use management's discussion and analysis and other public information to interpret economic events.
* Consider the cost components that underlie research and development expense.
* Compare and evaluate alternative accounting treatments of research and development costs.
* Understand how capitalizing previously expensed costs affects the balance sheet, the income statement, and the statement of cash flows.
* Adjust net income and balance sheet amounts to quantify the accounting effect of capitalizing previously expensed development costs.

Refer to the 2004 financial statements of Dr. Reddy's Laboratories and to the excerpt from Dr. Reddy's Annual Report on Form 20-F, which contains information about the company's research and development (R&D) program. Dr. Reddy's prepares financial statements under Indian GAAP as well as U.S. GAAP. The U.S. GAAP statements follow SFAS No. 2, which requires R&D costs be expensed as they are incurred.

✧ Concepts ✧

a. The 2004 statement of operations shows research and development expenses of Rs 1,991,629 (thousands of Rupees). What types of costs are likely included in these amounts?

b. If Dr. Reddy's followed international GAAP, its R&D accounting would be different. International GAAP is set by the International Accounting Standards Board (IASB) and promulgated through a series of International Accounting Standards (IAS) and International Financial Reporting Standards (IFRS). An excerpt from IAS 38—*Intangible Assets*, pertaining to R&D accounting, is provided.

In your opinion, which accounting principles provide more relevant balance sheet values, those of FASB's SFAS No. 2 or the IASB's IAS 38? Explain with particular reference to Dr. Reddy's research program.

✧ Process ✧

c. Provide the journal entry Dr. Reddy's Laboratories made to record 2004 R&D expense. Consider your answer to part *a* in determining which accounts are affected. (*Hint*: you will not be able to allocate specific amounts for each of the credited accounts, but you should be able to identify the accounts that are likely to be credited.)

✧ Analysis ✧

d. Assume that you are a financial analyst. You would like to compare Dr. Reddy's Laboratories to a company that follows IAS 38. As such, you decide to prepare proforma (i.e., "as if") information for Dr. Reddy's assuming they follow international GAAP (IAS 38).

To create the proforma information, assume the following.

- Consistent with the company's prior drug development strategy, all R&D costs incurred prior to fiscal 2002 were considered "research" costs under IAS 38.

- Beginning in fiscal 2002, 25% of the total R&D expenditures could be considered "development" costs and would be eligible for capitalization under IAS 38.

- Internal forecasts predict that capitalized development costs have an estimated useful life of five years. Had Dr. Reddy's followed IAS 38, they would have amortized the development costs on a straight-line basis over five years, beginning the year subsequent to their capitalization.

i. What would Dr. Reddy's Laboratories have reported as Operating Income in 2004, 2003, and 2002 under international GAAP? Comment on the trend. Are there other costs that might benefit from the same sort of proforma analysis?

ii. What gross asset amount for deferred development costs would be shown on the balance sheet at the end of each of the three years under international GAAP? What would the accumulated amortization be in each of the three years? What would the net asset be at the end of each year?

iii. How would cash be affected for fiscal 2004 if Dr. Reddy's Laboratories followed international GAAP? Would the cash flow statement be different?

e. Refer to the accompanying article, "Dr. Reddy's loses US patent court challenge." The article appeared in the March 2, 2004, issue of *The Financial Times*. If Dr. Reddy's Laboratories had followed IAS 38, what effect would the U.S. court decision have had on the fiscal 2004 financial statements?

f. Of late, the accounting for intangibles such as research and development has come under fire. Some people claim that current U.S. GAAP is deficient in measuring what they argue to be the United States' most important asset: knowledge. Comment on that position in light of the analyses you just completed.

DR. REDDY'S LABORATORIES LIMITED
EXCERPT FROM ANNUAL REPORT ON FORM 20-F
Year Ended March 31, 2004

Strategy

Our vision is to build a discovery-led global pharmaceutical company, with a strong pipeline of generics as well as innovative products. Our core businesses of active pharmaceutical ingredients and intermediates and formulations are well established with a track record of growth and profitability. In our generics business, we have built a pipeline of products that will help us drive growth in the medium-term. In addition, we are focusing our investments on innovation led businesses, including specialty pharmaceuticals and drug discovery. These businesses, while being investment intensive and with long lead times, have the potential to provide significant growth as well as sustained revenues and profitability for much longer periods due to patent protected franchises. As a result, we believe that, over the next few years, our fully established core businesses will fund the growth of our generics business and the establishment of our innovation businesses.

Research and Development

Our research and development activities can be classified into several categories, which rum (sic) parallel to the activities in our principal areas of operations:

- Formulations, where our research and development activities are directed at the development of product formulations, process validation, bioequivalency testing and other data needed to prepare a growing list of drugs that are equivalent to numerous brand name products for sale in the emerging markets.

- Active pharmaceutical ingredients and intermediates, where our research and development activities concentrate on development of chemical processes for the synthesis of active pharmaceutical ingredients for use in our generics and formulations segments and for sales in the emerging and developed markets to third parties.

- Generics, where our research and development activities are directed at the development of product formulations, process validation, bioequivalency testing and other data needed to prepare a growing list of drugs that are equivalent to numerous brand name products whose patents and regulatory exclusivity periods have expired or are nearing expiration in the regulated markets of the United States and Europe.

  During fiscal 2004, we integrated the product development capabilities in our API, generics and formulations segments to increase our focus on productivity and product delivery, by combining technical excellence with process excellence. We also strengthened our technical, intellectual property and legal skills to enhance our new product development process. This will help us leverage our core technology strengths in chemistry and formulation development with legal, regulatory and intellectual property management expertise to expand our product pipeline.

- Critical care and biotechnology, where research and development activities are directed at the development of oncology and biotechnology products for the emerging as well as regulated markets.

- Custom pharmaceuticals, where we intend to leverage the strength of our process chemistry skills to cater to the niche segment of the specialty chemical industry targeting innovator pharmaceutical companies. The research and development is directed toward supporting the business to focus on marketing of process development and manufacturing services to emerging and established pharmaceutical companies.

- Drug discovery, where we are actively pursuing discovery and development of NCEs. Our research programs focus on the following therapeutic areas:
  o Metabolic disorders
  o Cardiovascular disorders
  o Cancer
  o Bacterial infections

We are pursuing an integrated research strategy with our laboratories in the U.S. focusing on discovery of new molecular targets and designing of screening assays to screen for promising lead molecules. Discovery is followed by selection and optimization of lead molecules and further clinical development of those optimized leads at our laboratories in India.

FT FINANCIAL TIMES
World business newspaper

2 March 2004   20

Dr Reddy's loses US patent court challenge

By DAVID FIRN and KHOZEM MERCHANT

Dr Reddy's, the Indian drugs manufacturer, yesterday saw a fifth of its market value wiped out after a significant setback on a patent challenge in a US court.

The company's share price finished 18 per cent weaker at a two-year low and its capitalisation lighter by about $400m as India's leading patent-challenger said it would develop more speciality drugs despite the blow to its version of Pfizer's blockbuster drug Norvasc.

On Friday a US court overturned a lower-court judgment allowing Dr Reddy's to sell AmVaz, its version of Norvasc, a hypertension treatment that generates global revenues in excess of $2bn a year for Pfizer.

Dr Reddy's, India's second-largest drugs manufacturer, with sales of $380m in the year to March 2003, said it was "very disappointed" with the majority verdict that effectively brings to a halt its most ambitious drugs project. It had spent $10m developing AmVaz.

Dr Reddy's wants to develop value-added medicines to ease its dependency on generics, the bedrock of India's $6bn drugs industry.

AmVaz was the company's first foray into what Dr Reddy's calls speciality drugs but the strategy depended on persuading a US court that it was a genuinely new drug, not simply a slightly altered version of Norvasc.

Dr Reddy's has filed a second application on a new drug with US regulators, which should be decided in a year's time. But the company says future development will be based on drugs innovation rather than exploiting regulatory loopholes.

"This was a risky option but one we hope to mitigate by building our portfolio of speciality drugs," the company said.

A ruling in favour of Dr Reddy's would have had industry-wide implications.

"By using Pfizer's early experimental data, Dr Reddy's has been able to show bio-equivalence with a different salt of amlodipine (a chemical compound used for treating hypertension)," said Morgan Stanley in a report published before the court judgment.

"This could set a precedent for future new drug filings for alternative 'salt' versions of drugs."

Additional reporting by David Firn in London

Internally Generated Intangible Assets (excerpt from IAS 38—*Intangible Assets*)

39. It is sometimes difficult to assess whether an internally generated intangible asset qualifies for recognition. It is often difficult to:

    (a) identify whether, and the point of time when, there is an identifiable asset that will generate probable future economic benefits; and

    (b) determine the cost of the asset reliably. In some cases, the cost of generating an intangible asset internally cannot be distinguished from the cost of maintaining or enhancing the enterprise's internally generated goodwill or of running day-to-day operations.

    Therefore, in addition to complying with the general requirements for the recognition and initial measurement of an intangible asset, an enterprise applies the requirements and guidance in paragraphs 40-55 below to all internally generated intangible assets.

40. To assess whether an internally generated intangible asset meets the criteria for recognition, an enterprise classifies the generation of the asset into:

    (a) a research phase; and

    (b) a development phase.

    Although the terms "research" and "development" are defined, the terms "research phase" and "development phase" have a broader meaning for the purpose of this Standard.

41. If an enterprise cannot distinguish the research phase from the development phase of an internal project to create an intangible asset, the enterprise treats the expenditure on that project as if it were incurred in the research phase only.

Research Phase

42. *No intangible asset arising from research (or from the research phase of an internal project) should be recognized. Expenditure on research (or on the research phase of an internal project) should be recognized as an expense when it is incurred.*

43. This Standard takes the view that, in the research phase of a project, an enterprise cannot demonstrate that an intangible asset exists that will generate probable future economic benefits. Therefore, this expenditure is always recognized as an expense when it is incurred.

44. Examples of research activities are:

    (a) activities aimed at obtaining new knowledge;

    (b) the search for, evaluation and final selection of, applications of research findings or other knowledge;

    (c) the search for alternatives for materials, devices, products, processes, systems or services; and

    (d) the formulation, design, evaluation and final selection of possible alternatives for new or improved materials, devices, products, processes, systems or services.

Development Phase

45. *An intangible asset arising from development (or from the development phase of an internal project) should be recognized if, and only if, an enterprise can demonstrate all of the following:*

    (a) *the technical feasibility of completing the intangible asset so that it will be available for use or sale;*

    (b) *its intention to complete the intangible asset and use or sell it;*

    (c) *its ability to use or sell the intangible asset;*

    (d) *how the intangible asset will generate probable future economic benefits. Among other things, the enterprise should demonstrate the existence of a market for the output of the intangible asset or the intangible asset itself or, if it is to be used internally, the usefulness of the intangible asset;*

    (e) *the availability of adequate technical, financial and other resources to complete the development and to use or sell the intangible asset; and*

    (f) *its ability to measure the expenditure attributable to the intangible asset during its development reliably.*

46. In the development phase of a project, an enterprise can, in some instances, identify an intangible asset and demonstrate that the asset will generate probable future economic benefits. This is because the development phase of a project is further advanced than the research phase.

47. Examples of development activities are:

    (a) the design, construction and testing or pre-production or pre-use prototypes and models;

    (b) the design of tools, jigs, moulds and dies involving new technology;

    (c) the design, construction and operation of a pilot plant that is not of a scale economically feasible for commercial production; and

    (d) the design, construction and testing of a chosen alternative for new or improved materials, devices, products, processes, systems or services.

Report of Independent Registered Public Accounting Firm

The Board of Directors and Stockholders
Dr. Reddy's Laboratories Limited

We have audited the accompanying consolidated balance sheets of Dr. Reddy's Laboratories Limited and subsidiaries as at March 31, 2004 and 2003, and the related consolidated statements of operations, stockholders' equity and comprehensive income, and cash flows for each of the years in the three-year period ended March 31, 2004. These consolidated financial statements are the responsibility of the Company's management. Our responsibility is to express an opinion on these consolidated financial statements based on our audits.

We conducted our audits in accordance with the standards of the Public Company Accounting Oversight Board (United States). Those standards require that we plan and perform the audit to obtain reasonable assurance about whether the financial statements are free of material misstatement. An audit includes examining, on a test basis, evidence supporting the amounts and disclosures in the financial statements. An audit also includes assessing the accounting principles used and significant estimates made by management, as well as evaluating the overall financial statement presentation. We believe that our audits provide a reasonable basis for our opinion.

In our opinion, the consolidated financial statements referred to above present fairly, in all material respects, the financial position of Dr. Reddy's Laboratories Limited and subsidiaries as at March 31, 2004 and 2003, and the results of their operations and their cash flows for each of the years in the three-year period ended March 31, 2004, in conformity with U.S. generally accepted accounting principles.

As discussed in Note 4 to the consolidated financial statements, effective April 1, 2002, the Company adopted the provisions of Statement of Financial Accounting Standards (SFAS) No. 142, Goodwill and Other Intangible Assets. As discussed in Note 2(q) to the consolidated financial statements, effective April 1, 2003, the Company changed its method of accounting for stock-based employee compensation.

KPMG LLP
Manchester, United Kingdom
May 28, 2004

DR. REDDY'S LABORATORIES LIMITED AND SUBSIDIARIES
CONSOLIDATED BALANCE SHEETS
(in thousands, except share data)

	As of March 31,		
	2003	**2004**	**2004**
			Convenience translation into U.S.$ (unaudited)
ASSETS			
Current assets:			
Cash and cash equivalents	Rs.7,273,398	Rs.4,376,235	U.S.$100,835
Investment securities	-	2,536,223	58,438
Restricted cash	26,709	107,170	2,469
Accounts receivable, net of allowances	3,620,020	3,730,139	85,948
Inventories	2,781,384	3,031,651	69,854
Deferred income taxes	166,510	152,220	3,507
Due from related parties	22,863	22,437	517
Other current assets	1,235,999	1,712,864	39,467
Total current assets	15,126,883	15,668,939	361,035
Property, plant and equipment, net	4,830,480	6,331,135	145,879
Due from related parties	44,047	21,019	484
Investment securities	8,715	1,563,875	36,034
Investment in affiliates	170,184	279,182	6,433
Goodwill and intangible assets	2,867,567	2,665,620	61,420
Other assets	43,791	89,533	2,063
Total assets	Rs.23,091,667	Rs.26,619,303	U.S.$613,348

LIABILITIES AND STOCKHOLDERS' EQUITY

	2003	**2004**	**2004**
Current liabilities:			
Borrowings from banks	Rs.146,340	Rs.320,582	U.S.$ 7,387
Current portion of long-term debt	143,801	152,658	3,517
Trade accounts payable	1,685,382	2,174,295	50,099
Due to related parties	4,388	201,170	4,635
Accrued expenses	769,895	1,244,082	28,665
Other current liabilities	353,606	472,888	10,896
Total current liabilities	3,103,412	4,565,675	105,200
Long-term debt, excluding current portion	40,909	31,065	716
Deferred revenue	288,382	288,382	6,645
Deferred income taxes	700,274	571,558	13,170
Other liabilities	126,849	123,265	2,840
Total liabilities	Rs.4,259,826	Rs.5,579,945	U.S.$128,570

	2003	**2004**	**2004**
Stockholders' equity:			
Equity shares at Rs.5 par value; 100,000,000 shares authorized; Issued and outstanding; 76,515,948 shares and 76,518,949 shares as of March 31, 2003 and 2004 respectively	Rs.382,580	Rs.382,595	U.S.$8,816
Additional paid-in capital	10,085,004	10,089,152	232,469
Equity-options outstanding	135,694	256,748	5,916
Retained earnings	8,187,117	10,229,672	235,707
Equity shares held by a controlled trust: 41,400 shares	(4,882)	(4,882)	(112)
Accumulated other comprehensive income	46,328	86,073	1,983
Total stockholders' equity	18,831,841	21,039,358	484,778
Total liabilities and stockholders' equity	Rs.23,091,667	Rs.26,619,303	U.S.$613,348

See accompanying notes to the consolidated financial statements.

DR. REDDY'S LABORATORIES LIMITED AND SUBSIDIARIES
CONSOLIDATED STATEMENTS OF OPERATION
(in thousands, except share data)

	Year ended March 31,			
	2002	**2003**	**2004**	**2004**
				Convenience translation into U.S.$ (unaudited)
Revenues:				
Product sales, net of allowances for sales returns (includes excise duties of Rs.789,718, Rs.817,135 and Rs.870,079 for the years ended March 31, 2002, 2003 and 2004, respectively)	Rs.16,408,797	Rs.18,069,812	Rs.20,081,249	U.S.$462,702
License fees	124,757	-	-	-
Services	89,128	-	-	-
	16,622,682	18,069,812	20,081,249	462,702
Cost of revenues	6,868,958	7,847,573	9,346,117	215,348
Gross profit	9,753,724	10,222,239	10,735,132	247,353
Operating expenses:				
Selling, general and administrative expenses	3,674,058	5,103,213	6,562,856	151,218
Research and development expenses	742,384	1,411,838	1,991,629	45,890
Amortization expenses	487,715	419,439	382,857	8,822
Foreign exchange (gain)/loss	(208,965)	70,108	(282,419)	(6,507)
Total operating expenses	4,695,192	7,004,598	8,654,923	199,422
Operating income	5,058,532	3,217,641	2,080,209	47,931
Equity in loss of affiliates	(130,534)	(92,094)	(44,362)	(1,022)
Other (expense)/income, net	154,480	683,124	504,191	11,617
Income before income taxes and minority interest	5,082,478	3,808,671	2,540,038	58,526
Income taxes	(153,844)	(398,062)	(69,249)	(1,596)
Minority interest	(14,803)	(6,734)	3,364	78
Net income	Rs.4,913,831	Rs.3,403,875	Rs.2,474,153	U.S.$57,008
Earnings per equity share				
Basic	64.63	44.49	32.34	0.75
Diluted	64.53	44.49	32.32	0.75
Weighted average number of equity shares used in computing earnings per equity share				
Basic	76,027,565	76,515,948	76,513,764	76,513,764
Diluted	76,149,568	76,515,948	76,549,598	76,549,598

See accompanying notes to the consolidated financial statements.

DR. REDDY'S LABORATORIES LIMITED AND SUBSIDIARIES
CONSOLIDATED STATEMENT OF STOCKHOLDERS' EQUITY AND COMPREHENSIVE INCOME
(in thousands, except share data)

	Equity Shares		Additional Paid In Capital	Comprehensive Income	Equity Shares held by a Controlled Trust		Accumulated Other Comprehensive Income	Equity – Options Outstanding	Retained Earnings/(Accumulated Deficit)	Total Stockholders' Equity
	No. of shares	Amount			No. of Shares	Amount				
Balance as of March 31, 2001	63,177,560	315,889	4,296,154	-	41,400	(4,882)	6,166	-	627,137	5,240,464
Dividends	-	-	-	-	-	-	-	-	(561,676)	(561,676)
Common stock issued for ADS listing	13,225,000	66,125	5,716,600	-	-	-	-	-	-	5,782,725
Common stock issued for acquisition of minority interest	113,388	566	72,250	-	-	-	-	-	-	72,816
Comprehensive income										
Net income	-	-	-	Rs.4,913,831	-	-	-	-	4,913,831	4,913,831
Translation adjustment	-	-	-	2,337	-	-	2,337	-	-	2,337
Unrealized gain on investments, net	-	-	-	(276)	-	-	(276)	-	-	(276)
Comprehensive income				Rs.4,915,892						
Application of SFAS 123	-	-	-	-	-	-	-	7,211	-	7,211
Balance as of March 31, 2002	76,515,948	Rs.382,580	Rs.10,085,004		41,400	Rs.(4,882)	Rs.8,227	Rs.7,211	Rs.4,979,292	Rs.15,457,432
Dividends	-	-	-	-	-	-	-	-	(191,290)	(191,290)
Net loss for the quarter ended March 31, 2003 for the change in the fiscal year end of a consolidated subsidiary	-	-	-	-	-	-	-	-	(4,760)	(4,760)
Comprehensive income										
Net income	-	-	-	Rs.3,403,875	-	-	-	-	3,403,875	3,403,875
Translation adjustment	-	-	-	38,073	-	-	38,073	-	-	38,073
Unrealized gain on investments, net	-	-	-	28	-	-	28	-	-	28
Comprehensive income				Rs.3,441,976						
Application of SFAS 123	-	-	-	-	-	-	-	128,483	-	128,483
Balance as of March 31, 2003	76,515,948	Rs.382,580	Rs.10,085,004		41,400	Rs.(4,882)	Rs.46,328	Rs.135,694	Rs.8,187,117	Rs.18,831,841
Issuance of equity shares on exercise of options	3,001	15	4,148	-	-	-	-	(1,123)	-	3,040
Dividends	-	-	-	-	-	-	-	-	(431,598)	(431,598)
Comprehensive income										
Net income	-	-	-	Rs.2,474,153	-	-	-	-	2,474,153	2,474,153
Translation adjustment	-	-	-	24,725	-	-	24,725	-	-	24,725
Unrealized gain on investments, net	-	-	-	15,020	-	-	15,020	-	-	15,020
Comprehensive income				Rs.2,513,898						
Application of SFAS 123	-	-	-	-	-	-	-	122,177	-	122,177
Balance as of March 31, 2004	76,518,949	Rs.382,595	Rs.10,089,152		41,400	Rs.(4,882)	Rs.86,073	Rs.256,748	Rs.10,229,672	Rs.21,039,358
Convenience translation into U.S.$		U.S.$ 8,816	U.S.$ 232,469			U.S.$ (112)	U.S.$ 1,983	U.S.$ 5,916	U.S.$ 235,707	U.S.$ 484,778

See accompanying notes to the consolidated financial statements.

DR. REDDY'S LABORATORIES LIMITED AND SUBSIDIARIES
CONSOLIDATED STATEMENTS OF CASH FLOWS
(in thousands, except share data)

	Year ended March 31,			
	2002	2003	2004	2004
				Convenience translation into U.S.$ (unaudited)
Cash flows from operating activities:				
Net income	Rs.4,913,831	Rs.3,403,875	Rs.2,474,153	U.S.$ 57,008
Adjustments to reconcile net income to net cash from operating activities:				
Deferred tax expense/(benefit)	(268,589)	547	(134,867)	(3,108)
Gain on sale of investments	(19,420)	(6,284)	(24,786)	(571)
Depreciation and amortization	946,280	1,017,813	1,128,453	26,001
Loss on sale of property, plant and equipment	27,050	248	29,319	676
Provision for doubtful accounts receivable	78,700	93,883	19,871	458
Allowance for sales returns	92,130	193,229	169,511	3,906
Inventory write-downs.	103,141	34,239	31,898	735
Equity in loss of affiliates.	130,534	92,094	44,362	1,022
Write-down of investment.	8,209	1,679	-	-
Unrealised exchange (gain)/loss	(81,926)	79,947	(109,602)	(2,525)
Employees stock based compensation	7,211	128,483	147,730	3,404
Loss on sale of subsidiary interest	-	-	58,473	1,347
Minority interest	14,803	6,734	(3,364)	(78)
Changes in operating assets and liabilities:				
Accounts receivable	(1,451,643)	159,697	(379,413)	(8,742)
Inventories	(365,088)	(440,856)	(335,092)	(7,721)
Other assets	(180,960)	(665,278)	(276,467)	(6,370)
Due to / from related parties,net	(11,791)	5,997	148,576	3,423
Trade accounts payable	364,260	584,958	690,182	15,903
Accrued expenses	310,669	66,357	485,215	11,180
Deferred revenue	218,569	-	-	-
Taxes payable	(64,445)	(113,903)	(115,375)	(2,658)
Other liabilities	(118,740)	(276,727)	(49,547)	(1,142)
Net cash provided by operating activities	4,652,785	4,366,732	3,999,230	92,148
Cash flows from investing activities:				
Restricted cash	(6,515)	(1,524)	(67,221)	(1,549)
Expenditure on property, plant and equipment	(1,090,321)	(1,515,721)	(2,415,638)	(55,660)
Proceeds from sale of property, plant and equipment	49,301	4,311	33,558	773
Purchase of investment securities	(2,450,648)	(2,933,474)	(13,241,973)	(305,115)
Proceeds from sale of investment securities	2,363,680	2,939,603	9,167,150	211,225
Expenditure on intangible assets	(398,440)	(96,999)	(53,942)	(1,243)
Acquisition of minority interest	-	(3,208)	-	-
Proceeds from sale of subsidiary, net	-	-	81,464	1,877
Cash paid for acquisition, net of cash acquired	-	(347,684)	(9,453)	(218)
Net cash used in investing activities	(1,532,943)	(1,954,696)	(6,506,055)	(149,909)
Cash flows from financing activities:				
Proceeds from issuance of equity, net of expenses	5,782,725	-	3,040	70
Proceeds from issuance of equity, in subsidiary	-	-	2,435	56
Purchase of treasury stock	-	-	(115,990)	(2,673)
Proceeds from/(repayments of) borrowing from banks, net	(2,469,761)	43,700	184,519	4,252
Proceeds from issuance of long-term debt	6,141	1,009	-	-
Repayment of long-term debt	(1,335,546)	(6,440)	(11,072)	(255)
Principal payments under capital lease obligations	(109)	-	-	-
Dividends	(561,676)	(191,290)	(431,598)	(9,945)
Principal payments of short term loan	-	-	(7,448)	(172)
Net cash provided by/(used in) financing activities	1,421,774	(153,021)	(376,114)	(8,666)
Effect of exchange rate changes on cash	88,779	(94,991)	(14,224)	(328)
Net increase / (decrease) in cash and cash equivalents during the year	4,630,395	2,164,024	(2,897,163)	(66,755)
Cash and cash equivalents at the beginning of the year	478,979	5,109,374	7,273,398	167,590
Cash and cash equivalents at the end of the year	Rs.5,109,374	Rs.7,273,398	Rs.4,376,235	U.S.$ 100,835

91

Corning, Inc.—Current Liabilities and Contingencies

Corning is a global, technology-based corporation that operates in four business segments. Corning's Display Technologies segment (41% of total sales) manufactures glass substrates for active matrix liquid crystal displays (LCDs), that are used primarily in notebook computers, flat panel desktop monitors, and televisions. The Telecommunications segment (33% of total sales) produces optical fiber and cable, and hardware and equipment products for the worldwide telecommunications industry. Corning's environmental products (14% of total sales) include ceramic technologies and solutions for emissions and pollution control. Life Sciences laboratory products (6% of total sales) include microplate products, coated slides, filter plates for genomics sample preparation, plastic cell culture dishes, flasks, liquid handling instruments, Pyrex ® glass beakers, pipettors, centrifuge tubes and laboratory filtration products. (Excerpted from Corning's 2006 annual report.)

Learning Objectives
• Analyze current liability accounts.
• Account for multi-period warranties on products sold.
• Gain familiarity with environmental matters and accounting for contingencies.
• Read and interpret disclosures pertaining to current liabilities and contingencies.

Refer to the 2006 Corning, Inc., financial statements and selected footnotes.

 **Concepts**

a. What distinguishes a current liability from other liabilities? Why do companies report current and noncurrent liabilities separately?

b. What is a contingent liability? Explain, in your own words, when a company would record a contingent liability (i.e. a contingent loss) on its books. List some types of contingent liabilities. Do firms ever record contingent assets (i.e. contingent gains)?

c. Product warranties are a common contingent liability. From the perspective of a Corning customer, what is a product warranty? From Corning's perspective, what is a product warranty?

d. What judgments does management need to make to account for contingent liabilities?

Process

e. Consider Corning's current liabilities reported in the balance sheet and in Note 11.

   i. Explain briefly each of the following current liabilities: current portion of long-term debt, accounts payable, wages and employee benefits, asbestos settlement, income taxes and customer deposits.

   ii. Will Corning settle all of these current liabilities in cash? Explain why or why not.

f. Consider Note 14, "Commitments, Contingencies, and Guarantees."

   i. What amount does Corning report on its 2006 balance sheet for product warranties? Which balance sheet line item(s) likely captures the accrued product warranty liability?

   ii. Prepare journal entries to record Corning's warranty expense related to 2006 sales and to record the warranty settlements during 2006.

   iii. During 2006, Corning reduced the warranty liability by $6 million. Why?

g. Consider Note 1, "Significant Accounting Policies," and Note 14, "Environmental Liabilities."

i.   What amount does Corning report on its 2006 balance sheet for environmental liabilities? Explain, in your own words, what these liabilities represent. Which balance sheet line item(s) likely captures these liabilities?

ii.   How does Corning record potential reimbursements from the company's insurance providers for the environmental liabilities?

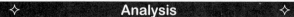

Analysis

h. Accounts payable often carry credit terms such as 3/15, net 45. These terms give the buyer, for example, 3% off the invoice price of goods purchased if paid within 15 days. Otherwise the entire invoice is payable within 45 days. What annual interest rate would Corning effectively pay if the company failed to take a discount such as the one described above? Is this a significant discount?

i. Accounts payable turnover and cash conversion cycle are measures that financial analysts commonly use to assess a company's liquidity and solvency.

i.   Calculate and interpret Corning's accounts payable turnover ratio for 2006. (*Hint*: Accounts payable turnover = Cost of sales / Average Accounts payable.) Is a lower accounts payable turnover ratio always preferable?

ii.   Calculate and interpret Corning's cash conversion cycle for 2006. (*Hint*: Cash conversion cycle, measured in days = Accounts receivable turnover, measured in days + Inventory turnover, measured in days – Accounts payable turnover, measured in days.) What steps can managers take to reduce their cash conversion cycle?

j. What percentage of total liabilities is Corning's warranty liability for 2006? Its reserve for environmental claims? Why does Corning specifically disclose these amounts given their relative magnitude?

k. Because accruals such as warranty reserves and environmental claims are based on managers' subjective estimates, they create earnings-management opportunities. Explain how managers could overstate current period income with accounts such as "Other liabilities" or "Contingencies." What effect would such actions have on income in future periods?

Consolidated Statements of Operations   Corning Incorporated and Subsidiary Companies

	For the years ended December 31,		
(In millions, except per share amounts)	2006	2005	2004
Net sales	$ 5,174	$ 4,579	$ 3,854
Cost of sales	2,891	2,595	2,439
Gross margin	2,283	1,984	1,415
Operating expenses:			
Selling, general and administrative expenses	857	756	653
Research, development and engineering expenses	517	443	355
Amortization of purchased intangibles	11	13	38
Restructuring, impairment and other charges and (credits) (Note 3)	54	(38)	1,789
Asbestos settlement (Note 8)	(2)	218	65
Operating income (loss)	846	592	(1,485)
Interest income	118	61	25
Interest expense	(76)	(108)	(133)
Loss on repurchases and retirement of debt, net (Note 12)	(11)	(16)	(36)
Other income, net	84	30	25
Income (loss) from continuing operations before income taxes	961	559	(1,604)
Provision for income taxes (Note 7)	(55)	(578)	(1,084)
Income (loss) before minority interests and equity earnings	906	(19)	(2,688)
Minority interests	(11)	(7)	(17)
Equity in earnings of affiliated companies, net of impairments (Note 8)	960	611	454
Income (loss) from continuing operations	1,855	585	(2,251)
Income from discontinued operation (Note 2)			20
Net income (loss)	$ 1,855	$ 585	$ (2,231)
Basic earnings (loss) per common share (Note 17):			
Continuing operations	$ 1.20	$ 0.40	$ (1.62)
Discontinued operation			0.01
Basic earnings (loss) per common share	$ 1.20	$ 0.40	$ (1.61)
Diluted earnings (loss) per common share (Note 17):			
Continuing operations	$ 1.16	$ 0.38	$ (1.62)
Discontinued operation			0.01
Diluted earnings (loss) per common share	$ 1.16	$ 0.38	$ (1.61)

The accompanying notes are an integral part of these consolidated financial statements.

Consolidated Balance Sheets

Corning Incorporated and Subsidiary Companies

	December 31,	
(In millions, except share and per share amounts)	**2006**	2005

Assets

Current assets:		
Cash and cash equivalents	**$ 1,157**	$ 1,342
Short-term investments, at fair value	**2,010**	1,092
Total cash, cash equivalents and short-term investments	**3,167**	2,434
Trade accounts receivable, net of doubtful accounts and allowances - $21 and $24	**746**	629
Inventories (Note 6)	**639**	570
Deferred income taxes (Note 7)	**47**	44
Other current assets	**199**	183
Total current assets	**4,798**	3,860
Investments (Note 8)	**2,522**	1,729
Property, net of accumulated depreciation - $4,087 and $3,632 (Note 9)	**5,193**	4,675
Goodwill and other intangible assets, net (Note 10)	**316**	338
Deferred income taxes (Note 7)	**114**	10
Other assets	**122**	595
Total Assets	**$13,065**	$ 11,207

Liabilities and Shareholders' Equity

Current liabilities:		
Current portion of long-term debt (Note 12)	**$ 20**	$ 18
Accounts payable	**631**	690
Other accrued liabilities (Note 11)	**1,668**	1,662
Total current liabilities	**2,319**	2,370
Long-term debt (Note 12)	**1,696**	1,789
Postretirement benefits other than pensions (Note 13)	**739**	593
Other liabilities (Note 11)	**1,020**	925
Total liabilities	**5,774**	5,677
Commitments and contingencies (Note 14)		
Minority interests	**45**	43
Shareholders' equity (Note 16):		
Common stock – Par value $0.50 per share; Shares authorized: 3.8 billion		
Shares issued: 1,582 million and 1,552 million	**791**	776
Additional paid-in capital	**12,008**	11,548
Accumulated deficit	**(4,992)**	(6,847)
Treasury stock, at cost; Shares held: 17 million and 16 million	**(201)**	(168)
Accumulated other comprehensive (loss) income	**(360)**	178
Total shareholders' equity	**7,246**	5,487
Total Liabilities and Shareholders' Equity	**$13,065**	$ 11,207

The accompanying notes are an integral part of these consolidated financial statements.

2006 Financials

1. Summary of Significant Accounting Policies (continued)

Allowance for Doubtful Accounts

The Company's allowance for doubtful accounts is determined based on a variety of factors that affect the potential collectibility of the related receivables, including length of time receivables are past due, customer credit ratings, financial stability of customers, specific one-time events and past customer history. In addition, in circumstances where the Company is made aware of a specific customer's inability to meet its financial obligations, a specific allowance is established. The majority of accounts are individually evaluated on a regular basis and appropriate reserves are established as deemed appropriate based on the above criteria. The remainder of the reserve is based on management's estimates and takes into consideration historical trends, market conditions and the composition of the Company's customer base.

Environmental Liabilities

The Company accrues for its environmental investigation, remediation, operating, and maintenance costs when it is probable that a liability has been incurred and the amount can be reasonably estimated. For environmental matters, the most likely cost to be incurred is accrued based on an evaluation of currently available facts with respect to each individual site, current laws and regulations and prior remediation experience. For sites with multiple potential responsible parties (PRP's), the Company considers its likely proportionate share of the anticipated remediation costs and the ability of the other parties to fulfill their obligations in establishing a provision for those costs. Where no amount within a range of estimates is more likely to occur than another, the minimum is accrued. When future liabilities are determined to be reimbursable by insurance coverage, an accrual is recorded for the potential liability and a receivable is recorded related to the insurance reimbursement when reimbursement is virtually certain. The uncertain nature inherent in such remediation and the possibility that initial estimates may not reflect the final outcome could result in additional costs.

Inventories

Inventories are stated at the lower of cost (first-in, first-out basis) or market.

Property, Net of Accumulated Depreciation

Land, buildings, and equipment are recorded at cost. Depreciation is based on estimated useful lives of properties using the straight-line method. Except as described in Note 3 (Restructuring, Impairment and Other Charges and (Credits)) related to accelerated depreciation arising from restructuring programs, the estimated useful lives range from 20 to 40 years for buildings and 3 to 20 years for equipment.

Included in the subcategory of equipment are the following types of assets:

Asset type	Range of useful life
Computer hardware and software	3 years
Manufacturing equipment	3 to 15 years
Furniture and fixtures	5 to 7 years
Transportation equipment	20 years

Included in manufacturing equipment are certain components of production equipment that are coated with or constructed of precious metals. These metals have an indefinite useful life because they will be returned to their elemental state and reused or sold.

Goodwill and Other Intangible Assets

Goodwill is the excess of cost of an acquired entity over the amounts assigned to assets acquired and liabilities assumed in a business combination. Goodwill is tested for impairment annually in the fourth quarter, and will be tested for impairment between annual tests if an event occurs or circumstances change that more likely than

11. Other Liabilities

Other accrued liabilities follow (in millions):

	December 31,	
	2006	2005
Current liabilities:		
Wages and employee benefits	**$ 363**	$ 325
Asbestos settlement	**656**	667
Income taxes	**125**	165
Customer deposits	**213**	164
Other current liabilities	**311**	341
Other accrued liabilities	**$1,668**	$1,662
Non-current liabilities:		
Asbestos settlement	**$ 160**	$ 152
Customer deposits	**420**	431
Other non-current liabilities	**440**	342
Other liabilities	**$1,020**	$ 925

Asbestos Settlement

The current liability is expected to be settled by contribution of our investment in PCE, assigned insurance proceeds, and 25 million shares of Corning common stock, if and when the PCC Plan becomes effective. As the timing of the settlement of the obligation under this portion of the PCC liability is outside of Corning's control, this liability is considered a "due on demand" obligation. Accordingly, this portion of the obligation has been classified as a current liability, even though it is possible that the contribution could be made in 2008 or later. The non-current liability represents the net present value of cash payments which will be contributed to the PCC Plan in six installments beginning one year after the PCC Plan is effective. Refer to Note 8 (Investments) for additional information on the asbestos settlement.

Customer Deposits

In 2005 and 2004, several of Corning's customers entered into long-term purchase and supply agreements in which Corning's Display Technologies segment will supply large-size glass substrates to these customers over periods of up to six years. As part of the agreements, these customers agreed to make advance cash deposits to Corning for a portion of the contracted glass to be purchased.

Upon receipt of the cash deposits made by customers, we record a customer deposit liability. This liability is reduced at the time of future product sales over the life of the agreements. As product is shipped to a customer, Corning recognizes revenue at the selling price and issues credit memoranda for an agreed amount of the customer deposit liability. The credit memoranda are applied against customer receivables resulting from the sale of product, thus reducing operating cash flows in later periods as these credits are applied for cash deposits received in earlier periods.

Customer deposits have been or will be received in the following periods (in millions):

	2005	2006	Estimated 2007	Total
Gross customer deposits received	$457	$171	$105	$733

In 2006 and 2005, we issued credit memoranda which totaled $126 million and $29 million for the years, respectively. These credits are not included (netted) in the above amounts.

11. Other Liabilities (continued)

Customer deposit liabilities were $633 million and $595 million at December 31, 2006 and 2005, respectively, of which $213 million and $164 million, respectively, were recorded in the current portion of other accrued liabilities in our consolidated balance sheets.

In the event customers do not make all customer deposit installment payments or elect not to purchase the agreed upon quantities of product, subject to specific conditions outlined in the agreements, Corning may retain certain amounts of the customer deposits. If Corning does not deliver agreed upon product quantities, subject to specific conditions outlined in the agreements, Corning may be required to return certain amounts of customer deposits.

12. Debt

(In millions):

	December 31,	
	2006	2005
Current portion of long-term debt	**$ 20**	$ 18
Long-term debt		
Notes, 6.3%, due 2009	**$ 54**	$ 150
Euro notes, 6.25%, due 2010	**270**	355
Debentures, 6.75%, due 2013	**100**	100
Debentures, 5.90%, due 2014	**200**	200
Debentures, callable, 6.05%, due 2015	**100**	100
Debentures, 6.20%, due 2016	**200**	200
Debentures, 8.875%, due 2016	**80**	81
Debentures, 8.875%, due 2021	**81**	82
Medium-term notes, average rate 7.66%, due through 2025	**45**	175
Debentures, 6.85%, due 2029	**150**	150
Debentures, callable, 7.25%, due 2036	**250**	
Other, average rate 3.2%, due through 2015	**186**	214
Total long-term debt	**1,716**	1,807
Less current portion of long-term debt	**20**	18
Long-term debt	**$1,696**	$1,789

At December 31, 2006 and 2005, the weighted-average interest rate on short-term borrowings was 2.4% and 2.2%, respectively.

Based on borrowing rates currently available to us for loans with similar terms and maturities, the fair value of long-term debt was $1.8 billion at December 31, 2006, and $1.9 billion at December 31, 2005.

The following table shows debt maturities by year at December 31, 2006 (in millions):

2007	2008	2009	2010	2011	Thereafter
$20	$20	$72	$297	$51	$1,247

In the first quarter of 2005, we completed negotiations with a group of banks on a new revolving credit facility. Concurrent with the closing of this credit facility, we terminated our previous $2 billion revolving line of credit that was set to expire in August 2005. The facility negotiated in 2005 provided us access to a $975 million unsecured multi-currency revolving line of credit and was set to expire in March 2010.

14. Commitments, Contingencies, and Guarantees (continued)

FASB Interpretation No. 45, "Guarantor's Accounting and Disclosure Requirements for Guarantees, Including Indirect Guarantees of Indebtedness of Others" (FIN 45), requires a company, at the time a guarantee is issued, to recognize a liability for the fair value or market value of the obligation it assumes. In the normal course of our business, we do not routinely provide significant third-party guarantees. Generally, third-party guarantees provided by Corning are limited to certain financial guarantees, including stand-by letters of credit and performance bonds, and the incurrence of contingent liabilities in the form of purchase price adjustments related to attainment of milestones. These guarantees have various terms, and none of these guarantees are individually significant.

We have agreed to provide a credit facility related to Dow Corning. The funding of the Dow Corning credit facility will be required only if Dow Corning is not otherwise able to meet its scheduled funding obligations in its confirmed Bankruptcy Plan. The purchase obligations primarily represent raw material and energy-related take-or-pay contracts. We believe a significant majority of these guarantees and contingent liabilities will expire without being funded.

Minimum rental commitments under leases outstanding at December 31, 2006 follow (in millions):

2007	2008	2009	2010	2011	2012 and thereafter
$62	$66	$28	$24	$24	$82

Total rental expense was $65 million for 2006, $67 million for 2005 and $54 million for 2004.

A reconciliation of the changes in the product warranty liability for the year ended December 31 follows (in millions):

	2006	2005
Balance at January 1	**$ 27**	$ 42
Adjustments for warranties issued for current year sales	**$ 7**	$ 5
Adjustments for warranties related to prior year sales	**$ (6)**	$ (6)
Foreign currency translation		$ (1)
Settlements made during the current year	**$ (2)**	$ (13)
Balance at December 31	**$ 26**	$ 27

Corning is a defendant in various lawsuits, including environmental, product-related suits, the Dow Corning and PCC matters discussed in Note 8 (Investments), and is subject to various claims which arise in the normal course of business. In the opinion of management, the ultimate disposition of these matters will not have a material adverse effect on Corning's consolidated financial position, liquidity, or results of operations.

We have been named by the Environmental Protection Agency under the Superfund Act, or by state governments under similar state laws, as a potentially responsible party for 18 active hazardous waste sites. Under the Superfund Act, all parties who may have contributed any waste to a hazardous waste site, identified by such Agency, are jointly and severally liable for the cost of cleanup unless the Agency agrees otherwise. It is our policy to accrue for the estimated liability related to Superfund sites and other environmental liabilities related to property owned and operated by us based on expert analysis and continual monitoring by both internal and external consultants. At December 31, 2006 and 2005, we had accrued approximately $16 million (undiscounted) and $13 million (undiscounted), respectively, for the estimated liability for environmental cleanup and related litigation. Based upon the information developed to date, we believe that the accrued amount is a reasonable estimate of our liability and that the risk of an additional loss in an amount materially higher than that accrued is remote.

Johnson & Johnson—Retirement Obligations

Johnson & Johnson was incorporated in the State of New Jersey in 1887 and is engaged in research and development, manufacture and sale of a broad range of products in the health care field. The company has three business segments: Consumer (over-the-counter body care, nutritional and pharmaceutical products), Pharmaceutical (therapeutic products that address cardiovascular, dermatology, gastrointestinal, and pain management problems) and Medical Devices and Diagnostics (products used by medical professionals and diagnostic laboratories). The company has approximately 119,200 employees worldwide and is listed on the NYSE. (Source: Company 2007 Form 10-K)

Learning Objectives
- Read and interpret retirement benefit (pension) footnotes.
- Understand the difference between expensing and funding retirement benefit obligations.
- Evaluate the impact of actuarial assumptions on pension expense, assets, and obligations.

Refer to the 2007 Johnson & Johnson financial statements and selected notes. Note that the company uses the term "retirement plan" to refer to its pension plan. The case uses the terms interchangeably.

✧ Concepts ✧

a. There are two general types of retirement (i.e. pension) plans—defined benefit plans and defined contribution plans.

   i. How do these two types of plans differ? Which type does Johnson & Johnson have?

   ii. Explain why retirement plan obligations are liabilities.

   iii. List some of the assumptions that are necessary in order to account for retirement plan obligations.

b. In general, companies' pension obligations are influenced each year by four main types of activities: service cost, interest cost, actuarial gains or losses, and benefits paid to retirees. Explain each of the four activities in your own words.

c. In general, companies' pension assets are influenced each year by three main types of activities: actual return on pension investments, company contributions to the plan, and benefits paid to retirees. Explain each of the three items in your own words.

d. In general, companies' pension expense and pension plan assets both have a "return on plan assets" component. How do the two returns differ? Explain the rationale for this difference.

e. Johnson & Johnson provides other benefits to retirees including health-care and insurance benefits. What is the primary difference between the company's other-benefits plans and its retirement plans?

✧ Process ✧

f. Consider Johnson & Johnson's pension expense detailed on page 61 of the company's annual report. Note that the company uses the term "net periodic benefit cost" to refer to pension expense.

   i. How much pension expense did Johnson & Johnson report on its 2007 income statement?

   ii. Prepare the journal entry to record the service cost and interest cost portion of the 2007 pension expense.

g. Consider Johnson & Johnson's retirement plan obligation, that is, the pension liability, as detailed on page 62 of the company's annual report.

i. What is the value at December 31, 2007, of the company's retirement plan obligation? What does this value represent? How reliable is this number?

ii. What is the pension-related interest cost for the year? Compute the average interest rate the company must have used to calculate interest cost during 2007. Does this rate seem reasonable? Explain.

iii. What amount of pension benefits were paid to retirees during the year? Did Johnson and Johnson pay cash for these benefits? How do the benefits paid affect the retirement plan obligation and the retirement plan assets?

h. Consider Johnson & Johnson' retirement plan assets that is, the pension plan asset, as detailed on page 62 of the company's annual report.

i. What is the value at December 31, 2007, of the retirement plan assets held by Johnson & Johnson's retirement plan? What "value" is this?

ii. Compare the amount of the expected return on plan assets to the amount of the actual return during 2006 and 2007. Are these differences significant? In your opinion, which return better reflects the economics of the company's pension expense?

iii. How much did Johnson & Johnson and their employees contribute to the retirement plan during 2007? How does that compare to contributions in 2006? (See page 63.)

iv. What types of investments are in Johnson & Johnson's retirement plan assets?

i. Is the company's retirement plan under funded or over funded at December 31, 2007? At December 31, 2006? Where does this funded status appear on the company's balance sheet?

j. Consider Johnson & Johnson's "Other benefits" plans, as detailed on page 62 of the company's annual report.

i. What is the total obligation for other benefits at December 2007? Is the other benefits plan under funded or over funded?

ii. Compare the funded status of the other benefits plan to that of the pension plan. Speculate on why the funded status of the two plans differs so dramatically.

Analysis

k. Pension accounting requires management to make a number of estimates about investment returns, discount rates, and future costs.

i. Consider Johnson & Johnson's retirement plan assets. Estimate the actual rate of return (in percentage terms) that the plan assets earned in 2007. How does that return compare to the expected return?

ii. During 2007, Johnson & Johnson changed the discount rate used to calculate its domestic projected retirement benefit obligation from 6% to 6½ %. How does this rate change affect the company's retirement obligation?

iii. Johnson & Johnson now projects compensation rate increases of 4% for international plans. How does this compare to prior years? How did the rate change the company's pension expense in 2007?

l. Calculate the combined retirement and other benefits expense over the past three years. (See page 61).

i. What general trend do you notice? Do you consider this trend persistent? That is, do you expect it to continue?

ii. Retirement and other benefits expense includes an operating component and a nonoperating component. Calculate both components for each of the three years. What trends do you notice in the components? Do you consider these trends persistent?

m. Under current U.S. GAAP, Johnson & Johnson includes on its balance sheet the net funded status of its retirement plans. Consider the balance sheet effects of instead including the gross assets of both the retirement plans and the other benefit plans and their respective gross obligations.

    i.   Use the table below to show how total assets and total liabilities on the balance sheet would be affected.

	Gross amount that would be added	Net amount currently included	Net amount that would be added
Retirement and Other benefit plan Assets			
Retirement and Other benefit plan Liabilities			

    ii.   Determine the amounts and ratios below using Johnson & Johnson's reported numbers. Then, recompute the amounts and ratios on a pro forma basis taking into account the restated assets and liabilities you calculated in part i above. For purposes of these calculations, use year-end balance sheet numbers and assume that the company's marginal tax rate, as approximated by the combined federal and state statutory rates is 35%.

	As reported	Pro forma
Total assets		
Total liabilities		
Liabilities to equity ratio		
Return on assets		
Return on equity		

    iii.   In your opinion, which set of ratios better reflects the economic reality, the as reported or the pro forma ratios? Explain.

Consolidated Balance Sheets

Johnson & Johnson and Subsidiaries

At December 30, 2007 and December 31, 2006 (Dollars in Millions Except Share and Per Share Data) (Note 1)	2007	2006
Assets		
Current assets		
Cash and cash equivalents (Notes 1 and 14)	$ 7,770	4,083
Marketable securities (Notes 1 and 14)	1,545	1
Accounts receivable trade, less allowances for doubtful accounts $193 (2006, $160)	9,444	8,712
Inventories (Notes 1 and 2)	5,110	4,889
Deferred taxes on income (Note 8)	2,609	2,094
Prepaid expenses and other receivables	3,467	3,196
Total current assets	**29,945**	**22,975**
Marketable securities, non-current (Notes 1 and 14)	2	16
Property, plant and equipment, net (Notes 1 and 3)	14,185	13,044
Intangible assets, net (Notes 1 and 7)	14,640	15,348
Goodwill, net (Notes 1 and 7)	14,123	13,340
Deferred taxes on income (Note 8)	4,889	3,210
Other assets (Note 5)	3,170	2,623
Total assets	**$80,954**	**70,556**
Liabilities and Shareholders' Equity		
Current liabilities		
Loans and notes payable (Note 6)	$ 2,463	4,579
Accounts payable	6,909	5,691
Accrued liabilities	6,412	4,587
Accrued rebates, returns and promotions	2,318	2,189
Accrued salaries, wages and commissions	1,512	1,391
Accrued taxes on income	223	724
Total current liabilities	**19,837**	**19,161**
Long-term debt (Note 6)	7,074	2,014
Deferred taxes on income (Note 8)	1,493	1,319
Employee related obligations (Notes 5 and 13)	5,402	5,584
Other liabilities	3,829	3,160
Total liabilities	**37,635**	**31,238**
Shareholders' equity		
Preferred stock — without par value		
(authorized and unissued 2,000,000 shares)	—	—
Common stock — par value $1.00 per share (Note 20)		
(authorized 4,320,000,000 shares; issued 3,119,843,000 shares)	3,120	3,120
Accumulated other comprehensive income (Note 12)	(693)	(2,118)
Retained earnings	55,280	49,290
	57,707	50,292
Less: common stock held in treasury, at cost (Note 20)		
(279,620,000 shares and 226,612,000 shares)	14,388	10,974
Total shareholders' equity	**43,319**	**39,318**
Total liabilities and shareholders' equity	**$80,954**	**70,556**

See Notes to Consolidated Financial Statements

Consolidated Statements of Earnings

Johnson & Johnson and Subsidiaries

(Dollars in Millions Except Per Share Figures) (Note 1)	2007	2006	2005
Sales to customers	$61,095	53,324	50,514
Cost of products sold	17,751	15,057	14,010
Gross profit	43,344	38,267	36,504
Selling, marketing and administrative expenses	20,451	17,433	17,211
Research expense	7,680	7,125	6,462
Purchased in-process research and development (Note 17)	807	559	362
Restructuring (Note 22)	745	—	—
Interest income	(452)	(829)	(487)
Interest expense, net of portion capitalized (Note 3)	296	63	54
Other (income) expense, net	534	(671)	(214)
	30,061	23,680	23,388
Earnings before provision for taxes on income	13,283	14,587	13,116
Provision for taxes on income (Note 8)	2,707	3,534	3,056
Net earnings	**$10,576**	**11,053**	**10,060**
Basic net earnings per share (Notes 1 and 19)	**$ 3.67**	3.76	3.38
Diluted net earnings per share (Notes 1 and 19)	**$ 3.63**	3.73	3.35

See Notes to Consolidated Financial Statements

Consolidated Statements of Equity

Johnson & Johnson and Subsidiaries

(Dollars in Millions) (Note 1)	Total	Comprehensive Income	Retained Earnings	Note Receivable From Employee Stock Ownership Plan (ESOP)	Accumulated Other Comprehensive Income	Common Stock Issued Amount	Treasury Stock Amount
Balance, January 2, 2005	**$32,535**		**35,945**	**(11)**	**(515)**	**3,120**	**(6,004)**
Net earnings	10,060	10,060	10,060				
Cash dividends paid	(3,793)		(3,793)				
Employee stock compensation and stock option plans	1,485		27				1,458
Conversion of subordinated debentures	369		(132)				501
Repurchase of common stock	(1,717)		203				(1,920)
Other comprehensive income, net of tax:							
Currency translation adjustment	(415)	(415)			(415)		
Unrealized losses on securities	(16)	(16)			(16)		
Employee benefit plans	26	26			26		
Gains on derivatives & hedges	165	165			165		
Reclassification adjustment		(15)					
Total comprehensive income		**9,805**					
Note receivable from ESOP	11			11			
Balance, January 1, 2006	**$38,710**		**42,310**	**—**	**(755)**	**3,120**	**(5,965)**
Net earnings	11,053	11,053	11,053				
Cash dividends paid	(4,267)		(4,267)				
Employee compensation and stock option plans	1,858		181				1,677
Conversion of subordinated debentures	26		(10)				36
Repurchase of common stock	(6,722)						(6,722)
Other	23		23				
Other comprehensive income, net of tax:							
Currency translation adjustment	362	362			362		
Unrealized losses on securities	(9)	(9)			(9)		
Employee benefit plans	(1,710)	(34)			(1,710)		
Losses on derivatives & hedges	(6)	(6)			(6)		
Reclassification adjustment		(9)					
Total comprehensive income		**11,357**					
Balance, December 31, 2006	**$39,318**		**49,290**	**—**	**(2,118)**	**3,120**	**(10,974)**
Net earnings	10,576	10,576	10,576				
Cash dividends paid	(4,670)		(4,670)				
Employee compensation and stock option plans	2,311		131				2,180
Conversion of subordinated debentures	9		(4)				13
Repurchase of common stock	(5,607)						(5,607)
Adoption of FIN 48	(19)		(19)				
Other	(24)		(24)				
Other comprehensive income, net of tax:							
Currency translation adjustment	786	786			786		
Unrealized gains on securities	23	23			23		
Employee benefit plans	670	670			670		
Losses on derivatives & hedges	(54)	(54)			(54)		
Reclassification adjustment		(5)					
Total comprehensive income		**11,996**					
Balance, December 30, 2007	**$43,319**		**55,280**	**—**	**(693)**	**3,120**	**(14,388)**

See Notes to Consolidated Financial Statements

Consolidated Statements of Cash Flows

Johnson & Johnson and Subsidiaries

(Dollars in Millions) (Note 1)	2007	2006	2005
Cash flows from operating activities			
Net earnings	$ 10,576	11,053	10,060
Adjustments to reconcile net earnings to cash flows:			
Depreciation and amortization of property and intangibles	2,777	2,177	2,093
Stock based compensation	698	659	540
Purchased in-process research and development	807	559	362
Intangible asset write-down (NATRECOR®)	678	—	—
Deferred tax provision	(1,762)	(1,168)	(235)
Accounts receivable allowances	22	(14)	(31)
Changes in assets and liabilities, net of effects from acquisitions:			
Increase in accounts receivable	(416)	(699)	(568)
Decrease/(increase) in inventories	14	(210)	(396)
Increase/(decrease) in accounts payable and accrued liabilities	2,642	1,750	(911)
(Increase)/decrease in other current and non-current assets	(1,351)	(269)	542
Increase in other current and non-current liabilities	564	410	343
Net cash flows from operating activities	**15,249**	**14,248**	**11,799**
Cash flows from investing activities			
Additions to property, plant and equipment	(2,942)	(2,666)	(2,632)
Proceeds from the disposal of assets	230	511	154
Acquisitions, net of cash acquired (Note 17)	(1,388)	(18,023)	(987)
Purchases of investments	(9,659)	(467)	(5,660)
Sales of investments	7,988	426	9,187
Other (primarily intangibles)	(368)	(72)	(341)
Net cash used by investing activities	**(6,139)**	**(20,291)**	**(279)**
Cash flows from financing activities			
Dividends to shareholders	(4,670)	(4,267)	(3,793)
Repurchase of common stock	(5,607)	(6,722)	(1,717)
Proceeds from short-term debt	19,626	6,385	1,215
Retirement of short-term debt	(21,691)	(2,633)	(732)
Proceeds from long-term debt	5,100	6	6
Retirement of long-term debt	(18)	(13)	(196)
Proceeds from the exercise of stock options/excess tax benefits	1,562	1,135	774
Net cash used by financing activities	**(5,698)**	**(6,109)**	**(4,443)**
Effect of exchange rate changes on cash and cash equivalents	275	180	(225)
(Decrease)/increase in cash and cash equivalents	3,687	(11,972)	6,852
Cash and cash equivalents, beginning of year (Note 1)	4,083	16,055	9,203
Cash and cash equivalents, end of year (Note 1)	**$ 7,770**	**4,083**	**16,055**
Supplemental cash flow data			
Cash paid during the year for:			
Interest	$ 314	143	151
Income taxes	4,099	4,250	3,429
Supplemental schedule of noncash investing and financing activities			
Treasury stock issued for employee compensation and stock option plans, net of cash proceeds	$ 738	622	818
Conversion of debt	9	26	369
Acquisitions			
Fair value of assets acquired	$ 1,620	19,306	1,128
Fair value of liabilities assumed	(232)	(1,283)	(141)
Net cash paid for acquisitions	**$ 1,388**	**18,023**	**987**

See Notes to Consolidated Financial Statements

12. Accumulated Other Comprehensive Income

Components of other comprehensive income/(loss) consist of the following:

(Dollars in Millions)	Foreign Currency Translation	Unrealized Gains/ (Losses) on Securities	Employee Benefit Plans	Gains/ (Losses) on Derivatives & Hedges	Total Accumulated Other Comprehensive Income/(Loss)
Jan. 2, 2005	$(105)	86	(346)	(150)	(515)
2005 changes					
Net change due to hedging transactions	—	—	—	112	
Net amount reclassed to net earnings	—	—	—	53	
Net 2005 changes	(415)	(16)	26	165	(240)
Jan. 1, 2006	$(520)	70	(320)	15	(755)
2006 changes					
Net change due to hedging transactions	—	—	—	17	
Net amount reclassed to net earnings	—	—	—	(23)	
Net 2006 changes	362	(9)	(1,710)	(6)	(1,363)
Dec. 31, 2006	$(158)	61	(2,030)	9	(2,118)
2007 changes					
Net change due to hedging transactions	—	—	—	(78)	
Net amount reclassed to net earnings	—	—	—	24	
Net 2007 changes	786	23	670	(54)	1,425
Dec. 30, 2007	$ 628	84	(1,360)	(45)	(693)

Total comprehensive income for 2007 includes reclassification adjustment gains of $7 million realized from the sale of equity securities and the associated tax expense of $2 million.

Total other comprehensive income for 2006 includes reclassification adjustment gains of $13 million realized from the sale of equity securities and the associated tax expense of $4 million.

Total other comprehensive income for 2005 includes reclassification adjustment gains of $23 million realized from the sale of equity securities and the associated tax expense of $8 million.

The tax effect on the unrealized gains/(losses) on the equity securities balance is an expense of $46 million, $33 million and $38 million in 2007, 2006 and 2005, respectively. The tax effect related to employee benefit plans was $349 million, $891 million and $160 million in 2007, 2006 and 2005, respectively. The tax effect on the gains/(losses) on derivatives and hedges are gains of $24 million in 2007, and losses of $4 million and $11 million in 2006 and 2005, respectively. See Note 15 for additional information relating to derivatives and hedging.

The currency translation adjustments are not currently adjusted for income taxes as they relate to permanent investments in international subsidiaries.

13. Pensions and Other Benefit Plans

The Company sponsors various retirement and pension plans, including defined benefit, defined contribution and termination indemnity plans, which cover most employees worldwide. The Company also provides postretirement benefits, primarily health care, to all U.S. retired employees and their dependents.

Many international employees are covered by government-sponsored programs and the cost to the Company is not significant.

Retirement plan benefits are primarily based on the employee's compensation during the last three to five years before retirement and the number of years of service. International subsidiaries have plans under which funds are deposited with trustees, annuities are purchased under group contracts, or reserves are provided.

The Company does not fund retiree health care benefits in advance and has the right to modify these plans in the future.

The Company uses the date of its consolidated financial statements (December 30, 2007 and December 31, 2006, respectively) as the measurement date for all U.S. and international retirement and other benefit plans.

In September 2006, Statement of Financial Accounting Standards (SFAS) No. 158, *Employers' Accounting for Defined Benefit Pension and Other Postretirement Plans* was issued and amends further the disclosure requirements for pensions and other postretirement benefits. This Statement was an amendment of FASB Statements No. 87, 88, 106 and 132(R). The incremental effect of applying FASB No. 158 was a $1.7 billion reduction in Shareholder's Equity, net of deferred taxes.

Net periodic benefit costs for the Company's defined benefit retirement plans and other benefit plans for 2007, 2006 and 2005 include the following components:

(Dollars in Millions)	Retirement Plans			Other Benefit Plans		
	2007	2006	2005	2007	2006	2005
Service cost	$ 597	552	462	$140	122	56
Interest cost	656	570	488	149	136	87
Expected return on plan assets	(809)	(701)	(579)	(2)	(3)	(3)
Amortization of prior service cost	10	10	12	(7)	(7)	(7)
Amortization of net transition asset	1	(1)	(2)	—	—	—
Recognized actuarial losses	186	251	219	66	74	25
Curtailments and settlements	5	4	2	—	—	—
Net periodic benefit cost	$ 646	685	602	$346	322	158

The net periodic benefit cost attributable to U.S. retirement plans was $379 million in 2007, $423 million in 2006 and $370 million in 2005.

Amounts expected to be recognized in net periodic benefit cost in the coming year for the Company's defined benefit retirement plans and other postretirement plans:

(Dollars in Millions)	
Amortization of net transition obligation	$ 2
Amortization of net actuarial losses	132
Amortization of prior service cost	5

The weighted-average assumptions in the following table represent the rates used to develop the actuarial present value of projected benefit obligation for the year listed and also the net periodic benefit cost for the following year.

(Dollars in Millions)	Retirement Plans			Other Benefit Plans		
	2007	2006	2005	2007	2006	2005
U.S. Benefit Plans						
Discount rate	6.50%	6.00	5.75	6.50%	6.00	5.75
Expected long-term rate of return on plan assets	9.00	9.00	9.00	9.00	9.00	9.00
Rate of increase in compensation levels	4.50	4.50	4.50	4.50	4.50	4.50
International Benefit Plans						
Discount rate	5.50%	5.00	4.75	6.50%	6.00	5.00
Expected long-term rate of return on plan assets	8.25	8.00	8.25	—	—	—
Rate of increase in compensation levels	4.00	3.75	3.75	4.50	4.50	4.25

The Company's discount rates are determined by considering current yield curves representing high quality, long-term fixed income instruments. The resulting discount rates are consistent with the duration of plan liabilities.

The expected long-term rate of return on plan assets assumption is determined using a building block approach, considering historical averages and real returns of each asset class. In certain countries, where historical returns are not meaningful, consideration is given to local market expectations of long-term returns.

The following table displays the assumed health care cost trend rates, for all individuals:

Health Care Plans	2007	2006
Health care cost trend rate assumed for next year	9.00%	9.00
Rate to which the cost trend rate is assumed to decline (ultimate trend)	5.00%	4.50
Year the rate reaches the ultimate trend rate	2014	2012

A one-percentage-point change in assumed health care cost trend rates would have the following effect:

(Dollars in Millions)	One-Percentage-Point Increase	One-Percentage-Point Decrease
Health Care Plans		
Total interest and service cost	$ 35	$ (27)
Postretirement benefit obligation	320	(259)

The following table sets forth information related to the benefit obligation and the fair value of plan assets at year-end 2007 and 2006 for the Company's defined benefit retirement plans and other postretirement plans:

(Dollars in Millions)	Retirement Plans 2007	Retirement Plans 2006	Other Benefit Plans 2007	Other Benefit Plans 2006
Change in Benefit Obligation				
Projected benefit obligation — beginning of year	$11,660	10,171	$ 2,668	2,325
Service cost	597	552	140	122
Interest cost	656	570	149	136
Plan participant contributions	62	47	—	—
Amendments	14	7	—	—
Actuarial (gains) losses	(876)	(99)	(1)	130
Divestitures & acquisitions	79	443	8	101
Curtailments & settlements	(46)	(7)	—	—
Benefits paid from plan	(481)	(402)	(255)	(147)
Effect of exchange rates	337	378	12	1
Projected benefit obligation — end of year	$12,002	11,660	$ 2,721	2,668
Change in Plan Assets				
Plan assets at fair value — beginning of year	$9,538	8,108	30	34
Actual return on plan assets	743	966	4	2
Company contributions	317	259	250	141
Plan participant contributions	62	47	—	—
Settlements	(38)	(7)	—	—
Divestitures & acquisitions	55	300	—	—
Benefits paid from plan assets	(481)	(402)	(255)	(147)
Effect of exchange rates	273	267	—	—
Plan assets at fair value — end of year	$10,469	9,538	$ 29	30
Funded status at — end of year	$ (1,533)	(2,122)	$(2,692)	(2,638)
Amounts Recognized in the Company's Balance Sheet consist of the following:				
Non-current assets	$ 481	259	—	—
Current liabilities	(43)	(26)	(262)	(81)
Non-current liabilities	(1,971)	(2,355)	(2,430)	(2,557)
Total recognized in the consolidated balance sheet — end of year	$ (1,533)	(2,122)	$(2,692)	(2,638)
Amounts Recognized in Accumulated Other Comprehensive Income consist of the following:				
Net actuarial loss (gain)	$ 1,027	1,996	$ 1,013	1,046
Prior service cost (credit)	51	44	(36)	(42)
Unrecognized net transition asset	7	7	—	—
Total before tax effects	$ 1,085	2,047	$ 977	1,004
Accumulated Benefit Obligations — end of year	$10,282	9,804		
Changes in Plan Assets and Benefit Obligations Recognized in Other Comprehensive Income				
Net periodic benefit cost	$ 646		$ 346	
Net actuarial loss (gain)	(555)		11	
Amortization of net actuarial loss	(435)		(13)	
Prior service cost	(9)		(34)	
Amortization of prior service cost	14		6	
Effect of exchange rates	23		3	
Total recognized in other comprehensive income, before tax	$ (962)		$ (27)	
Total recognized in net periodic benefit cost and other comprehensive income	$ (316)		$ 319	

Plans with accumulated benefit obligations in excess of plan assets consist of the following:

(Dollars in Millions)	Retirement Plans 2007	Retirement Plans 2006
Accumulated benefit obligation	$(4,914)	(3,085)
Projected benefit obligation	(5,233)	(3,561)
Plan assets at fair value	3,735	1,650

Strategic asset allocations are determined by country, based on the nature of the liabilities and considering the demographic composition of the plan participants (average age, years of service and active versus retiree status). The Company's plans are considered non-mature plans and the long-term strategic asset allocations are consistent with these types of plans. Emphasis is placed on diversifying equities on a broad basis combined with currency matching of the fixed income assets.

The following table displays the projected future benefit payments from the Company's retirement and other benefit plans:

(Dollars in Millions)	2008	2009	2010	2011	2012	2013-2017
Projected future benefit payments						
Retirement plans	$457	472	507	542	564	3,467
Other benefit plans — gross	$274	180	184	188	192	1,080
Medicare rebates	(9)	(11)	(12)	(13)	(14)	(94)
Other benefit plans — net	$265	$169	$172	$175	$178	$986

The Company was not required to fund its U.S. retirement plans in 2007 and is not required, nor does it anticipate funding in 2008 to meet minimum statutory funding requirements. International plans are funded in accordance with local regulations. Additional discretionary contributions are made when deemed appropriate to meet the long-term obligations of the plans. In certain countries other than the United States, the funding of pension plans is not a common practice as funding provides no economic benefit. Consequently the Company has several pension plans which are not funded.

The following table displays the projected future minimum contributions to the Company's U.S. and international unfunded retirement plans. These amounts do not include any discretionary contributions that the Company may elect to make in the future.

(Dollars in Millions)	2008	2009	2010	2011	2012	2013-2017
Projected future contributions						
Unfunded U.S. retirement plans	$28	30	33	35	38	238
Unfunded International retirement plans	$23	25	28	29	31	178

The Company's retirement plan asset allocation at the end of 2007 and 2006 and target allocations for 2008 are as follows:

	Percent of Plan Assets		Target Allocation
	2007	2006	2008
U.S. Retirement Plans			
Equity securities	79%	78%	75%
Debt securities	21	22	25
Total plan assets	100%	100%	100%
International Retirement Plans			
Equity securities	67%	67%	67%
Debt securities	32	32	33
Real estate and other	1	1	—
Total plan assets	100%	100%	100%

The Company's other benefit plans are unfunded except for U.S. life insurance contract assets of $29 million and $30 million at December 30, 2007 and December 31, 2006, respectively.

The fair value of Johnson & Johnson common stock directly held in plan assets was $462 million (4.4% of total plan assets) at December 30, 2007 and $452 million (4.9% of total plan assets) at December 31, 2006.

International Speedway Corporation—Deferred Taxes

International Speedway Corporation (ISC) dates back nearly 50 years, when Bill France Racing, Inc., signed the initial contract to secure the land for construction of Daytona International Speedway. Today, ISC is a leader in motorsports entertainment with 12 owned and operated motorsports facilities, as well as a 37.5% interest in Chicagoland Speedway and Route 66 Raceway. ISC manages over a million grandstand seats and has a presence in six of the USA's top ten media markets. (Source: Company 2003 Form 10-K)

Learning Objectives
- Understand the concepts underlying deferred income tax accounting.
- Interpret the income tax note to the financial statements.
- Use deferred tax asset and liability information to infer balances for tax purposes.
- Consider the tax consequences when revenue recognition differs for accounting and tax purposes.

Refer to the 2003 financial statements of International Speedway Corporation (ISC).

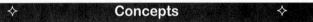
Concepts

a. Explain in general terms why the company reports deferred income taxes as part of their total income tax expense. Why don't companies simply report their current tax bill as their income tax expense?

b. Explain in general terms what deferred tax assets and deferred tax liabilities represent.

Process

c. According to Note 8—Federal and State Income Taxes, ISC had a net deferred tax liability balance of $113,414 at November 30, 2003. Explain where that balance is found on the balance sheet.

d. What journal entry did ISC record for income tax expense in fiscal 2003?

Analysis

e. The largest component of the deferred tax liability relates to "Amortization and depreciation."

    i. Explain how this deferred tax liability component arose.

    ii. Use the table below and information from the balance sheet and Note 8, to estimate ISC's net property and equipment (Net P&E) for tax purposes. Begin with step 1 and work up. For step 2, assume that the deferred tax liability was calculated with the company's 2003 effective tax rate.

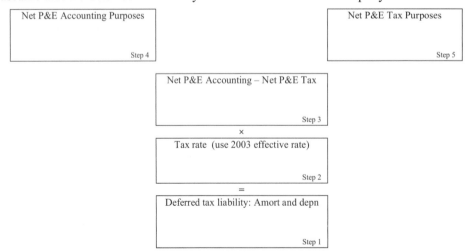

f. According to Note 1—Description of the Business, Basis of Presentation and Summary of Significant Accounting Policies, ISC's revenue recognition policy is:

REVENUE RECOGNITION/DEFERRED INCOME: Admission income and all race-related revenue is earned upon completion of an event and is stated net of admission and sales taxes collected. Advance ticket sales and all race-related revenue on future events are deferred until earned. Revenues from the sale of merchandise to retail customers, internet and catalog sales, and direct sales to dealers are recognized at the time of the sale.

Kansas Speedway Corporation ("KSC") offers Founding Fan Preferred Access Speedway Seating ("PASS") agreements, which give purchasers the exclusive right and obligation to purchase KSC season-ticket packages for certain sanctioned racing events annually for thirty years under specified terms and conditions. Among the conditions, licensees are required to purchase all season-ticket packages when and as offered each year. Founding Fan PASS agreements automatically terminate without refund should owners not purchase any offered season tickets.

Net fees received under PASS agreements are deferred and are amortized into income over the expected life of the PASS.

   i.   Why doesn't ISC record admission revenue when event tickets are purchased and paid for?

   ii.   How would receiving cash for tickets for the 2004 Daytona 500 auto race affect ISC's deferred tax assets and liabilities? Assume the tickets are sold in fiscal 2003 and that, for tax purposes, 10% of advance ticket receipts are immediately taxable and the remainder is taxable when the auto races take place.

   iii. Assume that the balance sheet item Deferred income, in the current liabilities section, relates entirely (and in equal amounts) to advance tickets sold to the Daytona 500 auto race to be held on February 15, 2004, and the Pepsi 400 auto race to be held on July 3, 2004, both at the Daytona International Speedway. Calculate the deferred tax asset or liability associated with the deferred revenue ISC recorded during fiscal 2003.

   iv.   Assume that during the first quarter of 2004, a further $10 million of tickets were sold, all for the Pepsi 400. Provide the journal entry to record the sale of the tickets. Also provide the journal entry to adjust the deferred tax account related to this additional deferred revenue.

   v.   Provide the adjusting entry that ISC will record at the end of first quarter 2004 to record the previously deferred revenues that were earned that quarter. Also provide the journal entry to adjust the deferred tax account related to deferred revenues. Assume that the company's 39% tax rate remains unchanged.

   vi.   Now assume that during the second quarter of fiscal 2004 no further advanced tickets were sold. However, a tax-law change was enacted lowering ISC's tax rate to 37%. Provide the adjusting journal entry related to the deferred tax asset associated with deferred income that ISC will record at the end of the second quarter.

g. One of ISC's deferred tax assets is labeled "Loss carryforwards."

   i.   What is a loss carryforward? How does it meet the definition of an asset?

   ii.   If ISC's loss carryforwards were expected to expire unused, would the related deferred tax assets still meet the definition of an asset?

h. One of ISC's deferred tax liabilities is labeled "Equity investment." Explain how accounting for investments in other companies using the equity method can give rise to deferred tax liabilities.

INTERNATIONAL SPEEDWAY CORPORATION

CONSOLIDATED BALANCE SHEETS

	November 30,	
	2002	**2003**
	(In Thousands)	
ASSETS		
Current Assets:		
Cash and cash equivalents	$ 109,263	$ 223,973
Short-term investments	200	201
Receivables, less allowance of $1,500 in 2002 and 2003	30,557	37,996
Inventories	4,799	5,496
Prepaid expenses and other current assets	3,784	4,078
Total Current Assets	148,603	271,744
Property and Equipment, net	859,096	884,623
Other Assets:		
Equity investments	31,152	33,706
Goodwill	92,542	92,542
Other	24,578	21,177
	148,272	147,425
Total Assets	$ 1,155,971	$ 1,303,792
LIABILITIES AND SHAREHOLDERS' EQUITY		
Current Liabilities:		
Current portion of long-term debt	$ 5,775	$ 232,963
Accounts payable	17,506	15,739
Deferred income	98,315	106,998
Income taxes payable	3,939	6,877
Other current liabilities	10,968	13,928
Total Current Liabilities	136,503	376,505
Long-Term Debt	309,606	75,168
Deferred Income Taxes	74,943	113,414
Long-Term Deferred Income	11,709	11,894
Other Long-Term Liabilities	885	346
Commitments and Contingencies	-	-
Shareholders' Equity:		
Class A Common Stock, $.01 par value, 80,000,000 shares authorized; 25,319,221 and 28,359,173 issued and outstanding in 2002 and 2003, respectively	253	283
Class B Common Stock, $.01 par value, 40,000,000 shares authorized; 27,867,456 and 24,858,610 issued and outstanding in 2002 and 2003, respectively	279	249
Additional paid-in capital	693,463	694,719
Retained (deficit) earnings	(67,641)	34,602
Accumulated other comprehensive loss	(874)	(333)
	625,480	729,520
Less unearned compensation-restricted stock	3,155	3,055
Total Shareholders' Equity	622,325	726,465
Total Liabilities and Shareholders' Equity	$ 1,155,971	$ 1,303,792

See accompanying notes

INTERNATIONAL SPEEDWAY CORPORATION

CONSOLIDATED STATEMENTS OF OPERATIONS

	Year Ended November 30,		
	2001	2002	2003
	(In Thousands, Except Per Share Amounts)		
REVENUES:			
Admissions, net	$ 214,494	$ 213,255	$ 210,535
Motorsports related income	238,208	259,609	284,902
Food, beverage and merchandise income	70,575	70,396	74,199
Other income	5,233	7,292	6,109
	528,510	550,552	575,745
EXPENSES:			
Direct expenses:			
Prize and point fund monies and NASCAR sanction fees	87,859	97,290	107,821
Motorsports related expenses	98,458	99,441	102,231
Food, beverage and merchandise expenses	38,251	38,109	41,250
General and administrative expenses	79,953	80,325	85,773
Depreciation and amortization	54,544	41,154	44,171
Homestead-Miami Speedway track reconfiguration	-	-	2,829
	359,065	356,319	384,075
Operating income	169,445	194,233	191,670
Interest income	3,446	1,211	1,821
Interest expense	(26,505)	(24,277)	(23,179)
Equity in net income from equity investments	2,935	1,907	2,553
Minority interest	992	-	-
Income before income taxes and cumulative effect of accounting change	150,313	173,074	172,865
Income taxes	62,680	66,803	67,417
Income before cumulative effect of accounting change	87,633	106,271	105,448
Cumulative effect of accounting change—company operations	-	(513,827)	-
Cumulative effect of accounting change—equity investment	-	(3,422)	-
Net income (loss)	$ 87,633	$ (410,978)	$ 105,448
Basic earnings per share before cumulative effect of accounting change	$ 1.65	$ 2.00	$ 1.99
Cumulative effect of accounting change	-	(9.75)	-
Basic earnings (loss) per share	$ 1.65	$ (7.75)	$ 1.99
Diluted earnings per share before cumulative effect of accounting change	$ 1.65	$ 2.00	$ 1.98
Cumulative effect of accounting change	-	(9.74)	-
Diluted earnings (loss) per share	$ 1.65	$ (7.74)	$ 1.98
Dividends per share	$ 0.06	$ 0.06	$ 0.06
Basic weighted average shares outstanding	52,996,660	53,036,552	53,057,077
Diluted weighted average shares outstanding	53,076,828	53,101,535	53,133,282

See accompanying notes

INTERNATIONAL SPEEDWAY CORPORATION

CONSOLIDATED STATEMENTS OF CASH FLOWS

	Year Ended November 30,		
	2001	2002	2003
	(In Thousands)		
OPERATING ACTIVITIES			
Net income (loss)	$ 87,633	$ (410,978)	$ 105,448
Adjustments to reconcile net income (loss) to net cash provided by operating activities:			
Cumulative effect of accounting change	-	517,249	-
Depreciation and amortization	54,544	41,154	44,171
Deferred income taxes	27,177	29,461	38,471
Homestead-Miami Speedway track reconfiguration	-	-	2,829
Amortization of unearned compensation	1,619	1,485	1,695
Amortization of financing costs	1,566	1,332	294
Undistributed income from equity investments	(2,935)	(1,907)	(2,553)
Minority interest	(992)	-	-
Other, net	722	(1,634)	(37)
Changes in operating assets and liabilities			
Receivables, net	(3,226)	(5,415)	(7,439)
Inventories, prepaid expenses and other current assets	3,394	2,209	(990)
Accounts payable and other current liabilities	1,815	2,873	1,040
Income taxes payable	-	4,544	2,939
Deferred income	(10,631)	(1,759)	8,868
Net cash provided by operating activities	160,686	178,614	194,736
INVESTING ACTIVITIES			
Capital expenditures	(98,379)	(53,521)	(72,587)
Proceeds from affiliate	-	4,045	4,075
Proceeds from short-term investments	400	400	400
Purchases of short-term investments	(400)	(400)	(400)
Proceeds from asset disposals	722	3,836	178
Proceeds from STAR bonds	-	5,589	-
Proceeds from restricted investments	33,930	1,263	-
Acquisition, net of cash acquired	(3,878)	-	-
Equity investments	(1,202)	-	-
Advances to affiliate	(1,500)	-	-
Other, net	(1,647)	(1,533)	(1,552)
Net cash used in investing activities	(71,954)	(40,321)	(69,886)
FINANCING ACTIVITIES			
Payment of long-term debt	(5,165)	(9,225)	(5,775)
Cash dividends paid	(3,190)	(3,191)	(3,193)
Reacquisition of previously issued common stock	(965)	(831)	(352)
Deferred financing fees	-	-	(820)
Payments under credit facilities	(71,000)	(90,000)	-
Proceeds under credit facilities	12,000	-	-
Proceeds from interest rate swap	-	3,213	-
Net cash used in financing activities	(68,320)	(100,034)	(10,140)
Net increase in cash and cash equivalents	20,412	38,259	114,710
Cash and cash equivalents at beginning of period	50,592	71,004	109,263
Cash and cash equivalents at end of period	$ 71,004	$ 109,263	$ 223,973

See accompanying notes

INTERNATIONAL SPEEDWAY CORPORATION

NOTES TO CONSOLIDATED FINANCIAL STATEMENTS, NOVEMBER 30, 2003

NOTE 8 - FEDERAL AND STATE INCOME TAXES

Deferred income taxes reflect the net tax effects of temporary differences between the carrying amounts of assets and liabilities for financial reporting purposes and the amounts used for income tax purposes.

Significant components of the provision for income taxes for the years ended November 30, are as follows (in thousands):

	2001	2002	2003
Current tax expense:			
Federal	$ 31,560	$ 29,441	$ 24,480
State	3,944	7,902	4,466
Deferred tax expense (benefit):			
Federal	23,986	29,526	36,329
State	3,190	(66)	2,142
Provision for income taxes	$ 62,680	$ 66,803	$ 67,417

The reconciliation of income tax computed at the federal statutory tax rates to income tax expense for the years ended November 30, are as follows (percent of pre-tax income):

	2001	2002	2003
Income tax computed at federal statutory rates	35.0%	35.0%	35.0%
State income taxes, net of federal tax benefit	3.1	3.6	3.1
Nondeductible goodwill	2.8	-	-
Other, net	0.8	-	0.9
	41.7%	38.6%	39.0%

INTERNATIONAL SPEEDWAY CORPORATION

NOTE 8 - FEDERAL AND STATE INCOME TAXES (continued)

The components of the net deferred tax assets (liabilities) at November 30 are as follows (in thousands):

	2002	2003
Amortization and depreciation	$ 48,138	$ 38,527
Deferred revenues	4,412	4,315
Loss carryforwards	2,672	2,840
Deferred expenses	2,645	2,454
Accruals	987	2,062
Compensation related	1,373	1,505
Other	275	199
Deferred tax assets	60,502	51,902
Amortization and depreciation	(130,916)	(157,664)
Equity investment	(4,210)	(7,322)
Other	(319)	(330)
Deferred tax liabilities	(135,445)	(165,316)
Net deferred tax liabilities	$ (74,943)	$ (113,414)

The Company has recorded deferred tax assets related to various state net operating loss carryforwards totaling approximately $69.3 million, that expire in varying amounts beginning in fiscal 2020.

NOTE 9 - CAPITAL STOCK

The Company's authorized capital includes 80 million shares of Class A Common Stock, par value $.01 ("Class A Common Stock"), 40 million shares of Class B Common Stock, par value $.01 ("Class B Common Stock"), and 1 million shares of Preferred Stock, par value $.01 ("Preferred Stock"). The shares of Class A Common Stock and Class B Common Stock are identical in all respects, except for voting rights and certain dividend and conversion rights as described below. Each share of Class A Common Stock entitles the holder to one-fifth (1/5) vote on each matter submitted to a vote of the Company's shareholders and each share of Class B Common Stock entitles the holder to one (1) vote on each such matter, in each case including the election of directors. Holders of Class A Common Stock and Class B Common Stock are entitled to receive dividends at the same rate if and when declared by the Board of Directors out of funds legally available therefrom, subject to the dividend and liquidation rights of any Preferred Stock that may be issued and outstanding. Class A Common Stock has no conversion rights. Class B Common Stock is convertible into Class A Common Stock, in whole or in part, at any time at the option of the

holder on the basis of one share of Class A Common Stock for each share of Class B Common Stock converted. Each share of Class B Common Stock will also automatically convert into one share of Class A Common Stock if, on the record date of any meeting of the shareholders, the number of shares of Class B Common Stock then outstanding is less than 10% of the aggregate number of shares of Class A Common Stock and Class B Common Stock then outstanding.

The Board of Directors of the Company is authorized, without further shareholder action, to divide any or all shares of the authorized Preferred Stock into series and fix and determine the designations, preferences and relative rights and qualifications, limitations, or restrictions thereon of any series so established, including voting powers, dividend rights, liquidation preferences, redemption rights and conversion privileges. No shares of Preferred Stock are outstanding. The Board of Directors has not authorized any series of Preferred Stock, and there are no plans, agreements or understandings for the authorization or issuance of any shares of Preferred Stock.

Rite Aid Corporation—Long-Term Debt

With 3,382 stores in 28 states, Rite Aid is the third largest retail pharmacy in the U.S. The company has a first or second market position in approximately 60% of the markets where it operates. In fiscal 2004, Rite Aid pharmacists filled more than 200 million prescriptions, which accounted for 63.6% of total sales. In addition, Rite Aid stores sell a wide assortment of other merchandise including over-the-counter medications, health and beauty aids, household items, beverages, convenience foods, greeting cards, as well as photo processing. The company also offers 2,100 products under the Rite Aid private brand. (Source: Company 2004 Form 10-K)

Learning Objectives
- Read and understand long-term debt footnote terminology.
- Understand discounts and premiums associated with long-term debt.
- Infer effective interest rates from footnote disclosures.
- Calculate and interpret common debt-related ratios.

Refer to the 2004 Rite Aid Corporation financial statements.

 Concepts

a. Consider the various types of debt the company describes in footnote 10.

    i.   Explain the difference between Rite Aid's secured and unsecured debt. Why would Rite Aid distinguish between these two types of debt?

    ii.   What is meant by the terms "senior," "fixed-rate," and "convertible"?

    iii.   Speculate as to why Rite Aid has many different types of debt with a range of interest rates?

 Process

b. Consider Note 10, Indebtedness. How much total debt does Rite Aid have at February 28, 2004? How much of this is due within the coming fiscal year? Reconcile the total debt reported in Note 10 with what Rite Aid reports on its balance sheet.

c. Consider the 9.5% senior secured notes due February 2011.

    i.   What is the face value (i.e. the principal) of these notes? How do you know?

    ii.   Prepare the journal entry that Rite Aid must have made when these notes were issued.

    iii.   Prepare the annual interest expense journal entry. Note that the interest paid on a note during the year equals the face value of the note times the stated rate (i.e., coupon rate) of the note.

    iv.   Prepare the journal entry that Rite Aid will make when these notes mature in 2011.

d. Consider the 4.75% convertible notes due December 2006. Assume that interest is paid annually.

    i.   What is the face value (or principal) of these notes? What is the carrying value (net book value) of these notes? Why do the two values differ?

    ii.   How much interest did Rite Aid pay on these notes during the fiscal 2004?

    iii.   Determine interest expense on these notes for the year ended February 28, 2004. Note that there are cash and noncash portion to interest expense on these notes because they were issued at a discount. The noncash portion of interest expense is the amortization of the discount during the year (that is, the amount by which the discount decreased during the year).

iv. Prepare the journal entry to record interest expense on these notes for 2004. Consider both the cash and discount (noncash) portions of the interest expense from part *iii* above.

e. Consider the 8.125% notes due 2010. Assume that Rite Aid issued these notes on May 1, 2003 and that the company pays interest on the last day of April each year.

i. According to a press release issued by Rite Aid at the time of the issuance, the proceeds of the notes issue were 98.688% of the face value of the notes. Prepare the journal entry that Rite Aid must have made when these notes were issued.

ii. At what effective annual rate of interest were these notes issued?

iii. Assume that Rite Aid uses the effective interest rate method to account for this debt. Use the guidance for the table that follows to prepare an amortization schedule for these notes. Use the last column to verify that each year's interest expense uses the same interest *rate* even though the *expense* changes.

Date	Interest Payment	Interest Expense	Bond Discount Amortization	Net Book Value of Debt	Effective Interest Rate
May 1, 2003				$ 355,276.80	
May 1, 2004	$ 29,250				
May 1, 2005					
May 1, 2006					
May 1, 2007					
May 1, 2008					
May 1, 2009					
May 1, 2010					

- May 1, 2003 Net Book Value is the initial proceeds of the bond issuance, net of costs. The face value of this debt is $360,000; the discount is $4,723.20; the coupon rate is 8.125% and the effective rate (including fees) is 8.3803%.

- Interest Payment is the face value of the bond times the coupon rate of the bond.

- Interest Expense equals opening book value of the debt times the effective interest rate.
  - The difference between the interest payment and interest expense is the amortization of the bond discount. This is equivalent to saying that interest expense equals the interest paid plus the amortization of the bond discount.
  - Amortizing the discount increases the net book value of the bond.

iv. Prepare the journal entry that Rite Aid must have recorded February 28, 2004, to accrue interest expense on these notes.

v. Based on your answer to part *iv.* what is the book value of the notes at February 28, 2004?

vi. Your answer to part *v.* will be different from the amount that Rite Aid reported because the company used the straight-line method to amortize the discount on these notes instead of the effective interest rate method. Use the guidance that follows to complete the following table using the straight-line method to amortize the bond discount. Use the last column in the table to record the interest rate each year. Under this method, does Rite Aid report the same interest *rate* on these notes each year?

Date	Interest Payment	Interest Expense	Bond Discount Amortization	Net Book Value of Debt	Straight-Line Interest Rate
May 1, 2003				$ 355,276.80	
May 1, 2004	$ 29,250				
May 1, 2005					
May 1, 2006					
May 1, 2007					
May 1, 2008					
May 1, 2009					
May 1, 2010					

- May 1, 2003, Net Book Value is the initial proceeds of the bond issuance, net of costs. The face value of this debt is $360,000; the discount is $4,723.20; the coupon rate is 8.125% and the effective rate (including fees) is 8.3803%.

- Interest Payment is the face value of the bond times the coupon rate of the bond.

- Interest Expense equals interest payment plus the amortization of the bond discount.

  o Under the straight-line method the bond discount is amortized on a straight-line basis over the life of the bond. That is, amortization is the same amount each year.

  o Amortizing the discount increases the net book value of the bond.

vii. Compare the year by year difference in interest expense derived from each method. What pattern do you observe? Is the difference material in any year?

f. Note 10 reports that Rite Aid engaged in some open-market debt transactions during year ended February 28, 2004 (see the part of note 10 marked "Debt Repurchased").

i. Prepare the journal entry required to record the repurchase of these notes.

ii. Why did Rite Aid not have to pay the face value to repurchase these notes on the open market?

iii. Explain why Rite Aid recorded a gain on all of the repurchased notes except on the 12.5% notes on which it recorded a loss?

g. Consider the 4.75% Convertible notes. How would Rite Aid's balance sheet be affected if these notes were converted? Why do firms issue convertible notes? Why do investors buy such notes?

h. Refer to Note 20, Financial Instruments.

i. What is the fair value of Rite Aid's fixed-rate debt at February 28, 2004? Why does it differ from the carrying amount?

ii. What is the fair value of the variable-rate debt at February 28, 2004? Why does it *not* differ from its carrying amount?

iii. Why would financial statement users want to know the fair value of Rite Aid's debt?

✦ Analysis ✦

i. You want to compare Rite Aid's leverage to other firms in the Retail Pharmaceutical industry. To assist you, the table below reports the industry averages for several common debt ratios. Calculate each of the ratios in the table for Rite Aid for the years ending February 28, 2004, and March 1, 2003. How does Rite Aid compare to the industry? What conclusion would you reach as a credit analyst?

Ratio	Definition	Industry average	Rite Aid FY2004	Rite Aid FY2003
Common-size debt	Total liabilities / Total assets	51.91%		
Common-size interest expense	Interest expense / Net sales	0.65%		
Debt to equity	Total liabilities / Total shareholders' equity	1.59		
Long-term debt to equity	Total long-term debt / Total shareholders' equity	0.58		
Proportion of long-term debt due in one year	Long-term debt due in one year / Total long-term debt	13.00%		
Times-interest-earned (interest coverage)	(Pretax income + interest expense) / Interest expense	9.98×		

RITE AID CORPORATION AND SUBSIDIARIES
CONSOLIDATED BALANCE SHEETS

(In thousands, except per share amounts)

	February 28, 2004	March 1, 2003
ASSETS		
Current assets:		
Cash and cash equivalents	$ 334,755	$ 365,321
Accounts receivable, net	670,004	575,518
Inventories, net	2,223,171	2,195,030
Prepaid expenses and other current assets	150,067	108,018
Total current assets	3,377,997	3,243,887
Property, plant and equipment, net	1,883,808	1,868,579
Goodwill	684,535	684,535
Other intangibles, net	176,672	199,768
Other assets	123,667	136,746
Total assets	$ 6,246,679	$ 6,133,515
LIABILITIES AND STOCKHOLDERS' EQUITY (DEFICIT)		
Current liabilities:		
Short-term debt and current maturities of convertible notes, long-term debt and lease financing obligations	$ 23,976	$ 103,715
Accounts payable	758,290	755,284
Accrued salaries, wages and other current liabilities	701,484	707,999
Total current liabilities	1,483,750	1,566,998
Convertible notes	246,000	244,500
Long-term debt, less current maturities	3,451,352	3,345,365
Lease financing obligations, less current maturities	170,338	169,048
Other noncurrent liabilities	885,975	900,270
Total liabilities	6,237,415	6,226,181
Commitments and contingencies	—	—
Redeemable preferred stock	—	19,663
Stockholders' equity (deficit):		
Preferred stock, par value $1 per share; liquidation value $100 per share; 20,000 shares authorized; shares issued — 4,178 and 3,937	417,803	393,705
Common stock, par value $1 per share; 1,000,000 shares authorized; shares issued and outstanding 516,496 and 515,115	516,496	515,115
Additional paid-in capital	3,133,277	3,119,619
Accumulated deficit	(4,035,433)	(4,118,119)
Stock based and deferred compensation	—	5,369
Accumulated other comprehensive loss	(22,879)	(28,018)
Total stockholders' equity (deficit)	9,264	(112,329)
Total liabilities and stockholders' equity (deficit)	$ 6,246,679	$ 6,133,515

The accompanying notes are an integral part of these consolidated financial statements.

41

RITE AID CORPORATION AND SUBSIDIARIES
CONSOLIDATED STATEMENTS OF OPERATIONS

(In thousands, except per share amounts)

	Year Ended		
	February 28, 2004	March 1, 2003	March 2, 2002
Revenues	$16,600,449	$15,791,278	$15,166,170
Costs and expenses:			
Cost of goods sold, including occupancy costs	12,568,405	12,035,537	11,697,912
Selling, general and administrative expenses	3,594,405	3,471,573	3,422,383
Stock-based compensation expense (benefit)	29,821	4,806	(15,891)
Goodwill amortization	—	—	21,007
Store closing and impairment charges	22,466	135,328	251,617
Interest expense	313,498	330,020	396,064
Interest rate swap contracts	—	278	41,894
Loss (gain) on debt modifications and retirements, net	35,315	(13,628)	221,054
Share of loss from equity investments	—	—	12,092
Loss (gain) on sale of assets and investments, net	2,023	(18,620)	(42,536)
	16,565,933	15,945,294	16,005,596
Income (loss) before income taxes	34,516	(154,016)	(839,426)
Income tax benefit	(48,795)	(41,940)	(11,745)
Net income (loss)	$ 83,311	$ (112,076)	$ (827,681)
Computation of income (loss) applicable to common stockholders:			
Net income (loss)	$ 83,311	$ (112,076)	$ (827,681)
Accretion of redeemable preferred stock	(102)	(102)	(104)
Preferred stock beneficial conversion	(625)	—	(6,406)
Cumulative preferred stock dividends	(24,098)	(32,201)	(27,530)
Net income (loss) applicable to common stockholders	$ 58,486	$ (144,379)	$ (861,721)
Basic and diluted income (loss) per share:			
Net income (loss) per share	$ 0.11	$ (0.28)	$ (1.82)

The accompanying notes are an integral part of these consolidated financial statements.

RITE AID CORPORATION AND SUBSIDIARIES
CONSOLIDATED STATEMENTS OF CASH FLOWS

(In thousands)

	Year Ended		
	February 28, 2004	March 1, 2003	March 2, 2002
Operating Activities:			
Net income (loss)	$ 83,311	$(112,076)	$ (827,681)
Adjustments to reconcile to net cash provided by operations:			
Depreciation and amortization	264,288	285,334	349,840
Store closings and impairment loss	22,466	135,328	251,617
Interest rate swap contracts	—	278	41,894
Loss (gain) on sale of assets and investments, net	2,023	(18,620)	(42,536)
Stock-based compensation expense (benefit)	29,821	4,806	(15,891)
Loss (gain) on debt modifications and retirements, net	35,315	(13,628)	221,054
Changes in operating assets and liabilities:			
Accounts receivable	(94,486)	14,803	(69,004)
Inventories	(48,014)	40,555	112,649
Income taxes receivable/payable	(61,209)	24,018	(14,635)
Accounts payable	(17,162)	(62,314)	(5,004)
Other assets and liabilities, net	11,162	6,899	14,040
Net cash provided by operating activities	227,515	305,383	16,343
Investing Activities:			
Expenditures for property, plant and equipment	(250,668)	(104,507)	(175,183)
Intangible assets acquired	(16,705)	(11,647)	(12,200)
Proceeds from the sale of AdvancePCS securities and notes	—	—	484,214
Proceeds from dispositions	25,223	43,940	45,700
Net cash (used in) provided by investing activities	(242,150)	(72,214)	342,531
Financing activities:			
Net proceeds from the issuance of long-term debt	—	—	1,378,462
Net change in bank credit facilities	(222,500)	(5,962)	—
Proceeds from the issuance of bonds	502,950	300,000	392,500
Principal payments on long-term debt	(264,324)	(477,466)	(2,277,431)
Change in zero balance cash account	(4,613)	(12,936)	(48,131)
Net proceeds from the issuance of common stock	3,541	279	530,589
Deferred financing costs paid	(30,985)	(15,818)	(83,098)
Net cash used in financing activities	(15,931)	(211,903)	(107,109)
Increase (decrease) in cash and cash equivalents	(30,566)	21,266	251,765
Cash and cash equivalents, beginning of year	365,321	344,055	92,290
Cash and cash equivalents, end of year	$ 334,755	$ 365,321	$ 344,055

The accompanying notes are an integral part of these consolidated financial statements.

RITE AID CORPORATION AND SUBSIDIARIES
NOTES TO CONSOLIDATED FINANCIAL STATEMENTS (continued)
For the Years Ended February 28, 2004, March 1, 2003 and March 2, 2002

(In thousands, except per share amounts)

10. Indebtedness and Credit Agreements

Following is a summary of indebtedness and lease financing obligations at February 28, 2004 and March 1, 2003:

	February 28, 2004	March 1, 2003
Secured Debt:		
Senior secured credit facility due April 2008	$1,150,000	$ —
Senior secured credit facility due March 2005	—	1,372,500
12.5% senior secured notes due September 2006 ($142,025 and $152,025 face value less unamortized discount of $4,158 and 6,143)	137,867	145,882
8.125% senior secured notes due May 2010 ($360,000 face value less unamortized discount of $4,168)	355,832	—
9.5% senior secured notes due February 2011	300,000	300,000
Other	5,125	6,540
	1,948,824	1,824,922
Lease Financing Obligations	183,169	176,186
Unsecured Debt:		
6.0% dealer remarketable securities due October 2003	—	58,125
7.625% senior notes due April 2005	198,000	198,000
6.0% fixed-rate senior notes due December 2005	38,047	75,895
4.75% convertible notes due December 2006 ($250,000 face value less unamortized discount of $4,000 and $5,500)	246,000	244,500
7.125% notes due January 2007	210,074	335,000
11.25% senior notes due July 2008	150,000	150,000
6.125% fixed-rate senior notes due December 2008	150,000	150,000
9.25% senior notes due June 2013 ($150,000 face value less unamortized discount of $2,221)	147,779	—
6.875% senior debentures due August 2013	184,773	200,000
7.7% notes due February 2027	295,000	300,000
6.875% fixed-rate senior notes due December 2028	140,000	150,000
	1,759,673	1,861,520
Total debt	3,891,666	3,862,628
Short-term debt and current maturities of convertible notes, long-term debt and lease financing obligations	(23,976)	(103,715)
Long-term debt and lease financing obligations, less current maturities	$3,867,690	$3,758,913

60

RITE AID CORPORATION AND SUBSIDIARIES
NOTES TO CONSOLIDATED FINANCIAL STATEMENTS (continued)
For the Years Ended February 28, 2004, March 1, 2003 and March 2, 2002

(In thousands, except per share amounts)

2004 Transactions:

New Credit Facility: On May 28, 2003, the Company replaced its senior secured credit facility with a new senior secured credit facility. The new facility consists of a $1,150,000 term loan and a $700,000 revolving credit facility, and will mature on April 30, 2008. The proceeds of the loans made on the closing of the new credit facility were, among other things, used to repay the outstanding amounts under the old facility and to purchase the land and buildings at the Company's Perryman, MD and Lancaster, CA distribution centers, which had previously been leased through a synthetic lease arrangement. On August 4, 2003, the Company amended and restated the senior secured credit facility, which reduced the interest rate on term loan borrowings under the senior secured credit facility by 50 basis points.

Borrowings under the new facility currently bear interest either at LIBOR plus 3.00% for the term loan and 3.50% for the revolving credit facility, if the Company chooses to make LIBOR borrowings, or at Citibank's base rate plus 2.00% for the term of the loan and 2.50% for the revolving credit facility. The Company is required to pay fees of 0.50% per annum on the daily unused amount of the revolving facility. Amortization payments of $2,875 related to the term loan will begin on May 31, 2004, and continue on a quarterly basis until February 28, 2008, with a final payment of $1,104,000 due April 30, 2008.

Substantially all of Rite Aid Corporation's wholly-owned subsidiaries guarantee the obligations under the new senior secured credit facility. The subsidiary guarantees are secured by a first priority lien on, among other things, the inventory, accounts receivable and prescription files of the subsidiary guarantors. Rite Aid Corporation is a holding company with no direct operations and is dependent upon dividends, distributions and other payments from its subsidiaries to service payments under the new senior secured credit facility. Rite Aid Corporation's direct obligations under the new senior secured credit facility are unsecured.

The new senior secured credit facility allows for the issuance of up to $150,000 in additional term loans or additional revolver availability. The Company may request the additional loans at any time prior to the maturity of the senior secured credit facility, provided that the Company is not in default of any terms of the facility, nor is in violation of any financial covenants. The new senior secured credit facility allows the Company to have outstanding, at any time, up to $1,000,000 in secured debt in addition to the senior secured credit facility. At February 28, 2004, the remaining additional permitted secured debt under the new senior credit facility is $197,975. The Company has the ability to incur an unlimited amount of unsecured debt, if the terms of such unsecured indebtedness comply with certain terms set forth in the credit agreement and subject to the Company's compliance with certain financial covenants. If the Company issues unsecured debt that does not meet the credit agreement restrictions, it reduces the amount of available permitted secured debt. The new senior secured credit facility also allows for the repurchase of any debt with a maturity prior to April 30, 2008, and for a limited amount of debt with a maturity after April 30, 2008, based upon outstanding borrowings under the revolving credit facility and available cash at the time of the repurchase.

The new senior secured credit facility contains customary covenants, which place restrictions on incurrence of debt, the payment of dividends, mergers, liens and sale and leaseback transactions. The new senior secured credit facility also requires us to meet various financial ratios and limits capital expenditures. For the twelve months ending February 26, 2005, the covenants require us to maintain a maximum leverage ratio of 6.05:1. Subsequent to February 26, 2005, the ratio gradually decreases to 3.8:1 for the twelve months ending March 1, 2008. We must also maintain a minimum interest coverage ratio of 2.05:1 for the twelve months ending February 26, 2005. Subsequent to February 26, 2005, the ratio gradually increases to 3.25:1 for the twelve months ending March 1, 2008. In addition, we must maintain a minimum fixed charge ratio of 1.10:1 for the twelve months ending February 26,

RITE AID CORPORATION AND SUBSIDIARIES
NOTES TO CONSOLIDATED FINANCIAL STATEMENTS (continued)
For the Years Ended February 28, 2004, March 1, 2003 and March 2, 2002

(In thousands, except per share amounts)

2005. Subsequent to February 26, 2005, the ratio gradually increases to 1.25:1 for the twelve months ending March 1, 2008. Capital expenditures are limited to $386,085 for the fiscal year ending February 26, 2005, with the allowable amount increasing in subsequent years.

The Company was in compliance with the covenants of the new senior secured credit facility and its other debt instruments as of February 28, 2004. With continuing improvements in operating performance, the Company anticipates that it will remain in compliance with its debt covenants. However, variations in operating performance and unanticipated developments may adversely affect the Company's ability to remain in compliance with the applicable debt covenants.

The new senior secured credit facility provides for customary events of default, including nonpayment, misrepresentation, breach of covenants and bankruptcy. It is also an event of default if any event occurs that enables, or which with the giving of notice or the lapse of time would enable, the holder of the Company's debt to accelerate the maturity of debt having a principal amount in excess of $25,000.

The Company's ability to borrow under the senior secured credit facility is based on a specified borrowing base consisting of eligible accounts receivable, inventory and prescription files. At February 28, 2004, the term loan was fully drawn and the Company had no outstanding draws on the revolving credit facility. At February 28, 2004, the Company had additional borrowing capacity of $584,804, net of outstanding letters of credit of $115,196.

As a result of the placement of the new senior secured credit facility, the Company recorded a loss on debt modification in fiscal 2004 of $43,197 (which included the write-off of previously deferred debt issue costs of $35,120).

On October 1, 2003, the Company paid, at maturity, its remaining outstanding balance on the 6.0% dealer remarketable securities.

In May 2003, the Company issued $150,000 aggregate principal amount of 9.25% senior notes due 2013. These notes are unsecured and effectively subordinate to the Company's secured debt. The indenture governing the 9.25% senior notes contains customary covenant provisions that, amount other things, include limitations on the Company's ability to pay dividends, make investments or other restricted payments, incur debt, grant liens, sell assets and enter into sale lease-back transactions.

In April 2003, the Company issued $360,000 aggregate principal amount of 8.125% senior secured notes due 2010. The notes are unsecured, unsubordinated obligations to Rite Aid Corporation and rank equally in right of payment with all other unsecured, unsubordinated indebtedness. The Company's obligations under the notes are guaranteed, subject to certain limitations, by subsidiaries that guarantee the obligations under our new senior secured credit facility. The guarantees are secured, subject to the permitted liens, by shared second priority liens, with the holders of the Company's 12.5% senior notes and the Company's 9.5% senior secured notes, granted by subsidiary guarantors on all of their assets that secure the obligations under the new senior secured credit facility, subject to certain exceptions. The indenture governing the Company's 8.125% senior secured notes contains customary covenant provisions that, among other things, include limitations on our ability to pay dividends, make investments or other restricted payments, incur debt, grant liens, sell assets and enter into sales lease-back transactions.

RITE AID CORPORATION AND SUBSIDIARIES
NOTES TO CONSOLIDATED FINANCIAL STATEMENTS (continued)
For the Years Ended February 28, 2004, March 1, 2003 and March 2, 2002

(In thousands, except per share amounts)

During fiscal 2004 the Company repurchased the following securities:

Debt Repurchased	Principal Amount Repurchased	Amount Paid	(Gain)/ loss
6.0% fixed rate senior notes due 2005	$ 37,848	$ 36,853	$ (865)
7.125% notes due 2007	124,926	120,216	(4,314)
6.875% senior debentures due 2013	15,227	13,144	(1,981)
7.7% notes due 2027	5,000	4,219	(715)
6.875% fixed rate senior notes due 2028	10,000	7,975	(1,895)
12.5% senior secured notes due 2006	10,000	11,275	1,888
Total	$203,001	$193,682	$(7,882)

2003 Transactions:

Senior Secured Notes: The Company issued $300,000 of 9.5% senior secured notes due 2011 in February 2003. The notes were unsecured, unsubordinated obligations of the Company and rank equally in right of payment with all of the Company's other unsecured, unsubordinated indebtedness. The Company's obligations under the notes are guaranteed, subject to certain limitations, by subsidiaries that guarantee the obligations under the senior secured credit facility. The guarantees are secured, subject to the permitted liens, by shared second priority liens with the holders of the 12.5% senior notes and the 8.125% senior secured notes, granted by subsidiary guarantors on all assets that secure the Company's obligations under the senior secured credit facility, subject to certain limitations. Proceeds from these notes were used to redeem all the $149,500 of the Company's senior secured (shareholders) notes due 2006 as well as to fund other debt repurchases and general corporate purposes.

Repurchase of Debt: The Company repurchased $25,425 of its 6.0% dealer remarketable securities due 2003, $118,605 of its 6.0% notes due 2005, and $15,000 of its 7.125% notes due 2007 during fiscal 2003. In addition to the debt repurchases noted above, the Company retired $150,500 of its 5.25% convertible subordinated notes at maturity in September 2002, and made quarterly mandatory repayments on the senior secured credit facility term loan totaling $27,500 during fiscal 2003. These fiscal 2003 transactions resulted in a gain of $13,628 on debt retirements and modifications.

2002 Refinancing and Other Transactions:

On June 27, 2001, the Company completed a major financial restructuring that extended the maturity dates of the majority of its debt to 2005 or beyond, provided additional equity and converted a portion of its debt to equity. These transactions are described below:

Senior Secured Credit Facility: The Company entered into a new $1,900,000 senior secured credit facility. This facility was replaced by the new senior secured credit facility discussed above.

High Yield Notes: The Company issued $150,000 of 11.25% senior notes due July 2008. These notes are unsecured and are effectively subordinate to the secured debt of the Company.

Debt for Debt Exchange: The Company exchanged $152,025 of its existing 10.5% senior secured notes due 2002 for an equal amount of 12.5% senior notes due September 2006. In addition, holders of these notes received warrants to purchase 3,000 shares of Company common stock at $6.00 per share. On June 29, 2001, the warrant holders exercised these warrants, on a cashless basis, and as a result approximately 982 shares of common stock were issued.

During the third quarter of fiscal 2004, the Company recorded a non-recurring income tax benefit, driven by the approval by the Congressional Joint Committee on Taxation on the conclusions of the Internal Revenue Service examination of the Company's federal tax returns for the fiscal years 1996 through 2000.

During the first quarter of fiscal 2004, the Company recorded a loss on debt modification of $43,197 related to the placement of its new senior secured credit facility.

During the fourth quarter of fiscal 2003, the Company incurred $78,277 in store closing and impairment charges. The Company also recorded a $27,700 million credit related to the elimination of several liabilities for former executives and a $19,502 million reduction of its LIFO reserve related to a lower level of inflation than originally estimated.

During the second quarter of fiscal 2003, the Company incurred $58,223 in store closing and impairment charges. In the first quarter of fiscal 2003, the company incurred a charge of $20,000 to reserve for probable loss related to the U.S. Attorney's investigation of former management's business practices. The Company also recorded a tax benefit of $44,011 related to a tax law change that increased the carryback period from two years to five for certain net operating losses.

20. Financial Instruments

The carrying amounts and fair values of financial instruments at February 28, 2004 and March 1, 2003 are listed as follows:

	2004		2003	
	Carrying Amount	Fair Value	Carrying Amount	Fair Value
Variable rate indebtedness	$1,150,000	$1,150,000	$1,372,500	$1,372,500
Fixed rate indebtedness	$2,558,497	$2,640,995	$2,313,942	$2,027,603

Cash, trade receivables and trade payables are carried at market value, which approximates their fair values due to the short-term maturity of these instruments.

The following methods and assumptions were used in estimating fair value disclosures for financial instruments:

LIBOR-based borrowings under credit facilities:

The carrying amounts for LIBOR-based borrowings under the credit facilities, term loans and term notes approximate their fair values due to the short-term nature of the obligations and the variable interest rates.

Long-term indebtedness:

The fair values of long-term indebtedness is estimated based on the quoted market prices of the financial instruments. If quoted market prices were not available, the Company estimated the fair value based on the quoted market price of a financial instrument with similar characteristics.

Continental Airlines, Inc.—Leases

Continental Airlines, Inc., is a major United States air carrier that transports passengers, cargo and mail. They are the fifth largest United States airline (as measured by the number of scheduled miles flown by revenue passengers, known as revenue passenger miles, in 2003). Together with ExpressJet Airlines, Inc. (operating as Continental Express), from which they purchase seat capacity, and the wholly owned subsidiary, Continental Micronesia, Inc., Continental serves 228 airports worldwide at December 31, 2003. (Source: Company Form 10-K)

Learning Objectives
- Understand the economic incentives of leasing versus buying assets.
- Interpret lease footnotes and discussion of commitments and contingencies.
- Relate lease footnote disclosures to balance sheet data.
- Understand the balance sheet and income statement effects of lease accounting.
- Perform present value calculations relating to lease obligations.
- Create pro-forma financial statements to capitalize leases previously treated as operating.
- Understand the economic consequences and quality of earnings issues related to lease accounting.

Refer to the 2003 financial statements of Continental Airlines, Inc.

◇   Concepts   ◇

a.   Why do companies lease assets rather than buy them?

b.   What is an operating lease? What is a capital lease? What is a direct financing lease? What is a sales-type lease? (*Hint*: if your textbook does not cover these lease complexities, use your favorite internet search engine to find definitions and examples.)

c.   Why do accountants distinguish between different types of leases?

◇   Process   ◇

d.   Consider Continental's operating lease payments and the information in Note 6, Leases.

  i.   Provide the summary journal entry that Continental made during fiscal 2003 for operating lease payments. Assume that half of the expense recorded on the income statement for landing fees and other rentals, pertains to landing fees.

  ii.   Provide the summary journal entry that Continental will make to record the anticipated operating lease payments for the year ended December 31, 2004 (that is, in the *next* fiscal year).

e.   The 2003 balance sheet shows "Owned property and equipment – Flight equipment" totaling $6,574 million and "Capital leases – Flight Equipment" of $107. What do these amounts represent? How many jet aircraft does each comprise?

f.   Note 1 provides information about owned aircrafts' residual value and useful lives. Assume that Continental uses 30 years for owned aircrafts' useful lives. Recalculate depreciation on these aircraft for 2003. Prepare the journal entry to record this depreciation. State any other assumptions you make.

g.   Consider the information in Note 1 concerning aircraft under capital lease. Assume that capital leases generally have terms of 20 years. Recalculate amortization on these leased aircraft for 2003. Prepare the journal entry to record this amortization. State any other assumptions you make.

h.   Note 6, Leases, indicates that the present value of capital lease obligations is $323. Explain where this figure is found on Continental's balance sheet.

i. Consider the future minimum lease payments made under the capital leases disclosed in Note 6, Leases. Assume that all lease payments are made on December 31 of the respective years. Also assume that payments made later than 2008 are made evenly over 10 years. That is, lease payments of $47.3 million will be made on December 31, 2009 through 2018, inclusive.

    i. Estimate the average interest rate for these leases. (*Hint*: Use the internal rate of return—IRR—function on a financial calculator or spreadsheet.)

    ii. Based on your calculation of the average interest rate, approximate the interest expense related to these leases for the year that will end December 31, 2004. Use the effective interest rate method. Under the effective interest rate method, interest expense is calculated as the present value of capital lease obligations measured at the beginning of each year times the average interest rate (the one you calculated in part i *i.* above).

    iii. How much cash will be paid for these leases in fiscal 2004?

    iv. Provide the journal entry to record the lease payment of December 31, 2004, based on your answers to parts i *ii.* and *iii.*

    v. Based on your journal entry in part i *iv.*, what portion of the Capital Lease liability is current as of December 31, 2003? Speculate as to why your estimate differs from the "current maturities of capital leases" in Note 6?

j. Consider how the financial statements would look had Continental capitalized all of its operating leases (that is, the aircraft and non-aircraft). Make the following assumptions:

- Continental enters into the leases on December 31, 2003, and annual payments are made at the end of each fiscal year beginning December 31, 2004.

- The implicit interest rate in these leases is 12%.

- Payments for "Later years" are made on December 31 each year for ten years.

    i. Calculate the present value of the future minimum lease payments.

    ii. Prepare the journal entry to capitalize these leases at December 31, 2003.

    iii. What would Continental have reported as the cost of "Equipment and Property Under Capital Leases: Flight equipment" at December 31, 2003? As "Total assets"?

    iv. What would Continental have reported as "Long-Term Debt and Capital Leases" at December 31, 2003? As "Total current liabilities"? And as total liabilities?

    v. What incentives does Continental Airlines, Inc.'s, management have to report its aircraft leases as operating leases? Comment on the effect of leasing on the quality of Continental's financial reporting.

k. Refer to your solution to part *j.* Had Continental capitalized their operating leases, key financial ratios would have been affected for 2003. Assume that the company's marginal tax rate is 35% for your calculations. State any other assumptions you make. Discuss how the current ratio, return on assets, return on equity, and debt to equity ratio would have been impacted. Is it true that the decision to capitalize will always yield weaker ratios?

l. Note 1 reveals that Continental assumes a 15% residual value for its planes and a useful life of between 25 and 30 years. By comparison, Delta Airlines assumes residual values as low as 5% and an average useful life of 20 years for owned aircraft. Which company has the more conservative depreciation policy? Had Continental Airlines adopted the same policy as Delta Airlines, how much depreciation would Continental have recorded in 2003? Compare this to the depreciation you calculated in part f above. Comment on the net income effect of Continental's policy choices.

CONTINENTAL AIRLINES, INC.
Form 10-K report
ITEM 2. PROPERTIES.

Flight Equipment

As shown in the following table, our operating aircraft fleet consisted of 355 mainline jets and 224 regional jets at December 31, 2003, excluding aircraft out of service. The regional jets are leased by ExpressJet from us and are operated by ExpressJet.

Aircraft Type	Total Aircraft	Owned	Leased	Firm Orders	Options	Seats in Standard Configuration	Average Age
777-200ER	18	6	12	-	1	283	4.3
767-400ER	16	14	2	-	-	235	2.3
767-200ER	10	9	1	-	-	174	2.8
757-300	4	4	-	5	-	210	2.0
757-200	41	13	28	-	-	183	6.9
737-900	12	8	4	3	24	167	2.3
737-800	81	26	55	40	35	155	3.6
737-700	36	12	24	15	24	124	5.0
737-500	63	15	48	-	-	104	7.7
737-300	51	14	37	-	-	124	17.3
MD-80	23	6	17	-	-	141	17.8
Mainline jets	355	127	228	63	84		7.6
ERJ-145XR	54	-	54	50	100	50	1.0
ERJ-145	140	18	122	-	-	50	3.6
ERJ-135	30	-	30	-	-	37	3.3
Regional jets	224	18	206	50	100		2.9
Total	579	145	434				5.8

As of December 31, 2003, we had the following mainline aircraft out of service:

Aircraft Type	Total Aircraft	Owned	Leased
DC 10-30	5	2	3
MD-80	14	9	5
737-300	2	-	2
Total	21	11	10

[Continental explains elsewhere that there are another 40 turboprop aircraft—32 leased, 8 owned—that are out of service.]

CONTINENTAL AIRLINES, INC.
CONSOLIDATED STATEMENTS OF OPERATIONS
(In millions, except per share data)

	Year Ended December 31,		
	2003	2002	2001
Operating Revenue:			
Passenger	$8,135	$7,862	$8,457
Cargo, mail and other	735	540	512
	8,870	8,402	8,969
Operating Expenses:			
Wages, salaries and related costs	3,056	2,959	3,021
Aircraft fuel	1,255	1,023	1,229
Aircraft rentals	896	902	903
Landing fees and other rentals	620	633	581
Maintenance, materials and repairs	509	476	568
Depreciation and amortization	444	444	467
Booking fees, credit card discounts and sales	377	380	445
Passenger servicing	297	296	347
Regional capacity purchase, net	153	-	-
Commissions	148	212	364
Other	988	1,135	1,193
Security fee reimbursement	(176)	-	-
Stabilization Act grant	-	12	(417)
Fleet impairment losses and other special charges	100	242	124
	8,667	8,714	8,825
Operating Income (Loss)	203	(312)	144
Nonoperating Income (Expense):			
Interest expense	(393)	(372)	(311)
Interest capitalized	24	36	57
Interest income	19	24	45
Gain on dispositions of ExpressJet Holdings shares	173	-	-
Equity in the income (loss) of affiliates	23	8	(20)
Other, net	152	(15)	(45)
	(2)	(319)	(274)
Income (Loss) before Income Taxes and Minority Interest	201	(631)	(130)
Income Tax Benefit (Expense)	(114)	208	35
Minority Interest	(49)	(28)	-
Net Income (Loss)	$ 38	$ (451)	$ (95)

CONTINENTAL AIRLINES, INC.
CONSOLIDATED BALANCE SHEETS
(In millions, except per share data)

	December 31,	
ASSETS	2003	2002
Current Assets:		
Cash and cash equivalents	$ 999	$ 983
Restricted cash and cash equivalents	170	62
Short-term investments	431	297
Accounts receivable, net of allowance for doubtful receivables of $19 and $30	403	378
Spare parts and supplies, net of allowance for obsolescence of $98 and $98	191	248
Deferred income taxes	157	165
Note receivable from ExpressJet Holdings, Inc.	67	-
Prepayments and other	168	145
Total current assets	2,586	2,278
Property and Equipment:		
Owned property and equipment:		
Flight equipment	6,574	6,762
Other	1,195	1,275
	7,769	8,037
Less: Accumulated depreciation	1,784	1,599
	5,985	6,438
Purchase deposits for flight equipment	225	269
Capital leases:		
Flight equipment	107	117
Other	297	262
	404	379
Less: Accumulated amortization	126	118
	278	261
Total property and equipment	6,488	6,968
Routes	615	615
Airport operating rights, net of accumulated amortization of $293 and $268	259	287
Intangible pension asset	124	144
Investment in affiliates	173	89
Note receivable from ExpressJet Holdings, Inc.	126	-
Other assets, net	278	260
Total Assets	$10,649	$10,641

CONTINENTAL AIRLINES, INC.
CONSOLIDATED BALANCE SHEETS
(In millions, except per share data)

LIABILITIES AND STOCKHOLDERS' EQUITY	2003	2002
Current Liabilities:		
Current maturities of long-term debt and capital leases	$ 422	$ 493
Accounts payable	840	930
Air traffic liability	957	882
Accrued payroll	281	285
Accrued other liabilities	366	336
Total current liabilities	2,866	2,926
Long-Term Debt and Capital Leases	5,558	5,471
Deferred Income Taxes	446	413
Accrued Pension Liability	678	723
Other	309	329
Commitments and Contingencies		
Minority Interest	-	7
Redeemable Preferred Stock of Subsidiary	-	5
Stockholders' Equity:		
Preferred stock - $.01 par, 10,000,000 shares authorized; one share of Series B issued and outstanding, stated at par value	-	-
Class B common stock - $.01 par, 200,000,000 shares authorized; 91,507,192 and 91,203,321 shares issued	1	1
Additional paid-in capital	1,401	1,391
Retained earnings	948	910
Accumulated other comprehensive loss	(417)	(395)
Treasury stock -25,471,881 and 25,442,529 shares, at cost	(1,141)	(1,140)
Total stockholders' equity	792	767
Total Liabilities and Stockholders' Equity	$10,649	$10,641

The accompanying Notes to Consolidated Financial Statements are an integral part of these statements.

CONTINENTAL AIRLINES, INC.
CONSOLIDATED STATEMENTS OF CASH FLOWS
(In millions)

	Year Ended December 31,		
	2003	2002	2001
Cash Flows from Operating Activities:			
Net income (loss)	$ 38	$ (451)	$ (95)
Adjustments to reconcile net income (loss) to cash from operations:			
Deferred income taxes	101	(179)	(40)
Depreciation and amortization	444	444	467
Fleet disposition/impairment losses	100	242	61
Gains on sales of investments	(305)	-	-
Equity in the (income) loss of affiliates	(23)	(8)	20
Other, net	(36)	12	31
Changes in operating assets and liabilities:			
(Increase) decrease in accounts receivable	(25)	(23)	73
(Increase) decrease in spare parts and supplies	4	4	(20)
Increase (decrease) in accounts payable	(19)	(79)	(8)
Increase (decrease) in air traffic liability	75	(132)	(111)
Increase (decrease) in other	(12)	124	189
Net cash provided by (used in) operating activities	342	(46)	567
Cash Flows from Investing Activities:			
Capital expenditures	(205)	(539)	(568)
Purchase deposits paid in connection with future aircraft deliveries	(29)	(73)	(432)
Purchase deposits refunded in connection with aircraft delivered	81	219	337
Purchase of short-term investments	(134)	(56)	(96)
Proceeds from sales of ExpressJet Holdings, net	134	447	-
Proceeds from sales of Internet-related investments	76	-	-
Proceeds from disposition of property and equipment	16	9	11
Other	53	(43)	(26)
Net cash used in investing activities	(8)	(36)	(774)

CONTINENTAL AIRLINES, INC.
CONSOLIDATED STATEMENTS OF CASH FLOWS
(In millions)

Cash Flows from Financing Activities:

Proceeds from issuance of long-term debt, net	559	596	436
Payments on long-term debt and capital lease obligations	(549)	(383)	(367)
Purchase of common stock	-	-	(451)
Proceeds from issuance of common stock	5	23	241
Increase in restricted cash to collateralize letters of credit	(108)	(32)	(22)
Other	-	-	(11)
Net cash (used in) provided by financing activities	(93)	204	(174)
Impact on cash of ExpressJet deconsolidation	(225)	-	-
Net Increase (Decrease) in Cash and Cash Equivalents	16	122	(381)
Cash and Cash Equivalents - Beginning of Period	983	861	1,242
Cash and Cash Equivalents - End of Period	$ 999	$ 983	$ 861

Supplemental Cash Flows Information:

Interest paid	$ 374	$ 345	$ 314
Income taxes paid (refunded)	$ 13	$ (31)	$ (4)
Investing and Financing Activities Not Affecting Cash:			
Property and equipment acquired through the issuance of debt	$ 120	$ 908	$ 707
Capital lease obligations incurred	$ 22	$ 36	$ 95
Contribution of ExpressJet stock to pension plan	$ 100	$ -	$ -

The accompanying Notes to Consolidated Financial Statements are an integral part of these statements.

CONTINENTAL AIRLINES, INC.

NOTE 1 - SUMMARY OF SIGNIFICANT ACCOUNTING POLICIES (excerpts)

g.   Property and Equipment -

Property and equipment are recorded at cost and are depreciated to estimated residual values over their estimated useful lives using the straight-line method. Jet aircraft are assumed to have an estimated residual value of 15% of original cost; other categories of property and equipment are assumed to have no residual value. The estimated useful lives for our property and equipment are as follows:

	Estimated Useful Life
Jet aircraft and simulators	25 to 30 years
Buildings and improvements	10 to 30 years
Food service equipment	6 to 10 years
Maintenance and engineering equipment	8 years
Surface transportation and ground equipment	6 years
Communication and meteorological equipment	5 years
Computer software	3 to 10 years
Capital lease - flight and ground equipment	Lease Term

NOTE 6 - LEASES

We lease certain aircraft and other assets under long-term lease arrangements. Other leased assets include real property, airport and terminal facilities, sales offices, maintenance facilities, training centers and general offices. Most aircraft leases include both renewal options and purchase options. The purchase options are generally effective at the end of the lease term at the then-current fair market value. Our leases do not include residual value guarantees. At December 31, 2003, the scheduled future minimum lease payments under capital leases and the scheduled future minimum lease rental payments required under operating leases, that have initial or remaining noncancelable lease terms in excess of one year, are as follows (in millions):

	Capital Leases	Operating Leases	
Year ending December 31,		Aircraft	Non-aircraft
2004	$ 44	$ 897	$ 360
2005	46	975	362
2006	39	864	365
2007	40	833	367
2008	45	811	354
Later years	473	6,988	5,675
Total minimum lease payments	687	$11,368	$7,483
Less: amount representing interest	364		
Present value of capital leases	323		
Less: current maturities of capital leases	25		
Long-term capital leases	$298		

At December 31, 2003, Continental had 469 aircraft under operating leases and seven aircraft under capital leases, including aircraft subleased to ExpressJet. These operating leases have remaining lease terms ranging up to 21½ years. Projected sublease income to be received from ExpressJet, not included in the above table, is approximately $3.7 billion.

Xilinx, Inc.—Stock-based Compensation

Xilinx, Inc. designs, develops, and markets complete programmable logic solutions, including advanced integrated circuits, software design tools, predefined system functions delivered as intellectual property cores, customer training, field engineering and technical support. Customers are electronic equipment manufacturers primarily in the telecommunications, networking, computing, industrial, and consumer markets. Products are sold globally through a direct sales management organization and through franchised domestic and foreign distributors. (Source: Company 2007 Form 10-K)

Learning Objectives
* Discuss the economic and corporate issues surrounding stock-based compensation.
* Understand how to account for stock-based compensation and how the activity is presented in the financial statements.
* Read and understand footnotes to the financial statements concerning stock-based compensation.
* Explain the financial statement tax effects of stock-based compensation.

Refer to the 2007 financial statements of Xilinx, Inc., and Note 3, Stock-Based Compensation. *Note*: following Xilinx's convention, the case refers to the year ended March 31, 2007, as "fiscal 2007" and to the year ended April 1, 2006, as "fiscal 2006."

✦ Concepts ✦

a. Consider the information on Employee Stock Option Plans (beginning on page 50 of Xilinx's annual report).

    i. Explain, in your own words, how this plan works. What incentives does this plan provide for Xilinx employees?

    ii. Explain briefly the following terms used in Note 3: grant date, exercise price, vesting period, expiration date, options granted, options exercised, and options forfeited.

b. Note 3 (page 47 of Xilinx's annual report) indicates that in fiscal 2007, Xilinx adopted a new accounting method for its stock options and other stock-based compensation as required by SFAS 123R. How does Xilinx now account for stock options? How does this differ from the method Xilinx used before adopting SFAS 123R?

c. In 2007, Xilinx used the modified-prospective method when it adopted SFAS 123R. Note 3 discloses that, ".. under the modified-prospective method the compensation cost recognized by the Company beginning in fiscal 2007 includes … compensation cost for all stock-based awards granted prior to, but not yet vested as of April 1, 2006." Before adopting the new standard, what actions could Xilinx have taken to minimize compensation cost for these unvested options at April 1, 2006?

d. Consider the information on Employee Qualified Stock Purchase Plan (page 52 of Xilinx's annual report). Explain, in your own words, how this plan works. What incentives does this plan provide for Xilinx employees? How do these incentives differ from the incentives created under the Employee Stock Option Plans?

✦ Process ✦

e. The table at the bottom of page 50 of Xilinx's annual report explains changes in the number of outstanding (unexercised) options during the year.

    i. How many options did Xilinx grant during fiscal 2007? What was the per-share average exercise (strike) price of these new options? Compare this price to the per-share average exercise price of grants in 2006 and 2005. What can we conclude from this comparison?

ii.   How many options did employees exercise during the year? Approximately how much cash did Xilinx receive from the exercise of these options? Where does this cash appear on the statement of cash flows? *Hint*: it is included with other share activity and not shown as its own separate cash-flow line item.

iii.   How many options did employees forfeit during the year? Why would employees not exercise all the options they held?

f. Consider Xilinx's 2007 Statement of Income, Statement of Cash Flows and the table on page 48 of Xilinx's annual report that discloses information about stock-based compensation expense.

i.   According to the table on page 48, what total expense does Xilinx report for stock-based compensation in 2007?

ii.   Where on the Statement of Income does Xilinx include this expense? Explain.

iii.   How does the 2007 expense affect the Statement of Cash Flows? Reconcile the Statement of Income and Statement of Cash Flows for this expense.

iv.   Explain in general terms, the income tax effects of Xilinx's 2007 stock-based compensation expense.

v.   Prepare the journal entry to record Xilinx's 2007 stock-based compensation expense. Your journal entry should include tax effects.

g. Note 3 discloses the following information about stock-option expirations, "Options currently granted (i.e., prior to 2007) … generally expire ten years from the grant date." (page 47 of annual report); and "The term for options granted under the 2007 Plan will be seven years." (page 51 of annual report). Explain how the change in option expiration from 10 years to seven years affects Xilinx's stock option expense.

Analysis

h. Consider the discussion of the fair values of stock options at the bottom of page 49 of the Xilinx annual report.

i.   How does Xilinx determine the fair values of stock options?

ii.   What is the per share average fair value of options granted during fiscal 2007?

iii.   Compare the per-share average fair value of options granted during 2007 to the average per-share exercise price of those option grants (from question e, i). Why are these two numbers different?

i. Note 3 (page 49) discloses that the company changed how it determines stock-price volatility from "historic" to "implied" volatility.

i.   In general, how does volatility affect stock-based compensation expense?

ii.   Compare Xilinx's volatility estimates from 2005 to 2007, disclosed on page 49 of Xilinx 2007 annual report. Does the change of volatility from historic to implied increase or decrease Xilinx's stock option expense in 2007 compared to 2005?

iii.   Quantify the effect of the change in volatility estimates on Xilinx's 2007 stock option expense. Use an option calculator (for example, a free calculator from the Chicago Board of Exchange at: http://www.ivolatility.com/calc/) to determine what Xilinx would have reported as stock option expense in 2007 if the company had used 2005 historic volatility instead of implied volatility. Is the difference significant?

j. Each year Xilinx receives a tax benefit related to exercises of employee stock options. This benefit arises because firms may deduct as an expense for tax purposes the intrinsic value of options *exercised* by employees.

i.   Using information in the Statement of Cash Flows, determine the amount of tax benefit Xilinx received during fiscal 2007.

ii. Why does this amount appear as a reconciling item in the operating section of the Statement of Cash Flows?

iii. What does the amount of "Excess tax benefit" that is reclassified from the operating to the financing section of the Statement of Cash Flows capture? *Hint*: see the discussion of "Excess tax benefits" in the first paragraph of Note 3.

iv. Prepare the journal entry to record Xilinx's 2007 tax benefit from employee exercises of stock options.

v. Compute your own estimate of the 2007 tax benefit to validate the amount reported by Xilinx. To do this, first estimate the intrinsic value of options *exercised* during the year and then apply the appropriate tax rate. Recall that an option's intrinsic value is the difference between its exercise price and the fair-value of the stock. Assume that the weighted average exercise price of options granted in 2007 provides a good measure of the fair-value of Xilinx stock when options were exercised during the year. Further assume that 35% is an appropriate marginal tax rate for Xilinx.

k. Consider the article from *Electronic News*. The SEC began an investigation of Xilinx to determine if the company had "backdated" stock options granted to employees. Explain what is meant by back-dating of option grants. Why would corporate executives backdate options? Why would shareholders object to such a practice?

Xilinx, Maxim Subject of More Stock-Option Litigation

Staff Reporter -- Electronic News, 6/15/2006*

A second lawsuit has been filed in the U.S. District Court for the Northern District of Calif. against certain officers and directors of Xilinx Inc. as a result of allegations concerning improper backdating of Xilinx options granted to company employees.

The first suit was filed on June 2.

The law firm Finkelstein, Thompson & Loughran said it is investigating similar claims at this time and welcomes inquiries from shareholders concerning their rights and interests in this matter.

This lawsuit in the wake of news reports indicating Xilinx appears to have backdated option grants so their exercise price correlated to a day on or near the day Xilinx stock hit its low price for the year, or directly in advance of sharp increases in the price of Xilinx stock, according to a statement by the firm today.

The complaint filed alleges the defendants mismanaged corporate assets and breached their fiduciary duties between 1998 and June 2 by authorizing or failing to halt the back-dating of certain stock options, and if true, could potentially require restatement of Xilinx's financial reports and could create additional tax and legal liabilities for the company, the firm also said.

In other stock-option-related news, the same firm said it has filed a lawsuit in the U.S. District Court for the Northern District of Calif. against certain officers and directors of Maxim Integrated Products Inc. as a result of allegations concerning improper backdating of Maxim options granted to Maxim employees.

The Securities and Exchange Commission (SEC) recently began an informal inquiry into Maxim's stock options grants and practices.

The inquiry against Maxim arose in the wake of news reports indicating Maxim appears to have backdated option grants so their exercise price correlated to a day on or near the day Maxim stock hit its low price for the year, or directly in advance of sharp increases in the price of Maxim stock, the firm noted.

These allegations, if true, could potentially require restatement of Maxim's financial reports and could create additional tax and legal liabilities for Maxim, the firm concluded.

These suits are a few of the latest in the growing number of semiconductor companies under scrutiny for their stock option granting practices.

* http://www.edn.com/article/CA6344184.html

ITEM 8. FINANCIAL STATEMENTS AND SUPPLEMENTARY DATA

XILINX, INC.
CONSOLIDATED STATEMENTS OF INCOME

	Years Ended		
	March 31, 2007(1)	April 1, 2006	April 2, 2005
	(In thousands, except per share amounts)		
Net revenues.	$1,842,739	$1,726,250	$1,573,233
Cost of revenues.	718,643	657,119	576,284
Gross margin	1,124,096	1,069,131	996,949
Operating expenses:			
Research and development.	388,101	326,126	307,448
Selling, general and administrative	375,510	316,302	303,595
Amortization of acquisition-related intangibles.	8,009	6,976	6,668
Litigation settlements and contingencies	2,500	3,165	—
Stock-based compensation related to prior years.	2,209	—	—
Write-off of acquired in-process research and development	—	4,500	7,198
Total operating expenses	776,329	657,069	624,909
Operating income	347,767	412,062	372,040
Impairment loss on investments	(1,950)	(1,418)	(3,099)
Interest and other, net	85,329	45,958	31,603
Income before income taxes	431,146	456,602	400,544
Provision for income taxes	80,474	102,453	87,821
Net income.	$ 350,672	$ 354,149	$ 312,723
Net income per common share:			
Basic.	$ 1.04	$ 1.01	$ 0.90
Diluted	$ 1.02	$ 1.00	$ 0.87
Shares used in per share calculations:			
Basic.	337,920	349,026	347,810
Diluted	343,636	355,065	358,230

(1) Cost of revenues and operating expenses for fiscal 2007 include stock-based compensation expenses. See Notes 2 and 3 for additional information.

Xilinx 2007 Form 10-K

See notes to consolidated financial statements.

XILINX, INC.
CONSOLIDATED BALANCE SHEETS

	March 31, 2007	April 1, 2006
	(In thousands, except par value amounts)	
ASSETS		
Current assets:		
Cash and cash equivalents	$ 635,879	$ 783,366
Short-term investments	502,036	201,551
Investment in United Microelectronics Corporation, current portion	—	37,285
Accounts receivable, net of allowances for doubtful accounts and customer returns of $3,737 and $3,697 in 2007 and 2006, respectively	182,295	194,205
Inventories	174,572	201,029
Deferred tax assets	100,344	110,928
Prepaid expenses and other current assets	104,976	119,884
Total current assets	1,700,102	1,648,248
Property, plant and equipment, at cost:		
Land	94,187	63,521
Buildings	281,334	246,550
Machinery and equipment	337,037	311,516
Furniture and fixtures	47,639	44,773
	760,197	666,360
Accumulated depreciation and amortization	(347,161)	(308,103)
Net property, plant and equipment	413,036	358,257
Long-term investments	675,713	616,296
Investment in United Microelectronics Corporation, net of current portion	67,050	239,209
Goodwill	117,955	125,084
Acquisition-related intangibles, net	14,626	22,651
Other assets	190,873	163,802
Total Assets	$ 3,179,355	$ 3,173,547
LIABILITIES AND STOCKHOLDERS' EQUITY		
Current liabilities:		
Accounts payable	$ 78,912	$ 71,004
Accrued payroll and related liabilities	83,949	79,260
Income taxes payable	24,210	30,048
Deferred income on shipments to distributors	89,052	126,558
Other accrued liabilities	27,246	38,154
Total current liabilities	303,369	345,024
Convertible debentures	999,597	—
Deferred tax liabilities	102,329	92,153
Other long-term liabilities	1,320	7,485
Commitments and contingencies		
Stockholders' equity:		
Preferred stock, $.01 par value; 2,000 shares authorized; none issued and outstanding	—	—
Common stock, $.01 par value; 2,000,000 shares authorized; 295,902 and 342,618 shares issued and outstanding in 2007 and 2006, respectively	2,959	3,426
Additional paid-in capital	849,888	1,375,120
Retained earnings	916,292	1,334,530
Accumulated other comprehensive income	3,601	15,809
Total stockholders' equity	1,772,740	2,728,885
Total Liabilities and Stockholders' Equity	$ 3,179,355	$ 3,173,547

See notes to consolidated financial statements.

Xilinx 2007 Form 10-K

XILINX, INC.
CONSOLIDATED STATEMENTS OF CASH FLOWS

	Years Ended		
	March 31, 2007	April 1, 2006	April 2, 2005
	(In thousands)		
Cash flows from operating activities:			
Net income	$ 350,672	$ 354,149	$ 312,723
Adjustments to reconcile net income to net cash provided by operating activities:			
Depreciation	55,998	53,326	51,921
Amortization	17,926	16,223	11,141
Amortization of deferred compensation	—	—	504
Stock-based compensation	90,292	—	—
Stock-based compensation related to prior years	2,209	—	—
Write-off of acquired in-process research and development	—	4,500	7,198
Net (gain) loss on sale of available-for-sale securities	(814)	4,981	(505)
Impairment loss on investments	1,950	1,418	3,099
Convertible debt derivatives – revaluation and amortization	(403)	—	—
Noncash compensation expense	—	735	—
Provision for deferred income taxes	7,091	26,032	59,552
Tax benefit from exercise of stock options	35,765	40,596	51,854
Excess tax benefit from stock-based compensation	(27,413)	—	—
Changes in assets and liabilities, net of effects from acquisition of businesses:			
Accounts receivable, net	11,911	19,380	35,490
Inventories	28,617	(15,307)	(83,268)
Deferred income taxes	3,532	(1,891)	(53,229)
Prepaid expenses and other current assets	35,652	(34,897)	4,509
Other assets	(15,636)	(29,910)	(32,116)
Accounts payable	7,908	7,811	(15,371)
Accrued liabilities	(10,939)	18,917	(5,976)
Income taxes payable	(5,244)	(687)	(23,572)
Deferred income on shipments to distributors	(37,506)	24,047	(48,468)
Net cash provided by operating activities	551,568	489,423	275,486
Cash flows from investing activities:			
Purchases of available-for-sale securities	(1,864,582)	(1,459,248)	(2,161,606)
Proceeds from sale and maturity of available-for-sale securities	1,693,152	1,812,580	2,196,321
Purchases of property, plant and equipment	(110,777)	(67,040)	(61,377)
Acquisition of businesses, net of cash acquired	—	(19,476)	(18,433)
Other investing activities	(1,564)	(24,436)	—
Net cash provided by (used in) investing activities	(283,771)	242,380	(45,095)
Cash flows from financing activities:			
Repurchases of common stock	(1,430,000)	(401,584)	(133,755)
Proceeds from issuance of common stock through various stock plans	128,136	100,949	85,064
Proceeds from issuance of convertible debentures, net of issuance costs	980,000	—	—
Payment of dividends to stockholders	(120,833)	(97,190)	(69,655)
Excess tax benefit from stock-based compensation	27,413	—	—
Net cash used in financing activities	(415,284)	(397,825)	(118,346)
Net increase (decrease) in cash and cash equivalents	(147,487)	333,978	112,045
Cash and cash equivalents at beginning of year	783,366	449,388	337,343
Cash and cash equivalents at end of year	$ 635,879	$ 783,366	$ 449,388
Supplemental schedule of non-cash activities:			
Accrual of affordable housing credit investments	$ —	$ 19,357	$ —
Supplemental disclosure of cash flow information:			
Income taxes paid, net of refunds	$ 39,330	$ 37,159	$ 52,026

See notes to consolidated financial statements.

XILINX, INC.
CONSOLIDATED STATEMENTS OF STOCKHOLDERS' EQUITY

	Common Stock Outstanding		Additional Paid-in Capital	Retained Earnings	Treasury Stock	Accumulated Other Comprehensive Income (Loss)	Total Stockholders' Equity
	Shares	Amount					
				(In thousands)			
Balance at April 3, 2004	346,962	$3,470	$ 903,991	$1,521,568	$ (1,031)	$ 55,064	$ 2,483,062
Components of comprehensive income:							
Net income	—	—	—	312,723	—	—	312,723
Change in net unrealized loss on available-for-sale securities, net of tax benefit of $38,471	—	—	—	—	—	(55,757)	(55,757)
Cumulative translation adjustment	—	—	—	—	—	897	897
Total comprehensive income							257,863
Issuance of common shares and treasury stock under employee stock plans	7,632	76	(49,420)	(1,763)	135,618	—	84,511
Repurchase of common stock	(4,433)	(44)	—	—	(134,587)	—	(134,631)
Deferred compensation-RocketChips	—	—	504	—	—	—	504
Cash dividends declared ($0.20 per common share)	—	—	—	(69,655)	—	—	(69,655)
Tax benefit from exercise of stock options	—	—	51,854	—	—	—	51,854
Balance at April 2, 2005	350,161	3,502	906,929	1,762,873	—	204	2,673,508
Components of comprehensive income:							
Net income	—	—	—	354,149	—	—	354,149
Change in net unrealized gain on available-for-sale securities, net of taxes of $10,540	—	—	—	—	—	17,179	17,179
Change in net unrealized gain on hedging transactions, net of taxes	—	—	—	—	—	118	118
Cumulative translation adjustment	—	—	—	—	—	(1,692)	(1,692)
Total comprehensive income							369,754
Issuance of common shares and treasury stock under employee stock plans	7,437	74	46,321	(13,009)	70,690	—	104,076
Reclassification of losses from reissuance of treasury stock	—	—	502,552	(502,552)	—	—	—
Repurchase and retirement of common stock	(15,011)	(150)	(159,429)	(169,741)	(70,690)	—	(400,010)
Noncash compensation expense	31	—	735	—	—	—	735
Cash dividends declared ($0.28 per common share)	—	—	—	(97,190)	—	—	(97,190)
Reversal of reserve for cost sharing as a result of Tax Court decision	—	—	44,713	—	—	—	44,713
Tax reconciliation and reclassification adjustments	—	—	(7,297)	—	—	—	(7,297)
Tax benefit from exercise of stock options	—	—	40,596	—	—	—	40,596
Balance at April 1, 2006	342,618	3,426	1,375,120	1,334,530	—	15,809	2,728,885
Components of comprehensive income:							
Net income	—	—	—	350,672	—	—	350,672
Change in net unrealized loss on available-for-sale securities, net of tax benefit of $8,267	—	—	—	—	—	(13,520)	(13,520)
Change in net unrealized loss on hedging transactions, net of taxes	—	—	—	—	—	(105)	(105)
Cumulative translation adjustment	—	—	—	—	—	1,417	1,417
Total comprehensive income							338,464
Issuance of common shares under employee stock plans	8,505	85	125,712	—	—	—	125,797
Repurchase and retirement of common stock	(55,221)	(552)	(781,371)	(648,077)	—	—	(1,430,000)
Stock-based compensation expense	—	—	90,292	—	—	—	90,292
Stock-based compensation capitalized in inventory	—	—	2,161	—	—	—	2,161
Stock-based compensation related to prior years	—	—	2,209	—	—	—	2,209
Cash dividends declared ($0.36 per common share)	—	—	—	(120,833)	—	—	(120,833)
Tax benefit from exercise of stock options	—	—	35,765	—	—	—	35,765
Balance at March 31, 2007	295,902	$2,959	$ 849,888	$ 916,292	$ —	$ 3,601	$ 1,772,740

See notes to consolidated financial statements.

40

XILINX, INC.
Notes to consolidated financial statements

Note 3. Stock-Based Compensation

Adoption of SFAS 123(R)

Effective April 2, 2006, the Company adopted SFAS 123(R). SFAS 123(R) requires the Company to measure the cost of all employee stock-based compensation awards that are expected to be exercised based on the grant-date fair value of those awards and to record that cost as compensation expense over the period during which the employee is required to perform service in exchange for the award (generally over the vesting period of the award). SFAS 123(R) addresses all forms of stock-based payment awards, including shares issued under employee stock purchase plans, stock options, restricted stock and stock appreciation rights. In addition, the Company is required to record compensation expense (as previous awards continue to vest) for the unvested portion of previously granted awards that remain outstanding at the date of adoption. The Company implemented the standard using the modified-prospective method and consequently has not retroactively adjusted results for prior periods. The Company previously accounted for stock-based compensation under APB 25 and related interpretations, using the intrinsic value method and, as such, generally recognized no compensation cost for employee stock options. Prior to adopting SFAS 123(R), the Company presented all tax benefits resulting from the exercise of stock options as operating cash flows in its statements of cash flows. SFAS 123(R) requires cash flows resulting from excess tax benefits to be classified as a part of cash flows from financing activities. Excess tax benefits are realized tax benefits from tax deductions for exercised options in excess of the deferred tax asset attributable to stock compensation costs for such options. In addition, the Company provided the required pro forma disclosures related to its stock plans prescribed by SFAS 123 as amended by SFAS No. 148.

Under the modified-prospective method of adoption for SFAS 123(R), the compensation cost recognized by the Company beginning in fiscal 2007 includes (a) compensation cost for all stock-based awards granted prior to, but not yet vested as of April 1, 2006, based on the grant-date fair value estimated in accordance with the original provisions of SFAS 123, and (b) compensation cost for all stock-based awards granted subsequent to April 1, 2006, based on the grant-date fair value estimated in accordance with the provisions of SFAS 123(R). The Company uses the straight-line attribution method to recognize stock-based compensation costs over the requisite service period of the award for stock-based awards granted after April 1, 2006. For stock-based awards granted prior to April 2, 2006, the Company continues to use the accelerated amortization method consistent with the amounts disclosed in the pro forma disclosure as prescribed by SFAS 123. Upon exercise, cancellation or expiration of stock options, deferred tax assets for options with multiple vesting dates are eliminated for each vesting period on a first-in, first-out basis as if each award had a separate vesting period. To calculate the excess tax benefits available for use in offsetting future tax shortfalls as of the date of implementation, the Company followed the alternative transition method discussed in FSP 123(R)-3.

Options currently granted by the Company generally expire ten years from the grant date. Options granted to existing and newly hired employees generally vest over a four-year period from the date of grant.

Stock-based compensation recognized in fiscal 2007 as a result of the adoption of SFAS 123(R) as well as pro forma disclosures according to the original provisions of SFAS 123 for periods prior to the adoption of SFAS 123(R) use the Black-Scholes option pricing model for estimating fair value of options granted under the Company's stock option plans and rights to acquire stock granted under the Employee Stock Purchase Plan.

XILINX, INC.
Notes to consolidated financial statements (continued)

The following table summarizes the effects of stock-based compensation resulting from the application of SFAS 123(R) to options granted under the Company's stock option plans and rights to acquire stock granted under the Employee Stock Purchase Plan:

(In thousands, except per share amounts)	2007	2006	2005
Stock-based compensation included in:			
Cost of revenues	$ 10,345	$ —	$ —
Research and development	41,610	—	—
Selling, general and administrative	38,337	—	—
Stock-based compensation related to prior years	2,209	—	—
Stock-based compensation effect on income before taxes	92,501	—	—
Income tax effect	(26,876)	—	—
Net stock-based compensation effect on net income	$ 65,625	$ —	$ —
Stock-based compensation effect on basic net income per common share	$ 0.19	$ —	$ —
Stock-based compensation effect on diluted net income per common share	$ 0.19	$ —	$ —
Stock-based compensation effect on cash flows from operations	$ (27,413)	$ —	$ —
Stock-based compensation effect on cash flows from financing activities	$ 27,413	$ —	$ —

In June 2006, under the direction of a Special Committee of the Board of Directors, outside counsel commenced an investigation of the Company's historical stock option-granting practices and found no evidence of fraud in the Company's practices in granting of stock options, nor any evidence of manipulation of the timing or exercise price of stock option grants. The investigation further found no issues of management integrity in the issuance of stock options. The investigation determined that in nearly all cases, stock options were issued as of pre-set dates. Based on the results of the investigation and the Company's analysis of the facts, the Company took a $2.2 million charge to its earnings for the first quarter of fiscal 2007 related to minor differences between recorded grant dates and measurement dates for certain stock option grants between 1997 and 2006. This one-time charge did not have a material effect on the Company's historical financial statements, and, thus, the Company did not restate its financial statements for prior years. See Note 15 for additional information about the conclusion of the investigation, which arose in response to the stockholder derivative complaints and a notification by the SEC of an informal inquiry into the Company's historical stock option-granting practices. The SEC subsequently terminated its informal inquiry of the Company's stock option-granting practices and the stockholder derivative complaints were consolidated and subsequently dismissed.

The amount that the Company would have capitalized to inventory as of April 1, 2006, if it had applied the provisions of SFAS 123(R) retrospectively, was $4.5 million. Under the provisions of SFAS 123(R), this $4.5 million has been recorded as a credit to additional paid-in-capital. The total stock-based compensation released from the inventory capitalization during fiscal 2007 was $2.3 million, which resulted in an ending inventory balance of $2.2 million related to stock-based compensation at March 31, 2007. During fiscal 2007, the tax benefit realized for the tax deduction from option exercises and other awards totaled $35.8 million. As of March 31, 2007, total unrecognized stock-based compensation costs related to stock options and Employee Stock Purchase Plan was $93.4 million and $19.0 million, respectively. The total unrecognized stock-based compensation cost for stock options and Employee Stock Purchase Plan is expected to be recognized over a weighted-average period of 2.6 years and 0.9 years, respectively.

XILINX, INC.
Notes to consolidated financial statements (continued)

Prior to the adoption of SFAS 123(R), the Company adopted the disclosure-only alternative allowed under SFAS 123, as amended by SFAS 148. Stock-based compensation expense recognized under SFAS 123(R) was not reflected in the Company's results of operations for fiscal 2006 or 2005 for stock option awards as all options were granted with an exercise price equal to the market value of the underlying common stock on the date of grant. In addition, the Employee Stock Purchase Plan was deemed non-compensatory under the provisions of APB 25. Forfeitures of awards were recognized as they occurred for the period prior to the adoption.

Pro forma information required under SFAS 123 for periods prior to fiscal 2007 as if the Company had applied the fair value recognition provisions of SFAS 123 to stock-based compensation, was as follows:

(In thousands, except per share amounts)	2006	2005
Net income as reported	$ 354,149	$ 312,723
Deduct: Stock-based employee compensation expense determined under fair value method for all awards, net of tax	(82,956)	(119,237)
Pro forma net income	$ 271,193	$ 193,486
Net income per common share:		
Basic-as reported	$ 1.01	$ 0.90
Basic-pro forma	$ 0.78	$ 0.56
Diluted-as reported	$ 1.00	$ 0.87
Diluted-pro forma	$ 0.76	$ 0.54

The fair values of stock options and stock purchase plan rights under the Company's stock option plans and Employee Stock Purchase Plan were estimated as of the grant date using the Black-Scholes option-pricing model. In the first quarter of fiscal 2006, the Company modified its volatility assumption to use implied volatility for options granted. Previously, the Company used only historical volatility in deriving its volatility assumption. Management determined that implied volatility is more reflective of market conditions and a better indicator of expected volatility than historical volatility. The expected life of options granted is based on the historical exercise activity as well as the expected disposition of all options outstanding. Calculated under SFAS 123(R) (SFAS 123 for fiscal 2006 and 2005), the per share weighted-average fair values of stock options granted during fiscal 2007, 2006 and 2005 were $9.02, $7.99 and $16.68, respectively. The per share weighted-average fair values of stock purchase rights granted under the Employee Stock Purchase Plan during fiscal 2007, 2006 and 2005 were $6.51, $7.89 and $12.59, respectively. The fair value of stock options and stock purchase plan rights granted in fiscal 2007, 2006 and 2005 were estimated at the date of grant using the following weighted average assumptions:

	Stock Options			Employee Stock Purchase Plan		
	2007	2006	2005	2007	2006	2005
Expected life of options (years)	6.3 to 6.4	4.8 to 5.0	4.7	0.5 to 2.0	0.5 to 2.0	0.5 to 2.0
Expected stock price volatility	0.31 to 0.39	0.29 to 0.36	0.66	0.27 to 0.38	0.27 to 0.46	0.36 to 0.51
Risk-free interest rate	4.4% to 5.2%	3.7% to 4.8%	3.6%	3.6% to 5.2%	1.9% to 4.6%	1.0% to 2.7%
Dividend yield	1.4% to 1.6%	1.0% to 1.1%	0.7%	1.4% to 1.8%	1.2% to 1.4%	0.6% to 0.7%

XILINX, INC.
Notes to consolidated financial statements (continued)

Options outstanding that have vested and are expected to vest in future periods as of March 31, 2007 are as follows:

	Number of Shares	Weighted-Average Exercise Price Per Share	Weighted-Average Remaining Contractual Term (Years)	Aggregate Intrinsic Value (1)
		(Shares and intrinsic value in thousands)		
Vested (i.e., exercisable)	41,803	$32.68	4.60	$110,381
Expected to vest	13,230	$26.64	8.61	16,602
Total vested and expected to vest	55,033	$31.23	5.56	$126,983
Total outstanding	55,942	$31.13	5.62	$128,369

---

(1) These amounts represent the difference between the exercise price and $25.73, the closing price per share of Xilinx's stock on March 30, 2007, for all in-the-money options outstanding.

Options outstanding that are expected to vest are net of estimated future option forfeitures in accordance with the provisions of SFAS 123(R), which are estimated when compensation costs are recognized. Options with a fair value of $103.2 million completed vesting during fiscal 2007.

Employee Stock Option Plans

Under the Company's stock option plans (Option Plans), options reserved for future issuance to employees and directors of the Company total 91.7 million shares as of March 31, 2007, including 35.8 million shares available for future grants. Options to purchase shares of the Company's common stock under the Option Plans are granted at 100% of the fair market value of the stock on the date of grant. Options granted to date expire ten years from date of grant and vest at varying rates over two or four years.

A summary of the Company's Option Plans activity and related information are as follows:

		Options Outstanding	
	Shares Available for Options	Number of Shares	Weighted Average Exercise Price Per Share
		(Shares in thousands)	
April 3, 2004	28,707	58,123	$27.13
Additional shares reserved	13,560	—	—
Granted	(9,810)	9,810	$37.12
Exercised	—	(5,993)	$ 8.75
Forfeited/cancelled/expired	1,297	(1,297)	$40.78
April 2, 2005	33,754	60,643	$30.18
Granted	(8,489)	8,489	$25.91
Exercised	—	(6,090)	$11.71
Forfeited/cancelled/expired	3,212	(3,212)	$38.64
April 1, 2006	28,477	59,830	$30.99
Additional shares reserved	10,000	—	—
Granted	(8,751)	8,751	$23.50
Exercised	—	(6,598)	$13.88
Forfeited/cancelled/expired	6,041	(6,041)	$37.51
March 31, 2007	35,767	55,942	$31.13

XILINX, INC.
Notes to consolidated financial statements (continued)

The above table includes additional shares that became available under a five-year evergreen program that was approved by stockholders in 1999. The final allotment of 13.6 million shares, approved by the Board on April 8, 2004, marked the end of the Company's five-year evergreen program. On July 26, 2006, the stockholders approved the adoption of the 2007 Equity Incentive Plan (2007 Plan) and authorized 10.0 million shares to be reserved for issuance thereunder. The types of awards allowed under the 2007 Plan include incentive stock options, non-qualified stock options, restricted stock units (RSUs), restricted stock and stock appreciation rights. The Company expects to issue primarily a mix of non-qualified stock options and RSUs under the 2007 Plan. The expected mix of stock options and RSU awards will change depending upon the grade level of the employees. Employees at the lower grade levels will receive mostly RSUs and may also receive stock options, whereas employees at the higher grade levels, including the Company's executive officers, will receive mostly stock options and may also receive RSUs. The term for options granted under the 2007 Plan will be seven years. Since the 2007 Plan became effective on January 1, 2007, the 10.0 million shares to be reserved for issuance are included as shares available for options in the table above, even though no awards had been granted under the new plan as of March 31, 2007. The 2007 Plan replaced both the Company's 1997 Stock Plan and the Supplemental Stock Option Plan and all available but unissued shares under these prior plans were cancelled as of April 1, 2007. At its 2007 annual stockholder meeting, the Company will seek stockholder approval of an increase in the number of shares reserved for issuance under the 2007 Plan by 5.0 million shares.

The total pre-tax intrinsic value of options exercised during fiscal 2007 was $75.5 million. This intrinsic value represents the difference between the fair market value of the Company's common stock on the date of exercise and the exercise price of each option.

Since the Company adopted the policy of retiring all repurchased shares of its common stock, new shares are issued upon employees' exercise of their stock options.

The following information relates to options outstanding and exercisable under the Option Plans at March 31, 2007:

Range of Exercise Prices	Options Outstanding			Options Exercisable	
	Options Outstanding	Weighted Average Remaining Contractual Life (Years)	Weighted Average Exercise Price Per Share	Options Exercisable	Weighted Average Exercise Price Per Share
	(Shares in thousands)				
$8.42 - $21.81	10,205	2.14	$16.22	9,768	$ 16.03
$21.85 - $23.49	10,563	7.69	$23.07	5,855	$ 23.27
$23.53 - $27.35	9,715	8.14	$25.62	3,909	$ 25.70
$27.45 - $37.57	10,901	5.28	$33.02	9,262	$ 33.61
$37.60 - $42.46	10,192	5.96	$40.50	8,643	$ 40.60
$42.88 - $96.63	4,366	3.15	$71.16	4,366	$ 71.16
$8.42 - $96.63	55,942	5.62	$31.13	41,803	$ 32.68

At April 1, 2006, 45.2 million options were exercisable at an average price of $31.39. At April 2, 2005, 45.4 million options were exercisable at an average price of $29.25.

XILINX, INC.
Notes to consolidated financial statements (continued)

Employee Qualified Stock Purchase Plan

Under the Employee Stock Purchase Plan, qualified employees can obtain a 24-month purchase right to purchase the Company's common stock at the end of six-month exercise periods. Participation is limited to 15% of the employee's annual earnings up to a maximum of $21 thousand in a calendar year. More than 80% of all eligible employees participate in the Employee Stock Purchase Plan. The purchase price of the stock is 85% of the lower of the fair market value at the beginning of the 24-month offering period or at the end of each six-month exercise period. Employees purchased 2.0 million shares for $34.2 million in fiscal 2007, 1.4 million shares for $33.0 million in fiscal 2006 and 1.6 million shares for $32.1 million in fiscal 2005. On July 26, 2006, the stockholders approved an amendment to increase the authorized number of shares available for issuance under the Employee Stock Purchase Plan by 2.0 million shares. At March 31, 2007, 8.0 million shares were available for future issuance out of 36.5 million shares authorized. At its 2007 annual stockholder meeting, the Company will seek stockholder approval of an increase in the number of shares reserved for issuance under the Employee Stock Purchase Plan by 2.0 million shares.

Merck & Co., Inc., and GlaxoSmithKline plc— Shareholders' Equity

Merck & Co., Inc., is a global research-driven pharmaceutical company that discovers, develops, manufactures and markets a broad range of products to improve human and animal health. Headquartered in New Jersey, the company employs 59,800 people worldwide, 11,700 of whom are engaged in research activities. The company's shares are listed on the New York and Philadelphia Stock Exchanges. (Source: Company 2007 Form 10-K)

GlaxoSmithKline plc is a global healthcare group engaged in the creation, discovery, development, manufacture and marketing of pharmaceutical and consumer health-related products. Headquartered in London, the company operates research and development facilities in the UK, the USA, Belgium, Italy, Japan and Spain and manufactures its products in 38 countries. The company's shares are listed on the London and New York Stock Exchanges. (Source: Company 2007 Annual Report)

Learning Objectives
• Read and interpret shareholders' equity disclosures.
• Explain why companies pay dividends.
• Explain why companies repurchase their stock.
• Compare accounting treatment of shareholders' equity accounts under U.S. and International GAAP.

Refer to the financial statements and notes of Merck & Co., Inc., and GlaxoSmithKline plc.

 Concepts

a. Consider Merck's common shares.

    i. How many common shares is Merck authorized to issue?

    ii. How many common shares has Merck actually issued at December 31, 2007?

    iii. Reconcile the number of shares issued at December 31, 2007, to the dollar value of common stock reported on the balance sheet.

    iv. How many common shares are held in treasury at December 31, 2007?

    v. How many common shares are outstanding at December 31, 2007?

    vi. At December 31, 2007, Merck's stock price closed at $57.61 per share. Calculate the total market capitalization of Merck on that day.

b. Consider GlaxoSmithKline's ordinary shares.

    i. How many ordinary shares is GlaxoSmithKline authorized to issue?

    ii. How many ordinary shares has GlaxoSmithKline actually issued at December 31, 2007?

    iii. How many ordinary shares are in free issue at December 31, 2007?

    iv. How many common shares are held in treasury at December 31, 2007?

    v. Explain the difference between "Share capital" and the "Share premium account" reported on GlaxoSmithKline's balance sheet. What does Merck call these types of accounts on their U.S. GAAP balance sheet?

c. Why do companies pay dividends on their common or ordinary shares? What normally happens to a company's share price when dividends are paid?

d. In general, why do companies repurchase their own shares?

e. Consider Merck's statement of cash flow and statement of retained earnings. Prepare a single journal entry that summarizes Merck's common dividend activity for 2007.

f. During 2007, GlaxoSmithKline paid ordinary dividends to shareholders.

    i. Use information in the statement of cash flow (financing activities) to prepare a single journal entry that summarizes GlaxoSmithKline' ordinary dividends to shareholders for 2007.

    ii. Note 16 Dividends reports total dividends declared of £2,905 for 2007. Reconcile this to the dividends recorded in the statement of cash flow.

g. During 2007, Merck repurchased a number of its own common shares on the open market.

    i. Describe the method Merck uses to account for its treasury stock transactions.

    ii. Refer to note 11 to Merck's financial statements. How many shares did Merck repurchase on the open market during 2007?

    iii. How much did Merck pay, in total and per share, on average, to buy back its stock during 2007? What type of cash flow does this represent?

    iv. Why doesn't Merck disclose its treasury stock as an asset?

h. During 2007, GlaxoSmithKline repurchased a number of its own shares on the open market.

    i. Refer to Note 33 of GlaxoSmithKline's annual report. How many shares did GlaxoSmithKline repurchase on the open market during 2007? Were all of these shares held in treasury?

    ii. How much did the company pay, on average, for each share repurchased during 2007?

    iii. Consider note 34 Movements in equity. What is the name of the comparable financial statement required under U.S. GAAP? Prepare a single journal entry that summarizes GlaxoSmithKline's share repurchases in 2007. How does this compare to the U.S. GAAP treatment?

i. Determine the missing amounts and calculate the ratios in the tables below. For comparability, use dividends paid for both companies rather than dividends declared. Use the number of shares outstanding at year end for per-share calculations. What differences do you observe in Merck's dividend-related ratios across the two years? What differences do you observe in the two companies' dividend-related ratios?

(in millions)	Merck ($) 2007	Merck ($) 2006	Glaxo (£) 2007
Dividends paid			
Shares outstanding			
Net income			
Total assets			
Operating cash flows			
Year-end stock price	57.61	41.94	97.39

| | Merck ($) | | Glaxo (£) |
	2007	2006	2007
Dividends per share			
Dividend yield (Dividends per share to Stock price)			
Dividend payout (Dividends to Net income)			
Dividends to Total assets			
Dividends to Operating cash flows			

j. At December 31, 2007, Merck's largest shareholder was FMR LLC, an institutional investor holding 103,253,386 Merck shares.

    i. What percent of Merck's total outstanding shares did FMR hold at year end?

    ii. Assume that on January 2, 2008, FMR wishes to own 6% of Merck's outstanding common stock. How many shares would FMR have to purchase on the open market to acquire a 6% interest in the company? What journal entry would Merck prepare to record the purchase of stock by FMR? Assume the stock price for this transaction was $56.87.

    iii. Now assume that Merck's Board of Directors supports FMR's bid to become a 6% shareholder. How many shares of its own common stock would Merck have to repurchase on the open market to result in a 6% stake for FMR? What journal entry would Merck prepare in this case? Again, assume that the average stock price for this transaction was $56.87 per share.

Item 8. Financial Statements and Supplementary Data.

(a) Financial Statements

The consolidated balance sheet of Merck & Co., Inc. and subsidiaries as of December 31, 2007 and 2006, and the related consolidated statements of income, of retained earnings, of comprehensive income and of cash flows for each of the three years in the period ended December 31, 2007, the Notes to Consolidated Financial Statements, and the report dated February 27, 2008 of PricewaterhouseCoopers LLP, independent registered public accounting firm, are as follows:

Consolidated Statement of Income
Merck & Co., Inc. and Subsidiaries
Years Ended December 31
($ in millions except per share amounts)

	2007	2006	2005
Sales	$24,197.7	$22,636.0	$22,011.9
Costs, Expenses and Other			
Materials and production	6,140.7	6,001.1	5,149.6
Marketing and administrative	7,556.7	8,165.4	7,155.5
Research and development	4,882.8	4,782.9	3,848.0
Restructuring costs	327.1	142.3	322.2
Equity income from affiliates	(2,976.5)	(2,294.4)	(1,717.1)
U.S. *Vioxx* Settlement Agreement charge	4,850.0	-	-
Other (income) expense, net	46.2	(382.7)	(110.2)
	20,827.0	16,414.6	14,648.0
Income Before Taxes	3,370.7	6,221.4	7,363.9
Taxes on Income	95.3	1,787.6	2,732.6
Net Income	$3,275.4	$4,433.8	$4,631.3
Basic Earnings per Common Share	$1.51	$2.04	$2.11
Earnings per Common Share Assuming Dilution	$1.49	$2.03	$2.10

Consolidated Statement of Retained Earnings
Merck & Co., Inc. and Subsidiaries
Years Ended December 31
($ in millions)

	2007	2006	2005
Balance, January 1	$39,095.1	$37,980.0	$36,687.4
Cumulative Effect of Adoption of FIN 48	81.0	-	-
Net Income	3,275.4	4,433.8	4,631.3
Dividends Declared on Common Stock	(3,310.7)	(3,318.7)	(3,338.7)
Balance, December 31	$39,140.8	$39,095.1	$37,980.0

Consolidated Statement of Comprehensive Income
Merck & Co., Inc. and Subsidiaries
Years Ended December 31
($ in millions)

	2007	2006	2005
Net Income	$3,275.4	$4,433.8	$4,631.3
Other Comprehensive Income			
Net unrealized (loss) gain on derivatives, net of tax and net income realization	(4.4)	(50.9)	81.3
Net unrealized gain on investments, net of tax and net income realization	58.0	26.1	50.3
Benefit plan net gain (loss) and prior service cost (credit), net of tax and amortization	240.3	-	-
Minimum pension liability, net of tax	-	22.5	(7.0)
Cumulative translation adjustment relating to equity investees, net of tax	44.3	18.9	(26.4)
	338.2	16.6	98.2
Comprehensive Income	$3,613.6	$4,450.4	$4,729.5

The accompanying notes are an integral part of these consolidated financial statements.

Consolidated Balance Sheet
Merck & Co., Inc. and Subsidiaries
December 31
($ in millions)

	2007	2006
Assets		
Current Assets		
Cash and cash equivalents	**$ 5,336.1**	$ 5,914.7
Short-term investments	**2,894.7**	2,798.3
Accounts receivable	**3,636.2**	3,314.8
Inventories (excludes inventories of $345.2 in 2007 and $416.1 in 2006 classified in Other assets — see Note 6)	**1,881.0**	1,769.4
Prepaid expenses and taxes	**1,297.4**	1,433.0
Total current assets	**15,045.4**	15,230.2
Investments	**7,159.2**	7,788.2
Property, Plant and Equipment (at cost)		
Land	**405.8**	408.9
Buildings	**10,048.0**	9,745.9
Machinery, equipment and office furnishings	**13,553.7**	13,172.4
Construction in progress	**795.6**	882.3
	24,803.1	24,209.5
Less allowance for depreciation	**12,457.1**	11,015.4
	12,346.0	13,194.1
Goodwill	**1,454.8**	1,431.6
Other Intangibles, Net	**713.2**	943.9
Other Assets	**11,632.1**	5,981.8
	$48,350.7	$44,569.8
Liabilities and Stockholders' Equity		
Current Liabilities		
Loans payable and current portion of long-term debt	**$ 1,823.6**	$ 1,285.1
Trade accounts payable	**624.5**	496.6
Accrued and other current liabilities	**8,534.9**	6,653.3
Income taxes payable	**444.1**	3,460.8
Dividends payable	**831.1**	826.9
Total current liabilities	**12,258.2**	12,722.7
Long-Term Debt	**3,915.8**	5,551.0
Deferred Income Taxes and Noncurrent Liabilities	**11,585.3**	6,330.3
Minority Interests	**2,406.7**	2,406.1
Stockholders' Equity		
Common stock, one cent par value		
Authorized — 5,400,000,000 shares		
Issued — 2,983,508,675 shares — 2007 — 2,976,223,337 shares — 2006	**29.8**	29.8
Other paid-in capital	**8,014.9**	7,166.5
Retained earnings	**39,140.8**	39,095.1
Accumulated other comprehensive loss	**(826.1)**	(1,164.3)
	46,359.4	45,127.1
Less treasury stock, at cost 811,005,791 shares — 2007 808,437,892 shares — 2006	**28,174.7**	27,567.4
Total stockholders' equity	**18,184.7**	17,559.7
	$48,350.7	$44,569.8

The accompanying notes are an integral part of this consolidated financial statement.

Consolidated Statement of Cash Flows
Merck & Co., Inc. and Subsidiaries
Years Ended December 31
($ in millions)

	2007	2006	2005
Cash Flows from Operating Activities			
Net income	$ **3,275.4**	$ 4,433.8	$ 4,631.3
Adjustments to reconcile net income to net cash provided by operating activities:			
U.S. *Vioxx* Settlement Agreement charge	**4,850.0**	-	-
Depreciation and amortization	**1,988.2**	2,268.4	1,708.1
Deferred income taxes	**(1,781.9)**	(530.2)	9.0
Equity income from affiliates	**(2,976.5)**	(2,294.4)	(1,717.1)
Dividends and distributions from equity affiliates	**2,485.6**	1,931.9	1,101.2
Share-based compensation	**330.2**	312.5	48.0
Acquired research	**325.1**	762.5	-
Taxes paid for Internal Revenue Service settlement	**(2,788.1)**	-	-
Other	**(64.7)**	18.1	647.5
Net changes in assets and liabilities:			
Accounts receivable	**(290.7)**	(709.3)	345.9
Inventories	**(40.7)**	226.5	125.6
Trade accounts payable	**117.7**	16.4	63.6
Accrued and other current liabilities	**451.1**	461.6	238.2
Income taxes payable	**987.2**	(138.2)	663.2
Noncurrent liabilities	**26.2**	(125.6)	(412.2)
Other	**105.1**	131.2	156.2
Net Cash Provided by Operating Activities	**6,999.2**	6,765.2	7,608.5
Cash Flows from Investing Activities			
Capital expenditures	**(1,011.0)**	(980.2)	(1,402.7)
Purchases of securities and other investments	**(10,132.7)**	(19,591.3)	(125,308.4)
Acquisitions of subsidiaries, net of cash acquired	**(1,135.9)**	(404.9)	-
Proceeds from sales of securities and other investments	**10,860.2**	16,143.8	128,981.4
Increase in restricted cash	**(1,401.1)**	(48.1)	-
Other	**10.5**	(3.0)	(3.1)
Net Cash (Used) Provided by Investing Activities	**(2,810.0)**	(4,883.7)	2,267.2
Cash Flows from Financing Activities			
Net change in short-term borrowings	**11.4**	(1,522.8)	1,296.2
Proceeds from issuance of debt	**-**	755.1	1,000.0
Payments on debt	**(1,195.3)**	(506.2)	(1,014.9)
Purchases of treasury stock	**(1,429.7)**	(1,002.3)	(1,015.3)
Dividends paid to stockholders	**(3,307.3)**	(3,322.6)	(3,349.8)
Proceeds from exercise of stock options	**898.6**	369.9	136.5
Other	**156.2**	(375.3)	(93.1)
Net Cash Used by Financing Activities	**(4,866.1)**	(5,604.2)	(3,040.4)
Effect of Exchange Rate Changes on Cash and Cash Equivalents	**98.3**	52.1	(128.8)
Net (Decrease) Increase in Cash and Cash Equivalents	**(578.6)**	(3,670.6)	6,706.5
Cash and Cash Equivalents at Beginning of Year	**5,914.7**	9,585.3	2,878.8
Cash and Cash Equivalents at End of Year	$ **5,336.1**	$ 5,914.7	$ 9,585.3

The accompanying notes are an integral part of this consolidated financial statement.

Notes to Consolidated Statements
Merck & Co., Inc. and Subsidiaries
Years Ended December 31
($ in millions)

11. Stockholders' Equity

Other paid-in capital increased by $848.4 million in 2007, $266.5 million in 2006 and $30.2 million in 2005. The increase in 2007 reflects the issuance of shares related to the acquisition of NovaCardia (see Note 4). The increases in all periods also reflect the impact of shares issued upon exercise of stock options and related income tax benefits, as well as the issuance of restricted shares. In addition, the increase in 2006 reflects the impact of recognizing share-based compensation expense as a result of the adoption of FAS 123R (see Note 12). A summary of treasury stock transactions (shares in millions) is as follows:

	2007		2006		2005	
	Shares	**Cost**	Shares	Cost	Shares	Cost
Balance as of January 1	**808.4**	**$27,567.4**	794.3	$26,984.4	767.6	$26,191.8
Purchases	**26.5**	**1,429.7**	26.4	1,002.3	33.2	1,015.3
Issuances *(1)*	**(23.9)**	**(822.4)**	(12.3)	(419.3)	(6.5)	(222.7)
Balance as of December 31	**811.0**	**$28,174.7**	808.4	$27,567.4	794.3	$26,984.4

(1) Issued primarily under stock option plans.

At December 31, 2007 and 2006, 10 million shares of preferred stock, without par value, were authorized; none were issued.

Consolidated balance sheet
at 31st December 2007

	Notes	2007 £m	2006 £m
Non-current assets			
Property, plant and equipment	17	**7,821**	6,930
Goodwill	18	**1,370**	758
Other intangible assets	19	**4,456**	3,293
Investments in associates and joint ventures	20	**329**	295
Other investments	21	**517**	441
Deferred tax assets	14	**2,196**	2,123
Derivative financial instruments	41	**1**	113
Other non-current assets	22	**687**	608
Total non-current assets		**17,377**	14,561
Current assets			
Inventories	23	**3,062**	2,437
Current tax recoverable	14	**58**	186
Trade and other receivables	24	**5,495**	5,237
Derivative financial instruments	41	**475**	80
Liquid investments	32	**1,153**	1,035
Cash and cash equivalents	25	**3,379**	2,005
Assets held for sale	26	**4**	12
Total current assets		**13,626**	10,992
Total assets		**31,003**	25,553
Current liabilities			
Short-term borrowings	32	**(3,504)**	(718)
Trade and other payables	27	**(4,861)**	(4,831)
Derivative financial instruments	41	**(262)**	(40)
Current tax payable	14	**(826)**	(621)
Short-term provisions	29	**(892)**	(1,055)
Total current liabilities		**(10,345)**	(7,265)
Non-current liabilities			
Long-term borrowings	32	**(7,067)**	(4,772)
Deferred tax liabilities	14	**(887)**	(595)
Pensions and other post-employment benefits	28	**(1,383)**	(2,339)
Other provisions	29	**(1,035)**	(528)
Derivative financial instruments	41	**(8)**	(60)
Other non-current liabilities	30	**(368)**	(346)
Total non-current liabilities		**(10,748)**	(8,640)
Total liabilities		**(21,093)**	(15,905)
Net assets		**9,910**	9,648
Equity			
Share capital	33	**1,503**	1,498
Share premium account	33	**1,266**	858
Retained earnings	34	**6,475**	6,965
Other reserves	34	**359**	65
Shareholders' equity		**9,603**	9,386
Minority interests	34	**307**	262
Total equity		**9,910**	9,648

Approved by the Board on 27th February 2008

Sir Christopher Gent
Chairman

FINANCIAL STATEMENTS
Consolidated balance sheet

Consolidated cash flow statement

for the year ended 31st December 2007

	Notes	2007 £m	2006 £m	2005 £m
Cash flow from operating activities				
Cash generated from operations	36	**8,080**	8,203	7,665
Taxation paid		**(1,919)**	(3,846)	(1,707)
Net cash inflow from operating activities		**6,161**	4,357	5,958
Cash flow from investing activities				
Purchase of property, plant and equipment		**(1,516)**	(1,366)	(903)
Proceeds from sale of property, plant and equipment		**35**	43	54
Proceeds from sale of intangible assets		**9**	175	221
Purchase of intangible assets		**(627)**	(224)	(278)
Purchase of equity investments		**(186)**	(57)	(23)
Proceeds from sale of equity investments		**45**	32	35
Share transactions with minority shareholders	38	**–**	(157)	(36)
Purchase of businesses, net of cash acquired	38	**(1,027)**	(273)	(1,026)
Disposal of businesses and interest in associates	38	**–**	5	(2)
Investments in associates and joint ventures	38	**(1)**	(13)	(2)
Interest received		**247**	299	290
Dividends from associates and joint ventures		**12**	15	10
Net cash outflow from investing activities		**(3,009)**	(1,521)	(1,660)
Cash flow from financing activities				
(Increase)/decrease in liquid investments		**(39)**	(55)	550
Proceeds from own shares for employee share options		**116**	151	68
Shares acquired by ESOP Trusts		**(26)**	–	–
Issue of share capital	33	**417**	316	252
Purchase of own shares for cancellation		**(213)**	–	–
Purchase of Treasury shares		**(3,538)**	(1,348)	(999)
Increase in long-term loans		**3,483**	–	982
Repayment of long-term loans		**(207)**	–	(70)
Net increase in/(repayment of) short-term loans		**1,632**	(739)	(857)
Net repayment of obligations under finance leases		**(39)**	(34)	(36)
Interest paid		**(378)**	(414)	(381)
Dividends paid to shareholders		**(2,793)**	(2,598)	(2,390)
Dividends paid to minority interests		**(77)**	(87)	(86)
Other financing cash flows		**(79)**	16	53
Net cash outflow from financing activities		**(1,741)**	(4,792)	(2,914)
Increase/(decrease) in cash and bank overdrafts	37	**1,411**	(1,956)	1,384
Exchange adjustments		**48**	(254)	233
Cash and bank overdrafts at beginning of year		**1,762**	3,972	2,355
Cash and bank overdrafts at end of year		**3,221**	1,762	3,972
Cash and bank overdrafts at end of year comprise:				
Cash and cash equivalents		**3,379**	2,005	4,209
Overdrafts		**(158)**	(243)	(237)
		3,221	1,762	3,972

FINANCIAL STATEMENTS
Consolidated cash flow statement

Consolidated statement of recognised income and expense
for the year ended 31st December 2007

	2007 £m	2006 £m	2005 £m
Exchange movements on overseas net assets	425	(390)	203
Tax on exchange movements	21	(78)	99
Fair value movements on available-for-sale investments	(99)	84	(1)
Deferred tax on fair value movements on available-for-sale investments	19	(15)	(10)
Exchange movements on goodwill in reserves	(14)	31	9
Actuarial gains/(losses) on defined benefit plans	671	429	(794)
Deferred tax on actuarial movements in defined benefit plans	(195)	(161)	257
Fair value movements on cash flow hedges	(6)	(5)	(4)
Deferred tax on fair value movements on cash flow hedges	2	2	1
Net profits/(losses) recognised directly in equity	824	(103)	(240)
Profit for the year	5,310	5,498	4,816
Total recognised income and expense for the year	6,134	5,395	4,576
Total recognised income and expense for the year attributable to:			
Shareholders	6,012	5,307	4,423
Minority interests	122	88	153
	6,134	5,395	4,576

Notes to the financial statements
continued

15 Earnings per share

	2007 pence	2006 pence	2005 pence
Basic earnings per share	94.4	95.5	82.6
Adjustment for restructuring costs	4.7		
Business performance earnings per share (basic)	99.1		
Diluted earnings per share	93.7	94.5	82.0
Adjustment for restructuring costs	4.6		
Business performance earnings per share (diluted)	98.3		

Basic and adjusted earnings per share have been calculated by dividing the profit attributable to shareholders by the weighted average number of shares in issue during the period after deducting shares held by the ESOP Trusts and Treasury shares.

Adjusted earnings per share is calculated using business performance earnings. The calculation of business performance, a supplemental non-IFRS measure, is described in Note 1 'Presentation of the financial statements'.

Diluted earnings per share have been calculated after adjusting the weighted average number of shares used in the basic calculation to assume the conversion of all potentially dilutive shares. A potentially dilutive share forms part of the employee share schemes where its exercise price is below the average market price of GSK shares during the period and any performance conditions attaching to the scheme have been met at the balance sheet date.

The numbers of shares used in calculating basic and diluted earnings per share are reconciled below.

Weighted average number of shares in issue	2007 millions	2006 millions	2005 millions
Basic	5,524	5,643	5,674
Dilution for share options	43	57	46
Diluted	5,567	5,700	5,720

Shares held by the ESOP Trusts are excluded. The trustees have waived their rights to dividends on the shares held by the ESOP Trusts.

16 Dividends

2007	First interim	Second interim	Third interim	Fourth interim	Total
Total dividend (£m)	670	667	708	860	2,905
Dividend per share (pence)	12	12	13	16	53
Paid/payable	12th July 2007	11th October 2007	10th January 2008	10th April 2008	

2006					
Total dividend (£m)	619	620	671	785	2,695
Dividend per share (pence)	11	11	12	14	48
Paid	6th July 2006	5th October 2006	4th January 2007	12th April 2007	

2005					
Total dividend (£m)	568	567	568	791	2,494
Dividend per share (pence)	10	10	10	14	44
Paid	7th July 2005	6th October 2005	5th January 2006	6th April 2006	

Under IFRS interim dividends are only recognised in the financial statements when paid and not when declared. GSK normally pays a dividend two quarters after the quarter to which it relates and one quarter after it is declared. The 2007 financial statements recognise those dividends paid in 2007, namely the third and fourth interim dividends for 2006 and the first and second interim dividends for 2007. The amounts recognised in each year are as follows:

	2007 £m	2006 £m	2005 £m
Dividends to shareholders	2,793	2,598	2,390

33 Share capital and share premium account

	Ordinary shares of 25p each		Share Premium
	Number	£m	£m
Share capital authorised			
At 31st December 2005	10,000,000,000	2,500	
At 31st December 2006	10,000,000,000	2,500	
At 31st December 2007	10,000,000,000	2,500	
Share capital issued and fully paid			
At 1st January 2005	5,937,688,831	1,484	304
Issued under share option schemes	25,162,425	7	245
At 31st December 2005	5,962,851,256	1,491	549
Issued under share option schemes	28,750,592	7	309
At 31st December 2006	5,991,601,848	1,498	858
Issued under share option schemes	37,307,678	9	408
Share capital purchased and cancelled	(16,322,500)	(4)	–
At 31st December 2007	6,012,587,026	1,503	1,266

	31st December 2007	31st December 2006	31st December 2005
Number ('000) of shares issuable under outstanding options (Note 42)	**218,182**	225,163	221,293
Number ('000) of unissued shares not under option	**3,769,231**	3,783,235	3,815,856

At 31st December 2007, of the issued share capital, 134,529,906 shares were held in the ESOP Trust, 504,194,158 shares were held as Treasury shares and 5,373,862,962 shares were in free issue. All issued shares are fully paid. The nominal, carrying and market values of the shares held in the ESOP Trust are disclosed in Note 42, Employee share schemes'.

In July 2007, the Group increased its share buy-back programme to £12 billion, which is expected to be completed over a two-year period. The exact amount and timing of future purchases, and whether repurchased shares will be held as Treasury shares or cancelled, will be determined by the company and is dependent on market conditions and other factors. In 2007, the Group also commenced close period share buy-backs by operating under specific, irrevocable agreements put in place with its brokers prior to the start of each close period.

A total of £11.6 billion has been spent by the company between 1st January 2001 and 31st December 2007 on buying its own shares for cancellation or to be held as Treasury shares, of which £3.8 billion was spent in 2007.

28.9 million shares have been purchased and cancelled in the period 1st January 2008 to 22nd February 2008 at a cost of £323 million. All purchases were made through the publicly announced buy-back programme.

The table below sets out the monthly purchases under the share buy-back programme:

Month	Number of shares 000	Average share price excluding commission and stamp duty £
January 2007	12,090	13.87
February 2007	9,910	14.48
March 2007	23,900	13.97
April 2007	8,800	14.45
May 2007	12,886	13.78
June 2007	22,480	13.05
July 2007	3,950	12.56
August 2007	47,528	12.76
September 2007	38,512	13.21
October 2007	55,775	12.76
November 2007	32,880	12.10
December 2007	16,323	12.99
Total	285,034	13.09

Of the shares purchased in 2007, 269 million (£3,537 million) are held as Treasury shares and 16 million (£213 million) have been cancelled. For details of substantial shareholdings refer to 'Substantial shareholdings' on page 176.

FINANCIAL STATEMENTS
Notes to the financial statements

Notes to the financial statements
continued

34 Movements in equity

	Share capital £m	Share premium £m	Retained earnings £m	Other reserves £m	Total £m	Minority interests £m	Total equity £m
					Shareholders' equity		
At 1st January 2005	1,484	304	4,448	(528)	5,708	217	5,925
Recognised income and expense for the year	–	–	4,426	(3)	4,423	153	4,576
Changes in minority shareholdings	–	–	(15)	–	(15)	(25)	(40)
Distributions to minority shareholders	–	–	–	–	–	(86)	(86)
Dividends to shareholders	–	–	(2,390)	–	(2,390)	–	(2,390)
Ordinary shares issued	7	245	–	–	252	–	252
Ordinary shares purchased and held as Treasury shares	–	–	(1,000)	–	(1,000)	–	(1,000)
Ordinary shares transferred by ESOP Trusts	–	–	–	68	68	–	68
Write-down of shares held by ESOP Trusts	–	–	(155)	155	–	–	–
Share-based incentive plans	–	–	240	–	240	–	240
Tax on share based incentive plans	–	–	25	–	25	–	25
At 31st December 2005	1,491	549	5,579	(308)	7,311	259	7,570
Recognised income and expense for the year	–	–	5,248	59	5,307	88	5,395
Changes in minority shareholdings	–	–	–	–	–	2	2
Distributions to minority shareholders	–	–	–	–	–	(87)	(87)
Dividends to shareholders	–	–	(2,598)	–	(2,598)	–	(2,598)
Ordinary shares issued	7	309	–	–	316	–	316
Ordinary shares purchased and held as Treasury shares	–	–	(1,348)	–	(1,348)	–	(1,348)
Ordinary shares transferred by ESOP Trusts	–	–	–	151	151	–	151
Write-down of shares held by ESOP Trusts	–	–	(163)	163	–	–	–
Share-based incentive plans	–	–	226	–	226	–	226
Tax on share-based incentive plans	–	–	21	–	21	–	21
At 31st December 2006	1,498	858	6,965	65	9,386	262	9,648
Recognised income and expense for the year	–	–	6,104	(92)	6,012	122	6,134
Distributions to minority shareholders	–	–	–	–	–	(77)	(77)
Dividends to shareholders	–	–	(2,793)	–	(2,793)	–	(2,793)
Ordinary shares issued	9	408	–	–	417	–	417
Ordinary shares purchased and cancelled	(4)	–	(213)	4	(213)	–	(213)
Ordinary shares purchased and held as Treasury shares	–	–	(3,537)	–	(3,537)	–	(3,537)
Ordinary shares acquired by ESOP Trusts	–	–	–	(26)	(26)	–	(26)
Ordinary shares transferred by ESOP Trusts	–	–	–	116	116	–	116
Write-down of shares held by ESOP Trusts	–	–	(292)	292	–	–	–
Share-based incentive plans	–	–	237	–	237	–	237
Tax on share-based incentive plans	–	–	4	–	4	–	4
At 31st December 2007	1,503	1,266	6,475	359	9,603	307	9,910

General Mills, Inc.—Analyzing Financial Performance
Traditional Multiplicative DuPont Model

General Mills, Inc., incorporated in Delaware in 1928, is a leading producer of packaged consumer foods. The company has three segments: U.S. Retail, International, and Bakeries and Foodservice. U.S. Retail sells ready-to-eat cereals, meals, frozen dough products, baking products, snacks, yogurt and organic foods. The International segment includes retail business in Canada, Europe, Latin America and the Asia/Pacific region. Bakeries and Foodservice sells to retail and wholesale bakeries, and convenience stores. (Source: Company 2006 Form 10-K)

Learning Objectives
- Understand how to use return metrics to assess performance.
- Calculate return on equity (ROE) and perform a simple DuPont analysis.
- Assess means to improve financial performance.

Refer to the General Mills financial statements for fiscal year 2006 (that is, the year ended May 28, 2006).

✦ Concepts ✦

A company's financial performance can be analyzed in many ways. Return on equity (ROE) is a widely used measure of financial performance that compares the profit the company made during the period (net income) to the resources invested and reinvested in the company by shareholders (stockholders' equity). The DuPont model systematically breaks ROE into components. One form of the DuPont model is:

$$ROE = \frac{NI}{Average\ Stockholders'\ equity}$$

$$ROE = \underbrace{\frac{NI}{EBT}}_{\substack{Cost \\ of\ taxes}} \times \underbrace{\frac{EBT}{EBIT}}_{\substack{Cost \\ of\ debt}} \times \underbrace{\frac{EBIT}{Sales}}_{\substack{Operating \\ profit}} \times \underbrace{\frac{Sales}{Average\ Total\ assets}}_{Asset\ turnover} \times \underbrace{\frac{Average\ Total\ assets}{Average\ Stockholders'\ equity}}_{Capital\ structure\ leverage}$$

Where:

- NI is Net income reported on the income statement.

- EBT is earnings before income tax expense.

- EBIT is earnings before interest expense, net and income tax expense. Interest expense includes any costs for debt issuances or repurchases and is net of interest income on financial assets.

- Sales are reported on the income statement.

- Total assets are reported on the balance sheet.

- Stockholders' equity is reported on the balance sheet and excludes any reported minority interest.

Note that once the common terms cancel in the second equation (the DuPont model), the right-hand side of the ROE equation collapses down to the first equation: Net income divided by the firm's Average Stockholders' equity.

a. What does return on equity (ROE) measure? Why is it important to consider ROE and not just net income in dollar terms?

b. In your own words, explain what each of the five ROE components measures.

◆ Analysis ◆

c. Compute return on equity (ROE) for fiscal 2006 and 2005. For simplicity, use year-end numbers rather than averages in your denominator.

d. Refer to General Mills' balance sheets and income statements.

   i. Calculate and interpret each of the five ROE components. Again, for simplicity, use year-end numbers in your calculations.

   ii. Verify that the product of the five components is equal to the ROE you calculated in part *c*.

e. Has the company's ROE improved or worsened over the two years? Explain why. *Hint*: use the DuPont analysis' five component parts and determine which part(s) explain the change in ROE.

f. In 2005, General Mills reported a divestiture gain of $499. What would ROE have been in 2005 without the effect of the divestiture gain? Assume that the company's marginal tax rate for 2005 was 38.3%. In your opinion, is this pro-forma ROE relevant to the financial statement users?

g. Assume that you have been hired by General Mills to help the company improve performance (ROE) in 2007. Suggest ways to accomplish this goal.

GENERAL MILLS, INC. AND SUBSIDIARIES
CONSOLIDATED STATEMENTS OF EARNINGS

In Millions, Except per Share Data

Fiscal Year Ended	May 28, 2006	May 29, 2005	May 30, 2004
Net Sales	$11,640	$11,244	$11,070
Costs and Expenses:			
Cost of sales	6,966	6,834	6,584
Selling, general and administrative	2,678	2,418	2,443
Interest, net	399	455	508
Restructuring and other exit costs	30	84	26
Divestitures (gain)	–	(499)	–
Debt repurchase costs	–	137	–
Total Costs and Expenses	10,073	9,429	9,561
Earnings before Income Taxes and After-tax Earnings from Joint Ventures	1,567	1,815	1,509
Income Taxes	541	664	528
After-tax Earnings from Joint Ventures	64	89	74
Net Earnings	$ 1,090	$ 1,240	$ 1,055
Earnings per Share – Basic	$ 3.05	$ 3.34	$ 2.82
Earnings per Share – Diluted	$ 2.90	$ 3.08	$ 2.60
Dividends per Share	$ 1.34	$ 1.24	$ 1.10

See accompanying notes to consolidated financial statements.

GENERAL MILLS, INC. AND SUBSIDIARIES
CONSOLIDATED BALANCE SHEETS

In Millions	May 28, 2006	May 29, 2005
ASSETS		
Current Assets:		
Cash and cash equivalents	$ 647	$ 573
Receivables	1,076	1,034
Inventories	1,055	1,037
Prepaid expenses and other current assets	216	203
Deferred income taxes	182	208
Total Current Assets	3,176	3,055
Land, Buildings and Equipment	2,997	3,111
Goodwill	6,652	6,684
Other Intangible Assets	3,607	3,532
Other Assets	1,775	1,684
Total Assets	$18,207	$18,066
LIABILITIES AND EQUITY		
Current Liabilities:		
Accounts payable	$ 1,151	$ 1,136
Current portion of long-term debt	2,131	1,638
Notes payable	1,503	299
Other current liabilities	1,353	1,111
Total Current Liabilities	6,138	4,184
Long-term Debt	2,415	4,255
Deferred Income Taxes	1,822	1,851
Other Liabilities	924	967
Total Liabilities	11,299	11,257
Minority Interests	1,136	1,133
Stockholders' Equity:		
Cumulative preference stock, none issued	–	–
Common stock, 502 shares issued	50	50
Additional paid-in capital	5,737	5,691
Retained earnings	5,107	4,501
Common stock in treasury, at cost, shares of 146 in 2006 and 133 in 2005	(5,163)	(4,460)
Unearned compensation	(84)	(114)
Accumulated other comprehensive income	125	8
Total Stockholders' Equity	5,772	5,676
Total Liabilities and Equity	$18,207	$18,066

See accompanying notes to consolidated financial statements.

GENERAL MILLS, INC. AND SUBSIDIARIES
CONSOLIDATED STATEMENTS OF CASH FLOWS

In Millions Fiscal Year Ended	May 28, 2006	May 29, 2005	May 30, 2004
Cash Flows – Operating Activities			
Net earnings	$ 1,090	$ 1,240	$ 1,055
Adjustments to reconcile net earnings to net cash provided by operating activities:			
Depreciation and amortization	424	443	399
Deferred income taxes	26	9	109
Changes in current assets and liabilities	184	258	(186)
Tax benefit on exercised options	41	62	63
Pension and other postretirement costs	(74)	(70)	(21)
Restructuring and other exit costs	30	84	26
Divestitures (gain)	–	(499)	–
Debt repurchase costs	–	137	–
Other, net	50	47	16
Net Cash Provided by Operating Activities	1,771	1,711	1,461
Cash Flows – Investing Activities			
Purchases of land, buildings and equipment	(360)	(434)	(653)
Investments in businesses	(26)	–	(10)
Investments in affiliates, net of investment returns and dividends	78	84	32
Purchases of marketable securities	–	(1)	(7)
Proceeds from sale of marketable securities	1	33	129
Proceeds from disposal of land, buildings and equipment	11	24	36
Proceeds from disposition of businesses	–	799	–
Other, net	4	(9)	2
Net Cash Provided (Used) by Investing Activities	(292)	496	(470)
Cash Flows – Financing Activities			
Change in notes payable	1,197	(1,057)	(1,023)
Issuance of long-term debt	–	2	576
Payment of long-term debt	(1,386)	(1,115)	(248)
Proceeds from issuance of preferred membership interests of subsidiary	–	835	–
Common stock issued	157	195	192
Purchases of common stock for treasury	(885)	(771)	(24)
Dividends paid	(485)	(461)	(413)
Other, net	(3)	(13)	(3)
Net Cash Used by Financing Activities	(1,405)	(2,385)	(943)
Increase (Decrease) in Cash and Cash Equivalents	74	(178)	48
Cash and Cash Equivalents – Beginning of Year	573	751	703
Cash and Cash Equivalents – End of Year	$ 647	$ 573	$ 751
Cash Flow from Changes in Current Assets and Liabilities:			
Receivables	$ (18)	$ (9)	$ (22)
Inventories	(6)	30	24
Prepaid expenses and other current assets	(7)	9	(15)
Accounts payable	14	(19)	(161)
Other current liabilities	201	247	(12)
Changes in Current Assets and Liabilities	$ 184	$ 258	$ (186)

See accompanying notes to consolidated financial statements.

General Mills, Inc.—Analyzing Financial Performance Return on Operating Assets Additive DuPont Model

General Mills, Inc., incorporated in Delaware in 1928, is a leading producer of packaged consumer foods. The company has three segments: U.S. Retail, International, and Bakeries and Foodservice. U.S. Retail sells ready-to-eat cereals, meals, frozen dough products, baking products, snacks, yogurt and organic foods. The International segment includes retail business in Canada, Europe, Latin America and the Asia/Pacific region. Bakeries and Foodservice sells to retail and wholesale bakeries, and convenience stores. (Source: Company 2006 Form 10-K)

Learning Objectives
*   Understand how to use return metrics to assess performance.
*   Calculate net operating profit after tax (NOPAT) and net operating assets (NOA).
*   Compute and interpret return on net operating assets (RNOA) and return on equity (ROE).
*   Assess means to improve corporate performance.

Refer to the General Mills financial statements for fiscal year 2006 (that is, the year ended May 28, 2006).

✦ Concepts ✦

A company's performance can be analyzed in many ways. Return on equity (ROE) is a widely used metric that compares the profit the company made during the period (net income) to the resources invested in the company by shareholders (shareholders' equity). We can break ROE into two components: return on net operating assets (RNOA), and nonoperating return. We can further break RNOA into two components: Net operating profit margin and Net operating asset turnover. The ROE breakdown can be written as:

$$ROE = \frac{Net\ income}{Average\ Stockholders'\ equity}$$

$$ROE = RNOA + Nonoperating\ return$$

$$RNOA = \underbrace{\frac{Net\ Operating\ Profit\ after\ Tax}{Sales}}_{Net\ operating\ profit\ margin} \times \underbrace{\frac{Sales}{Average\ Net\ Operating\ Assets}}_{Net\ operating\ asset\ turnover}$$

Where:

*   *Net income* is reported on the income statement.

*   Stockholders' equity is reported on the balance sheet and excludes any reported minority interest.

*   *Net operating profit after tax* is profit from the firm's main, ongoing operating activities. Net operating profit after tax excludes any nonoperating income or expenses such as interest, gains or losses from marketable securities or disposals of investments. It also excludes discontinued operations (they are not ongoing).

*   *Sales* are reported on the income statement.

*   *Net operating assets* are measured as all operating assets *less* all operating liabilities. Net operating assets exclude all nonoperating assets (including marketable securities and other passive investments) and all nonoperating liabilities (including short and long-term debt).

a. What does return on equity (ROE) measure? Why is it important to consider ROE and not just net income in dollar terms?

b. How do return on equity (ROE) and return on net operating assets (RNOA) differ? Explain in your own words what the nonoperating portion of ROE represents.

c. In general, what is a company's "marginal" tax rate? What is a tax shield?

Process

d. Refer to General Mills' 2006 balance sheet. Calculate net operating assets for 2006 and 2005. Assume that Other assets, Other current liabilities, and Other liabilities are operating items.

e. Refer to General Mills' 2006 income statement. Calculate net operating profit after tax for 2006 and 2005. Assume that the joint venture is operating income. Further assume that the company's marginal tax rate (as estimated by the combined federal and state statutory tax rates) is 38.3% for both years. How much of a tax shield did General Mills have in 2006?

Analysis

f. Compute return on net operating profit (RNOA) for 2006 and 2005. For simplicity, use year-end numbers and not averages in your denominator.

g. Has the company's RNOA improved or worsened over the two years? Explain why. *Hint*: disaggregate RNOA into its two main component parts (Net operating profit margin and Net operating asset turnover) and determine which part explains the change in RNOA.

h. Compute and interpret return on equity (ROE) for 2006 and 2005. For simplicity, use year-end numbers and not averages in your denominator. Calculate the difference between ROE and RNOA. What inference do you draw from this comparison?

i. The nonoperating return portion of ROE can be calculated directly as shown in the equation below. Calculate and interpret FLEV and Spread. For simplicity, use year-end numbers and not averages in your ratios. Footnote disclosures (not included) explain that the minority interest on General Mills' balance sheet relates to preferred stock issued by subsidiaries and that General Mills reports the distributions to these investors as interest expense. One approach is to treat the minority interest on the balance sheet as a nonoperating liability in computing FLEV and Spread. Using this approach, show that FLEV × Spread is equal to the nonoperating return you calculated in part h, above.

$$Nonoperating\ Return = FLEV \times Spread$$

$$FLEV = \frac{Average\ Net\ Nonoperating\ Liabilities}{Average\ Stockholders'Equity}$$

$$Spread = RNOA - \frac{Net\ Nonoperating\ Expense}{Average\ Net\ Nonoperating\ Liabilities}$$

Where:

- *FLEV* is a measure of financial leverage.

- *Spread* measures the amount by which operating return exceeds the cost of borrowing.

- *Net Nonoperating Liabilities* are measured as all nonoperating liabilities (including short and long-term debt) less all nonoperating assets (including marketable securities and other passive investments). As discussed above, you should include minority interest with nonoperating liabilities for General Mills.

- *Net Nonoperating Expense* is the after-tax nonoperating expenses such as interest and investment losses less any interest income and investment gains. It also includes discontinued operations.

j. Assume that you have been hired by General Mills to help the company improve RNOA in 2007. Suggest ways to accomplish this goal.

GENERAL MILLS, INC. AND SUBSIDIARIES
CONSOLIDATED STATEMENTS OF EARNINGS

In Millions, Except per Share Data

Fiscal Year Ended	May 28, 2006	May 29, 2005	May 30, 2004
Net Sales	$11,640	$11,244	$11,070
Costs and Expenses:			
Cost of sales	6,966	6,834	6,584
Selling, general and administrative	2,678	2,418	2,443
Interest, net	399	455	508
Restructuring and other exit costs	30	84	26
Divestitures (gain)	–	(499)	–
Debt repurchase costs	–	137	–
Total Costs and Expenses	10,073	9,429	9,561
Earnings before Income Taxes and After-tax Earnings from Joint Ventures	1,567	1,815	1,509
Income Taxes	541	664	528
After-tax Earnings from Joint Ventures	64	89	74
Net Earnings	$ 1,090	$ 1,240	$ 1,055
Earnings per Share – Basic	$ 3.05	$ 3.34	$ 2.82
Earnings per Share – Diluted	$ 2.90	$ 3.08	$ 2.60
Dividends per Share	$ 1.34	$ 1.24	$ 1.10

See accompanying notes to consolidated financial statements.

GENERAL MILLS, INC. AND SUBSIDIARIES
CONSOLIDATED BALANCE SHEETS

In Millions	May 28, 2006	May 29, 2005
ASSETS		
Current Assets:		
Cash and cash equivalents	$ 647	$ 573
Receivables	1,076	1,034
Inventories	1,055	1,037
Prepaid expenses and other current assets	216	203
Deferred income taxes	182	208
Total Current Assets	3,176	3,055
Land, Buildings and Equipment	2,997	3,111
Goodwill	6,652	6,684
Other Intangible Assets	3,607	3,532
Other Assets	1,775	1,684
Total Assets	$18,207	$18,066
LIABILITIES AND EQUITY		
Current Liabilities:		
Accounts payable	$ 1,151	$ 1,136
Current portion of long-term debt	2,131	1,638
Notes payable	1,503	299
Other current liabilities	1,353	1,111
Total Current Liabilities	6,138	4,184
Long-term Debt	2,415	4,255
Deferred Income Taxes	1,822	1,851
Other Liabilities	924	967
Total Liabilities	11,299	11,257
Minority Interests	1,136	1,133
Stockholders' Equity:		
Cumulative preference stock, none issued	–	–
Common stock, 502 shares issued	50	50
Additional paid-in capital	5,737	5,691
Retained earnings	5,107	4,501
Common stock in treasury, at cost, shares of 146 in 2006 and 133 in 2005	(5,163)	(4,460)
Unearned compensation	(84)	(114)
Accumulated other comprehensive income	125	8
Total Stockholders' Equity	5,772	5,676
Total Liabilities and Equity	$18,207	$18,066

See accompanying notes to consolidated financial statements.

GENERAL MILLS, INC. AND SUBSIDIARIES
CONSOLIDATED STATEMENTS OF CASH FLOWS

In Millions

Fiscal Year Ended	May 28, 2006	May 29, 2005	May 30, 2004
Cash Flows – Operating Activities			
Net earnings	$ 1,090	$ 1,240	$ 1,055
Adjustments to reconcile net earnings to net cash provided by operating activities:			
Depreciation and amortization	424	443	399
Deferred income taxes	26	9	109
Changes in current assets and liabilities	184	258	(186)
Tax benefit on exercised options	41	62	63
Pension and other postretirement costs	(74)	(70)	(21)
Restructuring and other exit costs	30	84	26
Divestitures (gain)	–	(499)	–
Debt repurchase costs	–	137	–
Other, net	50	47	16
Net Cash Provided by Operating Activities	1,771	1,711	1,461
Cash Flows – Investing Activities			
Purchases of land, buildings and equipment	(360)	(434)	(653)
Investments in businesses	(26)	–	(10)
Investments in affiliates, net of investment returns and dividends	78	84	32
Purchases of marketable securities	–	(1)	(7)
Proceeds from sale of marketable securities	1	33	129
Proceeds from disposal of land, buildings and equipment	11	24	36
Proceeds from disposition of businesses	–	799	–
Other, net	4	(9)	2
Net Cash Provided (Used) by Investing Activities	(292)	496	(470)
Cash Flows – Financing Activities			
Change in notes payable	1,197	(1,057)	(1,023)
Issuance of long-term debt	–	2	576
Payment of long-term debt	(1,386)	(1,115)	(248)
Proceeds from issuance of preferred membership interests of subsidiary	–	835	–
Common stock issued	157	195	192
Purchases of common stock for treasury	(885)	(771)	(24)
Dividends paid	(485)	(461)	(413)
Other, net	(3)	(13)	(3)
Net Cash Used by Financing Activities	(1,405)	(2,385)	(943)
Increase (Decrease) in Cash and Cash Equivalents	74	(178)	48
Cash and Cash Equivalents – Beginning of Year	573	751	703
Cash and Cash Equivalents – End of Year	$ 647	$ 573	$ 751
Cash Flow from Changes in Current Assets and Liabilities:			
Receivables	$ (18)	$ (9)	$ (22)
Inventories	(6)	30	24
Prepaid expenses and other current assets	(7)	9	(15)
Accounts payable	14	(19)	(161)
Other current liabilities	201	247	(12)
Changes in Current Assets and Liabilities	$ 184	$ 258	$ (186)

See accompanying notes to consolidated financial statements.

Kohl's Corporation and Dillard's, Inc. — Financial Statement Analysis

Kohl's Corporation was organized in 1988 and is a Wisconsin corporation. The company operates family-oriented department stores that sell moderately priced apparel, footwear and accessories for women, men and children; soft home products such as sheets and pillows; and housewares. Stores generally carry a consistent merchandise assortment with some differences attributable to regional preferences. As of February 2, 2008, the company operated 929 stores in 47 states. (Source: Company 2007 Form 10-K)

Originally founded in 1938 by William T. Dillard, Dillard's, Inc., now operates 326 stores in 29 states. The company's store base is diversified, with the character and culture of the community served determining the size of facility and, to a large extent, the merchandise mix. In general, stores offer a wide selection of merchandise including fashion apparel for women, men and children, accessories, cosmetics, home furnishings and other consumer goods. Most stores are located in suburban shopping malls but customers may also purchase merchandise online. (Source: Company 2007 Form 10-K)

Learning Objectives
- Read and compare financial statements for two companies in the same industry.
- Consider how different strategic choices lead to different financial statement relationships.
- Perform an analysis of financial information using common-size balance sheets and income statements, ratios, and other techniques.
- Critically evaluate two companies based on financial information.
- Evaluate a financial analysis to form investment recommendations.

Refer to the 2007 financial statements and notes of Kohl's Corporation and Dillard's, Inc.

✧ Analysis ✧

a. Describe the industry in which these two companies operate and assess the competitive environment. What current economic factors affect the companies' operations? Who are the main competitors in this industry? What threats do the companies face? What opportunities? How are the two companies similar? How are they different?

b. Consider the income statements of both companies. Are there any unusual or nonrecurring items that need to be considered in your analysis? That is, are the earnings of high quality? Are the earnings persistent?

c. Prepare common-sized income statements and balance sheets for each company for fiscal 2007 and 2006. To common size the income statement, divide each item by net sales. To common size the balance sheet, divide each item by total assets.

A company's financial performance can be analyzed in many ways. Return on equity (ROE) is a widely-used measure of financial performance that compares the profit the company made during the period (net income) to the resources invested and reinvested in the company by shareholders (stockholders' equity). The DuPont model systematically breaks ROE into components. One form of the DuPont model is:

$$ROE = \frac{NI}{Average\ Stockholders'\ equity}$$

$$ROE = \underbrace{\frac{NI}{EBT}}_{\substack{Cost \\ of\ taxes}} \times \underbrace{\frac{EBT}{EBIT}}_{\substack{Cost \\ of\ debt}} \times \underbrace{\frac{EBIT}{Sales}}_{\substack{Operating \\ profit}} \times \underbrace{\frac{Sales}{Average\ Total\ assets}}_{\substack{Asset\ turnover}} \times \underbrace{\frac{Average\ Total\ assets}{Average\ Stockholders'\ equity}}_{\substack{Capital\ structure\ leverage}}$$

$$\underbrace{\qquad\qquad\qquad\qquad\qquad\qquad\qquad}_{Operating\ Return\ on\ Assets}$$

Where:

- NI is Net income reported on the income statement.

- EBT is earnings before income tax expense.

- EBIT is earnings before interest expense, net, and income tax expense. Interest expense includes any costs for debt issuances or repurchases and is net of interest income on financial assets.

- Sales are reported on the income statement.

- Total assets are reported on the balance sheet.

- Stockholders' equity is reported on the balance sheet and excludes any reported minority interest.

Note that once the common terms cancel in the second equation (the DuPont model), the right-hand side of the ROE equation collapses down to the first equation: Net income divided by the firm's Stockholders' equity. Reading from left to right in the second equation, the first right-hand side ratio represents the fraction of pretax earnings that the shareholders keep. One minus that ratio is the average tax rate so the ratio decreases as the tax rate goes up. The second ratio represents the fraction of EBIT (i.e., operating profit) that the firm keeps after financing costs so the ratio decreases as the net cost of debt increases. The third ratio represents operating return on sales or the operating profit earned on each unit of revenue. The fourth term is the asset turnover ratio, a measure of overall efficiency in asset use. The product of the third and fourth terms is operating return on assets. The final ratio captures the leverage of the firm—a measure of how the firm has paid for its assets. The ratio increases as the firm takes on more debt (that is, for a fixed level of equity, more assets must mean more debt). Note that the final term is equal to 1 + (Total liabilities / Total stockholders' equity).

Normally, analysis of the financial statements begins with operating return on sales and asset turnover (thus, operating return on assets). Then it turns to leverage (liquidity and solvency) and the cost of leverage. Finally, a review of the tax burden is conducted. The ROE analysis can be followed up with an analysis of the company's cash flows.

d. Compute return on equity (ROE) for both companies for fiscal 2007 and 2006. Calculate the five components of ROE and verify that their product equals ROE.

e. Refer to the common-sized income statement you prepared in part *c* and your ROE decomposition from part *d*.

    i.   What trends do you notice in the ROE subcomponents for each firm over time?

    ii.   Which firm is more profitable? Consider profitability in terms of overall ROE, operating return on sales (and insights from common-size income statements), and operating return on assets.

f. Assess the companies' asset efficiency. Which firm is more efficient in its use of assets? Consider efficiency in terms of total asset turnover, receivables turnover (and average collection period), inventory turnover (and average holding period), payables turnover (and average time to payment), cash conversion cycle (i.e., receivables days + inventory days – payables days), and fixed asset turnover.

g. Assess the companies' liquidity and solvency. Are the companies likely to meet their debts as they come due? Consider ratios such as the current ratio, the quick ratio, and the debt-equity ratio. Also consider interest costs and the times interest earned ratio. Is there any "off-balance-sheet" financing that will constrain future cash flow? You should explicitly consider operating leases at both companies. Assume that the discount rate implicit in the capital leases is the appropriate discount rate for capitalizing the operating leases. Further, assume that the lease payments due in 2013 and beyond will be paid evenly over 20 years for Kohl's and paid entirely in 2013 for Dillard's.

h. Assess the cash flow of each company. Are cash flows from operations a source or a use of cash? How are operations and investments being financed? What differences do you note?

i. As a potential investor, would you be interested in seeking additional information about either of these companies? What sort of information would you want? Would you invest in either company?

KOHL'S CORPORATION
CONSOLIDATED BALANCE SHEETS
(In Thousands, Except Per Share Data)

ASSETS	February 2, 2008	February 3, 2007	January 28, 2006
Current assets:			
Cash	$ 180,543	$ 189,170	$ 126,839
Short-term investments	483,128	431,230	160,077
Merchandise inventories	2,855,733	2,578,378	2,237,568
Accounts receivable	--	-	1652,065
Deferred income taxes	71,069	40,190	23,677
Other	133,416	154,919	66,327
Total current assets	3,723,889	3,393,887	4,266,553
Property and equipment, net	6,509,819	5,352,974	4,616,303
Favorable lease rights, net	209,958	219,286	212,380
Goodwill	9,338	9,338	9,338
Other assets	107,078	58,539	48,920
Total assets	$10,560,082	$9,034,024	$ 9,153,494

LIABILITIES AND SHAREHOLDERS' EQUITY

	February 2, 2008	February 3, 2007	January 28, 2006
Current liabilities:			
Accounts payable	$ 835,985	$ 934,376	$ 829,971
Accrued liabilities	798,508	725,025	642,091
Income taxes payable	124,254	233,263	166,908
Current portion of long-term debt and capital leases	12,701	18,841	107,941
Total current liabilities	1,771,448	1,911,505	1,746,911
Long-term debt and capital leases	2,051,875	1,040,057	1046,104
Deferred income taxes	262,451	243,530	217,801
Other long-term liabilities	372,705	235,537	185,340
Common stock—$.01 par value, 800,000 shares authorized, 350,753; 348,502; and 345,088 shares issued	3,508	3,485	3,450
Paid-in capital	1,911,041	1,748,792	1,583,035
Treasury stock at cost, 40,285; 27,516; and 0 shares	(2,376,331)	(1,628,416)	--
Retained earnings	6,563,385	5,479,534	4,370,853
Total shareholders' equity	6,101,603	5,603,395	5,957,338
Total liabilities and shareholders' equity	$10,560,082	$9,034,024	$9,153,494

See accompanying Notes to Consolidated Financial Statements

F-3

KOHL'S CORPORATION
CONSOLIDATED STATEMENTS OF INCOME
(In Thousands, Except Per Share Data)

	2007	2006	2005
Net sales	$16,473,734	$15,596,910	$13,444,397
Cost of merchandise sold (exclusive of depreciation shown separately below)	10,459,549	9,922,073	8,664,077
Gross margin	6,014,185	5,674,837	4,780,320
Operating expenses:			
Selling, general, and administrative	3,696,841	3,422,600	2,980,853
Depreciation and amortization	452,145	387,674	338,916
Preopening expenses	60,722	49,762	44,370
Operating income	1,804,477	1,814,801	1,416,181
Other expense (income):			
Interest expense	82,412	66,743	73,925
Interest income	(19,996)	(26,387)	(3,534)
Income before income taxes	1,742,061	1,774,445	1,345,790
Provision for income taxes	658,210	665,764	503,830
Net income	$ 1,083,851	$ 1,108,681	$ 841,960
Net income per share:			
Basic	$ 3.41	$ 3.34	$ 2.45
Diluted	$ 3.39	$ 3.31	$ 2.43

See accompanying Notes to Consolidated Financial Statements

F-4

KOHL'S CORPORATION
CONSOLIDATED STATEMENT OF CHANGES IN SHAREHOLDERS' EQUITY
(In Thousands)

	Common Stock		Paid-In Capital	Treasury Stock	Retained Earnings	Total
	Shares	Amount				
Balance at January 29, 2005	343,345	$3,433	$1,501,572	$ —	$3,528,893	$ 5,033,898
Exercise of stock options	1,743	17	22,841	—	—	22,858
Income tax benefit from exercise of stock options	—	—	14,458	—	—	14,458
Share-based compensation expense	—	—	44,164	—	—	44,164
Net income	—	—	—	—	841,960	841,960
Balance at January 28, 2006	345,088	3,450	1,583,035	—	4,370,853	5,957,338
Exercise of stock options	3,414	35	94,559	—	—	94,594
Income tax benefit from exercise of stock options	—	—	25,707	—	—	25,707
Share-based compensation expense	—	—	45,491	—	—	45,491
Treasury stock purchases	—	—	—	(1,628,416)	—	(1,628,416)
Net income	—	—	—	—	1,108,681	1,108,681
Balance at February 3, 2007	348,502	3,485	1,748,792	(1,628,416)	5,479,534	5,603,395
Exercise of stock options	2,251	23	97,389	—	—	97,412
Income tax benefit from exercise of stock options	—	—	6,151	—	—	6,151
Share-based compensation expense	—	—	58,709	—	—	58,709
Treasury stock purchases	—	—	—	(747,915)	—	(747,915)
Net income	—	—	—	—	1,083,851	1,083,851
Balance at February 2, 2008	350,753	$3,508	$1,911,041	$(2,376,331)	$6,563,385	$ 6,101,603

See accompanying Notes to Consolidated Financial Statements

F-5

KOHL'S CORPORATION
CONSOLIDATED STATEMENTS OF CASH FLOWS
(In Thousands)

	2007	2006	2005
Operating activities			
Net income	**$ 1,083,851**	$ 1,108,681	$ 841,960
Adjustments to reconcile net income to net cash provided by operating activities:			
Depreciation and amortization, including debt discount	**453,171**	388,515	339,826
Share-based compensation	**53,607**	44,699	43,941
Excess tax benefits from share-based compensation	**(6,151)**	(25,707)	(14,458)
Deferred income taxes	**(11,958)**	9,216	18,793
Other non-cash revenues and expenses	**33,700**	22,940	24,792
Changes in operating assets and liabilities:			
Accounts receivable, net	**—**	1,652,065	(262,433)
Merchandise inventories	**(275,025)**	(349,663)	(289,684)
Other current and long-term assets	**(44,329)**	(65,348)	(19,643)
Accounts payable	**(98,391)**	104,405	125,316
Accrued and other long-term liabilities	**148,746**	138,358	95,521
Income taxes	**(102,858)**	92,062	4,184
Net cash provided by operating activities	**1,234,363**	3,120,223	908,115
Investing activities			
Acquisition of property and equipment and favorable lease rights	**(1,541,683)**	(1,163,092)	(854,564)
Purchases of short-term investments	**(7,746,231)**	(13,509,169)	(2,978,529)
Sales of short-term investments	**7,694,333**	13,238,936	2,907,219
Proceeds from sale of property, plant and equipment	**30,197**	—	—
Other	**(4,387)**	(6,856)	(4,333)
Net cash used in investing activities	**(1,567,771)**	(1,440,181)	(930,207)
Financing activities			
Proceeds from issuance of debt	**996,031**	—	—
Payments of long-term debt	**(19,611)**	(109,596)	(5,102)
Deferred financing fees	**(7,287)**	—	—
Treasury stock purchases	**(747,915)**	(1,628,416)	—
Excess tax benefits from share-based compensation	**6,151**	25,707	14,458
Proceeds from stock option exercises	**97,412**	94,594	22,858
Net cash provided by (used in) financing activities	**324,781**	(1,617,711)	32,214
Net (decrease) increase in cash	**(8,627)**	62,331	10,122
Cash at beginning of year	**189,170**	126,839	116,717
Cash at end of year	**$ 180,543**	$ 189,170	$ 126,839

See accompanying Notes to Consolidated Financial Statements

KOHL'S CORPORATION
NOTES TO CONSOLIDATED FINANCIAL STATEMENTS

1. Business and Summary of Accounting Policies

Business

As of February 2, 2008, Kohl's Corporation operated 929 family oriented, department stores located in 47 states that feature exclusive and national brand apparel, footwear, accessories, soft home products and housewares targeted to middle-income customers.

Our authorized capital stock consists of 800 million shares of $0.01 par value common stock and 10 million shares of $0.01 par value preferred stock.

Consolidation

The consolidated financial statements include the accounts of Kohl's Corporation and its subsidiaries. All intercompany accounts and transactions have been eliminated.

Accounting Period

Our fiscal year end is the Saturday closest to January 31. Unless otherwise noted, references to years in this report relate to fiscal years, rather than to calendar years. Fiscal year 2007 ("2007") ended on February 2, 2008 and was a 52-week year. Fiscal year 2006 ("2006") ended on February 3, 2007 and was a 53-week year. Fiscal year 2005 ("2005") ended on January 28, 2006 and was a 52-week year.

Use of Estimates

The preparation of consolidated financial statements in conformity with accounting principles generally accepted in the United States requires management to make estimates and assumptions that affect the amounts reported in the consolidated financial statements and accompanying notes. Actual results could differ from those estimates.

Reclassifications

Certain reclassifications have been made to prior years' financial statements to conform to the 2007 presentation.

Short-term Investments

Short-term investments consist primarily of municipal auction rate securities. Short-term investments are classified as available-for-sale securities and are stated at cost, which approximates market value.

As of February 2, 2008, we held $447.2 million in auction rate securities ("ARS") which are classified as short-term investments. ARS are long-term debt instruments with interest rates reset through periodic short term auctions. If there are insufficient buyers, then the auction "fails" and holders are unable to liquidate their investment through the auction. A failed auction is not a default of the debt instrument, but does set a new interest rate in accordance with the original terms of the debt instrument. A failed auction limits liquidity for holders until there is a successful auction or until such time as another market for ARS develops. ARS are generally callable at any time by the issuer. Scheduled auctions continue to be held until the ARS matures or until it is called.

Subsequent to February 2, 2008, we sold five ARS issues, at a total par value of $75.5 million and acquired three ARS issues with a total par value of $52.8 million. From February 11 through March 18, 2008, all of the auctions that were held for ARS in our portfolio failed. Our ARS portfolio consists entirely of "AAA" rated, insured student loan backed securities. Approximately 95% of the principal and interest is insured by the federal government and the remainder is insured by "AAA" rated insurance companies. At this time, we have no reason to believe that any of the underlying issuers of our ARS or their insurers are presently at risk or that the underlying credit quality of the assets backing our ARS investments has been impacted by the reduced liquidity of these investments.

KOHL'S CORPORATION
NOTES TO CONSOLIDATED FINANCIAL STATEMENTS (continued)

Merchandise Inventories

Merchandise inventories are valued at the lower of cost or market using a first-in, first-out method ("FIFO"). We record a reserve when the future estimated selling price is less than cost. We changed our method of accounting for inventory from the last-in, first-out method ("LIFO") to the FIFO method during 2005. We believe that adopting the FIFO method provides more transparent financial reporting and is consistent with our changing business environment with respect to the sourcing of goods and the nature of our inventory. The cumulative effect of the change was a $2.4 million increase to gross margin recorded in the quarter ended July 30, 2005. Because the accounting change was not material to our financial statements for any of the years presented, no retroactive restatement of prior years' financial statements was made.

Property and Equipment

Property and equipment consist of the following:

	February 2, 2008	February 3, 2007
	(In Thousands)	
Land	$ 870,775	$ 745,517
Buildings and improvements	4,859,477	3,967,988
Store fixtures and equipment	1,954,008	1,643,657
Property under capital leases	214,370	185,871
Construction in progress	353,406	243,435
Capitalized software	287,709	220,241
Total property and equipment	8,539,745	7,006,709
Less accumulated depreciation	(2,029,926)	(1,653,735)
	$ 6,509,819	$ 5,352,974

Construction in progress includes land and improvements for locations not yet opened and for the expansion and remodeling of existing locations in process at the end of each year.

Property and equipment is recorded at cost, less accumulated depreciation. Depreciation is calculated using the straight-line method over the estimated useful lives of the assets. Property rights under capital leases and improvements to leased property are amortized on a straight-line basis over the term of the lease or useful life of the asset, whichever is less. Depreciation expense for property and equipment, including property under capital leases and capitalized software, totaled $440.6 million for 2007, $375.1 million for 2006 and $326.4 million for 2005.

The annual provisions for depreciation and amortization generally use the following ranges of useful lives:

Buildings and improvements	8-40 years
Store fixtures and equipment	3-15 years
Property under capital leases	5-40 years
Computer hardware and software	3-8 years

Property and equipment acquired through capital leases totaled $28.9 million in 2007, $13.6 million in 2006 and $52.0 million in 2005.

Capitalized Interest

We capitalize interest on the acquisition and construction of new locations and expansion of existing locations and depreciate that amount over the lives of the related assets. The total interest capitalized was $16.3 million for 2007, $7.7 million for 2006 and $7.3 million for 2005.

KOHL'S CORPORATION
NOTES TO CONSOLIDATED FINANCIAL STATEMENTS (continued)

Favorable Lease Rights

Favorable lease rights are generally amortized on a straight-line basis over the remaining base lease term plus certain options with a maximum of 50 years. Accumulated amortization was $95.7 million at February 2, 2008 and $84.1 million at February 3, 2007. Amortization begins when the respective stores are opened. Amortization expense was $11.5 million for 2007, $12.6 million for 2006 and $12.5 million for 2005.

Amortization expense for current favorable lease right assets for the next five years is estimated to be as follows:

	2008	2009	2010	2011	2012
			(In Thousands)		
Amortization expense	$11,505	$11,499	$10,969	$10,394	$10,295

Long-Lived Assets

All long-lived assets (including favorable lease rights) are reviewed when events or changes in circumstances indicate that the asset's carrying value may not be recoverable. If such indicators are present, it is determined whether the sum of the estimated undiscounted future cash flows attributable to such assets is less than their carrying amounts. We evaluated the ongoing value of our property and equipment and other long-lived assets as of February 2, 2008, February 3, 2007, and January 28, 2006, and determined that there was no significant impact on our results of operations.

Goodwill

We completed our annual goodwill impairment tests for 2007, 2006 and 2005 and determined there was no impairment of existing goodwill. The goodwill balance is $9.3 million as of both February 2, 2008 and February 3, 2007.

Accrued Liabilities

Accrued liabilities consist of the following:

	February 2, 2008	February 3, 2007
	(In Thousands)	
Various liabilities to customers	$ 201,361	$ 171,672
Accrued construction costs	121,190	92,929
Sales, property and use taxes	113,337	92,351
Due to JPMorgan Chase	85,107	83,876
Payroll and related fringe benefits	69,304	140,308
Accrued interest	36,500	14,098
Other accruals	171,709	129,791
	$ 798,508	$ 725,025

The various liabilities to customers include gift cards and merchandise return cards that have been issued but not presented for redemption.

Self-Insurance

We use a combination of insurance and self-insurance for a number of risks including workers' compensation, general liability and employee-related health care benefits, a portion of which is paid by our associates. Liabilities associated with these losses include estimates of both reported losses and losses incurred but not yet reported. We use a third-party actuary, which considers historical claims experience, demographic factors, severity factors and other actuarial assumptions, to estimate the liabilities associated with these risks. We retain the initial risk of $500,000 per occurrence under our workers' compensation insurance policy and $250,000 per occurrence under our general liability policy. We also have a lifetime medical payment limit of $1.5 million. Total estimated liabilities for workers' compensation, general liability and employee-related health benefits, excluding administrative expenses and before pre-funding, were approximately $70 million at February 2, 2008 and $60 million at February 3, 2007.

KOHL'S CORPORATION
NOTES TO CONSOLIDATED FINANCIAL STATEMENTS (continued)

Long-term Liabilities

The major components of other long-term liabilities consist of the following:

	February 2, 2008	February 3, 2007
	(In Thousands)	
Property related liabilities	$ 221,381	$ 184,924
Unrecognized tax benefits, including accrued interest and penalties	97,877	—
Deferred compensation	39,817	32,818
Other long-term liabilities	13,630	17,795
	$ 372,705	$ 235,537

Treasury Stock

We account for repurchases of common stock using the cost method with common stock in treasury classified in the Consolidated Balance Sheets as a reduction of shareholders' equity.

Comprehensive Income

Net income for all years presented is the same as comprehensive income.

Revenue Recognition

Revenue from the sale of merchandise at our stores is recognized at the time of sale, net of any returns. E-commerce sales are recorded upon the shipment of merchandise. Net sales do not include sales tax as we are considered a pass-through conduit for collecting and remitting sales taxes. Revenue from gift card sales is recognized when the gift card is redeemed.

Gift card breakage revenue is based on historical redemption patterns and represents the balance of gift cards for which we believe the likelihood of redemption by a customer is remote. We began recognizing gift card breakage revenue in 2006. Total sales for 2006 include $15.0 million related to this initial recognition of gift card breakage revenue.

Cost of Merchandise Sold and Selling, General and Administrative Expenses

The following table illustrates the primary costs classified in Cost of Merchandise Sold and Selling, General and Administrative Expenses:

Cost of Merchandise Sold	Selling, General and Administrative Expenses
• Total cost of products sold including product development costs, net of vendor payments other than reimbursement of specific, incremental and identifiable costs	• Compensation and benefit costs including: • Stores • Corporate headquarters, including buying and merchandising • Distribution centers
• Inventory shrink	• Occupancy and operating costs of our retail, distribution and corporate facilities
• Markdowns	
• Freight expenses associated with moving merchandise from our vendors to our distribution centers	• Freight expenses associated with moving merchandise from our distribution centers to our retail stores, and among distribution and retail facilities
• Shipping and handling expenses of E-commerce sales	• Advertising expenses, offset by vendor payments for reimbursement of specific, incremental and identifiable costs
• Terms cash discount	• Other administrative costs

The classification of these expenses varies across the retail industry.

KOHL'S CORPORATION
NOTES TO CONSOLIDATED FINANCIAL STATEMENTS (continued)

Vendor Allowances

We receive consideration for a variety of vendor-sponsored programs, such as markdown allowances, volume rebates and promotion and advertising support. The vendor consideration is recorded either as a reduction of inventory costs or Selling, General and Administrative ("S,G&A") expenses based on the application of Emerging Issues Task Force No. 02-16, *Accounting by a Customer (including a Reseller) for Certain Consideration Received from a Vendor*. Promotional and advertising allowances are intended to offset our advertising costs to promote vendors' merchandise. Markdown allowances and volume rebates are recorded as a reduction of inventory costs.

Advertising

Advertising costs, which include primarily television and radio broadcast and newspaper circulars, are expensed when the advertisement is first seen. Advertising costs, net of related vendor allowances, were $839.0 million for 2007, $768.1 million for 2006 and $647.3 million for 2005. Advertising vendor allowances were $141.6 million for 2007, $112.4 million for 2006 and $115.7 million for 2005.

Preopening Costs

Preopening expenses relate to the costs associated with new store openings, including advertising, hiring and training costs for new employees, processing and transporting initial merchandise and rent expense. Preopening costs are expensed as incurred.

Income Taxes

Income taxes are accounted for under the asset and liability method. Under this method, deferred tax assets and liabilities are recorded based on differences between the amounts of assets and liabilities recognized for financial reporting purposes and such amounts recognized for income tax purposes. Deferred tax assets and liabilities are calculated using the enacted tax rates and laws that are expected to be in effect when the differences are expected to reverse. We establish valuation allowances for tax benefits when we believe it is more likely than not that the related expense will be deductible for tax purposes.

On February 4, 2007, we adopted Financial Accounting Standards Board ("FASB") Interpretation No. 48, *Accounting for Uncertainty in Income Taxes—an interpretation of FASB Statement No. 109* ("FIN 48"), which clarifies the accounting and disclosure for uncertainty in tax positions, as defined. FIN 48 seeks to reduce the diversity in practice associated with certain aspects of the recognition and measurement related to accounting for income taxes.

Net Income Per Share

Basic net income per share is net income divided by the average number of common shares outstanding during the period. Diluted net income per share includes incremental shares assumed to be issued upon exercise of stock options. The information required to compute basic and diluted net income per share is as follows:

	2007	2006	2005
	(In Thousands, except per share data)		
Numerator—net income	$1,083,851	$1,108,681	$841,960
Denominator—weighted average shares			
Basic	318,123	332,323	344,172
Impact of dilutive employee stock options (a)	1,964	2,448	2,600
Diluted	320,087	334,771	346,772
Net income per share:			
Basic	$ 3.41	$ 3.34	$ 2.45
Diluted	$ 3.39	$ 3.31	$ 2.43

(a) Excludes 7.9 million options for 2007, 7.2 million options for 2006 and 6.4 million options for 2005 as the impact of such options was antidilutive.

KOHL'S CORPORATION
NOTES TO CONSOLIDATED FINANCIAL STATEMENTS (continued)

Stock Options

Stock-based compensation transactions, including stock options and nonvested stock awards, are accounted for in accordance with the provisions of Statement of Financial Accounting Standards No. 123(R), *Share-based Payment* ("SFAS 123(R)"). Under SFAS 123(R), we recognize expense related to the fair value of new, modified and unvested share-based awards which are expected to vest on a straight-line basis over the vesting period. The fair value of all share-based awards is estimated on the date of grant, which is defined as the date the award is approved by the Board of Directors (or management with the appropriate authority).

New Accounting Pronouncements

On December 4, 2007, the FASB issued FASB Statement No. 141 (Revised 2007), *Business Combinations* ("SFAS 141(R)"). SFAS 141(R) will significantly change the accounting for business combinations. We will need to apply the provisions of SFAS 141(R) to any business combinations with an acquisition date after January 31, 2009. Earlier adoption is prohibited. As we typically acquire single properties rather than businesses, we do not expect the adoption of this statement will have a material impact on our financial statements.

The FASB has also released two statements which address fair value accounting. FASB Statement No. 157, *Fair Value Measurements* ("SFAS 157"), defines fair value, establishes a framework for measuring fair value and expands disclosure about fair value measurements. FASB Statement No. 159, *The Fair Value Option for Financial Assets and Financial Liabilities—Including an Amendment of FASB Statement No. 115* ("SFAS 159"), permits an entity to choose to measure many financial instruments and certain other items at fair value. Portions of both statements are effective for our fiscal 2008. The remaining portions of both statements are effective for our fiscal 2009. We do not expect the adoption of either of these statements will have a material impact on our financial statements.

3. Debt

Long-term debt consists of the following:

Maturing	Weighted Average Effective Rate	February 2, 2008	Weighted Average Effective Rate	February 3, 2007
		($ in Thousands)		
Notes and debentures:				
Senior debt (a)				
2011	6.59%	$ 400,000	6.59%	$ 400,000
2017	6.31%	650,000	—	—
2029	7.36%	200,000	7.36%	200,000
2033	6.05%	300,000	6.05%	300,000
2037	6.89%	350,000	—	—
Total notes and debentures	6.55%	1,900,000	6.58%	900,000
Capital lease obligations		172,385		163,052
Unamortized debt discount		(7,809)		(4,172)
Other		—		18
Less current portion		(12,701)		(18,841)
Long-term debt and capital leases		$2,051,875		$1,040,057

(a) Non-callable and unsecured notes and debentures.

On September 28, 2007, we issued $1 billion of long-term debt, which included $650 million in aggregate principal amount of our 6.25% Notes due 2017 and $350 million in aggregate principal amount of our 6.875% Notes due 2037. Interest-only payments are due on these notes semi-annually on June 15 and December 15 beginning on June 15, 2008. The notes are subject to various customary covenants.

KOHL'S CORPORATION
NOTES TO CONSOLIDATED FINANCIAL STATEMENTS (continued)

Based on quoted market prices, the estimated fair value of our notes and debentures was approximately $1.86 billion at February 2, 2008 and $920 million at February 3, 2007.

We have various facilities upon which we may draw funds. As of year-end 2007, these facilities included a $900 million senior unsecured revolving facility and two demand notes with availability of $50 million. No amounts were outstanding under our short-term credit facilities at year-end 2007 or 2006. Depending on the type of advance under these facilities, amounts borrowed bear interest at competitive bid rates; LIBOR plus a margin, depending on our long-term unsecured debt ratings; or the agent bank's base rate. The $900 million senior unsecured revolving credit facility agreement matures on October 12, 2011. Information related to our revolving facilities is as follows:

	February 2, 2008	February 3, 2007
	($ in Thousands)	
Maximum outstanding during year	$392,000	$194,000
Average outstanding during year	62,745	19,045
Outstanding at year end	—	—
Weighted average interest rate	6.0%	5.3%

We reached our highest short-term borrowing level for 2007 on September 27, 2007 and for 2006 on April 20, 2006.

Our debt agreements contain various covenants including limitations on additional indebtedness and certain financial tests. As of February 2, 2008, we were in compliance with all covenants of the debt agreements.

We also have outstanding letters of credit and stand-by letters of credit totaling approximately $37.8 million at February 2, 2008.

Interest payments, net of amounts capitalized, were $59.0 million for 2007, $68.1 million for 2006 and $73.2 million for 2005.

4. Commitments

We lease certain property and equipment. Rent expense is recognized on a straight-line basis over the expected lease term. The lease term begins on the date we become legally obligated for the rent payments or we take possession of the building or land for initial setup of fixtures and merchandise or land improvements, whichever is earlier. The lease term includes cancelable option periods where failure to exercise such options would result in an economic penalty. Failure to exercise such options would result in the recognition of accelerated depreciation expense of the related assets.

Rent expense charged to operations was $417.2 million for 2007, $388.8 million for 2006 and $343.6 million for 2005. Rent expense includes contingent rents, which are based on sales, of $3.9 million for 2007, $4.4 million for 2006 and $3.7 million for 2005. In addition, we are often required to pay real estate taxes, insurance and maintenance costs. These items are not included in the rent expenses listed above. Many store leases include multiple renewal options, exercisable at our option, that generally range from two additional five-year periods to eight ten-year periods.

Assets held under capital leases are included in property and equipment and depreciated over the term of the lease. Assets under capital leases consist of the following:

	February 2, 2008	February 3, 2007
	(In Thousands)	
Buildings and improvements	$197,378	$164,739
Equipment	16,992	21,132
Less accumulated depreciation	(54,367)	(39,829)
	$160,003	$146,042

KOHL'S CORPORATION
NOTES TO CONSOLIDATED FINANCIAL STATEMENTS (continued)

Depreciation expense related to capital leases totaled $14.4 million for 2007, $10.6 million for 2006 and $7.6 million for 2005.

Future minimum lease payments at February 2, 2008, are as follows:

	Capital Leases	Operating Leases
	(In Thousands)	
Fiscal Year:		
2008	$ 25,175	$ 410,735
2009	23,734	414,032
2010	20,596	404,246
2011	19,040	394,968
2012	17,159	392,710
Thereafter	188,219	7,429,841
	293,923	$9,446,532
Less amount representing interest	121,538	
Present value of lease payments	$172,385	

SCHEDULE II

Valuation and Qualifying Accounts

	2007	2006	2005
		(In Thousands)	
Accounts Receivable—Allowances:			
Balance at beginning of year	$—	$ 26,335	$ 24,657
Charged to costs and expenses	—	—	53,505
Deductions—bad debts written off, net of recoveries and other allowances	—	—	(51,827)
Elimination of reserve in connection with sale of accounts receivable	—	(26,335)	—
Balance at end of year	$—	$ —	$ 26,335

F-23

DILLARD'S, INC.
CONSOLIDATED BALANCE SHEETS

	February 2, 2008	February 3, 2007	January 28, 2006
		Dollars in Thousands	
Assets			
Current assets:			
Cash and cash equivalents	$88,912	$193,994	$299,840
Accounts receivable	10,880	10,508	12,523
Merchandise inventories	1,779,279	1,772,150	1,802,695
Other current assets	66,117	71,194	35,421
Total current assets	1,945,188	2,047,846	2,150,479
Property and equipment:			
Land and land improvements	83,346	89,451	90,879
Buildings and leasehold improvements	3,117,292	2,931,244	2,792,417
Furniture, fixtures and equipment	1,969,343	2,160,190	2,143,914
Buildings under construction	96,057	56,856	92,336
Buildings and equipment under capital leases	48,910	48,910	81,496
Less accumulated depreciation and amortization	(2,124,504)	(2,140,025)	(2,053,419)
	3,190,444	3,146,626	3,147,623
Goodwill	31,912	34,511	34,511
Other assets	170,585	167,752	173,026
Total assets	$5,338,129	$5,396,735	$5,509,755
Liabilities and stockholders' equity			
Current liabilities:			
Trade accounts payable and accrued expenses	$753,309	$797,806	$858,082
Current portion of long-term debt	196,446	100,635	198,479
Current portion of capital lease obligations	2,613	3,679	5,929
Other short-term borrowings	195,000	—	--
Federal and state income taxes including deferred taxes	36,802	74,995	84,902
Total current liabilities	1,184,170	977,115	1,147,392
Long-term debt	760,165	956,611	1,058,946
Capital lease obligations	25,739	28,328	31,806
Other liabilities	217,403	206,122	259,111
Deferred income taxes	436,541	448,770	479,123
Operating leases and commitments			
Guaranteed preferred beneficial interests in the Company's subordinated debentures	200,000	200,000	200,000
Stockholders' equity:			
Common stock, Class A – 116,445,495; 116,217,645; and 115,237,382 shares issued; 71,155,347; 76,130,196; and 75,283,433 shares outstanding	1,165	1,162	1,153
Common stock, Class B (convertible) – 4,010,929 shares issued and outstanding	40	40	40
Additional paid-in capital	778,987	772,560	749,068
Accumulated other comprehensive loss	(22,211)	(21,229)	(14,574)
Retained earnings	2,680,690	2,640,224	2,407,327
Less treasury stock, at cost, Class A– 45,290,148, 40,087,449 and 39,953,949 shares	(924,560)	(812,968)	(809,637)
Total stockholders' equity	2,514,111	2,579,789	2,333,377
Total liabilities and stockholders' equity	$5,338,129	$5,396,735	$5,509,755

DILLARD'S, INC.
CONSOLIDATED STATEMENTS OF OPERATIONS

	Years Ended		
	February 2, 2008	February 3, 2007	January 28, 2006
	(Dollars in Thousands, Except Per Share Data)		
Net sales	$7,207,417	$7,636,056	$7,551,697
Service charges and other income	163,389	174,011	142,948
	7,370,806	7,810,067	7,694,645
Cost of sales	4,786,655	5,032,351	5,014,021
Advertising, selling, administrative and general expenses	2,065,288	2,096,018	2,041,481
Depreciation and amortization	298,927	301,147	301,864
Rentals	59,987	55,480	47,538
Interest and debt expense, net	91,556	87,642	105,570
Gain on disposal of assets	(12,625)	(16,413)	(3,354)
Asset impairment and store closing charges	20,500	—	61,734
Income before income taxes and equity in earnings of joint ventures	60,518	253,842	125,791
Income taxes	13,010	20,580	14,300
Equity in earnings of joint ventures	6,253	12,384	9,994
Net income	$ 53,761	$ 245,646	$ 121,485
Earnings per common share:			
Basic	$ 0.69	$ 3.09	$ 1.49
Diluted	0.68	3.05	1.49

See notes to consolidated financial statements.

F-7

DILLARD'S, INC.
CONSOLIDATED STATEMENTS OF STOCKHOLDERS' EQUITY AND COMPREHENSIVE INCOME (LOSS)

Dollars in Thousands, Except Per Share Data

	Common Stock		Additional Paid-in Capital	Accumulated Other Comprehensive Loss	Retained Earnings	Treasury Stock	Total
	Class A	Class B					
Balance, January 29, 2005, as restated (See Note 2)	$1,146	$ 40	$739,620	$ (13,333)	$2,298,829	$(708,769)	$2,317,533
Net income	—	—	—	—	121,485	—	121,485
Minimum pension liability adjustment, net of tax of $698	—	—	—	(1,241)	—	—	(1,241)
Total comprehensive income							120,244
Issuance of 655,858 shares under stock option plan	7	—	9,448	—	—	—	9,455
Purchase of 4,567,100 shares of treasury stock	—	—	—	—	—	(100,868)	(100,868)
Cash dividends declared:							
Common stock, $0.16 per share	—	—	—	—	(12,987)	—	(12,987)
Balance, January 28, 2006, as restated (See Note 2)	1,153	40	749,068	(14,574)	2,407,327	(809,637)	2,333,377
Net income	—	—	—	—	245,646	—	245,646
Minimum pension liability adjustment, net of tax of $153	—	—	—	266	—	—	266
Total comprehensive income							245,912
Adoption of FAS 158, net of tax of $3,995	—	—	—	(6,921)	—	—	(6,921)
Issuance of 980,263 shares under stock option and stock bonus plans	9	—	23,492	—	—	—	23,501
Purchase of 133,500 shares of treasury stock	—	—	—	—	—	(3,331)	(3,331)
Cash dividends declared:							
Common stock, $0.16 per share	—	—	—	—	(12,749)	—	(12,749)
Balance, February 3, 2007, as restated (See Note 2)	1,162	40	772,560	(21,229)	2,640,224	(812,968)	2,579,789
Net income	—	—	—	—	53,761	—	53,761
Change in unrecognized losses and prior service cost related to pension plans, net of tax of $567	—	—	—	(982)	—	—	(982)
Total comprehensive income							52,779
Issuance of 227,850 shares under stock option and stock bonus plans	3	—	6,427	—	—	—	6,430
Purchase of 5,202,699 shares of treasury stock	—	—	—	—	—	(111,592)	(111,592)
Cumulative effect of accounting change related to adoption of FIN 48	—	—	—	—	(803)	—	(803)
Cash dividends declared:							
Common stock, $0.16 per share	—	—	—	—	(12,492)	—	(12,492)
Balance, February 2, 2008	$1,165	$ 40	$778,987	$ (22,211)	$2,680,690	$(924,560)	$2,514,111

See notes to consolidated financial statements.

F-8

DILLARD'S, INC.
CONSOLIDATED STATEMENTS OF CASH FLOWS

	Years Ended		
	February 2, 2008	February 3, 2007	January 28, 2006
	Dollars in Thousands		
Operating activities:			
Net income	$ 53,761	$ 245,646	$ 121,485
Adjustments to reconcile net income to net cash provided by operating activities:			
Depreciation and amortization of property and deferred financing cost	300,859	303,256	304,376
Share-based compensation	77	1,002	—
Excess tax benefits from share-based compensation	(325)	(5,251)	—
Deferred income taxes	(2,399)	(32,807)	(32,862)
Gain on sale of joint venture	—	(13,810)	—
(Gain) loss on disposal of property and equipment	1,484	(2,603)	(3,354)
Asset impairment and store closing charges	20,500	—	61,734
Gain from hurricane insurance proceeds	(18,181)	—	(29,715)
Proceeds from hurricane insurance	5,881	—	83,398
Changes in operating assets and liabilities:			
(Increase) decrease in accounts receivable	(372)	2,015	(2,872)
(Increase) decrease in merchandise inventories	(7,129)	30,545	(123,345)
(Increase) decrease in other current assets	(7,366)	(60,283)	17,138
Increase in other assets	(4,243)	(2,421)	(6,201)
Decrease in trade accounts payable and accrued expenses, other liabilities and income taxes	(88,098)	(104,707)	(20,640)
Net cash provided by operating activities	254,449	360,582	369,142
Investing activities:			
Purchase of property and equipment	(396,337)	(320,640)	(456,078)
Proceeds from sale of property and equipment	48,249	6,479	103,637
Proceeds from hurricane insurance	16,101	27,826	26,708
Proceeds from sale of joint venture	—	19,990	—
Proceeds from sale of subsidiary	—	—	14,000
Return of capital from joint venture	—	—	14,125
Net cash used in investing activities	(331,987)	(266,345)	(297,608)
Financing activities:			
Principal payments on long-term debt and capital lease obligations	(104,291)	(205,907)	(163,919)
Payment on line of credit fees and expenses	(522)	(595)	(1,623)
Cash dividends paid	(12,492)	(12,749)	(12,987)
Proceeds from issuance of common stock	6,028	17,248	9,455
Excess tax benefits from share-based compensation	325	5,251	—
Purchase of treasury stock	(111,592)	(3,331)	(100,868)
Increase in short-term borrowings	195,000	—	—
Net cash used in financing activities	(27,544)	(200,083)	(269,942)
Decrease in cash and cash equivalents	(105,082)	(105,846)	(198,408)
Cash and cash equivalents, beginning of year	193,994	299,840	498,248
Cash and cash equivalents, end of year	$ 88,912	$ 193,994	$ 299,840
Non-cash transactions:			
Tax benefit from exercise of stock options	$ —	$ —	$ 3,683
Capital lease transactions	—	—	19,518
(Prepaid) accrued capital expenditures	(516)	10,052	23,351
Note received from sale of subsidiary	—	—	3,000

See notes to consolidated financial statements.

DILLARD'S, INC.
NOTES TO CONSOLIDATED FINANCIAL STATEMENTS

1. Description of Business and Summary of Significant Accounting Policies

Description of Business—Dillard's, Inc. (the "Company") operates retail department stores located primarily in the Southeastern, Southwestern and Midwestern areas of the United States. The Company's fiscal year ends on the Saturday nearest January 31 of each year. Fiscal years 2007, 2006 and 2005 ended on February 2, 2008, February 3, 2007 and January 28, 2006, respectively. Fiscal year 2006 included 53 weeks and fiscal years 2007 and 2005 included 52 weeks.

Consolidation—The accompanying consolidated financial statements include the accounts of Dillard's, Inc. and its wholly owned subsidiaries. Intercompany accounts and transactions are eliminated in consolidation. Investments in and advances to joint ventures in which the Company has a 50% ownership interest are accounted for by the equity method.

Use of Estimates—The preparation of financial statements in conformity with accounting principles generally accepted in the United States of America requires management to make estimates and assumptions that affect the reported amounts of assets and liabilities and disclosure of contingent assets and liabilities at the date of the financial statements and the reported amounts of revenues and expenses during the reporting period. Significant estimates include inventories, sales return, self-insured accruals, future cash flows for impairment analysis, pension discount rate and taxes. Actual results could differ from those estimates.

Seasonality—The Company's business is highly seasonal, and historically the Company has realized a significant portion of its sales, net income and cash flow in the second half of the fiscal year, attributable to the impact of the back-to-school selling season in the third quarter and the holiday selling season in the fourth quarter. Additionally, working capital requirements fluctuate during the year, increasing in the third quarter in anticipation of the holiday season.

Guarantees—The Company accounts for certain guarantees in accordance with FASB Interpretation No. 45, *Guarantor's Accounting and Disclosure Requirements for Guarantees, Including Indirect Guarantees of Indebtedness to Others, an Interpretation of FASB Statements No. 5, 57 and 107 and a Rescission of FASB Interpretation No. 34* ("FIN 45"). FIN 45 elaborates on the disclosures to be made by a guarantor in its interim and annual financial statements about its obligations under guarantees issued. FIN 45 also clarifies that a guarantor is required to recognize, at inception of a guarantee, a liability for the fair value of certain obligations undertaken. The Company recognized a liability related to indebtedness incurred by certain joint ventures as of January 28, 2006. No guarantees existed as of February 2, 2008 or February 3, 2007.

Cash Equivalents—The Company considers all highly liquid investments with an original maturity of three months or less when purchased to be cash equivalents. The Company considers receivables from charge card companies as cash equivalents because they settle the balances within two to three days.

Accounts Receivable—Accounts receivable primarily consists of the monthly settlement with GE for Dillard's share of revenue from the long-term marketing and servicing alliance.

Merchandise Inventories—The retail last-in, first-out ("LIFO") inventory method is used to value merchandise inventories. At February 2, 2008 and February 3, 2007, the LIFO cost of merchandise was approximately equal to the first-in, first-out ("FIFO") cost of merchandise.

Property and Equipment—Property and equipment owned by the Company is stated at cost, which includes related interest costs incurred during periods of construction, less accumulated depreciation and amortization. Capitalized interest was $6.3 million, $4.4 million and $6.1 million in fiscal 2007, 2006 and 2005, respectively. For financial reporting purposes, depreciation is computed by the straight-line method over estimated useful lives:

Buildings and leasehold improvements	20 – 40 years
Furniture, fixtures and equipment	3 -10 years

Properties leased by the Company under lease agreements which are determined to be capital leases are stated at an amount equal to the present value of the minimum lease payments during the lease term, less accumulated amortization. The properties under capital leases and leasehold improvements under operating leases are amortized

DILLARD'S, INC.
NOTES TO CONSOLIDATED FINANCIAL STATEMENTS (continued)

on the straight-line method over the shorter of their useful lives or the related lease terms. The provision for amortization of leased properties is included in depreciation and amortization expense.

Included in property and equipment as of February 2, 2008 are assets held for sale in the amount of $6.8 million. During fiscal 2007, the Company realized losses on the disposal of property and equipment of $1.5 million. During fiscal 2006 and 2005, the Company realized gains on the disposal of property and equipment of $2.6 million and $3.4 million, respectively.

Depreciation expense on property and equipment was $299 million, $301 million and $302 million for fiscal 2007, 2006 and 2005, respectively.

Long-Lived Assets Excluding Goodwill—The Company follows SFAS No. 144, *Accounting for the Impairment or Disposal of Long-Lived Assets*, which requires impairment losses to be recorded on long-lived assets used in operations when indicators of impairment are present and the undiscounted cash flows estimated to be generated by those assets are less than the assets' carrying amount. In the evaluation of the fair value and future benefits of long-lived assets, the Company performs an analysis of the anticipated undiscounted future net cash flows of the related long-lived assets. This analysis is performed at the store unit level. If the carrying value of the related asset exceeds the undiscounted cash flows, the carrying value is reduced to its fair value which is based on real estate values or expected discounted future cash flows. Various factors including future sales growth and profit margins are included in this analysis. Management believes at this time that the carrying value and useful lives continue to be appropriate, after recognizing the impairment charges recorded in fiscal 2007 and 2005, as disclosed in Note 15.

Goodwill—The Company follows SFAS No. 142, *Goodwill and Other Intangible Assets*, which requires that goodwill be reviewed for impairment annually or more frequently if certain indicators arise. The Company tests for goodwill impairment annually as of the last day of the fourth quarter using the two-step process prescribed in SFAS No. 142. The Company identifies its reporting units under SFAS No. 142 at the store unit level. The fair value of these reporting units are estimated using the expected discounted future cash flows and market values of related businesses, where appropriate. Management believes at this time that the carrying value continues to be appropriate, recognizing the impairment charges recorded in fiscal 2007 and 2005 as disclosed in Notes 3 and 15.

Other Assets—Other assets include investments in joint ventures accounted for by the equity method. These joint ventures, which consist of malls and a general contracting company that constructs Dillard's stores and other commercial buildings, had carrying values of $100 million and $98 million at February 2, 2008 and February 3, 2007, respectively. The malls are located in Toledo, Ohio; Denver, Colorado and Bonita Springs, Florida. The Company received $14.1 million as a return of capital from a joint venture during fiscal 2005. The Company recorded a $13.8 million pretax gain during the year ended February 3, 2007 for the sale of its interest in the Yuma Palms joint venture for $20.0 million.

Vendor Allowances—The Company receives concessions from its vendors through a variety of programs and arrangements, including cooperative advertising and margin maintenance programs. The Company has agreements in place with each vendor setting forth the specific conditions for each allowance or payment. These agreements range in periods from a few days to up to a year. If the payment is a reimbursement for costs incurred, it is offset against those related costs; otherwise, it is treated as a reduction to the cost of the merchandise.

For cooperative advertising programs, the Company generally offsets the allowances against the related advertising expense when incurred. Many of these programs require proof-of-advertising to be provided to the vendor to support the reimbursement of the incurred cost. Programs that do not require proof-of-advertising are monitored to ensure that the allowance provided by each vendor is a reimbursement of costs incurred to advertise for that particular vendor. If the allowance exceeds the advertising costs incurred on a vendor-specific basis, then the excess allowance from the vendor is recorded as a reduction of merchandise cost for that vendor.

Margin maintenance allowances are credited directly to cost of purchased merchandise in the period earned according to the agreement with the vendor.

DILLARD'S, INC.
NOTES TO CONSOLIDATED FINANCIAL STATEMENTS (continued)

The accounting policies described above are in compliance with Emerging Issues Task Force 02-16, *Accounting by a Customer (Including a Reseller) for Certain Considerations Received from a Vendor*.

Insurance Accruals—The Company's consolidated balance sheets include liabilities with respect to self-insured workers' compensation and general liability claims. The Company estimates the required liability of such claims, utilizing an actuarial method, based upon various assumptions, which include, but are not limited to, our historical loss experience, projected loss development factors, actual payroll and other data. The required liability is also subject to adjustment in the future based upon the changes in claims experience, including changes in the number of incidents (frequency) and changes in the ultimate cost per incident (severity).

Operating Leases—The Company leases retail stores, office space and equipment under operating leases. Most store leases contain construction allowance reimbursements by landlords, rent holidays, rent escalation clauses and/or contingent rent provisions. The Company recognizes the related rental expense on a straight-line basis over the lease term and records the difference between the amounts charged to expense and the rent paid as a deferred rent liability.

To account for construction allowance reimbursements from landlords and rent holidays, the Company records a deferred rent liability included in trade accounts payable and accrued expenses and other liabilities on the consolidated balance sheets and amortizes the deferred rent over the lease term, as a reduction to rent expense on the consolidated income statements. For leases containing rent escalation clauses, the Company records minimum rent expense on a straight-line basis over the lease term on the consolidated income statement. The lease term used for lease evaluation includes renewal option periods only in instances in which the exercise of the option period can be reasonably assured and failure to exercise such options would result in an economic penalty.

Revenue Recognition—The Company recognizes revenue at the "point of sale." Allowance for sales returns are recorded as a component of net sales in the period in which the related sales are recorded.

GE Consumer Finance ("GE") owns and manages Dillard's proprietary credit cards ("proprietary cards") under a long-term marketing and servicing alliance ("alliance") that expires in fiscal 2014. The Company's share of income earned under the alliance with GE is included as a component of service charges and other income. The Company received income of approximately $119 million, $125 million and $105 million from GE in fiscal 2007, 2006 and 2005, respectively. Further pursuant to this agreement, the Company has no continuing involvement other than to honor the proprietary cards in its stores. Although not obligated to a specific level of marketing commitment, the Company participates in the marketing of the proprietary cards and accepts payments on the proprietary cards in its stores as a convenience to customers who prefer to pay in person rather than by mailing their payments to GE. Amounts received for providing these services are included in the amounts disclosed above.

Gift Card Revenue Recognition—The Company establishes a liability upon the sale of a gift card. The liability is relieved and revenue is recognized when gift cards are redeemed for merchandise and for estimated breakage. The Company uses a homogeneous pool to recognize gift card breakage and will recognize income over the period when the likelihood of the gift card being redeemed is remote and the Company determines that it does not have a legal obligation to remit the value of unredeemed gift cards to the relevant jurisdiction as abandoned property. The Company determined gift card breakage income based upon historical redemption patterns. At that time, the Company will recognize breakage income over the performance period for those gift cards (i.e. 60 months). As of February 2, 2008 and February 3, 2007, gift card liabilities of $76.9 million and $74.9 million, respectively, were included in trade accounts payable and accrued expenses and other liabilities.

Advertising—Advertising and promotional costs, which include newspaper, television, radio and other media advertising, are expensed as incurred and were $197 million, $205 million and $229 million, net of cooperative advertising reimbursements of $67.1 million, $67.1 million and $57.8 million for fiscal years 2007, 2006 and 2005, respectively.

Income Taxes—Income taxes are accounted for in accordance with Statement of Financial Accounting Standards No. 109, *Accounting for Income Taxes* ("SFAS No. 109"). Under SFAS No. 109, income taxes are recognized for the amount of taxes payable for the current year and deferred tax assets and liabilities for the future tax consequence of events that have been recognized differently in the financial statements than for tax purposes.

DILLARD'S, INC.
NOTES TO CONSOLIDATED FINANCIAL STATEMENTS (continued)

Deferred tax assets and liabilities are established using statutory tax rates and are adjusted for tax rate changes. Effective at the beginning of the first quarter of fiscal 2007, we adopted FASB Interpretation No. 48, *Accounting for Uncertainty in Income Taxes* ("FIN 48"). This interpretation clarifies the accounting for uncertainty in income tax recognized in an entity's financial statements in accordance with SFAS No. 109. FIN 48 requires companies to determine whether it is "more likely than not" that a tax position will be sustained upon examination by the appropriate taxing authorities before any part of the benefit can be recorded in the financial statements. For those tax positions where it is "not more likely than not" that a tax benefit will be sustained, no tax benefit is recognized. Where applicable, associated interest and penalties are also recorded.

Shipping and Handling—In accordance with Emerging Issues Task Force ("EITF") 00-10, *Accounting for Shipping and Handling Fees and Costs*, the Company records shipping and handling reimbursements in Service Charges and Other Income. The Company records shipping and handling costs in cost of sales.

Stock-Based Compensation—On January 29, 2006, the first day of our 2006 fiscal year, the Company adopted the provisions of Statement of Financial Accounting Standards No. 123(R), *Share-Based Payment* ("SFAS 123(R)"), a revision of SFAS No. 123, Accounting for Stock-Based Compensation, as interpreted by SEC Staff Accounting Bulletin No. 107. Under SFAS 123(R), all forms of share-based payment to employees and directors, including stock options, must be treated as compensation and recognized in the income statement. Previous to the adoption of SFAS 123(R), the Company accounted for stock options under the provisions of Accounting Principles Board Opinion No. 25, Accounting for Stock Issued to Employees, and, accordingly, did not recognize compensation expense in our consolidated financial statements.

Retirement Benefit Plans—The Company's retirement benefit plan costs are accounted for using actuarial valuations required by SFAS No. 87, *Employers' Accounting for Pensions,* and SFAS No. 106, *Employers' Accounting for Postretirement Benefits Other Than Pensions.* The Company adopted SFAS No. 158, *Employer's Accounting for Defined Benefit Pension and Other Postretirement Plans—an amendment of FASB Statements No. 87, 88, 106, and 132(R)* ("SFAS 158") as of February 3, 2007. SFAS 158 requires an entity to recognize the funded status of its defined pension plans on the balance sheet and to recognize changes in the funded status that arise during the period but are not recognized as components of net periodic benefit cost, within other comprehensive income, net of income taxes.

Equity in Earnings of Joint Ventures—Equity in earnings of joint ventures includes the Company's portion of the income or loss of the Company's unconsolidated joint ventures.

Segment Reporting—The Company reports in a single operating segment—the operation of retail department stores. Revenues from customers are derived from merchandise. The Company does not rely on any major customers as a source of revenue. The Company purchases merchandise from many suppliers, none of which accounted for more than 5% of the Company's net purchases during fiscal 2007.

The following table summarizes the percentage of net sales by each major product line:

	Percentage of Net Sales		
	Fiscal 2007	Fiscal 2006	Fiscal 2005
Cosmetics	15%	15%	15%
Ladies' Apparel and Accessories	37	36	36
Juniors' and Children's Apparel	9	10	10
Men's Apparel and Accessories	18	18	18
Shoes	13	13	12
Home and Other	8	8	9
Total	100%	100%	100%

New Accounting Pronouncements

In December 2007, the Financial Accounting Standards Board ("FASB") issued the Statement of Financial Accounting Standards ("SFAS") No. 141(R), *Business Combinations* ("SFAS 141(R)"). SFAS 141(R)'s objective is to improve the relevance, representational faithfulness, and comparability of the information that a reporting entity

DILLARD'S, INC.
NOTES TO CONSOLIDATED FINANCIAL STATEMENTS (continued)

provides in its financial reports about a business combination and its effects. SFAS 141(R) applies prospectively to business combinations for which the acquisition date is on or after December 31, 2008. We expect that the adoption of SFAS 141(R) will not have a material impact on our consolidated financial statements.

In December 2007, the FASB issued the SFAS No. 160, *Noncontrolling Interest in Consolidated Financial Statements* ("SFAS 160"). SFAS 160's objective is to improve the relevance, comparability, and transparency of the financial information that a reporting entity provides in its consolidated financial statements by establishing accounting and reporting standards for the noncontrolling interest in a subsidiary and for the deconsolidation of a subsidiary. SFAS 160 will be effective for fiscal years and interim periods within those fiscal years, beginning on or after December 15, 2008. We expect that the adoption of SFAS 160 will not have a material impact on our consolidated financial statements.

In February 2007, the FASB issued SFAS No. 159, *The Fair Value Option for Financial Assets and Financial Liabilities—Including an amendment of FASB Statement No. 115* ("SFAS 159"). This statement permits entities to choose to measure many financial instruments and certain other items at fair value. SFAS 159 is effective at the beginning of an entity's first fiscal year that begins after November 15, 2007. We expect that the adoption of SFAS 159 will not have a material impact on our consolidated financial statements.

In September 2006, the FASB issued SFAS No. 157, *Fair Value Measurements* ("SFAS 157"). This statement defines fair value, establishes a framework for measuring fair value in generally accepted accounting principles, and expands disclosures about fair value measurements. This statement applies under other accounting pronouncements that require or permit fair value measurements, the FASB having concluded in those other accounting pronouncements that fair value is the relevant measurement attribute. This statement is effective for financial assets and liabilities in financial statements issued for fiscal years beginning after November 15, 2007. It is effective for non-financial assets and liabilities in financial statements issued for fiscal years beginning after November 15, 2008. We expect that the adoption of SFAS 157 will not have a material impact on our consolidated financial statements.

In December 2007, the Securities and Exchange Commission ("SEC") issued Staff Accounting Bulletin ("SAB") No. 110 to extend the use of "simplified method" for estimating the expected terms of "plain vanilla" employee stock options for the awards valuation. The method was initially allowed under SAB 107 in contemplation of the adoption of SFAS 123(R) to expense the compensation cost based on the awards grant date fair value. SAB 110 does not provide an expiration date for the use of the method. However, as more external information about exercise behavior will be available over time, it is expected that this method will not be used when more relevant information is available.

2. Restatement

Subsequent to the issuance of the Company's consolidated financial statements for the year ended February 3, 2007, the Company identified an error in accounting for its share of the equity in earnings of CDI Contractors LLC ("CDI"), a 50%-owned, equity method joint venture investment of the Company that is also a general contractor that constructs stores for the Company. In connection with a potential transfer of the other 50% shareholder's interest, the Company performed a review of CDI's internal financial records. During this review process, the Company discovered that CDI had recorded profit on the Company's construction projects in excess of what CDI had previously reported and which, therefore, was not properly eliminated. The cumulative impact on beginning retained earnings and stockholders' equity as of January 29, 2005 of this error was a decrease of $7.2 million.

The following table reflects the effects of the restatement on the Statement of Stockholders' Equity as of January 28, 2006 (in thousands):

| | January 28, 2006 | | |
	As Previously Reported	Restatement Adjustments	As Restated
Retained earnings	$2,414,491	$ (7,164)	$2,407,327
Total stockholders' equity	2,340,541	(7,164)	2,333,377

DILLARD'S, INC.
NOTES TO CONSOLIDATED FINANCIAL STATEMENTS (continued)

The following table reflects the effects of the restatement on the Consolidated Balance Sheet and Statement of Stockholders' Equity as of February 3, 2007 (in thousands):

	February 3, 2007		
	As Previously Reported	Restatement Adjustments	As Restated
Property and equipment	$3,157,906	$ (11,280)	$3,146,626
Total assets	5,408,015	(11,280)	5,396,735
Deferred income taxes	452,886	(4,116)	448,770
Retained earnings	2,647,388	(7,164)	2,640,224
Total stockholders' equity	2,586,953	(7,164)	2,579,789
Total liabilities and stockholders' equity	5,408,015	(11,280)	5,396,735

The Company's net income for fiscal 2006 and 2005 was not materially impacted by this error; accordingly, a decrease of $2.9 million to correct the effect of the error on fiscal 2006 and 2005 was recorded in fiscal 2007.

5. Long-Term Debt

Long-term debt consists of the following:

	February 2, 2008	February 3, 2007
	(in thousands of dollars)	
Unsecured notes		
At rates ranging from 6.30% to 9.50%, due 2008 through 2028	$ 952,392	$ 1,052,392
Mortgage note, payable monthly through 2013 and bearing interest at a rate of 9.25%	4,219	4,854
	956,611	1,057,246
Current portion	(196,446)	(100,635)
	$ 760,165	$ 956,611

There are no financial covenants under the debt agreements. Building, land, and land improvements with a carrying value of $5.7 million at February 2, 2008 were pledged as collateral on the mortgage notes. Maturities of long-term debt over the next five years are $196 million, $25 million, $1 million, $57 million and $56 million. Outstanding letters of credit aggregated $72.5 million at February 2, 2008.

Net interest and debt expense consists of the following:

	Fiscal 2007	Fiscal 2006	Fiscal 2005
	(in thousands of dollars)		
Long-term debt:			
Interest	$82,037	$ 99,644	$104,003
Loss on early retirement of long-term debt	—	—	478
Amortization of debt expense	1,932	2,274	2,826
	83,969	101,918	107,307
Interest on capital lease obligations	2,319	1,817	2,138
Revolving credit facility expenses	9,387	3,721	3,442
Investment interest income	(4,119)	(9,314)	(7,317)
Interest on income tax settlement	—	(10,500)	—
	$91,556	$ 87,642	$105,570

Interest paid during fiscal 2007, 2006 and 2005 was approximately $96.2 million, $123.3 million and $113.7 million, respectively.

DILLARD'S, INC.

NOTES TO CONSOLIDATED FINANCIAL STATEMENTS (continued)

13. Leases and Commitments

Rental expense consists of the following:

	Fiscal 2007	Fiscal 2006	Fiscal 2005
	(in thousands of dollars)		
Operating leases:			
Buildings:			
Minimum rentals	$25,798	$29,640	$30,611
Contingent rentals	5,997	6,558	6,775
Equipment	28,192	19,282	10,152
	$59,987	$55,480	$47,538

Contingent rentals on certain leases are based on a percentage of annual sales in excess of specified amounts. Other contingent rentals are based entirely on a percentage of sales.

The future minimum rental commitments as of February 2, 2008 for all noncancelable leases for buildings and equipment are as follows:

Fiscal Year	Operating Leases	Capital Leases
	(in thousands of dollars)	
2008	56,065	4,684
2009	50,014	3,628
2010	37,325	3,569
2011	45,026	3,509
2012	34,118	13,787
After 2012	33,143	12,066
Total minimum lease payments	$255,691	41,243
Less amount representing interest		(12,892)
Present value of net minimum lease payments (of which $2,613 is currently payable)		$ 28,351

Renewal options from three to 25 years exist on the majority of leased properties. At February 2, 2008, the Company is committed to incur costs of approximately $153 million to acquire, complete and furnish certain stores and equipment.